Project Portfolio Management

A Practical Guide to Selecting Projects, Managing Portfolios, and Maximizing Benefits

Harvey A. Levine

Foreword by Max Wideman

JOSSEY-BASS
A Wiley Imprint
www.josseybass.com

Published by Jossey-Bass
A Wiley Imprint
989 Market Street, San Francisco, CA 94103-1741   www.josseybass.com

Jossey-Bass books and products are available through most bookstores. To contact Jossey-Bass directly call our Customer Care Department within the U.S. at 800-956-7739, outside the U.S. at 317-572-3986, or fax 317-572-4002.

Jossey-Bass also publishes its books in a variety of electronic formats. Some content that appears in print may not be available in electronic books.

Library of Congress Cataloging-in-Publication Data

Levine, Harvey A.
    Project portfolio management : a practical guide to selecting projects, managing portfolios, and maximizing benefits / by Harvey A. Levine; foreword by Max Wideman.—1st ed.
        p. cm.—(The Jossey-Bass business & management series)
    Includes bibliographical references and index.
    ISBN-13 978-0-7879-7754-2 (alk. paper)
    ISBN-10 0-7879-7754-3 (alk. paper)
    1. Project management. I. Title. II. Series.
    HD69.P75L485 2005
    658.4'04—dc22
                                                                    2005013189

Printed in the United States of America
FIRST EDITION
HB Printing   10 9 8 7 6 5 4

The Jossey-Bass
Business & Management Series

Contents

Foreword

With all that has been written on and about project management over the past decade, you might be forgiven for thinking that surely there cannot be anything new to say. Indeed, some eminent practitioners have even stated categorically that little has advanced in these ten years. But in the past five, the management of projects has risen to a new prominence. Projects are seen as critical to success in all three sectors: public, private, and nonprofit.

The impact of projects on contemporary society is immense, but the evident wastage through improper selection of projects or their improper formulation (or both) is equally immense. Collectively this represents a serious diminution of our collective capital assets and consequent drag on our economy. To deal with this challenge, there *is* something new, though it is still evolving. The solution is to be found in project portfolio management (PPM), and it is not just a trendy label or fad.

Some may view PPM as just another technique of project management, but it is not that. PPM is literally above and beyond project management because it spans all the way from the vision of those in the executive suite, through project management, to the realization of benefits to the enterprise and its successful competitive positioning. Key to this new project portfolio life span is selection of the right projects in the first place.

It should come as no surprise that Harvey Levine, author of several books and literally hundreds of articles on almost every aspect of project management, has thrown himself into the fray on this one. As Harvey explains in the Introduction, "The emergence of PPM as a recognized set of practices may be considered the biggest leap in project management technology since the development of PERT and CPM in the late 1950s."

Harvey is no slouch. He does not go along with new trends and fads—those that are short on substance and practical use, but no doubt designed to enhance a consultant's repertoire. Rather, Harvey has spent the past five years studying this topic, gaining insight from knowledgeable people, and finding out what companies actually do. He has surveyed the best of the best and collected their knowledge and wisdom. This book is the result of that effort.

Books on this subject, certainly ones that provide profound, up-to-date, and practical information, are rare, making this one an essential addition to the list.

Perhaps the first thing to understand is why all the fuss. It is interesting to follow the genesis of project management itself. Although not recognized as such, project management was clearly practiced in the great building endeavors of the ancient world. In the twentieth century, it emerged as a management discipline in its own right, essentially from the traditional heartlands of construction and engineering, where it has a well-established process and track record. But the sizes of such projects are such that they generally tend to be not only truly unique but also relatively unconnected.

With the advent of business automation through the use of information systems, computer technology, and software development, all that has changed. In recent years, there has been a tremendous upsurge in project-based work. This is typically associated with new challenges and opportunities brought about by other technological developments, shifting boundaries of knowledge, dynamic market conditions, environmental regulations, and changes in organizational thinking and strategic directions. The challenges that these bring have been compounded by the drive toward shorter product life cycles, customer involvement, and increased scope and complexity of interorganizational relationships.

Today organizations have embraced project management, in principle at least, as the way to address these challenges. So all these areas have entered the project management domain; indeed they have swamped it. Consequently, it is not unusual for companies to be faced with hundreds of projects annually and even more to choose from. It can be shown mathematically that supposing you have, say, fifteen projects from which you have to choose some, but not all, then you have around thirty thousand choices.[1] Obviously the optimum selection within the constraints of the enterprise's resources is a serious challenge. This book explains how to tackle this problem and what information you need to do so.

The second thing to recognize is that we are dealing here with a different group of people who don't speak the same language. They even have a different mind-set compared to project management types. These are the people who run the enterprise within which projects take place, and they are the ones responsible for keeping the organization afloat. That is, Harvey is addressing business executives such as chief executive officers, chief operating officers, chief financial officers, chief information officers, senior functional managers, or even strategic planners. Certainly, to them, "on time" and "within budget" is important, but their real interest lies in the answer to the question, "What benefits will this project bring to the organization, when, and how risky is it?"

The important point here is that the answers to these questions are typically beyond the purview of the average project manager. Certainly, timely delivery of the right product at the right level of quality is essential, but the correct deployment of that resulting product is what will determine whether the project is really successful. So Harvey introduces readers to a new idea, the project portfolio life span (PPLS). This is the feature that makes the whole thing make sense. PPLS links project benefits back to the original selection decision and provides the basis for continuous organizational learning.

The third lesson to be gained from this book is that it makes a cogent case for consistency in project management methodology, without which it is not possible to collect the requisite project selection decision-making data. It makes an even stronger case for establishing a central project or program office to facilitate the collection and transfer of those data and provide unification of project direction, priority assignment of limited resources, and so on. Such an office must also facilitate the transfer of requisite information back to the various project managers so that they have the information available for making rational corporate-beneficial decisions rather than just project-beneficial decisions.

As Harvey says in Chapter 1.1, "What is so obviously needed is a basis for addressing project selection issues, deciding on project termination, facilitating reallocation of resources, changing of priorities, and evaluation of alternatives. And, without this capability, there is no project portfolio management." Furthermore, he says, "Periodically, we need to review [each] project to test assumptions, update givens, and monitor progress. We need to periodically examine alternatives and consider remodeling the portfolio." And he continues in Chapter 2.4, "The core mistake is to think that PPM is fundamentally the management of multiple projects. This definitely is not so. PPM is the management of the project portfolio so as to maximize the contribution of projects to the overall welfare and success of the enterprise."

Finally, as Harvey writes in his Foreword to my most recent book: "The recognition and structuring of PPM during the last five years or so has raised the value of projects and project management to a new level. We are now in a position to bridge the gap between the projects and the operations sides of our business. PPM enables us to not only do projects right, but to select and do the right projects in the first place."

Throughout this book, Harvey tackles the many problems associated with PPM, such as ranking value and benefits, the size of the portfolio pipeline, the impact of uncertainty on projects and portfolios, the benefit-risk relationship, and how to implement PPM.

He has divided the book into two major parts, the first containing the results of his own findings and the second with chapters contributed by major players in the field. A significant portion of the book is devoted to a practical look at precise details for effective PPM implementation.

The whole is a valuable and instructive read and should be on the bookshelf of every executive and senior manager involved in or contemplating the elusive but finer art of project portfolio management.

Vancouver, B.C., Canada   Max Wideman
May 2005

Max Wideman is a Project Management Institute Fellow and past PMI chair. Among his publications are *A Management Framework for Project, Program and Portfolio Integration* (2004) and *Cost Control of Capital Projects and the Project Cost Management System Requirements* (2nd edition, 1995).

Acknowledgments

With forty-three years of intensive involvement in project management (PM), it's only natural that I would build a large network of colleagues who have also been significant contributors to the PM state-of-the-art. What has been a major joy is the sharing among us. We post our research and discussions on open Web sites. We meet, in person or electronically, to discuss, argue, challenge, and test our theories. We gladly share our findings and experiences. With mutual respect, we express our dedication to this exponentially growing field through our publications.

I have had the honor several times to provide a guest chapter to publications by my colleagues. Now it's payback time. In Part Two of this book, about two dozen leaders in the field of project portfolio management (PPM) have contributed their knowledge, experience, and expertise by providing valuable content. Some of them are long-time friends. Others are recent additions to the network. Still others are new associates—those whom I contacted after reading impressive and valuable articles that they authored. Some are polished writers. Others had to be mentored to get past some writer's block or style issues.

What is common to all of them is that they have, through their earlier work and through their writings for this book, left a legacy for the growing PPM community. Without their thoughtful contributions, we would not have published this book. I am deeply indebted to them for their support and for helping to make this book a valuable resource for the PPM community. A big thank-you to K. C. Yelin, Ray Trotta, Christopher Gardner, Jim Devlin, Mike Gruia, Cliff Cohen, Randy Englund, Matt Light, David Hurwitz, Bob Cooper, Larry Leach, Rebecca Seibert, Don Kingsberry, Rich Dougherty, Vanessa McMillan, Bob Graham, Dennis Cohen, James Schlick, Andrew Longman, Gil Matleff, Jim Pennypacker, and Patrick Sepate for their contributions.

When I first proposed this book, Jossey-Bass, the publisher, was looking for some validation that there would be buyers for it. This is becoming a very competitive market. My first reaction was to invite a few PM software vendors to participate as sponsors. The response was immediate and overwhelming. I thank Expert Choice, Sciforma, Dekker, Welcom, and PlanView for their support. These valued PM software developers have made many contributions to the practice of PM and PPM. Some of them have also provided material for the book, and all will help get the book out to the readers. I also thank them for their faith in my ability to produce a valuable reference book. It is most gratifying.

A special thank-you to SmartDraw, developers of the wonderful program by that name used for creating charts and diagrams. I used SmartDraw's complimentary copy to produce several diagrams for Part One of this book.

A very special thank-you to R. Max Wideman for contributing the Foreword for this book. Max has been a leader in the project management community and has served as president and chair of the Project Management Institute and is a PMI Fellow. For several decades, we have shared a passion for project management and for the development of standards and a body of knowledge. His recently published *A Management Framework for Project, Program and Portfolio Integration* is his latest gift to this body of knowledge. I value his career-long dedication and his friendship. Max also provided significant and valuable comments and advice that helped to make this a better book.

A very, very special thank-you to my spouse of forty-seven years, Judy Levine. In addition to the important encouragement and support, Judy also volunteered to read the manuscript before I submitted it to the publisher. As an author in her own right, she made numerous helpful suggestions to improve grammar and readability. As a retired management professional, she read with interest and understanding this treatise on project portfolio management (not her field) and offered perceptive comments for further improvement of the text. If, when you read this book, you can get through the difficult passages with understanding, tip your hat to Judy.

Finally, after a long career in practicing project management and especially in sharing my knowledge and views, this thought comes to mind: to teach is to learn. After doing hundreds of seminars, speeches, and writings, I find that the payoff is what I learn from each of these experiences. So to all of those who have worked with me on this project, thanks for contributing to my knowledge and making me wiser.

The Author

Harvey A. Levine is in his forty-fourth year of service to the project management profession, providing applications, system design, and consulting services in project planning and control, mostly with the General Electric Company. He has served on the board of directors of the Project Management Institute, including as president and chairman of the board, and is a PMI Fellow. Levine has been adjunct professor of project management at Rensselaer Polytechnic Institute and at Boston University. Since 1986, he has provided consulting services in a wide range of project management areas, across all industries and sectors. His book *Practical Project Management: Tips, Tactics, and Tools* (2002) has won wide recognition for its pragmatism and readability. He has also published over two hundred articles and papers.

Introduction

> Project portfolio management is a set of business practices that brings the world of projects into tight integration with other business operations. It brings projects into harmony with the strategies, resources, and executive oversight of the enterprise and provides the structure and processes for project portfolio governance.

I have never been one to jump on the bandwagon. Much to the contrary, I tend to resist and question new trends and fads, finding that many of them are only a flash in the pan—short on substance and practical use. However, when it comes to PPM, I eagerly join the stampede. PPM is more than an expanded application of project management. The emergence of PPM as a recognized set of practices may be considered the biggest leap in project management technology since the development of Program Evaluation and Review Technique and Critical Path Method in the late 1950s. However, it is important to recognize that this newer technique goes way beyond the simple expansion of project management practices. PPM revolutionizes the way that we look at projects, the impact that projects have on the health of the business, and even the governance of projects.

Understanding What PPM Is Not

Don't confuse PPM recent popular concepts, such as enterprise project management and professional services automation. These are an expansion of project management, but in a totally different direction. And neither addresses the alignment of projects with strategies or the science of selecting the right projects. Neither of these provides for project portfolio governance.

Another key misconception is to think of PPM as the management of multiple projects. Yes, PPM does address this. But the primary and unique aspect of PPM is what it does to formalize and assist in the selection of projects.

We talk about why we need PPM in Chapter 1.1 and about what PPM is and is not in Chapter 1.2. But here's a brief look.

The What and Why of PPM

PPM is a set of business practices that brings the world of projects into tight integration with other business operations. In the past, the absence of this integration has resulted in a large disconnect between the projects' function and the rest of the operations of the enterprise. Without this essential connectivity, a lot of effort goes into doing projects right—even if they are not the right projects.

We have projects proposed and approved that do not deliver the promised benefits. We have projects that are wrong; they are not in sync with the goals of the enterprise. We have projects that have excessive risk, yet the risk is set aside when the project is considered for approval. We have projects that get approved solely because of the political power of the project sponsor. These projects drain valuable and scarce resources from more beneficial projects.

We have projects that are failing at an early stage. Yet they are continued until total failure is recognized and the team admits that the product cannot be delivered. We have projects that are designed to generate income (or cost savings), but because of various kinds of failures, they become a burden instead. We have projects that slip so badly in time that they miss the window of opportunity. Yet they are continued when they should be terminated.

So what we have here are two distinct and costly problems:

- Projects that should not have been selected to be in the pipeline
- Projects that remain in the pipeline even after they no longer serve the company's best interests

The result is that many projects are not delivering on their promises or are not supporting the goals of the enterprise.

The Impact of PPM

Fortunately, as widespread and as costly as these problems are, the solution is simple and inexpensive: it requires very little in the way of acquisitions and has very little impact on head count. It does require a few new skills and some small additions to management software. Moving to a PPM culture will require a top-level commitment and a mature and cooperative environment for the project and governance teams.

For this small investment, you can have a significant impact on the way that the organization deals with projects and business initiatives. PPM will push the corporate culture in a new direction— one in which it really wants to go if it could only articulate it.

Success will require the development and implementation of new practices. While the new process flow will be comprehensive, it will actually streamline the selecting and managing of projects. The new processes will be executed primarily with current staffing.

Perhaps the biggest change will be in communication and decision making. And these changes will be for the better.

Do you remember the Six Sigma movement? It propelled us ever closer to zero defects. The PPM process will move us closer to zero failed projects. The objective is to reduce terminated projects to zero. It's hard to argue with the premise that the earlier that you can weed out a bad project, the better. Best yet is not wasting any time on such a project in the first place.

The Components of PPM

The PPM process starts with a rational prioritization and selection procedure. By evaluating a proposed project against a set of selection criteria, bad projects get weeded out (or modified to meet the criteria). If a proposed project can't pass the minimal criteria, there is no need even to rank it for selection. If we don't let the wild horse out of the corral, we don't have to go and chase it back.

PPM is about having the right information so you can make the right decisions to select the right projects. It's about bridging the gap between projects and operations. It's about communicating and connecting the business strategy to the project selection process. It's about making sure that intended opportunities are real opportunities. By evaluating value and benefits, by modifying benefit calculations on the basis of risk, and by forcing such analyses to take place under structured and consistent procedures, we prevent problem projects from sneaking in with real opportunities. (See Chapter 3.2 on project prequalification.)

By evaluating benefits, risks, alignment, and other business and project factors, we can prioritize candidate projects and select the higher-ranking ones to get first crack at the organization's limited economic and human resources. This is the set of practices associated with project prioritization and selection, addressed in Chapter 2.1.

By monitoring performance of active projects against both the project goals and the selection criteria, we can adjust the portfolio to maximize return. This means being willing to restructure, delay, or even terminate projects with performance deficiencies. The ability to monitor such performance exists in all traditional project management systems. All we add in PPM is the routine to do so and the ability to feed these data into the PPM system. This is the set of practices associated with maintaining the project pipeline (Chapter 2.2).

The Voice of the Skeptic

This book does not profess to have all of the answers. Early adopters of PPM, an emerging art and science, are reporting phenomenal results. Nevertheless, as proven in the Hawthorne experiments, almost any kind of change can bring about initial improvements. Do we need more time to be sure that the improvements that have been experienced are directly related to the adoption of PPM practices? I think not. The first decade of PPM development and application has produced numerous stories of enormous success. We present four of these success stories in the case studies in Section Nine.

If there is any doubt about the value of PPM, it is whether PPM is equally effective across all project environments. In Chapter 3.2 on project prequalification, we look at three typical classifications of projects and discuss the applicability of PPM to each of these.

We have no doubt that there is a vastly increased awareness of the forces that help projects to contribute to business success. Through PPM, noticeable improvements in communication and cooperation between the various disciplines of the enterprise are being achieved.

Nevertheless, there are those who believe that some of the processes offer a simple formula for a complex condition. Some of these processes deal with financial valuations of the proposed projects, such as benefits, return on investment, or net present value without directing much effort toward how these values can be determined. Many PPM tools offer extended abilities to display such values without support for creating valid data. Other tools, such as analytic hierarchy process (AHP), are specifically designed to assist in simplifying the prioritization of complex issues and data. AHP is widely recognized and employed as an aid to the decision-making process (see Chapter 4.3). Still, the skeptic in me pauses to ask whether even this admirable technique might focus too much on the details and miss the big picture.

And then there is the other extreme: where supposedly very precise data are displayed with attractive, advanced graphic techniques.

These techniques, such as the increasingly popular bubble chart, are superb vehicles for presenting extensive, multidimensional data in intelligent, usable formats. They are so impressive as to allow us to overlook the possibility that the data displayed may not sit on a solid foundation.

In a recent discussion, a colleague raised this question:

> I find my skepticism to be directly proportional to the PPM software hype curve. The root of my skepticism lies in the benefit and benefit-risk side of PPM. I see bubble charts and Web forms as too simple and shallow to support the depth needed to analyze significant undertakings. Significant undertakings require in-depth business plans with market positioning, detailed financial models, trade-off studies, and competitive analysis. This analysis takes place well before any projects are initiated and continues throughout the life cycle. The approval process is interactive and face-to-face with many PowerPoint briefings. Now, one could argue that the PPM discipline embraces all this, but this embracing is more a declaration of hoped-for ownership rather than value-added.
>
> Because PPM software is limited to simple projects, it is relatively well positioned for internal work like information technology projects. I don't think I will ever see the day when Ford executives look at a project portfolio bubble chart to pick which cars to build. I do think that an IT exec could decide on a Web-based expense report over an upgrade to Office 2999 or vice versa using the PPM tools (but maybe not even here).

One message that we can derive from my colleague's declaration is that (as in any other discipline) we need to understand the available processes and tools and be prepared to apply them where practicable—but not blindly. Every data-based process is subject to somebody fouling up the numbers. Diligence and dutiful wariness must be built into the process.

Nothing in the PPM process precludes preparing traditional business plans and analyses. In fact, they are strongly endorsed.

Where PPM helps is in dealing with multiple business plans and opportunities.

Remember also that portfolio planning is based extensively on forecasting. I once read that forecasting is like driving an automobile while blindfolded and taking directions from someone who is looking out of the back window. You certainly want to be careful in betting the future of the company on data such as these.

To avoid falling into the trap of accepting faulty assumptions and data, everyone involved in PPM should become a devil's advocate. By this, I mean that we need to question things that look too good. Someone has to ask the difficult and probing questions. We need to be careful not to get swept up in the current of popular opinion. It may not take you where you want to go.

Even having said this, I am confident of the value of PPM as the best means of addressing the issues of aligning projects with strategies and attempting to select the best projects for the health of the business.

This book presents the many sides of PPM. The other authors and I offer an extensive overview of the fundamentals and why and where they can be employed. We provide several discussions of specific issues and techniques. Throughout the process, we maintain a skeptic's eye so as not to overly promote any part of this emerging discipline. We have noted that PPM is already delivering positive benefits and results. This book does not offer the final word on PPM because it is a work in progress. Still, it is fully ready for prime time, and we sincerely recommend that you consider putting these practices into action. We will also be maintaining a watchful eye on these applications, ever ready to report and implement improvements based on such feedback.

An Executive's Guide to Project Portfolio Management

As you read through the Contents and this Introduction, you may notice that there is considerable mention of projects. We also discuss the project management office, the management of projects in general, and some popular techniques that we use in managing projects.

However, the real focus of this book is how to ensure that projects contribute to a successful enterprise, so the target readership goes well beyond the project management community. In fact, it is the business executive who will gain the most from this material. If you are a senior manager, such as a chief executive officer, chief operations officer, chief financial officer, chief information officer, or a strategic planner, you are surely concerned about picking the right projects and getting the most out of your resources. The answers are in PPM. If you are an executive charged with the responsibility for information technology, application development, or new product development, this book was written for you.

Perhaps your executive duties limit the time that you have to read everything. For a comprehensive look at PPM, I suggest that you read all of Sections One and Two. Then you can select other chapters that attract your interest. Among these I recommend Chapters 3.1, 3.3, 3.4, 4.1, 5.1, 5.2, and 5.3. Information technology managers will want to read Section Six. Section Seven is a must for new product development managers. And don't miss the case studies in Section Nine. The overview chapters in Section Ten are excellent.

PPM brings the projects community and the operations community together to achieve business success. We hope that this book will facilitate a better partnership.

Navigating This Book

This book is organized into two parts and ten sections. Each section presents from one to six chapters.

Part One consists of thirteen chapters that I have written. Section One introduces PPM, describing what it is and why we need it. Section Two contains the meat of the discussion on PPM, with five chapters on selecting projects for the pipeline, maintaining the pipeline, executing PPM, integrating tools, and implementing PPM. If you can't find the time to read the entire book, you will find the essentials in these first two sections. The chapters in Section

Three address several important issues and techniques. These are some of the finer points of PPM.

Part Two presents twenty-one chapters contributed by experts in the field. Many of these are people who have extensive experience in PPM and have published their developments and research as well as their successes. A few have been induced to write for the first time about their subject and have delivered some of the best material, no doubt because of their closeness to the subject and their dedication to the application of PPM. To all, I express my deepest appreciation for the time and effort that they took to share their knowledge and expertise with us.

Each contributing author has his or her own view of PPM and usually a particular focus. At times, they use different terms or models to present their material. The differences, if any, do not refute anyone else's way of presenting PPM. Some authors simply present their material and let it speak for itself. Others state their point of view emphatically. These contributors were selected not because they all have a like mind toward PPM but rather for their independent focus. We believe that they have valuable expertise and a respected position that is well worth reading. Without endorsing any single point of view, I believe that all readers will benefit from the wider view of PPM.

Section Four contains four chapters on PPM techniques and issues, focusing on portfolio planning. These are topics that I touch on in Section Two and are covered here in greater detail by subject experts. The authors continue discussing PPM techniques and issues in Section Five, focusing on organizing and implementing PPM.

Sections Six and Seven look at PPM applications, first in information technology and then for new product development. The guest author for the two chapters on new product development applications is the recognized guru in this area, Robert G. Cooper.

The chapters in Section Eight discuss at length the application of PPM for advocates of theory of constraints (TOC) and critical chain project management (CCPM). TOC expert Larry Leach provides a primer on TOC and shows how PPM is a natural extension of TOC and CCPM practices.

Section Nine presents four case studies. The first two are written by the individuals who lead the successful development and implementation of PPM in their companies. They share insightful and proprietary wisdom as they have us follow along with their experiences. The other two case studies have been prepared by tool vendors who participated with their clients in developing and implementing PPM. What you can take away from these four case studies is more than worth the price of the book.

Finally, the five chapters in Section Ten sample what others are saying about PPM. The authors here are among the recognized experts in project management.

Thus, in Part Two, I have surveyed the best of the best and collected these practitioners' knowledge and wisdom so that you can find it all in one place. Our collective aim is to make this the only book that you will ever need on project portfolio management.

PART ONE

A Practical Guide to Project Portfolio Management

The thirteen chapters in Part One offer my personal view of PPM based on over forty years in the field of project management as a practitioner and a consultant. I am very exited about what PPM is bringing to the projects community in both the public and private sectors. I am especially pleased with how PPM serves the executives of any organization, providing a means of synchronizing the vast effort in projects with the expressed mission of the enterprise. I'm very upbeat about the benefits that are being realized by early adopters. But what I like about it the most is how practical it is.

Project portfolio management is not a highly scientific, theorem-oriented concept. It is just plain common sense. It is easy to implement and practical to employ. *Practical* is a key operative word here, and this is the approach that I take in bringing PPM to you.

First, we discuss what PPM is and why we need it. Then we get into the fundamentals of PPM: project prioritization and selection, maintaining the project pipeline, organizational considerations, integrating PPM tools with traditional project management tools, and implementing PPM. Finally, we cover some special issues and provide further guidance on how to make PPM work.

SECTION ONE

What Is Project Portfolio Management, and Why Do We Need It?

The project portfolio life span extends well beyond the project life cycle to include identification of needs and opportunities on the front end and the realization of benefits at the other end. PPM recognizes this, bridging the traditional gap between the projects and operations functions and delivering maximum value from limited resources. Every executive should demand that PPM practices be put in place, and they should lead in their development and execution.

The first three sections of this book cover the topic of PPM in increasing detail. Section 1 introduces PPM, discussing why it is so valuable and providing an overview of what PPM is. Section Two goes into the meat of PPM, providing complete coverage of what it takes to create a PPM capability and to implement it. Section Three covers some of the finer points pertinent to PPM.

When you read Chapter 1.1, it should become readily apparent that something has been missing in how we view the place of projects in the enterprise. It will also come as no surprise that PPM is growing exceptionally fast and that virtually all of the software vendors that support the project management discipline have revamped their offerings to support PPM.

I'll introduce you to the project portfolio life span. You'll learn why PPM is much more than just an extension to project management. You'll start to question whether your firm is working on the right projects. You'll discover that there is a significant gap between the projects function and the operations functions of most firms, and I'll show how to use PPM as a means to bridge that gap.

In Chapter 1.2, you'll see specifics on how to do just that. You'll get your first look at the things that you can accomplish with PPM and the processes that support these accomplishments. In addition, you'll find an overview of how to organize for PPM.

After four decades of being completely engrossed in project management, I thought that I fully understood its power and value. But as I learned about PPM, it opened an entirely new world of capabilities to exponentially increase our ability to use projects to build business value and fully integrate the projects environment with the ongoing business. After reading this section, I hope that you will feel the same way.

1.1

Why Do We Need Project Portfolio Management?

> Do traditional measures of project success miss the true business objectives? Scope, Time, Cost and Quality are only components of the objective, rather than independent measures of success.
>
> Harvey Levine, June 2000

Could what I said five years ago be considered blasphemous? Imagine going against conventional wisdom at a time when project portfolio management (PPM) was just emerging as a body of thought. Project management was finally getting its well-deserved recognition, and everyone was focusing on spreading the gospel of bringing projects in on time, within budget, and meeting scope and quality objectives. Well, almost everyone.

Why would anyone want to shoot holes in the acceptance of project management? No one is suggesting that project management is wrong. However, limiting our focus to the critical measures of project success confuses the means to an end with the end itself.

Almost everything written about measurements of project success dwells on the four pillars of success: scope, time, cost, and quality. We have been taught to identify the goals for success in each of these areas and then to create plans that balance these objectives.

Then we implement practices and use computer-based tools to measure how well we are accomplishing these objectives. When we meet these objectives and satisfy the project stakeholders, we consider the project to have been successful.

However, most executives are not interested in these areas of measurement. Instead, they talk about profitability, return on investment, delivery of benefits, and taking advantage of windows of opportunity. We used to say that executives are interested in just two things about projects: when they will be finished and what they will cost. Not anymore. Now (in the for-profit arena) they ask:

- What mix of potential projects will provide the best utilization of human and cash resources to maximize long-range growth and return on investment for the firm?
- How do the projects support strategic initiatives?
- How will the projects affect the value of corporate shares (stock)?

Similar issues apply to the nonprofit and government operations where optimizing the use of limited funds and resources and support of missions and strategies is vital. While PPM can be effectively applied to both the public and private sectors, most of the examples in this book use a for-profit enterprise as the model. With minor adjustments, PPM can be adapted to nonprofit and government operations.

Perhaps this is an oversimplification. However, if we start with this premise and examine its meaning, we can begin to realize the tremendous impact of this observation on the way that we conduct project management and even in the way that we select and implement project management tools.

The Emergence of Project Portfolio Management

Certainly it is not news to anyone that the basic concept of project management has evolved to what we call *enterprise project management*. At first, many people in the PM community thought that this shift was more of a way of aggrandizing project management—sort of a pompous elevating of project management to a higher level of importance. Later we came to realize that enterprise project management was a reflection of the importance of consolidating and integrating all of the organization's projects—for universal access and evaluation. Now we come to find that enterprise project management entails consideration of potential projects as well as approved projects. We also find that the emphasis has shifted from traditional project-centric objectives to higher-level operational objectives.

Projects, executives have come to realize, are the basis for the future profitability of the firm. Hence, they have a growing interest in how projects are selected and managed. They are precipitating an increased demand for more standardization and automation of project management. But what they are asking for is different from the requests from traditional project management sources. And what they are calling this emerging project management protocol has also changed. It is no longer just *project management* or even *enterprise project management*. It is now called *project portfolio management*.

Bridging the Gap Between Operations Management and Projects Management

Project portfolio management is the bridge between traditional operations management and project management (see Chapter 3.1). For organizations that will be depending on project success for the success of the overall enterprise, a well-structured bridge, built on a good foundation, is the preferred way to overcome the traditional gap between operations and projects management.

In PPM, it is assumed that the enterprise positions itself for increased strength and profitability through its selection and execution of projects and ensures that it continues to thrive in a world of constant change and the threat of competition.

The basic elements of PPM are not new, nor is the environment in which it is applied. However, before the emergence of PPM as a defined discipline, these elements were the responsibility of two distinct groups: operations management and projects management, each with its specific role:

Operations Management	Projects Management
Strategies	Schedule/time
Objectives, goals	Project cost
Business performance	Project performance
Stockholder satisfaction	Stakeholder satisfaction
Project selection and mix	Scope/change control
Resource availability	Resource utilization
Cash flow, income	Cash usage

The Traditional Organization

When the execution of projects is a normal part of the organization's business, typically the organization establishes, in parallel with the operations function, a function to manage the projects. This normally includes a central project office or project management office (PMO) and specialized personnel to manage projects. The PMO, under a chief project officer (or similar title), develops standards and practices directed at the effective execution of projects and the attainment of schedule, cost, scope, and quality objectives. In doing so, a project management planning and information system is put in place, and periodic measurements of project progress and performance are conducted.

In traditional organizations, responsibility for determining and achieving the organization's goals is assigned to the operations function. Senior managers with titles such as chief operating officer, chief technology officer, chief information officer, chief financial officer, and strategic planner establish objectives and goals and develop strategies to achieve these. When there are projects associated with these goals, these senior managers are expected to select from a menu of proposed and pending projects. The objective is to create the mix of projects most likely to support the achievement of the organization's goals within the preferred strategies and within the organization's resource (people and funding) constraints.

A problem common to many organizations is that there is no connection between the operations and projects functions and no structured, consistent, and meaningful flow of information between these two groups. The organization's objectives (enterprise-level goals) are hardly ever communicated to the project office, and the periodic measurements made by the projects group cannot be related to these objectives.

What a waste! Both groups are off in their own world, working to do the best that they can but not knowing if their efforts are effective or efficient. Are the projects that are being worked on (assuming that they were properly selected in the first place) still the best ones to support the objectives? How well are they supporting the objectives? Are there performance issues associated with meeting the objectives? How would the operations people know?

And over in the project office, when the project performance data is evaluated, what knowledge is available to influence the corrective action decisions? If the individual project objectives are in danger, what should the project manager know to work on balancing schedule, cost, scope, and quality parameters? Can this be effectively done in the absence of operations inputs?

Bridging the Gap Between Portfolio Planning and Portfolio Management

There is a second gap with which to contend. Our traditional approach is to separate the function of project selection from that of managing the project pipeline. The traditional assumption is that once a project is approved, it is separated from the parental umbilical cord. The criteria on which the selection was based are lost. The only criteria remaining for monitoring project performance are specific to the individual project goals rather than the portfolio as a whole.

And how shall we deal with project and portfolio assessment? Is a project a static item or a dynamic system? If a project is dynamic in nature (its scope, timing, and cost are subject to change), then what effect does this have on the project portfolio? The typical project has a range of possible outcomes and costs. There is the base case and potential upside and downside. If the project was selected on the basis of a set of assumptions (stated in the base case), does that project still belong in the portfolio when its attributes change? Periodically we need to review the project to test assumptions, update givens, and monitor progress; examine alternatives; and consider remodeling the portfolio.

Thus, we can see that there are potential weaknesses in the typical project management implementation:

- The organization's objectives and goals, as supported by the project portfolio, are not communicated to the people responsible for project performance.
- The project performance, as monitored by the project managers, is not communicated to the portfolio managers, strategic planners, and senior managers.
- The gap that exists between these two groups, in both communication and available information, prevents active management of the portfolio based on the current, changing status of the component projects.

What is needed is a basis for addressing project selection issues, deciding on project termination, facilitating reallocation of resources, changing of priorities, and evaluating alternatives. Without this capability, there is no project portfolio management.

The Project Portfolio Life Span

Perhaps the strongest way to delineate the differences between project management and PPM is to look at the true life span of projects within the PPM environment. We usually consider the life span of a project to be from authorization to delivery. In some models, we start earlier, with a proposal.

With PPM, this life span is expanded, on both ends. According to Max Wideman, the project portfolio life span (PPLS) consists of the following phased components (see Figure 1.1-1):[1]

1. Identification of needs and opportunities
2. Selection of best combinations of projects (the portfolios)
3. Planning and execution of the projects (project management)
4. Product launch (acceptance and use of deliverables)
5. Realization of benefits

Looking at this model, you can see that the purview of the project office is concentrated on item 3. The expansion of the life span and scope to include all five items requires the involvement and leadership of the executive side of the organization and the development of a portfolio governance culture, processes and tools.

Furthermore, the measurement of success does not stop with project delivery. The project was designed to deliver certain defined benefits. The true measure of success must extend to the evaluation of whether these benefits were in fact obtained.

FIGURE 1.1-1 First Three Steps of the Project Portfolio Life Span

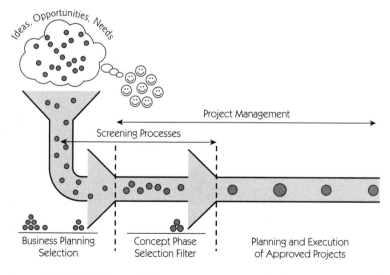

Source: R. M. Wideman, *A Management Framework for Project, Program and Portfolio Integration* (New Bern, N.C.: Trafford Publishing, 2004), p. 169.

1.2

What Is Project Portfolio Management?

> Project portfolio management is the management of the project portfolio so as to maximize the contribution of projects to the overall welfare and success of the enterprise.

Now that organizations have discovered the importance of projects and project management, the next logical step is to move toward the recognition of PPM. However, it is a very big mistake to think that PPM is merely an extension of project management. These two equally important functions are not alike at all.

As more and more firms adopt project management central office or project management office (PMO) methods, it would not surprise me to see responsibility for PPM thrust fully into the hands of the chief project officer (CPO). This too would be a mistake.

This chapter presents an overview of what PPM is as well as what it is not. Each of these topics is discussed in greater detail in Section Two.

Project Portfolio Management Is Not Just Enterprise Project Management

A critical mistake is to think that PPM is fundamentally the management of multiple projects. This is not so. PPM is the management of the project portfolio so as to maximize the contribution of projects to the overall welfare and success of the enterprise. This means that:

- Projects must be aligned with the firm's strategy and goals.
- Projects must be consistent with the firm's values and culture.
- Projects must contribute (directly or indirectly) to a positive cash flow for the enterprise.
- Projects must effectively use the firm's resources—both people and other resources.
- Projects must not only provide for current contributions to the firm's health but must help to position the firm for future success.

This cannot be accomplished solely within the projects domain. PPM, to be fully effective, requires the participation of several core components of the firm. Furthermore, it requires the integration of several systems within the organization. Let's look at each of these first from an organizational point of view and then from a systems point of view.

What Processes Comprise PPM?

We can subdivide PPM into two primary phases: the first focusing on the prioritization and selection of projects for the portfolio and the second dealing with managing the projects within the portfolio. Although these two components require different practices and are separate in nature, each affects the other, so they must be integrated.

Phase 1: Selecting Projects for the Pipeline

This phase deals with proposed projects and provides a structured process to:

- Guide the preparation of project proposals (business case) so that they can be evaluated.
- Evaluate project value and benefits.
- Appraise the risks that might modify these benefits.
- Align candidate projects with enterprise strategies.
- Determine the most favorable use of resources.
- Rank projects according to a set of selection criteria.
- Select projects for the portfolio.

In order to perform the ranking and selection of projects, it will also be necessary to:

- Execute a strategic plan and subsequent tactical planning guidelines.
- Maintain an inventory of available resources.
- Establish budget buckets for the portfolios.
- Decide on an optimum or acceptable size of the project pipeline.
- Establish a set of weighted scoring criteria.
- Set some boundaries or guidance for acceptable risk.

Details of the prioritization and selection phase are presented in Chapter 2.1.

Phase 2: Maintaining the Project Pipeline

After selecting projects, we manage these projects with an eye toward achieving two sets of objectives: to meet the *project* objectives (this is the traditional project tracking and control process that we used even before we implemented PPM) and to meet the *portfolio* (business) objectives.

When we execute the ranking and selection phase, we match the characteristics of the proposed projects with a set of selection criteria. Then when we execute the projects, we need to monitor and evaluate any conditions that might alter either of these (project characteristics or selection criteria). Periodically we need to update or confirm the criteria used for project selection. On a regular basis, we evaluate the status and performance of each project. If the performance will change the values that we assumed at the proposal stage (in the business case), we need to consider whether the project should remain in the portfolio. Although delaying or terminating an active project may not always be possible or prudent, we should always consider those options as part of managing the portfolio.

To facilitate the periodic evaluation of project status and performance, we can rely on two well-known techniques: earned value analysis and the Stage-Gate® process.[1] (Both techniques are discussed in Chapter 2.2. In addition, Chapter 3.6 is devoted to earned value analysis and Chapter 7.1 to the Stage-Gate® Process.

Organizing for PPM

The responsibility for leading the PPM function falls to the person responsible for operations management within the firm. In most organizations, this is the individual who brings together the strategies, measurements, and cash management. It may be someone with the title of chief operating officer (COO) or vice president of operations. It also could be the chief executive officer or president. Also playing key roles on the PPM team are the chief financial officer or vice president of finance, and the CPO, or vice president of projects. While the project management office would have the major role in operating and supporting the PPM practices, it would not own the final decision role. In a firm where information technology is the primary business, the chief information officer would certainly have a significant role. Rounding out the PPM team are representatives of the various functional operations and the marketing function.

Here, we are assuming that the functional departments own the critical resources that will be used on projects. Hence, the importance of their participation on the PPM team. In addition, because the management of the projects portfolio will require consideration of future engagements and resource demands, the marketing operation will have to contribute forecasting data to the PPM function.

Note that there are no new functional positions defined for PPM. Rather, we are viewing PPM as a *process*, to be supported by the PMO and senior personnel already in place in the firm. The PPM process will be added to the responsibilities of these senior members, who will function as a team to manage the projects portfolio under the leadership of the COO (or equivalent). It's not as if these newly defined (or redefined) responsibilities are changed. What is different within the PPM process is that the individual responsibilities for the project portfolio are executed within a structured, integrated PPM team.

A growing popular term for the process of guiding the portfolio is *governance*. This is especially so in the information technology area, where the term *IT governance* is becoming synonymous with PPM. Further discussion of organization and roles is presented in Chapter 2.3. IT governance is also addressed in Chapters 5.3 and 6.2.

Supporting Processes

So far we have brought several functions together under the umbrella of PPM: projects, operations, financial, functional departments and resources, and marketing. Each of these is supported by automated information systems. A challenge under PPM is to bring these computer-based systems together. Furthermore, extended capabilities must be added to support the intended benefits of PPM and to support integration of the individual systems.

If you have an enterprise resource management (ERP) system or a multifunction project management system, you probably have the underlying structure to move in the desired direction. But even then, new processes and functions will be needed. We look at the tools for PPM and tool integration in Chapter 2.4.

SECTION TWO

The Fundamentals of a Project Portfolio Management Process

Executives expect projects to be aligned with strategies, make effective use of limited resources, and deliver certain benefits. The processes associated with PPM bring the operations and projects functions together to fulfill these expectations.

We started this book with a discussion of why we need PPM, followed by an overview of what PPM is and what PPM is not. To really appreciate PPM, we need to take a good look at the fundamentals.

The five chapters in this section provide a complete review of PPM that will help you decide if PPM is for you. If the answer is yes, it will help you understand what you need to do to set up a PPM capability. Once you buy into the process, you can move on to detailed discussions of specific PPM areas in the sections that follow.

In Chapters 2.1 to 2.5, we will assume that you can accept certain key premises and conditions:

- A basic project management capability is in place, managed and supported by a professional staff. It is preferable that this function be centralized (for standardization and consistency). In our discussion, we will refer to such a function as the project management office (PMO).

• There is a desire to develop a structured approach to selecting projects, based on a fair and balanced ranking system. The projects that are selected will be aligned with business strategies and placed in portfolios that represent the tactical implementation of such strategies. (Any discussion in this book about a portfolio may also apply to one of several portfolios or subportfolios that are created to support the strategies.)

• After projects are selected for the portfolio, they will be managed to achieve two sets of objectives. One set consists of objectives that are associated with specific project goals and commitments. The second set consists of evaluating project performance so as to assess the ability of the project to continue to meet the original selection criteria (that is, to realize the expected benefits). A culture and practices will be developed to consider delaying or terminating projects that no longer represent adequate value or efficient use of resources.

• New roles will be created to support PPM. This would include the naming of a team responsible for portfolio governance. This team will be able to act for senior executives (or may include the executives) to oversee the portfolios. In this section, the governance team is referred to as the *governance council*.

• The PMO will review its current project management tool set for support of the new PPM functions. If the existing tool set has not added such support, the PMO will evaluate additional software capabilities to be integrated with the project management tools.

Discussion of a PPM process must consider five major areas:

• Selecting projects for the pipeline, that is, what goes in the pipeline (Chapter 2.1)
• Maintaining the pipeline, that is, what stays in the pipeline (Chapter 2.2)
• Executing PPM, that is, who does it (Chapter 2.3)
• Tools for data gathering and analysis and other PPM processes (Chapter 2.4)
• Implementing PPM (Chapter 2.5)

Where Do We Start?

Getting started in implementing a PPM process is a bit like the chicken-and-egg question. Do we first attack the existing portfolio and then implement an improved project selection process? Or do we accept the current portfolio and go right after the selection of new projects? There is no prescribed order. However, reports from the field indicate that many firms have first reviewed their current portfolio, eliminating a significant portion of their project load (due to redundancy, nonalignment with strategies, poor value, or inefficient use of resources), thus making room to add more valuable projects.

In reality, the two phases are inseparable. The processes form a loop: build the project portfolio; manage the project portfolio; adjust the project pipeline, if indicated, based on project performance and reevaluation; consider proposed projects to fill availabilities due to completed, delayed, or terminated projects; update the project portfolio; and so on. Since we cannot address all of these parts at once, we will look at the process for selecting new projects first. Then we'll look at managing the pipeline, followed by discussion of issues of PPM execution, including adjustments to organizational roles and responsibilities.

Purpose and Types of Projects

When we talk about "projects" in a portfolio, what do we mean by *projects?* The flavor of a project portfolio management process will depend somewhat on the kinds of projects involved. Although most firms are now heavily involved in projects, the purposes and types of projects vary—for instance:

• The project is for the benefit of an external client. The primary benefit to the project producer is income (profit). Secondary benefits may include making use of surplus resources, building a reputation in a new area, or creating reusable technology or knowledge. Examples of these are architectural, engineering, and construction projects; consulting; temporary labor sources; and professional services organizations.

- The project is for the benefit of the performing company: to create new products and services that will be sold (at a profit). Examples are manufacturing and process companies, software developers, and pharmaceutical firms.
- The project is for the benefit of the performing company: to improve or maintain capabilities required to operate the business effectively. These would include internal information technology projects, manufacturing processes, facilities improvements, or expansions.
- The project is for the benefit of the performing company: to improve a competitive position. All of the previous examples apply here.

We can see that a project portfolio management process for Bechtel or Halliburton, involved in architectural, engineering, and construction work, would have a different focus from the internal IT department at Citicorp.

Just as traditional project management can be effectively applied to all types of industries and technologies, PPM has a universal applicability. There will be variations in the process and the roles, but the fundamentals are similar. What follows here is equally applicable to new product development, information technology, and dozens of other business areas. With some modification, it is equally applicable to nonprofits and the public sector.

We can also see that the funnel of proposed projects could be filled from many sources. Project requests may come in through the firm's opportunity management program, product managers or other internal requests, or senior management (to support strategic initiatives). The challenge of PPM is to filter the project requests so that the projects that pass through the funnel into the pipeline best serve the long-term interests of the firm.

2.1

Selecting Projects for the Pipeline

> The objective is to create the mix of projects most likely to support the achievement of the organization's goals, aligned with the preferred strategies, and within the organization's resource (people and funding) constraints.

There are thousands of true stories that illustrate what is wrong with how most organizations determine which projects to approve. It is obvious that the pointy-haired guy (Dilbert's boss in the cartoon *Dilbert*) has gotten around. Here's an example of just one of these situations:

The company was a major manufacturer of paper goods. When it added a new project to the pipeline, the process began when a client of the paper company called her sales rep and asked if the company could provide a product to a new specification. The sales rep called the product line manager, who in turn called the development engineer responsible for that technology. The engineer decided whether he would like to work on creating a version of the product to the new specification. He has the option (solely on his own) to accept or decline the product line manager's solicitation. If he decides to work on the project, he has the right to draw on several of the firm's resources.

Here is what is wrong with this picture:

- The engineer has no idea how this modified product fits into the firm's strategies.
- He has no data on marketability or profitability.
- He has no process for performing a value/benefits evaluation.
- He probably hasn't considered the capability to support the revised specification.
- He has not considered risk issues.
- He is committing other resources, which may be needed for higher-priority projects.
- There really isn't a practice for determining project priorities.

What about the customer? Is she really serious about the revised product? Will she buy it at a price that is not yet determined? Will she take her business elsewhere if the current supplier does not deliver a new version? Can she get a product to the new spec from someone else? A development engineer would be unlikely to ask these questions or have the answers. Yet this information is essential in making the project decision and should be an integral part of the project selection process.

The project pipeline for this firm was a disaster. Resources were shifted from project to project, many of which should never have been in the pipeline in the first place. Resources were diverted from high-value, low-risk, strategically aligned projects to someone's pipe dream. Many of these projects never reached completion. Meanwhile, opportunities were lost and money was wasted.

Evaluating Candidate Projects

We'll assume that the objective of the PPM process is to prioritize work that brings the most value to the firm. The definition of *value* will certainly differ in accordance with the firm's focus, strategies, and types of projects. Regardless of these differences, a project portfolio management process should address the following:

- A ranking of value and benefits
- An appraisal of risk (in achieving these benefits)
- An inventory of resource availability and allocation
- An idea of an optimum or acceptable size of the project pipeline

The criteria for each of these factors will have to be customized by the firm that is implementing the PPM process. This definition will be driven by the firm's strategic focus. The project portfolio is one of the layers of tactical planning that are executed in support of the strategic plan. So we must add to the list above:

- Publication of the strategic plan to the project portfolio management governance council. (In defining the PPM process, we assume that the process will involve some type of governance council, usually a team of senior people designated by top management to make decisions about the project portfolio. The roles and organization for PPM are addressed in Chapter 2.3.)
- Development of tactical plans that would involve projects in support of the strategic plan
- Definitions of value and benefits as they apply to the tactical plans
- Some boundaries on acceptable risk parameters
- A long-range projection of resource strategies

Ranking Value and Benefits

Assuming that the number of potential projects exceeds the number that can be effectively executed in a reasonable time, there must be a means of prioritizing each project. This process must be structured and conducted by a team in order to eliminate the tendency to select projects by political means, power plays, or emotion.

Conceptually this ranking process is simple, although the individual parameters will vary according to strategies, resources, profit motive, and other categories. The process is not unlike that used in selecting items for an investment portfolio. In fact, this is an investment portfolio: you are investing in projects with the objective of maximizing the return.

One of the primary ranking factors will be expected return on investment (ROI). However, there are qualifiers associated with this process. You can't prioritize projects using ROI alone. You need to also consider:

- Alignment with strategic and tactical plans
- Balance between maintenance projects and investment projects
- Allocation of R&D expenditures and resources
- Allocation of marketing expenditures and resources
- Effective use of resources
- Probability of delivering the project on time, within budget, and with the designed work scope
- Ancillary benefits (nonfinancial)

The ranking practice should use a balanced scorecard approach, with each of the factors listed and weighted. As each factor is rated, an aggregate score for each project is obtained. The rating of each factor can be prompted by a series of questions, with the answers noted in a narrative format and then converted to a numerical score based on the level of the answer against a guideline. (For additional discussion and details on ranking and prioritization of projects, see Section Four and Chapter 7.2.)

Risk

The value/benefits ranking may be modified by risk: the risk that the perceived benefits might not be realized. A potential million-dollar return with a 10 percent chance of happening is probably not as desirable as a potential quarter of a million-dollar return with a 90 percent probability. A new technology with a 20 percent chance of success may not fit with the strategy. A project that is vulnerable to critical delays might be a lower-ranked candidate than one that is certain to be delivered in time to produce the expected benefit.

A typical value formula takes the expected benefits, minus the total cost of ownership, divided by the risk. The risk factor takes time into consideration, acknowledging that a longer duration to ROI increases the potential risk. (See Chapter 4.2 for a detailed discussion on how to determine the value of a project and Chapter 3.3 for more on risk and uncertainty.)

A common practice is to display the value/benefit ranking and the risk ranking on a grid (Figure 2.1-1). Preference would be given to projects that appear in the high value–low risk quartile.

As the typical project environment moves away from repetitive-type projects to unique and original challenges, risk assessment and management becomes an essential part of PPM.

Resources

If we acknowledge that the availability of resources is a constraint on the number of projects in the pipeline, then why can't we just increase resources as we need them? There are a number of obvious answers to this question:

- Resources cost money. They have an impact on cash flow. In a well-managed organization, the size of a firm's labor force is dictated

FIGURE 2-1.1 Risk-Benefits Ranking Grid Diagram

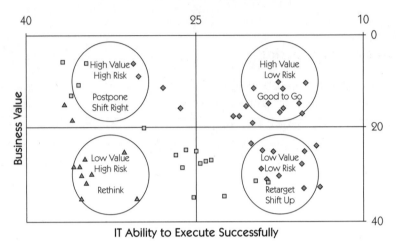

HP IT Program Selection Process

Source: Don Kingsberry, Hewlett-Packard. See the case study in Chapter 9.2.

by the firm's revenue. In a growing organization, the amount of resources are increased incrementally as the revenues increase, usually by a set proportion. They are not increased just because there are more projects in the pipeline than can be supported by current resources.

- Effective and efficient use of resources calls for a stable workforce—a group of people who understand how the organization works and communicates and who fit the organization's culture and can work well as teams on projects. Although there are times when temporary or transient resources can be used to meet specific needs, it is best to avoid this as a standard source of resources. The cost of supervision, coordination, and learning curve issues will often negate the benefits.

- One of the key objectives of a managed portfolio is balance. This is a well-respected strategy in investment portfolios and should also be an objective in project portfolios. Resource balancing is one aspect of a balanced project portfolio. This is a bidirectional process. The mix of projects and the mix of resources should be manipulated to best use the firm's resources on work that is well matched to the available strengths and skills.

Size of the Pipeline

How much project work is enough? How much is too much? If we proceed on the basis that projects generate value and benefits, then doesn't it follow that the more projects that we have in the pipeline, the better off we will be? *Ridiculous!* you say! Well, of course, it is. But that doesn't stop many organizations from shooting at everything that moves.

The opportunities (or demand) for projects usually exceed the capacity to execute them all. We all have stories in which project deliverables were significantly delayed because the pipeline was overloaded. In almost every case, the delays eroded the value and benefits of the venture (as well as alienated the client).

There is significant feedback from successful firms that tends to show that doing fewer projects actually improves the bottom line. Committed resources are staying on the assigned job and doing the assigned work in support of established target dates. The income or benefits start earlier, and everyone is happier. Furthermore, because the projects are not drawn out, new projects can be added sooner, and just as many projects may eventually find their way into the pipeline and under improved conditions.

The message here is very clear: limiting the amount of work in the pipeline so that the projects can be completed as quickly as possible results in increased profits or savings and more satisfied clients, and it leads to executing more projects without increasing resources.

Adding an Approved Project to the Pipeline

A structured approach toward project initiation is critical to managing a successful portfolio of projects. Here are some critical first steps.

Issue a Project Charter

Although often omitted from the project process, there should be a formal project authorization practice. This is best instituted by means of a project charter document that contains much of the early description of project content, objectives, and budget. It is both a starting point for the project initiation process and the basis for guidance and measurement during execution. It specifies the project sponsor, the intended benefits and benefactors, and the source of funding. The project charter serves as the spending authorization. Time or expenses should not be charged to a project until such charges are authorized. The authorization document should specify who may charge and to what accounts the charges can go. Spending authorizations may be granted by phases. The project team should set up the Stage-Gate® criteria for the specific project, based on the established life cycle standard.[1] These are used to evaluate project progress before proceeding to the next major phase. (We introduce Stage-Gates in Chapter 2.2. Stage-Gate developer Robert Cooper describes the process in even greater detail in Chapter 7.1.)

Establish Critical Parameters

This includes targets, limits, and thresholds. The basis for these parameters is the values that were used to evaluate the project during the selection phase. For instance, what is the target delivery date? What amount of time extension can be tolerated? When do projected delays dictate that continuation of the effort be evaluated? Milestone dates may also be important and can help to identify out-of-tolerance conditions earlier in the project. Target and limit values should also be established for cost items, technology accomplishments, window-of-opportunity issues, and any area where performance is critical to supporting the criteria associated with the original goals. This process is crucial to prevent wishful-thinking projects from sapping the resources of the firm.

Determine What Is to Be Measured and by Whom

What gets measured to monitor the targets, limits, and thresholds? What is the mechanism for making the measurements? Who makes the measurements, who evaluates them against the measurement parameters, and who reports out-of-tolerance situations?

In Chapter 2.2, we'll look at the fundamentals of managing the pipeline with respect to maintaining the optimal portfolio.

2.2

Maintaining the Pipeline

> The identification of opportunities and the selection of the best projects are only the beginning. It is the realization of benefits that is the end objective. The portfolio must be managed to deliver those benefits.

Due to our effective application of the project selection process, we have established a portfolio of projects that are aligned with the firm's strategies, maximize potential benefits, and make the most effective use of the firm's resources. At least that was the situation when the projects were chosen and initiated. Now that the projects are underway, has anything happened that would lead us to want to change these decisions?

In the practice of PPM, one fundamental is to treat projects as if their selection was conditional. That's not to say that every project is on continual probation. We plan and execute each project with the intention of bringing it to a successful completion. But there is no blank check. There are numerous conditions that could warrant a reevaluation of a project's position in the portfolio.

This being the case, the normal process of project control must undergo some change in order to recognize the increased importance of the project status and performance as a part of the PPM process. In this chapter, we look at the fundamentals of maintaining the project pipeline (that is, what stays in the pipeline):

- Periodic measurement of status and performance
- Evaluation of status and performance against critical parameters
- Reporting of items that don't support targets, limits, or thresholds
- Stage-Gate® and bounding box concepts[1]

Modern Project Management (Past Its Prime?)

For about the past forty-five years (the era of modern project management), the focus of project management was on successfully completing projects, delivering project content, and satisfying project stakeholders. We paid significant attention to issues of schedule, resource use, cost, and quality. We employed specialized computer-based tools such as critical path scheduling, critical chain, risk analysis, resource allocation and leveling, and multiproject reporting engines. Project management grew from an arcane practice to a widespread and respected profession. And we took these scattered project management practitioners and brought them into centralized project management offices (PMO).

While those of us in the project management discipline were joyful when we helped to achieve project management success, we were dismayed to learn that project success did not always equate to business success. Across the hall from the PMO, senior operating personnel were often disconnected from the projects scene, as if the hallway were the Maginot Line. "Why," they would ask, "are so many projects not contributing to the firm's bottom line?" "Why," they would query, "are critical and scarce resources being allocated to work that is not aligned with strategic objectives?" They searched to find the "value" in these projects.

Across the hall in the PMO, they would ask, "What strategic objectives?" "Value? That's not in our purview. Isn't it enough to bring the project in on schedule and within budget? How can we perform so well and still fail to produce the results that senior management demands?"

The schism is even greater than that. What about the projects that don't make it to the end? Or the projects that do make it all the way through but deliver an unusable product? Finally, we have begun to question whether the projects should have been approved or continued past a point of limited value. So it is time to enter the era of postmodern project management, or what we now call project portfolio management (PPM).

PPM Is More Than Selecting Projects

PPM is primarily the process of determining which projects should be in the firm's project portfolio. In Chapter 2.1, we discussed the process of selecting projects for the portfolio. In this chapter, we turn to maintenance of the portfolio.

During the selection process, we make assumptions about the value of candidate projects. We look at the opportunities and balance them against potential risks. We predict the effect of the project on revenue and cash flow and consider the costs of the project. We make many assumptions about key criteria at the completion of the project (and major segments of the project) according to a forecasted time line.

But the project and business environments are not cast in concrete. These are not static environments. Projects don't always go as planned. The assumptions may become less valid with time. Windows of opportunity close, and sometimes unpredictably.

Managing the Pipeline

During the project selection process, we match the assumptions about the project with the assumptions about the business needs and opportunities. Once the projects are in the pipeline, we update both sets of assumptions. On the projects side, we periodically measure project status and performance. On the business side, we periodically validate or adjust strategies and the assumptions about value, risk, resources, budgets, opportunity, and need.

Two popular and proven techniques that are available to support management of the project pipeline are (1) earned value analysis and (2) the Stage-Gate process. Each of these processes is introduced in this chapter to provide an overview of their contribution to PPM. (For a more detailed discussion of earned value analysis, see Chapter 3.6, and of the Stage-Gate process, see Chapter 7.1.)

Earned Value Analysis

How can we tell if a project is proceeding according to plan? If we are employing critical path scheduling techniques (CPM), diminishing float or slack is an indication of schedule slippage. However, with its focus on the critical path activities, this doesn't always reveal how badly the entire scope of work is falling behind. It also doesn't measure the actual costs against the amount of work that has been accomplished. The bottom line is that monitoring float or slack is not an adequate device for evaluating project performance.

A better way is the earned value analysis technique (EVA). EVA can even be used in the absence of a critical path schedule, but it works best in conjunction with the CPM. To use EVA, there should be a list of the work to be performed, a weight factor for each item on the list, and a planned schedule of accomplishment. When we use a CPM, these items become a natural part of the process. The weight factor can be the budget in either cost or labor-hours. This budget is expressed as the budget at completion (BAC). When the work is scheduled, we can generate the budgeted cost of work scheduled (BCWS), which is the planned effort at any point in time.

In order to track status and performance, we need to periodically provide two pieces of information for each work item. The first is the item percent complete (%C). By multiplying the %C times the BAC, we can compute the budgeted cost of work performed (BCWP). This is the earned value. I prefer to call it the earned value of the work performed. By comparing the value of the work performed (BCWP) to the value of the work that we had planned to accomplish (BCWS), we can calculate the schedule variance (SV) at any point in time. If we had planned to do 50 percent of the work item and accomplished only 20 percent, then we can clearly tell that the item is behind. By using the budget values in the calculation, we are able to roll up the SV to any level of the work breakdown structure (WBS). By dividing the BCWP by the BCWS, we produce the schedule performance index (SPI). In this example, the SPI would indicate that we are making only 40 percent of the progress that we had planned. (The acronyms used here are the traditional terms for EVA. A simplified set of terms is gaining popularity and is introduced in Chapter 3.6.)

To repeat, the first progress data item is BCWP (based on the %C). The second progress item is actual cost for work performed (ACWP). With these two data items (synchronized time-wise), we can evaluate cost performance. To generate a cost variance (CV), we compare what we have spent (the ACWP) to the budget for the work that we actually accomplished (BCWP). This is an important improvement over older accounting methods. Before we had earned value data, it was common to compare actual costs to planned costs. But this can produce a misleading story when the progress has not kept up with the plan. In the example, if we had actually spent 30 percent of the budget to accomplish 20 percent of the defined work, we are really overspent by 50 percent. By dividing the BCWP by the ACWP, we produce the schedule performance index (SPI).

For a more detailed discussion on EVA techniques, see Chapter 3.6. It's really much more straightforward than it sounds.

Updating Critical Parameters

The EVA data provides information about project performance against the plan. With this information, the team can evaluate whether certain deficient performance warrants consideration of terminating the project prior to completion, changing the priority of the project, or reallocating resources to other work.

However, there will generally be an additional set of factors to consider. Has there been any change in the need for this project? Is the window of opportunity still open? Has critical technology changed? Have the firm's strategies changed? On a periodic basis, all of the criteria that were examined when putting a value on the project should be validated and updated.

The project management office (PMO) will publish reports indicating where defined targets, limits, and thresholds have been violated. The PPM governance council will consider this information, together with the updated critical parameters, to evaluate all projects for continuation or termination.

There is a special case where a structured reevaluation of the projects in the portfolio against the selection criteria is of paramount importance. This is when there is a major departure from the published strategic plan, such as when there is a merger of two firms. In this situation, the newly merged entity will publish a revised strategic plan and the PMO and GC will review the entire portfolio for alignment with the new plan. It would not be surprising to find cause to eliminate 5 to 25 percent of the project volume due to duplication of efforts or nonalignment with emerging strategies.

The Stage-Gate Process

If you hang around with some new product development (NPD) people, it won't be very long before someone reverently invokes the name "Cooper." This is a reference to Robert G. Cooper, widely recognized as an NPD guru, and father of the Stage-Gate process, who has much to contribute to the discipline of PPM.

The typical NPD project consists of a series of steps starting with project conception and leading to product delivery/launch. These steps can usually be grouped into a series of phases. Each phase will have a number of activities, possibly performed in multiple disciplines, leading to an interim milestone or goal.

The Stage-Gate concept was developed primarily to enhance the efforts involved in new product development. It is a natural practice to apply to PPM. (In Chapter 7.1, Cooper thoroughly covers this topic as originally developed for NPD and technology development.)

In the Stage-Gate process, each phase (called a *stage*) is separated by a decision point (called a *gate*). As described by Cooper for the NPD environment, Stage-Gate is applied across the entire project life cycle. Conditions for passing through a gate are defined. At the end of a stage, a cross-functional team evaluates the status against the pass/no-pass conditions.

I believe that the process can be expanded in the development and testing stages to improve management of projects during those phases. This would entail declaring development milestones as mini-gates that would be monitored by the PMO. In this way, the project doesn't have to wait until development is completed before evaluating it for a kill or delay decision.

Therefore, active projects within the portfolio continue to be subject to a Stage-Gate control process. Just as there is a set of criteria for determining if the project is to be selected for the active portfolio, each gate will have a set of metrics by which the project can be evaluated. The PMO reviews each project at each gate, before making a go/no-go recommendation to the governance council. Funding may be cut off or the project put on hold if the evaluation data shows that the project performance is not supporting the original plan or is no longer making sound use of limited resources. Other reasons for killing the project include technical limitations or failure, a change in financial considerations, or inability to meet the allowable time window.

The governance council is the gatekeeper. The council is made up of senior representatives of the functions responsible for business success. Evaluations are made against predetermined criteria and decisions are made by comparing the metrics to those criteria. Gut feelings or territorial protectionism should be resisted.

Stage-Gate techniques need not be limited to NPD projects. These practices can be applied effectively to any type of project that has identifiable phases.

The Bounding Box Approach

What if your project doesn't fit well into a phased mode? Perhaps there are significant overlaps between basic phases. Or the project contains some looping components, as might be found in pure research projects.

In this case, you might want to pass up the Stage-Gate process for the *bounding box approach*. This process calls for setting selected critical parameters (boundaries) and is a type of management-by-exception technique. The governance council approves a set of targets or limits, such as delivery dates, cash flow, projected returns, and performance metrics. As long as the project stays within the boundaries, the project team will control most of the action and decisions. However, if a critical target or limit is compromised, then the situation must be identified by the PMO and brought to the attention of the governance council. The PMO and governance council then review the project to consider project termination or continuation with reset targets and limits.

Managing Projects with a High Degree of Uncertainty

We have acknowledged that two of the primary application candidates for PPM are the fields of information technology and NPD. These two fields share a common challenge: they often have projects with a high degree of uncertainty.

These high-uncertainty projects create two distinct problems in regard to PPM. The first is a high and complex risk condition, which we address at length in Chapter 3.3. The second problem is that of setting performance targets and metrics for projects where what is learned from each phase defines the succeeding phase. This issue is addressed by establishing two sets of targets by phase. One set consists of long-range soft targets, based on the business case that was presented with the project proposal. As with the bounding box, we look for project performance issues that would indicate that the project might not be delivering the benefits that were expected as a condition of selection. The second set is shorter-term hard targets that would be used for the EVA. These targets would be updated at the end of each phase. As each phase clarifies the efforts and objectives of the next phase, a set of specific target metrics is produced. What we avoid by this method is having the project being measured against an obsolete set of metrics. (For discussion on phased baselining and other aspects of managing the EVA baseline and scope changes, see Practical Project Management: Tips, Tactics, and Tools, Chapter 7.1.)[2]

Success Stories

Organizations can benefit in several ways by employing a structured termination process—for example:

- During the first ninety days of the merger between HP and Compaq, the global project management office stopped over one hundred projects or programs that were not aligned with the emerging strategy or made poor use of resources. (See Chapter 9.2.)

- In 2003, AOL built an entirely new project management culture around its implementation of PPM. It set up seven portfolio management teams, each centered on a line of business. For the 2004 planning cycle, AOL was able to achieve a 40 percent reduction in demand hours (from the initial portfolio), allowing it to balance resource capacity versus demand without additional head count. (See Chapter 9.3.)

- There are reported claims that the best-performing companies averaged 40 percent early cancellation of projects using Stage-Gate techniques to review value against risk.

- Critical resources are freed up for higher-value projects.
- Projects that are not performing well, whether due to technical, schedule, cost, or scope problems, do not continue to drain resources and dollars.

2.3

Executing Project Portfolio Management

> PPM is an enterprise-wide process involving a wide range of participants. It is also an extremely visible and sensitive process. How well this process is executed will have the greatest possible impact on the viability and success of the firm for an extended time.

Any implementation of a PPM capability needs strong and visible sponsorship of the defined processes by the senior executives and new or revised roles and responsibilities for the people who will make it happen. In this chapter, we discuss the execution of PPM, focusing on who does what.

Extending the Boundaries

The process for PPM extends well beyond the scope of traditional project management. Consider, for example, some of the following functions that are usually beyond the typical purview of project managers or the project management office (PMO) in the traditional project management process:

- Identifying opportunities and needs
- Selecting which projects are to be undertaken
- Selecting which projects are to be terminated or deferred
- Establishing project priorities
- Projecting revenue and effect on cash flow
- Aligning projects with strategic objectives
- Evaluating the value and benefits of the project to the firm
- Making a determination as to whether there are adequate benefits from the opportunity to overcome predicted risks
- Ensuring balance among various types of projects (maintenance, opportunity, competitive edge) so as to protect and enhance the firm's future

These are primarily the purview of financial managers, strategic planners, operations executives, and other senior officers. The processes listed above may also warrant inputs and participation from the marketing, purchasing and outsourcing, and human resource departments, as well as the various functional departments.

PPM is an enterprise-wide process involving a wide range of participants. It is also an extremely visible and sensitive process. How well this process is executed will have the greatest possible impact on the viability and success of the firm for an extended time.

Level of Participation

PPM not only has a wide breadth across the organization, requiring a wide range of participation, it also extends deeply into the hierarchy. At the upper end, the leadership and direction must come from the very highest levels of the enterprise: the chief executive officer (CEO), chief operating officer (COO), and chief financial officer (CFO). In an organization where information technology (IT) is a primary business, we can expect the chief information officer (CIO) to play a significant role. Certainly the vice president of projects or chief projects officer is a key player.

Depending on the type of business, there might be participation by the director of manufacturing, the chief chemist, the chief engineer, or the director of construction. In the pharmaceutical industry, the director of regulatory affairs should be involved. The key factor here is to identify the parts of the organization that have major stakeholder responsibility and make sure that their leaders are part of the PPM leadership.

PPM Governance Council

One of the impediments to having a PPM process is that most of the people mentioned above have their specific territories to oversee. They typically are not motivated to spend their time on PPM and are unlikely to have the specific skills, practices, and tools to participate fully in this important function.

Although this senior management group must carry full responsibility for PPM and approve all major decisions, the process can be centered just below this level, at the PPM governance council. (In information systems organizations, this group is often called the *IT governance council* or the *IT business management team*.) The governance council can consist of any of the senior positions noted above or high-level designated representatives of these officer-level people. It is the PPM governance council that is charged with the responsibility for the key decisions that affect the project portfolio.

The senior officers, in adopting a PPM process, must provide the overall leadership of the process. In this regard, the CEO, with the support and participation of other key officials, will announce the implementation of the PPM process. A PPM charter declaration will be issued, explaining the need for and purpose of the PPM process, the roles of all participants, and the makeup of the initial governance council. The PPM charter declaration will spell out the specific responsibilities of the governance council and note when the council must elevate issues and decisions to senior management. PPM orientation sessions will be conducted to present the new PPM processes and answer questions about each defined role.

The governance council, working with the PMO, will meet and communicate regularly to ensure that the information needed to select projects and manage the pipeline is available and that decisions are made based on this data.

Project Management Office

PPM is a process that brings together the projects and operations sides of the enterprise. The operations side, consisting of the general business departments, plus the financial, and strategic and tactical planning functions, is represented by the PPM governance council. The projects side is represented by the PMO.

The PMO is responsible for the oversight of all projects. This includes monitoring project accomplishments against established criteria and advising the governance council of status and issues that would affect the planned benefits of any project. The placement of any project in the portfolio was based on a set of expectations of the value of the project, the potential contribution of the project to the welfare of the enterprise, and the expected impact on and use of the firm's resources. Whenever any of these expectations is compromised due to poor schedule or cost performance, technical impediments, reduced technical performance, and so forth, the PMO prepares a report and recommendations for consideration by the governance council.

The governance council, coordinating with the PMO, will need to reevaluate the effect of the situation on revenues and cash flow, as well as reviewing risk issues, project priority, and support for strategic initiatives. It is the governance council that then has the responsibility to decide if the affected project should be terminated, delayed, or continued under a revised set of expectations.

Although most PPM implementations have a PMO and a governance council, the balance of power and responsibility between the two will vary from organization to organization. In some implementations, the PMO carries most of the evaluation and decision responsibility, escalating to the governance council only in critical situations. In other implementations, the PMO prepares all of the analytical data, but the governance council makes all of the selection, delay, and termination decisions. In either case, it is important that both groups remember that they are not the owners of the projects or the portfolios. There are clients or sponsors who fill this bill. The challenge to the PPM team is to balance the needs of the owners with the strategies of the firm.

Integration

PPM is a way of facilitating the integration of several critical enterprise functions. Without PPM, the business of managing projects is conducted with the sense that the ultimate objective is to achieve project success. That is, if the schedule, cost, technical, scope, and quality objectives of a project have been met, then it is assumed that the project is of value. Yet early implementers of PPM have frequently found that many projects that are approved and allocated scarce resources do not fit very well with the strategic objectives of the firm, do not contribute (as well as other projects) to the cash flow, and do not represent the best use of resources.

The project portfolio represents part of the tactical planning that is implemented to support the strategic plan. Therefore, the governance council, in selecting projects for the portfolio and in managing what stays in the portfolio, is in fact an integral part of the strategic and tactical planning process.

The projects that comprise the project portfolio have a significant impact on the financial condition of the firm. Most projects incur costs during their execution and generate revenue (or reduce costs) on completion (or during execution, in the case of progress payments). Projects thus have an impact on the cash flow and the projection of financial condition. Today's regulatory atmosphere demands that financial reports represent a current and true picture of the asset value of projects.

Traditionally, project reporting has focused on costs (ignoring other financial items such as revenue and cash flow). Therefore, the PMO has to integrate with the financial function to update revenue and cash flow data based on project status and performance. The tools employed to support the PPM process either have to add revenue and cash flow capabilities or be integrated with tools that can fill the void.

Decisions on the makeup of the project portfolio should take into consideration not only the projects at hand but also prospective projects, which may be represented by marketing initiatives or as a result of top-down initiatives coming out of the strategic plan. Forecasting, based on data furnished by the strategic planning committee and the opportunities management system, should be integrated with the PPM process.

Project Managers and Executives Don't Speak the Same Language

In this new world of PPM, we are looking not only for projects that are managed well but also for projects that are right for the firm. So we have formed a partnership between the project-oriented people in the PMO and the business-oriented people, represented by the governance council. My experience has been that the design and implementation of a PPM capability has often been derailed for the simple reason that the two groups do not speak the same language (as well as having a different focus).

To illustrate this, picture yourself as working within the PMO. When you report to others about how your project is going, do you focus on schedule and costs? Do you talk about resource utilization or scope changes? Surely these are important items. As project managers, we are taught to communicate these key items to management as a measure of whether the project is progressing successfully. They still are important—a gauge of project health. But they don't always reflect the project's true impact on the business.

When communicating to executives, you need to focus on the terms that reflect how the project is contributing to the larger set of objectives of the enterprise. How is the project contributing to growth, competitive advantage, revenue and cash flow, effective use of all resources, and key strategic initiatives? Focus more on benefits, revenue, and return on investment than on costs. The project end date may not be as important as the window of opportunity.

For each person with whom you communicate, think about how that person gets measured and views success. Then design custom communications for each in the language that he or she uses. One of the first tasks of the governance council will be to develop a set of terms and metrics that will form the basis of the communication stream that supports the PPM process.

Summary

Implementation of the PPM process involves three groups of people:

- Senior management, for providing leadership and direction and designating their representatives to the PPM governance council
- The members of the PPM governance council, who will manage the selection of projects for the portfolio and review projects for possible deselection
- The project management office, which monitors approved projects and advises the governance council where projects are deviating from expected benefits and value

The PPM process leads to improved integration of projects with strategic and tactical plans, financial projections and reporting, and opportunity management.

2.4

Tools for Project Portfolio Management

> PPM extends traditional project management practices and tools to situations beyond the planning and control of approved projects. It requires the development and application of some new practices and tools. Effective integration of new and existing practices and tools is essential to PPM success.

Project portfolio management is a set of processes, usually supported by a set of tools (software). Support for PPM requires some supplementary tool support, in addition to the tools that you are already using for traditional project management. But don't throw away the tools that you have been using. You'll still need them. PPM integrates traditional project and business functions. You'll need to integrate your support tools as well.

We start with a brief summary of the first three chapters as a review of the PPM processes and a guide for our evaluation of software requirements for support of PPM. We then use this framework to look at how PPM fits in with other project management practices. Finally, we look at how the various project management and PPM tools work together to support project portfolio management.

An Overview of the Project Portfolio Management Processes

PPM is more than an extension of project management to deal with multiple projects. Although it addresses different needs, it is very important to have full integration with traditional project management capabilities.

As more and more firms adopt project management office (PMO) methods, it would not surprise us to see responsibility for PPM thrust fully into the hands of the chief project officer. This, too, would be a mistake. *PPM requires governance at the executive level.* And the tools need to be optimized to support these changing roles.

The core mistake is to think that PPM is fundamentally the management of multiple projects. This definitely is not so. PPM is the management of the project portfolio so as to maximize the contribution of projects to the overall welfare and success of the enterprise. What this means is:

- Projects must be aligned with the firm's strategy and goals.
- Projects must be consistent with the firm's values and culture.
- Projects must contribute to a positive cash flow for the enterprise.
- Projects must effectively use the firm's resources—both people and other resources.
- Projects must not only provide for current contributions to the firm's health but must help to position the firm for future success.

We repeat this list here so that we can think about the impact of these attributes of PPM on tool support for the process. Our application of traditional project management processes and tools has focused on managing projects. Now we need to extend our practices and tools to support project prioritization and selection. We also have to integrate the project management tools with the portfolio management tools.

Extending Management Processes to Include PPM

There are two primary components of the PPM process. Although they are intertwined, each has its specific objectives and practices:

- Prioritization and selection of candidate projects for the portfolio
- Maintaining the pipeline: continuing, delaying, or terminating approved projects

Both of these segments of PPM compel us to apply structured, repeatable, proactive practices to the selection and continuance of projects:

- PPM extends traditional project management practices and tools to situations beyond the planning and control of approved projects.
- PPM requires the development and application of new practices and tools.

If you already have processes and tools to support planning and scheduling, earned value management, risk management, and communication, you are well on your way to having a PPM capability. But you will need additional capabilities to complete your PPM arsenal.

Defining the New PPM Processes

This chapter reviews the workings of the PPM processes, to describe the tools that are available to support these processes and to explain the interrelationships between the core planning and control components and newer facilities needed for PPM.

Phase One: Prioritization and Selection of Candidate Projects

In this phase, we identify and evaluate candidate projects. The evaluation requires us to consider the opportunity (value and benefits) as well as the risks (which modify the expected benefits). We also have to consider our ability to handle the project loads, much of which is dependent on resource availability.

Evaluating Candidate Projects. We'll assume that the objective of the PPM process is to prioritize work that brings the most value to the firm. The definition of *value* will certainly differ in accordance with the firm's focus, strategies, and types of projects. Regardless of these differences, a project portfolio management process will have to address the following:

- A ranking of value and benefits
- An estimate of the total costs
- An appraisal of risk (in achieving these benefits)
- An inventory of resource availability and allocation (capacity planning)
- An idea of an optimum or acceptable size of the project pipeline

While we will have a defined process specifically designed to guide and support the evaluation of candidate projects, we may rely on established tools to aid in some of these steps—for instance:

- Your standard planning and control tool would be a convenient source of the resource availability and allocation data.
- Your risk management tool would be used to address the risk component of the evaluation.
- Your enterprise resource planning (ERP) tools would cover financial and human resources (HR) functions, and possibly opportunity management.

- Using an integrated collection of project management tools, where available, minimizes redundancy (and conflicting data) and provides efficient, seamless flow of information.

However, most PM tools were not designed to hold the ranking data or to display it in ways that facilitate portfolio decisions by the governance team (although such capabilities are being added to some). For this, you will need a specifically designed PPM tool. In addition, some recognized decision support tools have been optimized for application to PPM.

Ranking Value and Benefits. Assuming that the number of potential projects exceeds the number that can be effectively executed in a reasonable time, there must be a means of prioritizing each project. Conceptually, this ranking process is simple, although the individual parameters will vary according to strategies, resources, profit motive, and other categories. Earlier, we noted that the process is not unlike that used in selecting items for an investment portfolio. In fact, this *is* an investment portfolio: you are investing in projects with the objective of maximizing the return.

One of the primary ranking factors will be expected return on investment (ROI) or net present value (NPV), or some variation of these traditional financial measurements. However, there are qualifiers associated with this process. You can't prioritize projects using ROI or NPV alone. You also need to consider:

- Alignment with strategic and tactical plans
- Balance between maintenance projects and investment projects
- Allocation balance of R&D or marketing expenditures and resources
- Effective use of resources
- Probability of delivering the project on time, within budget, and with the designed work scope

- Ancillary benefits (nonfinancial)
- Impact of potential risk
- Cost of performing the project

The last two items are often considered in a formula such as: Value = NPV × probability of technical success/costs. (See Chapter 4.2 for an illustration of a typical formula for value. See Chapter 7.2 for additional examples.) There are almost endless approaches toward developing a value figure. Your software should support your preferences in this area.

Risk. Risk is a modifier of opportunity. (See Chapter 3.3 for detailed discussion of risk.) Any estimate of the benefits of a project must be adjusted for the consideration of risk. There is always the issue of technical risk. What is the probability that the technical objectives won't be met? What are the consequences of that happening? Can anything be done to mitigate or otherwise contain the risk? If so, what is the impact of the mitigation action on benefits and costs? If the project is intended to generate income, what is the probability that the commercial objectives won't be met? If the project deliverables are targeted for a specific window of opportunity, what is the probability that the time objective will be missed? Again, there are the questions of mitigation and effect on benefits and costs.

This is a lot of information and data to keep in one's head or on the back of an envelope. As with any other project management and PPM processes, it is best to have a standardized, repeatable process for evaluating and managing risk, supported by appropriate software. And it is preferable to integrate the risk software with the other PPM tools.

Balanced and Weighted Ranking. The ranking practice should use a balanced scorecard approach, where each of the factors is listed and weighted. As each factor is rated, an aggregate score for each project is obtained. The rating of each factor can be prompted by a series of questions, with the answers noted in a narrative format and then converted to a numerical score based on the level of the answer against a guideline.

A common practice is to evaluate the value/benefit ranking and the risk ranking on a grid. Preference would be given to projects that appear in the high-value/low-risk quartile.

Analytic Hierarchy Process. The issue of ranking has brought an established, mathematics-based, decision-making process called analytic hierarchy process (AHP) to the PPM tool market. AHP involves the use of voting groups using paired comparisons to create weighted rankings for multiple objectives. For instance, the group may compare the importance of short-range income to long-range income, and then long-range income to technical standing, and so on. AHP software tallies all of the results to derive weight factors for each objective. Then the group may use the pairwise comparisons to judge how well each project matches up with the objectives. The result is a fairly weighted prioritization of the projects.

While the AHP method might appear (to some) to be overkill, it allows everyone to have an equal and complete voice in the ranking and selection process and minimizes the effect of personal biases. (See Chapter 4.3 for a detailed discussion of AHP.)

In addition to the formal application of AHP, other vendors have adopted similar capabilities aimed at optimizing the decision-making process. These include the use of pairwise comparison matrices, efficient frontier, and other structured decision analysis methodologies. (See Chapter 4.4 for a detailed discussion of the efficient frontier concept.)

Displaying the Ranking and Selection Data. Regardless of the techniques employed to weigh the selection criteria and prioritize the candidate projects, you will eventually have to display and communicate these data to the decision makers. This capability is supported by almost all PPM software solutions. In some cases, it is the primary PPM-specific feature in products that were developed with a PPM focus.

Common display mechanisms are bubble charts, spreadsheets, four-quadrant grids, X-Y charts, bar charts, matrix comparison charts, executive dashboards (see Figure 2.4-1), and an interesting graph called the Efficient Frontier, a portfolio optimization tool. They all support multidimensional analysis of data to provide multidimensional presentations. Through the use of axes, variable bubble size, colors, and shapes, some bubble charts can display as many as six different variables on one chart. Many products allow you to display multiple charts on a single page or screen.

FIGURE 2.4-1 An Executive Dashboard

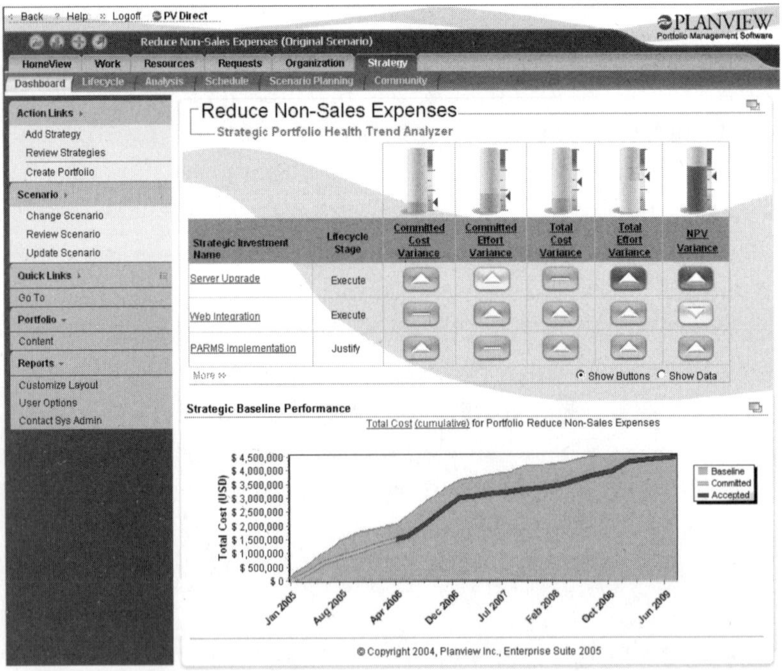

Note: The figure displays summary information about the projects in a portfolio. Typically, colored "traffic lights" (green, yellow, red) call attention to the health (schedule and cost) of the projects. Thresholds for yellow and red are established by the user.

Most of these display methods support "what-if" analysis to test various scenarios. There is tremendous power and utility in these display methods. But a little caution is called for. The quality of the display is not a direct indication of the quality of the data. Without a meticulous, structured approach toward developing the data, you might be manipulating and displaying only junk.

One way to reduce the likelihood of bad data is to have a seamless connection from the data generators to the data displays. That is, the data is developed using accepted practices that provide an audit trail back to the source. You can be assured that the selection committee will frequently look at the data in a display and say, "Where did that come from?" Will you be able to answer?

Phase Two: Maintaining the Pipeline

The old conventional wisdom was that once a project has been initiated, it is active until completion (or failure). The new conventional wisdom is that a project is active as long as it continues to support the criteria that were established for its selection and acceptable performance. In this respect, projects are periodically evaluated against these criteria.

The evaluation considers two basic aspects of the project: project performance and an updating of the project critical parameters. Some of the things that we want to know are:

- Is the project still aligned with the strategies?
- What is the current probability that the project will be technically successful?
- What is the current probability that the project will be commercially successful?
- How is the project performing against the target criteria?
- What are the performance trends? Improving or worsening?
- Does the project still represent effective use of the firm's resources?

Measuring Project Performance.   If you are directly involved with project management, you have been working with most of the project tracking practices. If we have a critical path (CPM) schedule, we maintain the project progress in the CPM software and monitor schedule milestones and float. Diminishing float is an indication of schedule slippage, but that value doesn't always reveal how much the work is falling behind. It focuses on the most critical schedule items.

A better way to look at performance is with earned value analysis (EVA), a process for evaluating schedule and cost performance on a project. It produces schedule variance data by comparing actual accomplishment to planned accomplishment. It produces cost variance data by comparing the actual cost for the work that has actually been accomplished to the budgeted cost for that quantity of work. EVA usually generates these values at a detailed level and then rolls the data up to summary levels for evaluation.

EVA provides an early warning system for schedule and cost overruns. When the EVA data indicates that certain work is not keeping up with the schedule target or is running over budget, the project team is expected to investigate the problem and, if possible, recommend corrective action. When the data (after considering corrective action) indicates that schedule or cost overruns jeopardize achievement of the project objectives, the PMO will communicate this to the portfolio governance council.

EVA capabilities are available in almost all conventional project management software. If you have planned a project using such software, the core data for EVA is already in place. If you use this software for project tracking, entering percent complete values will provide the data needed for automatic calculation of schedule variance (SV). If you track actual costs, you'll have what you need for calculation of cost variance (CV). (For a more detailed discussion of EVA, see Chapter 3.6.)

Updating Critical Parameters.   The EVA data provides information about project performance against the plan. When the results show that project performance is deficient, the team should conduct an evaluation to consider terminating the project prior to completion, changing the priority of the project, or reallocating resources to other work.

There are generally additional factors to consider. Has there been any change in the need for this project? Is the window of opportunity still open? Has critical technology changed? Have the firm's strategies changed? On a periodic basis, all of the criteria that were examined when putting a value on the project should be validated and updated.

The PMO publishes reports indicating where defined targets, limits, and thresholds have been violated. As part of the periodic project selection cycle, it makes recommendations regarding rescheduling or terminating projects with deteriorating performance or that no longer rank well against the selection criteria. The PMO, as part of these recommendations, identifies funding and resources that could be freed up for new, more beneficial projects. The PPM software must be able to process and publish all of these data.

The PPM governance council considers this information, together with the updated critical parameters, to evaluate all projects for continuation or termination.

Defining PPM and the Tools for PPM

Getting a clear, unified definition of PPM and PPM tools is virtually impossible. Consider this statement from a leading consulting firm (one of many on this topic):

> We define PPM as software that streamlines outward functions and inward processes of project-intensive departments, industries and organizations. Integrating multiple business processes and point solutions into one application suite, PPM features integrated management of pipeline, scope, time, resource, skills, cost, procurement, communication, reporting and forecasting, and risk management functions.

I propose a different definition:

PPM is a set of *processes*, supported by people and tools, to guide the enterprise in selecting the right projects and the right number of projects, and in maintaining a portfolio of projects that will maximize the enterprise's strategic goals, efficient use of resources, stakeholder satisfaction, and the bottom line.

Although PPM does not directly encompass the traditional PM processes and tools mentioned in the first statement, they are part of the process flow. PPM is integrated with these processes and tools and relies on inputs from them for its success.

First, we note that PPM is a set of processes, supported by tools, rather than being the tools themselves. Second, the PPM tool set (in my definition) includes software that helps us to automate specific PPM processes. There are many other tools used in the process of managing projects or the business operations of the enterprise that would also be used in conjunction with PPM tools to serve the entire operations and projects needs. That these various tools work together is a major objective of implementing a PPM capability.

In discussing the software for PPM, we describe several configurations of tool sets. Although each category contains powerful and valuable capabilities, none of them offers every capability that could be used to support PPM. Yet most of these are being advertised as PPM solutions.

Software for Project Management and PPM. Tools for PPM are being offered in many varieties and from various vendors who have focused on different needs. Among the traditional offerings (before adding support for PPM) are the following:

- *Critical Path Scheduling (CPM) programs*. These are the basic tools for scheduling and tracking projects. They allow you to define the project work items, define task relationships, assign task durations, assign resources, and calculate base critical path schedules and resource-constrained schedules. These programs also usually have excellent support for work breakdown structures (WBS) and simple applications of EVA. All offer multiple means of reporting plans and status. Additional features may include simplified risk planning and tracking, issue tracking, and time keeping.

- *Critical chain project management (CCPM)*. This is a variation on traditional CPM methods, focusing on methods for sharing contingency. CCPM has created almost a cult following of adopters who praise its benefits. As with the traditional CPM advocates, CCPM supporters are also moving to embrace PPM. (See Chapter 8.1.)

- *Earned value method (EVM) programs*. These support advanced EVA applications, especially for defense system projects and other programs where EVM is mandated. These EVM programs have a strong focus on cost control and strong support for multiple WBS's (used for directed cost buckets).

- *Risk management programs*. These usually go well beyond the skeleton risk capabilities in traditional CPM programs. These are valuable where a highly structured, proactive risk-management culture is required. There are two quite different foci to risk management. One is often called the PERT approach. It addresses only schedule risk and uses three time estimates per task and Monte Carlo simulation to determine project durations and probability of meeting specified completion dates. Currently more in vogue is the risk assessment and management approach. This calls for identification of potential risk events, an assessment of the probability that the event will occur, and the probable impact of the event if it does occur. The user is then expected to consider mitigation options to contain the risks.

- *Slice-and-dice software*. Originally created as separate software, these capabilities are commonly found in most project management tools. The objective is to access and present large volumes of data in meaningful ways. Many of these use online analytical processing techniques.

- *Enterprise resource planning (ERP) tools*. ERP software combines integrated support for project management and many business operations. The most common components (for project management applications) are accounting and human resource software. Customer relations management (CRM) and opportunities management modules can also be integrated with the PM systems.

- *Professional services automation (PSA) tools.* This is another integration of project management and business components. Developed primarily for firms that provide outsourced IT services, PSA components include project management, billing, time accounting, CRM, engagement management, and cross-charging. There are several terms being used for this class of tools, including enterprise services automation (ESA).

- *Structured objectives planning software.* This is an unusual program that helps to structure a statement of strategic objectives. Starting with the strategic plan, you can build down to individual objectives and align them with projects or parts of projects. When integrated with traditional project planning software, the project work can be associated with specific strategy-based objectives.

- *Analytic hierarchy process (AHP).* AHP is a mathematics-based decision-making process. It has been used in a wide variety of applications and is now being applied to PPM. It uses voting groups using pairwise comparisons to create weighted rankings for multiple objectives.

Adding PPM Software to the Mix. Do you remember the old story about a group of blind people attempting to describe an elephant? Each person surveyed a different area of the elephant by feel, and each came up with a different description.

Trying to describe PPM software is not unlike describing the elephant. In this case, the vast majority of PPM tool vendors had already been market players with tools that provided capabilities as noted above. In some cases, PPM capabilities were added to the existing tool sets. In other cases, the product line was revamped and refocused to center on PPM.

So what we have are CPM vendors offering PPM tools, ERP vendors offering PPM tools, PSA vendors offering PPM tools, AHP vendors offering PPM tools, data presentation (slice-and-dice) vendors offering PPM tools, and so on. No single vendor is providing 100 percent of the functions that are available for PPM. But many come very close and offer an extensive set of capabilities.

The primary additions to the capabilities (to support PPM) include:

- A repository for proposed and active projects
- Guidelines for presenting project proposals for ranking and selection
- Project selection criteria
- Decision engines to develop weight factors for selection criteria
- A repository for financial and resource allocation data
- Tools to assist in computing potential project benefits, including the ability to incorporate the impact of costs and risks
- Tools to support project prioritization and ranking
- Tools to display ranking results
- Tools to aid in project selection
- What-if capabilities to explore alternatives
- The ability to integrate these capabilities with other operations and projects tools

Examples of an Integrated Tool Set

From the various configurations noted earlier, I have selected a few representative vendor offerings for the purpose of providing illustrations of integrated tool sets. The selection of any of the vendors for these illustrations is not an indication of my preference for any specific solution. Each firm should evaluate and choose software to meet its specific needs.

The Welcom Family of Tools. Welcom offers a suite of five tools that support the PPM process. These are two recent additions, WelcomPortfolio and WelcomRisk, which join WelcomHome,

Open Plan, and Cobra. In addition, Microsoft Project can be substituted for Open Plan (for planning and control). The complete PPM process uses all five tools, with WelcomPortfolio serving as the primary repository for the portfolio data.

Projects to be considered for the portfolio would be initiated in WelcomPortfolio, and capabilities within this tool are designed to facilitate data collection and manipulation leading to evaluation-based rankings. Additional capabilities will display this information to facilitate selection decisions.

WelcomRisk can produce risk scores for the candidate projects and feed this data into WelcomPortfolio. However, risk values can also be determined outside WelcomRisk and entered directly into WelcomPortfolio.

Open Plan (or Microsoft Project) can be used in two ways to support portfolio planning. It can help with capacity planning by calculating and holding data relative to the maximum project pipeline size and the available resource pool. It can also be used to produce preliminary, high-level plans to compute schedule, resource, and cost data needed for the portfolio evaluation process.

WelcomHome can be used throughout any of the processes as a global communication tool. WelcomHome facilitates collaboration by supporting bidirectional communication among all parties. It would be used to publish the project charter and to officially open the project to all interested parties.

Once a project is approved, detailed planning would begin, using Open Plan (or Microsoft Project). Project plans would be maintained, and data affecting capacity planning would be fed back to WelcomPortfolio.

Once the project is in progress, we will need to monitor project performance as well as reviewing the criteria used for selection. A key performance measuring technique is EVA, supported in its simplest form by Open Plan (and Microsoft Project) and at an advanced level by Cobra. The PMO monitors project performance with these tools and feeds information and recommendations to the governance council when such information indicates that the status of the project should be reexamined.

Coming full circle, recommendations regarding active projects will be routed back into WelcomPortfolio to produce an updated list of ranked projects.

The entire process is dynamic and ongoing. All Welcom components are used as needed to support the process, with periodic WelcomPortfolio outputs being provided to the governance council for portfolio decisions.

Oracle, SAP, and PeopleSoft. Leading ERP vendors Oracle, SAP, and PeopleSoft have added PPM attributes to support project ranking and selection, skills analysis and resource deployment, collaboration, and the popular dashboard and bubble chart display modes. These capabilities are integrated with all of the other previously integrated functions for projects and business management that are typical in the ERP models.

Niku and Other PSA Vendors. Niku is one of the original providers of PSA software. Its package featured integration of several business components linked to the Workbench Results Management package (project management) that it acquired from ABT. It was developed primarily for firms that provide outsourced IT services. Niku 6 components included a collection of project management and financial management modules, resource management, demand management, opportunity management, and work flow and collaboration facilities. Niku 6 also introduced Niku's first portfolio manager module.

Upgraded and rebadged as Clarity 7 in 2004, it covers a wide span of capabilities with eight modules. Portfolio Manager, upgraded and moved up to anchor the system, is a repository for project evaluation data and is used to develop and display data for ranking and selection. There are three choices for project management: a new Web-based Project Manager module and the ability to use Workbench or Microsoft Project. The Resource Planner is used to help assign resources, balance capacity and demand, and identify and track skills information. The Financial Manager handles charge backs, billing and invoicing, cost and rate management, and financial reporting. The

Process Manager features a work flow capability to automate business processes and standardize them.

Similar integrated offerings are available from vendors such as Lawson and Changepoint (now called "Compuware IT Governance by Changepoint").

IT Governance. Several project management and PPM vendors have specifically focused on IT applications. It is not that their offerings could not be used for other applications. However, these have been packaged and advertised for the IT market. Many of these choose to label their solutions as IT governance solutions, containing PPM and allied functions. Niku and Changepoint fall into this group. Others are ProSight, Mercury Interactive, and PlanView. Even PeopleSoft, with a wide market, has packaged its integrated PPM solution as ESA (Enterprise Services Automation) for IT.

ProSight. The centerpiece of ProSight is a portfolio analysis and prioritization tool that provides strong data manipulation and presentation. This is an example of a PPM product that is not attempting to cover a wide range of project management and PPM capabilities. Rather, it prefers to act as a hub for data that it then processes to support portfolio analysis. Any project management functionality is provided through a bridge to Microsoft Project Server.

Expert Choice and United Management Technologies. United Management Technologies (UMT) and Expert Choice go deeper into mathematical engines to assist with assigning collaborated weights to the selection criteria and supporting prioritization and selection. In Expert Choice, this is accomplished through the use of the analytic hierarchy process, an effective decision support tool.

These capabilities are integrated with components that help to optimize resource use and to evaluate and select projects. Strong presentation components are featured. Neither product has a project scheduling engine. UMT has a gateway connection to Microsoft Project Server. Expert Choice connects through Microsoft Access or SQL Server.

Project Management with Expanded PPM Processing and Displays. Primavera, PlanView, and Sciforma are long-time key players in traditional project and resource management software systems. PlanView has added an extensive set of PPM functions anchored by its PRISMS for IT Governance and Resource Management process set. Primavera and Sciforma offer extensive user configuration of database and computational functions that effectively support PPM needs. Their key strengths (as with Welcom) are strong traditional scheduling and resource engines and good support for EVA, risk analysis, resource allocation, and reporting.

Implementing a PPM Capability

PPM is a valuable process to aid in the selection of projects that will best further the organization's mission considering risks, capacity limits, and project value. In order to implement such a capability, the firms must:

- Develop a PPM process.
- Establish a governance team.
- Acquire PPM and other project management support tools.
- Integrate the PPM process and tools with other project management processes and tools.

2.5

Implementing Project Portfolio Management

> The first step in the new PPM process is to evaluate the existing project inventory. Excising nonaligned, redundant, or nonbeneficial projects will release scarce resources for better opportunities.

Do you remember the chicken-or-egg question? Now that we're ready to implement a PPM capability, which should we do first? Do we use the portfolio planning process to prioritize or select projects for the portfolio? Or do we evaluate the currently active projects?

In most cases, the firm will already have a portfolio of projects (or multiple portfolios), although they might not call it by that name. Field experience has shown that this is a good place to start. New implementers of PPM have found that a structured review and evaluation of the existing portfolio can turn up numerous instances of deficiencies in that portfolio. In taking inventory of current project activity, they found projects that should never have been approved and projects that were failing to the point that they would not deliver anything close to their expected benefits.

We mentioned the HP/Compaq inventory of their combined project loads and their decision to eliminate over one hundred projects. This reduced the overall cost burden of the projects and opened up resources for more beneficial opportunities. (See Chapter 9.2.) AXA Financial reports a similar success:

> When I took an as-is snapshot of what the lay of the land looked like, I discovered there were a number of projects behind schedule and over budget and, more important, that all projects were created equal. There was no hierarchy of improvement. There was no sense of how these projects related to our vision, mission, long-term, short-term—any kind of objective you wanted to define.
>
> I bet we saved $5 million to $10 million in the first year alone, on projects that would have automatically gone through before. But, now the business units knew what could get killed, so they killed it first. It just became immediately apparent how much junk we weeded out of the system.[1]

Evaluating the Current Portfolio

It would certainly appear that a good place to start is by taking an inventory of the current project burden. It is not unlikely that the results of such an inventory will more than pay for the efforts invested in implementing the new PPM capability.

As noted in Chapter 2.2, the evaluation process for projects in the pipeline has two dimensions. The first is performance of the project. Here, we evaluate the project performance against targets that have been set for the project, normally including metrics regarding schedule, resource utilization, costs, deliverables, and quality. The data would include planned status, current status, and forecast performance. Indications of poor performance would be a cause of concern, but it's not the only condition to be considered.

The second dimension to be evaluated is the criteria that were used to select the project in the first place. Has anything changed? Are the project deliverables still needed? Can they be delivered in an acceptable time frame? Are the cost benefits still acceptable? Is the project still aligned with the strategies? Has a competitor beaten you to the punch? Has the market fizzled? Has the technology changed, making this design obsolete?

Actually, many of the projects currently in the pipeline probably were selected without a structured portfolio process, so there are no criteria to be evaluated. It will have to be constructed after the fact (sort of reverse-engineering).

So if the first step in the new PPM process is to evaluate the existing project inventory, the first job of the team is to establish the decision criteria, establish thresholds, and clarify responsibilities for the decisions.

Culture and Project Weeding

Developing a culture that supports the excising of poor projects is not easy. Sometimes you can try to impose a bogey (quota) for reductions, to give it a push. This works with forced personnel cutbacks. Why not for projects? As an alternative, you can impose some key pass-fail criteria associated with items like strategy alignment or budgetary resource or risk limits.

Project Prioritization and Selection

There are some essential steps for initiating the selection phase of PPM. A key step is to make sure that the governance council is in place and that its roles and responsibilities are clear. Another key item is to make sure that the governance council is fully aware of the firm's strategic plans and the tactical options to support the strategies.

There should be a standardized practice for submitting proposed projects to the system. Guidelines spelling out information required from the project sponsor should be published. (See Chapter 3.2.)

What are the optimum and maximum sizes of the project pipeline? This will be based in part on the availability of resources. You'll want to know these limits before you complete the selection process.

In Chapter 2.1, we described several options for ranking candidate projects. You can use any or all of these in your PPM system. The team will want to decide which methods to use and make sure that practices and tools are available to support these methods.

PPM Implementation Tips

Instead of deploying the new PPM system across the board all at once, try it out with a pilot program. Make sure that the initial people involved are adventurous supporters (and not reactionaries). Use the pilot to fine-tune the practices before you broadcast them as company standards.

When you're ready to implement the PPM process, the effort would be well served if you employ a checklist, perhaps similar to the questionnaire shown in Exhibit 2.5-1, prepared by United Management Technologies (UMT).

Executive Support

Finally, let's make sure that there is full executive support. There are several ways to validate that level of support. One is to have the top executive authenticate all of the key role modifications. The roles and responsibilities should show up in revised position guides and in any management-by-objectives metrics. People so affected should receive a letter from the CEO acknowledging the importance of their role in the new PPM process.

Kick the process off with a bang, even if it's just a pilot program. Let people know that this is big. Make it clear to everyone (in a message from the CEO) that "PPM is a way of life in the organization and that support for PPM is a condition of employment."

Implementing PPM Is a Project

People often fail to realize that the development and implementation of a PPM capability is in itself a project and should be handled

EXHIBIT 2.5-1 Program Management Questionnaire

Governance

- We have a formal procedure to review projects, approve (funding decisions) submitted project proposals and business case changes, as well as to rationalize our investment portfolio.

- We have clear lines of responsibility and accountability for the technical and financial performance of our projects.

- We use a consistent set of policies to guide the development of estimates (costs, benefits, etc.), to assess progress and to manage projects.

- Every project has a senior business manager/sponsor, who oversees the project definition and budget, and takes responsibility for its success.

Business Case

- Each project proposal identifies the specific business goals and objectives it will support.

- Each submittal includes a description of the scope (what's included, what's omitted) of the proposed effort and the approach (methodology) to be employed, as well as the identification of project overlaps and dependencies.

- We require that each proposal include a detailed work plan consisting of a task breakdown structure, timeline, resources, deliverables and milestones.

- We have a standard framework to quantify the benefits of proposed projects that includes non-financial elements

- A project proposal identifies and assesses all risks associated with the development plan as well as those associated with achieving the promised benefits.

Culture Compatible with Program Management

- We are accustomed to managing multiple projects across business units and/or the regular functional organizational structure.

- We have a recognized, documented standard procedure for capturing and formalizing project ideas from all stakeholders (IT, business, others).

EXHIBIT 2.5-1 Program Management Questionnaire, Cont'd.

- Our program management office is well-established and respected for its contributions to the organization.
- In our company, key decision makers have demonstrated the judgment and practical experience to interpret status reports, foresee obstacles and react in a timely fashion.

Infrastructure Supportive of Program Management

- We use standardized processes for key project management events—planning, initiation, change control, reporting, etc.
- Our financial system provides an infrastructure of accounts, internal pricing and resource cost transfer policies compatible with a multi-project environment.
- The projects in our portfolio are selected on the basis of their relative impact on our company's strategic goals and objectives.
- We employ automation tools for project status information collection, aggregation and portfolio analysis.
- We provide training for new project managers and program management office staff.

Analysis and Tracking Processes

- We have a clear strategy and process for the sources of information and the distribution of project portfolio status reports to appropriate decision-making levels.
- Our tracking process includes milestones, budget and resource usage against the approved project plan.
- At the portfolio level, we ensure that inter-project dependencies, overlaps and coordination do not generate scope, timing and resource conflicts.
- Our procedures are designed to ensure consistent quality of all project deliverables.
- We have a robust process for identifying, tracking, analyzing and escalating issues to the appropriate decision makers.
- We periodically replan the entire portfolio of projects to reflect changes in individual projects (scope, benefits, budget, timing) as well as overall business conditions.

Source: United Management Technologies.

just like any other major project. Among the significant items and issues to be addressed within this project are these:

- Prepare and issue an approved project charter.
- Prepare and distribute the project plan.
- Prepare a responsibilities matrix, and clarify all roles.
- Develop the PPM processes.
- Select the support tools, and integrate them with existing tools.
- Conduct orientation and training.
- Provide mentoring and conduct implementation audits.
- Begin with pilot portfolios and then expand.

SECTION THREE

The Finer Points of Project Portfolio Management

Integrating operations and projects, fostering better proposals, dealing with risk and uncertainty, applying work breakdown structures to risks and strategies, and understanding earned value analysis: these are topics that will aid in the effective implementation of PPM.

Section Two presented the essentials of PPM without dwelling too long on any particular element. In the sections that follow, we delve into some of the finer points of PPM. Specifically, the six chapters in Section Three contain practical advice for optimizing the benefits that you are certain to gain from implementing a PPM methodology.

Earlier, we suggested that PPM is a way of bridging the gap between the projects and operations sides of the enterprise. In Chapter 3.1, we expand on that premise by considering that PPM is in reality a hub rather than a bridge. We see PPM as a means of eliminating the gap. We see PPM as the center of a process that brings these two diverse groups together in harmony and purpose to promote the health of the business.

One of the problems with selecting projects for the pipeline is that too many projects are proposed that shouldn't be. A casual meeting at the water cooler ends up producing a pet project for some executive. An innocent phone call from a client generates a request for a modified gizmo assembly. Proposals are instigated for some half-baked idea without prior thought to costs, schedules, impact on resources, value, alignment with strategies, technical feasibility, commercial feasibility, or risk.

Such proposals clog the funnel into the pipeline. Each proposal puts demands on the project management office and the governance council, requiring them to evaluate the proposal prior to rejecting it for any of the deficiencies noted above. In Chapter 3.2, we propose a process for project prequalification. This process helps to generate improved proposals and significantly reduce the submittal of proposals for bad projects. The use of the prequalification procedure often induces project sponsors to improve their project value and alignment. If they can't find such improvement, they may stop short of forwarding the proposal because they can see that it doesn't support the selection criteria.

Uncertainty and risk are constant companions for any project. We need not fear them, but we must respect them. Suggestions for dealing with uncertainty and risk are presented in Chapter 3.3. Risk will have an impact on value and benefits. If risk is not considered, the proposed project value and benefits will be erroneous. A project that would get a high priority may very well be rejected if the risk elements are honestly considered. Risk is especially present in development and transformation projects. We need not abandon a project because of high risk, but we will want to look into options to mitigate the risks.

Not all projects are equal. Three typical classifications of projects are utility or maintenance, growth or enhancement, and transformation. The latter is a project for which the goal is to capture a new market or a leap ahead in technology. It has the potential of yielding monumental benefits but requires very special handling. We discuss this in Chapter 3.4.

Have you been using work breakdown structures (WBSs)? They are extremely valuable and typically are used to develop hierarchies for tasks, resources, budgets, and so on. In Chapter 3.5, we expand the concept of WBSs to risk and to strategies.

In Chapter 2.2, we noted the importance of evaluating project performance. We mentioned the concept of earned value analysis and earned value management as practical and powerful methods to monitor project performance. For readers who are not familiar with EVA, we present a primer in Chapter 3.6.

3.1

Defining PPM

A Bridge or a Hub?

> If embraced and supported by senior management, PPM becomes the core of a set of combined business and projects processes, leading to much improved effectiveness in the use of limited cash and human resources.

Some six years ago, I started writing about PPM. With some of my early-adapter colleagues, I recognized the potential power and benefits of this emerging art and science. I then saw PPM as a bridge, connecting the world of projects with the world of business operations.

As I noted in Chapter 1.1, the basic elements of PPM and the environment in which it is applied are not new. However, before the emergence of PPM as a defined discipline, these elements were the responsibility of two distinct groups, operations management and projects management, each with its specific role:

Operations Management	Projects Management
Strategies	Schedule/time
Objectives/goals	Project cost
Business performance	Project performance

Stockholder satisfaction	Stakeholder satisfaction
Project selection and mix	Scope/change control
Resource availability	Resource utilization
Cash flow/income	Cash usage

The gap between these two worlds was very apparent. The projects world was diligently pursuing excellence in project performance, virtually totally oblivious to the strategies of the enterprise and whether its projects were in line with these strategies. The operations side of the business was called on to support these projects with funding and resources, not understanding how or whether these were really the projects that it wanted or needed. There was no way of knowing this.

In the absence of a repeatable structure, neither group could communicate with the other in a meaningful way to make the connection. Communication was further hampered by the lack of a common language. A bridge was needed.

Today I see PPM not as a bridge but as a hub (Figure 3.1-1). PPM is the nucleus of a system that brings projects and operations together. It is the core of an integrated collection of processes that represent both operations and projects functions. It is also the engine that drives the production of project deliverables to enhance the total health of the enterprise.

Building a bridge between these two functions will not do the job. A bridge acknowledges that a gap exists and does nothing to eliminate the gap. A connection between these two entities is not enough. They must be brought together in unity as distinct roles working in harmony, within a shared system and for a common cause.

PPM ties these distinct functions into an efficient business machine that increases the value and purpose of projects so as to contribute to the overall health and success of the enterprise. It does much more than bridge a gap. It eliminates the gap by bringing these diverse functions together.

FIGURE 3.1-1 Project Portfolio Management as a Hub

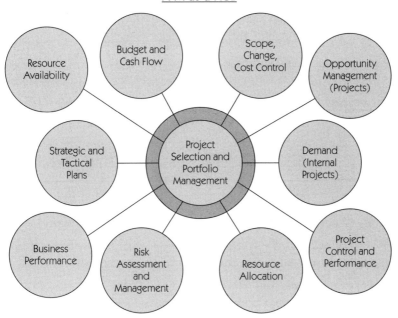

The basis for PPM is a rational decision system with these components:

- Having all of the information
- Having analytical processes for effective use of the information
- Having means of communicating with all stakeholders in their language

- Aligning opportunities with objectives
- Conditioning opportunities by assessing and controlling risk
- Eliminating or minimizing office politics and personal favoritism
- Getting all of the disciplines of the enterprise on the same page
- Promoting the use of common sense

PPM provides the motivation and the vehicle for all of this. If embraced and supported by senior management, PPM becomes the core of a set of combined business and projects processes, leading to much improved effectiveness in the use of limited cash and human resources. With PPM as the hub for these linked processes, better project portfolios are developed, affording greater opportunities for increased benefits. Feeding the results of project status and performance back into the portfolio management system provides a loop ensuring that the project selection process encompasses both proposed and active projects.

All of these processes have to be connected. The PPM hub is a means to accomplish this. It serves as a place holder for proposed and active projects. It serves as a database for PPM data and a link to other associated data. It serves as a reporting and communication system for information regarding projects and business items. It contains the engines to support rational analysis and decision making.

PPM encompasses several project and operations management processes. It is not just a new piece of the project management picture (a common misconception) or an extension of project management. It is an entirely new discipline that includes project management as an important component. PPM is the hub of a system that makes all of this happen, and it is the glue that holds it all together.

3.2

A Prequalification Process for Selecting Projects for the Portfolio

> The prequalification process provides a structured routine that guides the sponsor through the preparation of the proposal, for ranking. Once this is done, the proposal or business case must pass certain tests before the project can get on the candidate list.

The process for prioritizing and selecting projects for inclusion in one or more project portfolios requires the development of a set of data for each project, representing an appraisal of value, benefits, risk, and impact on resources. These data should also consider alignment with strategies, technical feasibility, and miscellaneous other ranking items. This is a lot of work to be performed before a project is even proposed and considered for approval. The project management office (PMO) and the governance council (GC) then invest additional effort in reviewing these data.

All of this effort is for a good cause: building a good portfolio of projects or, better yet, weeding out the bad proposals. Even so, wouldn't it be better to minimize the submission of poor projects and reduce the preparation and review effort for candidate projects? Wouldn't it be better to guide people to consider the critical criteria before running the projects up the flagpole to see if they get a salute?

Prequalification

An effective way to accomplish these goals is using a prequalification process. The idea is to follow a structured routine that guides the sponsor through the preparation of the ranking material. Once this is done, the proposal or business case must pass certain tests before the project can get on the candidate list.

As part of the development of the PPM process, the PMO creates a prequalification template. This template has a section for each subject area of the proposal to be considered with questions to guide the sponsor's responses. Periodically (in conjunction with the strategic planning cycle) the prequalification template is updated with the current ranking and selection criteria to reflect the latest thinking relative to strategic buckets, risk philosophy, and financial and resource constraints.

As each project is conceived, a proposal (or business case) is prepared that will include the response to the current prequalification questionnaire. The first objective is one of self-regulation. It is expected that many inappropriate proposals will be withdrawn before being issued because the sponsor will recognize that it doesn't meet the acceptance criteria, or it will be ranked so low as not to make the cut.

At this juncture, projects should be withdrawn for these reasons:

- Not in line with available resources, mission, or other criteria
- Not sound politically, socially, or for business relationships
- Feasible technologically but not economically
- Feasible economically but not technologically
- Involve excessive risk or are not within the risk culture

The prequalification criteria should not be rigid. However, if there are exceptions, the business case must present arguments to pass the prequalification criteria.

Because the prequalification criteria have been published and distributed, sponsors are obligated to address potential issues early. The result is a reduction in the number of bad proposals.

Proposals that are not withdrawn are now reviewed within the PMO for pass-fail against prequalification criteria. The PMO may reject proposals that do not meet the criteria or may pass on recommendations to the GC. The project sponsor may appeal the PMO decision to the GC. A review team will judge whether anyone has a reason to override the prequalification criteria for a particular proposal. They will have to convince others on the committee. The committee may recommend modifications to the proposed project to allow it to pass the prequalification test.

Once the proposed project passes the prequalification test, it is placed in the hopper for the ranking review, the next step. Failed proposals may be fully withdrawn or placed in a second-tier group as backups.

This prequalification routine will save the time and effort to rank proposed projects that don't really have a chance. It will also help to make the number of proposed projects more manageable. Figure 3.2-1 is a flow diagram of the prequalification process within a PPM system.

The Prequalification Criteria

I suggest that a prequalification template be designed that can be updated with specific values and conditions in accordance with the latest strategies, tactical plans, and corporate culture.

Actually, most operations will have multiple prequalification models. As an example, let's consider an organization that manages three types of projects: maintenance and utility projects, growth or enhancement projects, and transformation projects. It therefore has a portfolio for each type of project and a separate prequalification model for each category.

Maintenance or Utility Projects

Maintenance or utility projects generally support ongoing products and services. When we prioritize these, they might not register as high on the benefits-value scale as some other types of projects.

FIGURE 3.2-1 The Prequalification Process

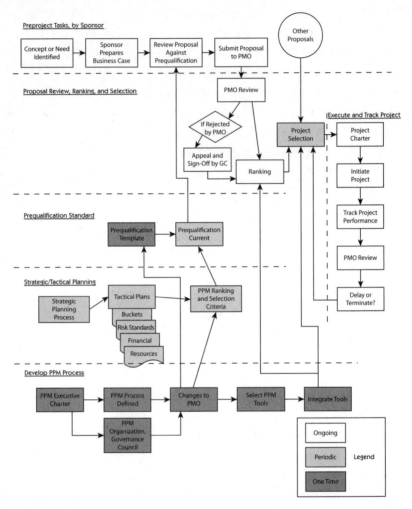

Nevertheless, most organizations earmark funding and resources for these projects. But which ones shall be undertaken?

We can't use the same selection evaluation criteria because these projects will be evaluated to a different standard and set of objectives than the other types of projects. For instance, there may not be a directly measurable value for return on investment (ROI) or net present value (NPV). If we set a single threshold for NPV, maintenance projects might never pass the prequalification test. The strategic plan probably doesn't show anything for maintenance and utility efforts, although we would certainly expect the tactical plans to allocate resources and a budget.

For this category, the prequalification criteria consist more of need and justification data as opposed to cash-based benefits and alignment to strategies. The prequalification questionnaire might ask for evidence of what would suffer if the project were bypassed. It might look for data that shows interdependence with other projects. Some statement of benefits is certainly called for. Alignment criteria cannot be totally ignored. Would we want to select a maintenance project to make improvements to a product or capability that is no longer supported by the firm's strategies? Even for this group, the general PPM practices apply.

Growth or Enhancement Projects

Growth or enhancement projects are likely to fall nicely into medium-to-high benefit and high-alignment segments of the ranking criteria. By design, these should be projects that support strategic initiatives and represent increasing value. Such projects are needed to keep the firm in a solid competitive position.

For most organizations that employ PPM techniques, the growth or enhancement projects will comprise the bulk of the projects. You can expect serious competition among the proposed projects, making the portfolio planning process critical to efficient and effective project selection. The development of sound prequalification guidelines will help to keep the project sponsors focused on the business objectives and the selection criteria. It will also make it more difficult for them to get carried away with desired benefits, mistaking them for carefully evaluated benefits.

Setting thresholds and ranges that are aligned with the strategies and the tactical plans will be helpful. These should reflect budget and resource allocation objectives, as well as risk guidelines. The process requires that the high-level strategies be transformed into specific tactical plans, with clearly stated objectives and constraints.

Transformation Projects

Transformation projects are the opportunities to move the firm to a new level or to introduce new products or services that will dominate the marketplace. This category requires extraordinary diligence starting at the proposal phase. A prequalification model can also be used here, but only as part of the evaluation process. Assuming that the proposed project is aligned with the strategies and guidelines, it will require the preparation of a full business case, complete with three scenarios: most likely, potential upside, and potential downside.

We can expect these projects to exhibit a higher risk profile. However, the potential benefits can be so great as to place the project off the scale when we plot NPV or ROI. There is also a greater sensitivity to the benefits and risk data for transformation projects, especially when there is an indefinite window of opportunity. Multiple scenarios, as presented in the business case, will produce considerably different values for benefits and risk. The range of these values is in itself a value to be considered. A conservative strategy, if that is the culture, would have you rank the more sensitive projects (those with a higher differential between case extremes) a bit lower than a project that has less uncertainty. You can't mix transformation-type projects with growth projects or use the same prequalification criteria for both types of projects.

Transformation projects may be "bet the firm's future" projects. Failure to select the right projects in this category will lead not only to failure of the project, but will also waste the monetary and human resources that could have been used for a better opportunity. It is difficult to sustain business growth without periodic transformation projects. To choose wisely is to protect the future of the enterprise.

3.3

The Impact of Uncertainty on Projects and the Portfolios

> Uncertainty is an element of all projects. Risk in projects must be recognized, evaluated, and considered as part of the project prioritization and selection process, as well as during the execution of selected projects. In managing risk, the goal is to minimize the potential for failure to achieve the project's benefits.

When we execute any of the ranking and prioritization schemes, we are basing our decisions on data that is assumed to be precise. In fact, almost all of the data is fraught with uncertainty.

Uncertainty is part of the definition of a project. We are either doing something for the first time or are inventing or developing or designing or experimenting. We are operating in a variable environment, where some of the conditions are beyond our direct control. We are depending on the contributions of others. A slight delay, a change in the exchange rate, a failure of an experiment, an act of nature: each of these can turn a promising project into a disappointment.

Disregarding all of this, we take the assumed values and submit the data to a very exacting routine, generating a set of numerical values that we take to the bank. What we are likely to have is erroneous because it assumes results that are based on a specific set of circumstances that have little chance of occurring exactly as planned. Then we extend this data to four decimal places, based on the assumed results, which will only give us a very precise error.

Developing a Range of Values

So what are we to do? I would not for a moment suggest abandoning the effort to quantify the value of proposed projects. But we do have to look at this data as a function of the surrounding environment. We have to recognize that uncertainty exists. We have to evaluate the source and degree of uncertainty. We have to attempt to reduce uncertainty and contain the effects of risk events. We have to look at the data as a range of values rather than a single precise value.

Throughout this book, there are references to viewing a project portfolio as we would an investment portfolio. In the world of investments, we acknowledge that there are risks. We usually choose investments with some recognition of the events that can affect the results and what the acceptable range of results is. Many business decisions require the preparation of a business case. Each case will contain three scenarios: a most likely, a best case (potential upside), and a worst case (potential downside). A wise decision is based on considering all three scenarios. The proposal may be rejected if the potential downside has more than a remote probability and the worst-case results would make the business opportunity too unattractive.

We need to apply a similar approach to proposed projects—for instance:

1. Conduct a formal risk evaluation of the project and all of its segments.

2. Identify potential risk events.

3. Weigh the probability of the risk event occurrence.

4. Estimate the impact of the risk event, should it occur.

5. Identify possible ways to reduce risk (mitigation).

6. Calculate the cost of mitigation actions and the effect of these actions on the risk impact.

7. Incorporate the variables into the project valuation.

8. Extend the valuation to a range of expected results.

9. Consider each of the scenarios.

Defining a Policy for Uncertainty

The consideration of risk is a normal component of the portfolio-planning process. But we have to be careful about how the risk is factored in. For instance, some of the formulas call for modifying the expected benefits by the risk percentage. This can be misleading. Let's use the *Titanic* for an example. We'll say that the net present value (NPV) of the investment is calculated as $50 million. There is a 10 percent chance that the ship will hit an iceberg during the first year and sink. Is it reasonable to modify the NPV to $45 million?

No! What we have here is a case where the risk event would totally eliminate any return on the investment. The issue is not how much to modify the benefit. It is whether the governance council is willing to consider a project that might fail entirely.

This is an issue that has to be addressed by those responsible for implementing the tactical plans in support of the strategic plan. If we recognize that uncertainty is part of the game and that in some cases the degree of uncertainty can seriously negate the expected benefits, then surely a risk policy is needed.

At the executive level, guidance should be provided relative to how much risk is acceptable. The guidelines might spell out a risk balance, with a mix of high-risk and low-risk projects within a portfolio or a limit to one (or a specified number) of high-risk projects.

Getting back to the *Titanic* illustration, what if we mitigate the risk? We insure the ship. Certainly that is an option. But now we have to consider the effect of the mitigation on the income model. First, there is the cost of the insurance. If it is $2 million, we have to factor that cost into the NPV for the base case. We still have to have a figure for the effect of destruction of the ship from collision with an iceberg. The insurance is not likely to cover the income that would be lost, only the loss of the property. So we would still have a risk-based income model that is substantially below the $50 million.

Dealing Honestly with Risk

Uncertainty is an ever-present element of the project environment. Risk is not necessarily bad. In fact, many of the best opportunities have considerable risk. The key is to make sure that the risk is fully disclosed and considered. This can be ensured only if there is a proactive culture to address risk, backed up by mandated and audited practices. There is considerable danger that enthusiastic or biased project sponsors will hide potential risks or discount the impact of potential risks.

Here's a scene played out regularly in the corporate world. The project case is presented. There is a most likely scenario, plus a potential upside and a potential downside. The sponsor then says to ignore the downside because the downside won't happen. No one can will the downside to go away. You not only have to be honest enough to recognize the risk. You also have to acknowledge the necessity to deal with risk.

Remember the saying, "If you can't stand the heat, then stay out of the kitchen"? For projects, it can be reworded as, "If you can't stand uncertainty, then stay out of the projects business." But don't let the uncertainty be an enemy. Recognize it and deal with it.

Dealing with Uncertainty and Change in the Active Portfolio

Think about digital photography for a moment. There are two types. One is the still shot, a photograph of something taken at a specific point in time. The other is the video, a continual photograph taken over a span of time.

What does this have to do with PPM? Diagnostic and reporting tools essentially take snapshots. They provide a view of projects and portfolios at a single point in time. Yet projects and portfolios are not stagnant. They are dynamic and ever changing. In a perfect world, we would toss out our still camera and replace it with a video camera. But this is not practical.

What we can do is to recognize the dynamics and be prepared to deal with change and uncertainty. Uncertainty is a by-product of change and exists in every project. We make plans and generate estimates, then make decisions based on these plans and estimates.

If you look at an active portfolio, it consists of projects that were selected based on data that was available before the projects were activated. Once the project is initiated, the uncertainties start to move us in directions that were not planned. Periodically, we have to ask, "Would we have made the same decision on the basis of the data that we have now?"

So the first few things to acknowledge are these:

- The projects selected will have risk and uncertainty.
- This risk and uncertainty will result in change, either unplanned or corrective.
- The changes (including performance issues) may negate the basis for the original selection decision.
- Our picture is changing. Are we satisfied with the direction that it is taking us?

What About Projects with High Uncertainty?

Many projects, especially in the new product development area (this includes software development), have a high degree of uncertainty. It is the very nature of these types of projects to exhibit increased uncertainty in the later phases. That is, it is the objective of the earlier phases to define the later ones. As the project moves through the phases, the degree of uncertainty should diminish. At the proposal phase, can the technical or commercial success be ensured, or is this just the desired objective, subject to risk?

The worse thing we can do in this case is to say that "the project is too uncertain" to apply risk assessment techniques. In fact, it is these types of projects that need risk assessment the most. The challenge is not so much in identifying potential risks as it is in quantifying them with any precision.

So rather than ignoring the matter, we can best address the problem by processing the risk assessment in stages. At the proposal stage, we need to identify as many of the potential risks as possible. For each, we rough out a potential range of probability and impact, specifically noting the risk areas that can ruin the project. We also note if there are any options to contain these risks and when we would have to know to implement these options. Once the project is initiated, the risk items should be revisited at the end of each phase, especially as each phase helps to define the succeeding phases.

Managing Risk Mitigation Options

Before we address the effect of change on decisions, I want to stay a bit longer with the discussion of risk and uncertainty. We addressed this earlier when we evaluated risk on proposed projects and took into account the impact of risk on the benefits model. If we did not reject the project outright due to unacceptable risk, we identified potential risk events and potential risk mitigation options. Some of these options will have been chosen prior to project selection. Others may have been backup mitigation options, to be employed sometime during the project execution, based on risk events.

Therefore, managing risk in the active portfolio requires:

- Identifying the points in time where decisions regarding mitigation options should be made. These should be noted in the project schedule.

- Allowing some lead time just prior to the decision point for the review and decision process.

- Incorporating the effect of the risk/mitigation decision issue into the project valuation data to allow reconsideration of the selection decision.

- Repeatedly asking, "Are we satisfied with the direction that the project is taking?"

Three Levels of Review and Action

Now let's visit the issue of evaluating changes in timing, costs, resource demand, benefits, or deliverables. When do we do this? We can't do it on a continuing basis, as with a video camera. So how often should we take a snapshot? There is no single right answer to this question. However, we can let three levels of review and decision making serve as a guide.

Level 1: Periodic Project Status Review

The first level, the periodic project status review, will probably be performed monthly, but it should be performed more often for short-duration or highly sensitive (critical) projects. At this level, the typical review consists of comparing current status to the plan. Have key milestones been met? Are technical or design issues threatening project success? Variances to schedule and cost will be evaluated. Trend data showing a continuing degradation of performance should be highlighted. The effect of excessive variances (outside a declared tolerance level) should be evaluated, and, if warranted, brought to the attention of higher management. The project manager should maintain an awareness of the decision criteria on which the project selection was based. However, unless there is an obvious indication of a critical degradation, the portfolio selection process is not invoked at this time. (See Chapter 3.6 for a description of the earned value analysis method for evaluating project performance.)

Level 2: Phase-Level Review

Most projects should be broken down into segments called phases or stages. The end point of each phase usually represents a point where the entire project should undergo review of all aspects. For instance, a typical early project phase is the feasibility study. The deliverable of this phase is an appraisal of the likelihood that the defined project objectives will be met. If the result is a recommendation that the project objectives are unattainable, then the decision is simple. But in all likelihood, the results are that the objectives can be met with some higher degree of difficulty, or that part of the solution is not feasible, or that the technical objectives can be met but at a higher cost.

This is a critical point in the PPM process. If the results of any phase-level review indicate that the original business case for the project is no longer supported, then the business case needs to be amended and reevaluated. This process of evaluating projects at the end of each phase is often called Stage-Gate® or phase-gate.[1] (See Chapter 7.1 for more on this process.)

The Stage-Gate reviews should also include a checklist of all associated risk mitigation option items. We are managing projects with uncertainty. We need to maintain vigilance over performance and risk issues.

Level 3: Periodic Project Selection Review

This is a regular review of proposed projects and the selection of projects for the portfolio. During this review process, all ongoing projects that are in danger of not meeting set objectives should be put through the review. It is at this time that current projects (those that have not previously been paused or dropped as a result of the Stage-Gate review) may be considered for delay or termination, and replaced by proposed projects that better support the business goals.

Summary

Uncertainty is an element of all projects. Risk in projects must be recognized, evaluated, and considered as part of the project prioritization and selection process, as well as during the execution of selected projects. In managing risk, the goal is to minimize the potential for failure to achieve the project's benefits. The risk-based process has these key elements:

- Evaluate proposed projects against the selection criteria using each business case scenario: once with the base case and again with the potential upside and downside case data.

- Consider bypassing a proposed project that has excessive risk. Make sure that there is a clear policy for risk, and then adhere to it.

- Reduce the ranking of a proposed project where the range of risk-based results is large. A high level of uncertainty is not a desirable condition.

- Where risk is large enough to demote a project, consider risk mitigation options to contain such risk.

- Add the cost of mitigation actions (if any) to the project proposal data.

- Balance risk, that is, don't put too many high-risk projects in a portfolio.

- Don't stop with project selection. Consider the effect of risk and change in ongoing projects.

- Conduct periodic project status reviews. Note any items that can influence the decision to have that project in the portfolio. Consider delay or termination where warranted.

- Conduct periodic Stage-Gate reviews. Include significant risk milestones.
- Consider active projects as well as proposed projects when conducting the periodic ranking, selection, and resource allocation exercises.

3.4

Is There a Gorilla in Your Portfolio?

Turning Opportunity into Value

> Gorillas are products that dominate a market, placing the company in an extraordinarily powerful position. Companies with gorilla products or services can experience 30 to 40 percent growth per quarter. Gorilla projects require special handling.

Most discussions of the project portfolio describe several different types of projects for the makeup of portfolios. In Chapter 3.2, we introduced three general types: maintenance or utility projects, growth or enhancement projects, and transformation projects.

These discussions suggested that the typical portfolio consists of a balance of these types of projects. The nature of the business will dictate the proper makeup and balance of its portfolio. Balance does not mean that the portfolios are equal. For instance, the three examples stated here have a considerably different effect on the business, with the potential impact of the transformation projects being higher than the other types.

Maintenance or utility projects generally support ongoing products and services. When we prioritize these, they might not register as high on the benefits-value scale as some other type of projects. Yet they can be important even if they are not especially attractive or exciting. These types of projects are essential to maintaining current capabilities even if they don't show a direct return on investment (ROI).

Growth or enhancement projects are likely to fall into medium- to high-benefit and high-alignment segments of the ranking criteria. By design, these should be the projects that support strategic initiatives and represent increasing value. Such projects are needed to keep the firm in a solid competitive position. In today's technological environment, no business can succeed by maintaining the status quo.

Therefore, the typical business will have at least two project portfolios (or divisions of their portfolio): one for utility projects and another for enhancement projects. Strategy buckets will be established with goals and budgets attached to each, as well as resources allocated to each.

A third bucket will often be established for transformation projects. These are the opportunities to move the firm to a new level or to introduce new products or services that will dominate the marketplace. Although the projects in this category might exhibit a higher risk profile, the potential benefits can be so great as to place the project off the scale when plotting net present value or ROI. However, these numbers are extremely sensitive to market timing and success and must be treated with some skepticism.

Transformation projects require special handling. When we compute a benefits number for these projects, we are assuming a particular return based on a specific market position. Whether this assumed market position is attained depends on several factors, and whether this assumed market position is attained will have a monumental effect on benefits. I refer to these as gorilla projects, based on research conducted and reported by Geoffrey Moore.[1]

What Is a Gorilla?

According to Moore, gorillas are products that dominate a market, placing the company in an extraordinarily powerful position. Companies with gorilla products (or gorilla services) can experience 30 to 40 percent growth per quarter. Gorillas can be so strong as to force any potential competitor to search for a niche market instead.

Managing the Gorilla Project

The gorilla project, if it is to be successful, requires every possible advantage that can come from superior project management diligence. Here are some special characteristics to consider.

Planning

Although it is quite possible that the plans will change, it is essential at least to start with a plan. However, the planning process must be very dynamic. The gorilla project will often be based on leading-edge technology. As the project moves along, we may find that we must deviate from the initially preferred path and should be ready to select alternate strategies. The ability to have alternate plans and to perform what-if evaluations quickly and frequently is essential in this environment.

Timing

For the gorilla project, speed is of the essence. The second firm to offer the new product or service does not become the gorilla. Only the first gets to claim that title and the spoils that go with it. The plan must consider every possible way to shorten the time-to-market cycle. Every exception to the defined plan or any delay must be evaluated for effect on the opportunity to be first to market. Therefore, the plan must be carefully monitored, and pressure must be maintained to prevent loss of critical time.

Decision Points

The gorilla project has a finite time window. If the window of opportunity is missed, even the most successful and advanced technical accomplishment may lose out to a lesser product or service that makes it to the market first. This overall time window must be broken down into smaller units, marking key decision points along the way. The plan must identify these decision points. The team must be aware of upcoming decision points (or gates) and be prepared to make the decisions that are required to keep the project on track.

Risk

Significant risk is a normal component of the gorilla project. However, such risk can be managed. To do so, the potential risks must first be identified and then quantified as to probability of occurrence and consequence of occurrence. For all high-impact risks, a mitigation plan should be prepared. After these tasks have been performed (risk identification, quantification, and mitigation), we evaluate whether the risk is acceptable (for example, are there less risky approaches to the same objective?). Finally, we monitor all risk areas, being prepared to apply mitigation strategies where warranted.

Schedule Risk

Schedule risk is especially sensitive for the gorilla project. Tools are available to evaluate critical path schedules for the probability of meeting calculated project completion dates. Traditional critical path scheduling techniques will deliver a plan having 50 percent or less probability of being executed by the dates calculated. If your project can't accept this low confidence factor, you can use Monte Carlo scheduling techniques to develop and evaluate schedules having a higher degree of safety. (Monte Carlo–based risk software is available from several companies, including Pertmaster, Palisade, and C/S Solutions.) A common alternative is to insert selective schedule contingency elements. These are dummy tasks, placed in strategic paths that represent a shared contingency for the work along that path. Avoid adding contingency to individual tasks. It will be construed to mean that there is additional time available to complete these tasks. An alternate scheduling technique (employing shared contingency) is the critical chain method, based on the theory of constraints (see Chapter 8.1).

Communication

Communication is the greatest in importance. Communication, especially for the gorilla project, will have great impact on project success. Frequent communication among all stakeholders, in formats that convey essential information and in ways that promote and facilitate the desired responses to action items, must be the foundation of any project management system for gorilla projects. Decisions can't be made in a vacuum. Nor can they be made if no one knows that the decision is required. A system of alarms and alerts that highlight items needing attention and that are distributed promptly to the proper parties is a part of such a system.

Time-to-Market

You might be thinking, *Aren't these things that should be done for all projects?* Of course, they are. However, on many projects, you might get away without being very diligent in applying these basic project management principles. When it comes to the gorilla project, there is no room for being casual about it.

Getting back to the significance of being the first to market, Moore has some interesting figures to offer on this. He says that when a new product is created for a new market, the first one getting to market is most likely to garner at least 50 percent of the total market. The remaining 50 percent is all that will remain for all of the other players. No wonder that there is so much pressure on new developments (and perhaps why some developers are willing to skimp on quality rather than chance delays).[2]

There's more. If the first vendor to the market garners 50 percent of possible sales, while vendor 2 picks up, say, 20 percent, that is not the probable ratio for income. That is because vendor 1 sets the price, which, without competition, allows maximizing profits and return on investment. By the time the other vendors join the battle, profit margins will drop (but only after vendor 1 has made its killing). Moore figures that vendor 1 will garner at least 70 percent of the profits pie in this model.

Is that enough motivation to drive schedule compression and management?

Every day that can be squeezed out of the schedule improves the developer's chances of grabbing the lion's share of the market. Every day of slippage that is avoided due to diligent management of the project can bring the spoils of being the gorilla closer to home. The new product developer must not only invest effort in creating fast-track schedules, but must also continually tweak the schedule looking for ways to shorten the time cycles. The payoff for getting there first can be monumental.

Gorillas in the Portfolio

Recognizing the extreme sensitivity of time-to-market, we have to be very careful of the values that we declare for the potential benefits from transformation projects. If we assume that we will be first-to-market (the gorilla), the declared benefits will be exceedingly higher than not being the leader. If we do use the higher figures, we have to make sure that the project has enough visibility and priority to meet the window of opportunity. As long as the project remains on track to be a gorilla, it should rate the highest priority for critical resources.

We have to continually monitor the position of the project against the window of opportunity. If it looks as if the window will be missed and corrective actions are not available, the benefit calculations will have to be revised. This may change the ranking of the project.

The gorilla portfolio should have continual executive attention. The success of its component projects represents the highest benefit-to-cost potential among all projects and portfolios. Time-to-market is a critical aspect of these projects. The one who scores first almost always wins.

3.5

Work Breakdown Structures for Risk and Strategies

Work breakdown structures are popular mechanisms for creating hierarchical arrangements for project tasks, resources, cost buckets, and organizations. In this chapter, we expand the WBS concept to risk and strategies.

Most practitioners of project management are familiar with work breakdown structures (WBS). We use the WBS format to create a hierarchical structure of the work in a project. We have also adapted WBS technology to organizations (OBS), resources (RBS), and finances. Let's look at applying WBS concepts to aligning projects with strategies.

A WBS for Strategies

Figure 3.5-1 presents a matrix-style WBS for strategies. In this example, we show a one-layer vertical WBS and a one-layer horizontal WBS. (There can be additional layers, but we've tried to keep this example simple.)

FIGURE 3.5-1 Strategies Work Breakdown Structure in a Matrix Format

STRATEGIC INITIATIVES

Alignment Matrix	Generate Income	Reduce Costs	Reduce Head Count	Establish New Market Beachhead
Desktop and Notebook Computers	Add build-to-order capability	Outsource customer support to India	Outsource customer support to India	Add build-to-order capability
Specialty Computers (PDA, Pocket PC)				New leading-edge pocket PC
Servers and Networks		Move European plants to China		
Printers		Outsource customer support to India	Outsource customer support to India	
Displays	Add plasma line	Build new plant in Mexico		
Other	Develop new advertising program	R&D for packaging	Outsource surveys and marketing research	

STRATEGIC BUSINESS UNIT

The vertical WBS represents strategic business units (SBUs) or product lines. Here it is assumed that each SBU will be aligning its projects with the various strategic buckets. The horizontal WBS represents four business strategies.

Each proposed project is placed in the matrix to show alignment with an SBU and a strategic bucket. Note that it is possible to have a project support more than one strategy. In this example, we show two SBUs with plans to outsource customer support. This tactical initiative (to be conducted jointly by the two SBUs) supports two strategies: "Reduce Costs" and "Reduce Head Count."

The strategies WBS serves as a visual display of how projects are aligned with SBUs and strategic buckets. If desired, the project boxes can be color-coded to distinguish proposed projects from approved projects, and additional data can be added (for example, ranking scores, internal or external client, or internal or external resources).

The matrix-style display also provides a visual indication of which strategies are not being supported and which SBUs are not participating.

Figure 3.5-2 presents the strategies WBS in a bubble chart format. This chart contains all of the information as the matrix in Figure 3.5-1, plus data on the size (net present value) of each of the candidate projects. Through the use of bubble sizing and color, such a chart can present up to four aspects of the data (x-axis, y-axis, bubble size, and bubble color).

A WBS for Risk

Using the WBS approach for risk works even better than the SBS. In the example provided in Figure 3.5-3, we use the WBS primarily as a structured checklist.

At the first level of the risk WBS, we list seven categories for risk consideration: time, people, costs, deliverables, quality, contract, and market. (Obviously there can be others.) For each of these categories, we list any areas where there could be a risk issue. For instance, under the category of cost, we might ask, "Are there any risk issues

FIGURE 3.5-2 Strategies Work Breakdown Structure as a Bubble Chart

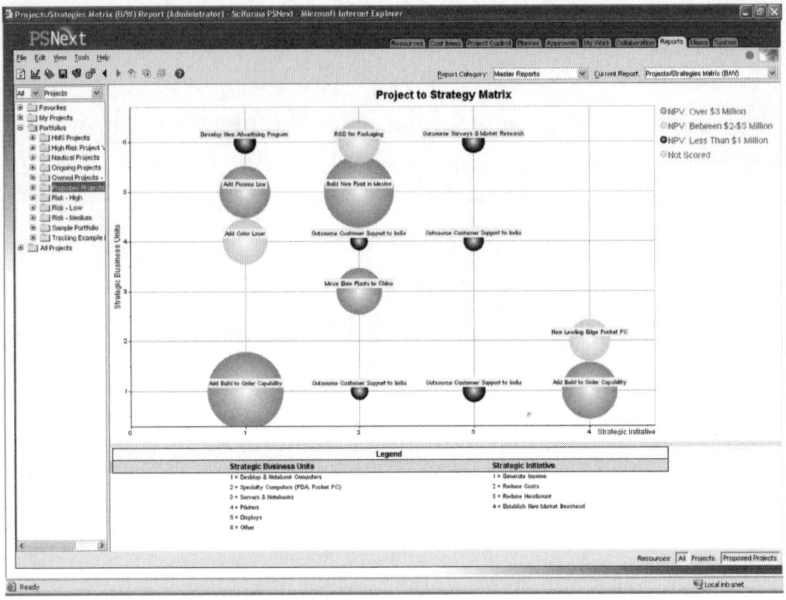

associated with escalation, estimating errors, penalty exposure, or exchange rates?" These are the areas where issues often arise that can upset the cost projections developed to support the project proposal.

In developing a cost figure, we assume a number for escalation. In the risk assessment exercise, we have to ask, "What is the range of possible escalation on items that are sensitive to such escalation?" Then we ask, "What is the effect on cost?" We would also probe the project estimating data, looking for areas that might be sensitive to an estimating error. Is this a risk item?

Is there a penalty condition in the contract? What risks to cost (or income) does this present? Are we dealing with multiple currencies? Is there a risk to cost (or income) because of unexpected exchange rate changes? I have experienced a major international project where all aspects of the project were completed with great success and the firm lost money on it because of significant and damaging changes in the exchange rate.

FIGURE 3.5-3 Risk Breakdown Structure Diagram

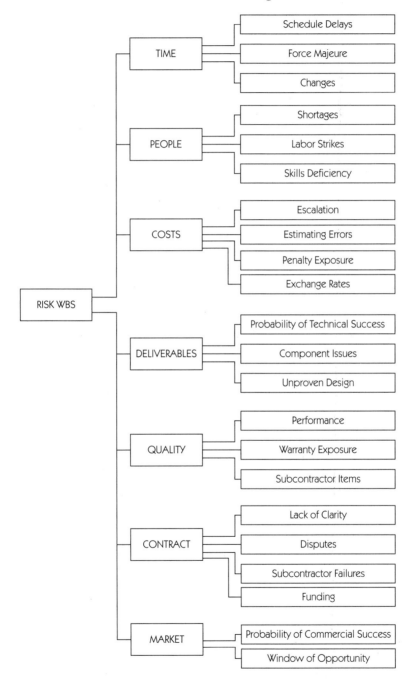

Using the WBS as a Checklist

There's a good chance that your project does not have exchange rate or penalty exposure. No problem! You just cross that off the checklist that the risk WBS represents. It is much easier to start with a list of all possible items and to delete those that do not apply rather than start out with a blank sheet of paper (or a blank screen) and try to think of risk items.

Templates can be developed for each type of common project. The proposal manager deletes items that don't apply and adds items that are unique to that project. Actually, even better than deleting nonapplicable items is to mark them N/A. This serves as an audit trail, showing that the item was considered.

Some of the second-level items can easily belong in more than one place. This is not important. What is important is that they show up somewhere and are not overlooked.

Assessing and Mitigating Risk

On each of these second-level items, the first question is, "Does it apply?" If the answer is yes, then describe the potential risk event. For each event, you then need to assess the potential effect on schedule, cost, resources, deliverables, technical objectives, and commercial objectives. The potential effect is the product of two estimates. First, what is the probability that the event will occur? Second, what is the impact of the event if it does happen?

Finally, you consider options for containing the risks. Look for options to reduce the probability of risk occurrence and minimize the impact of risk events should they occur.

Steps in Dealing with Risk Issues

1. Determine the probability of the event.
   - Consider the ability to reduce probability.
   - Can you insure, find an alternative, or reduce the risk?

2. Determine the impact of the event.

- Consider the ability to reduce the impact.
- Can you insure, find an alternative, or reduce the risk?

3. What is the cost to mitigate the risk?

4. What is the ability to absorb the impact?

- Consider schedule contingency, cost contingency, and the design margin, for example.

5. Can the impact be shifted to others?

- Consider cost plus, extras, or that the client or sponsor might accept a lesser product.

Summary

- More people have written about risk management than have practiced it. Risk management is a way of dealing with uncertainty in projects. Every project has some degree of uncertainty. Therefore, every project requires risk management.
  - ➤ Risk assessment and management (RAM) requires a structured, proactive approach.
  - ➤ A risk WBS is a valuable element of a structured RAM system.
- An "accurate estimate" is an oxymoron.
  - ➤ How reliable is your information?
- How sensitive is the project to the risks?
  - ➤ What is the ability to absorb impacts? For example, being late for a dinner reservation can be tolerated. Being late for a cruise ship departure cannot.
- Avoid redundant or cumulative contingency.
  - ➤ Contingency is important. Without it, you will finish late and over budget. However, there is a tendency to pile on contingencies so that they are redundant. To avoid this,

consider shared contingency. Apply contingency to groups rather than individual items. For instance, apply schedule contingency for a string of tasks rather than to each task. Apply cost contingency to work packages, not individual line items.

- A guarantee against all risk may not be practical or economically feasible.

- Risk is dynamic.

  ➤ The probability and impact of risk can change as the project progresses. Consider the time dimensions of risk and when to address the risk issues.

- Maintain a risk issues directory.

  ➤ Log all risk items. Identify a responsible party for each risk issue. Maintain an audit trail of all communications and actions. Flag open risk items.

- Don't forget the big picture.

  ➤ Consider risk issues at the project level. How well is the organization situated to do this project? What is the organization's risk culture? What risk guidelines have been established at the strategic level?

3.6

An Introduction to Earned Value Analysis

A key component of PPM is improved management of the project pipeline. We conduct performance reviews of active projects with the objective of considering termination of projects that no longer support the conditions on which approval was granted. An essential capability for such performance reviews is the process of Earned Value Analysis. The ability to monitor schedule and cost variances in a consistent, structured manner provides key data for performance reviews and removes personal biases from the evaluation.

Do you cringe when someone brings up the subject of Earned Value Management (EVM) or Earned Value Analysis (EVA)? Do you see yourself drowning in torrents of seemingly obscure data, generated by some space age software that has run amok? And what about all that alphabet soup? What the heck are BCWS, SPI, and ACWP?

If you're into project management, you've probably heard of EVA and maybe even tinkered with it. Unfortunately, there is a widespread misconception that EVA is only for the big aerospace and defense jobs, where the customer is the government. If you're working on these kinds of projects, you've probably read up on earned value, perhaps the highly recognized text by EVM guru Quentin Fleming, which is crammed with 560 pages of really good stuff on "Cost/Schedule Control Systems Criteria" (the Department of Defense's version of EVM).[1] Or maybe you are familiar with the downsized discussion on "Earned Value Project Management," published by Project Management Institute (PMI), still inviting the reader to digest 140 pages.[2]

The good news is that you can pick up the essentials of EVA in about five pages, and you don't have to use all of the available EVA features in order to benefit from EVA.

EVA Made Easy

I am a real believer in EVA. Although I fully understand its intricacies and power, I can also sympathize with the novice project management practitioner who feels overwhelmed by the seemingly complicated EVA concepts. I also have found through actual field experience that the concepts of EVA can be effectively applied in virtually every project situation, from very complex to the absurdly simple.

There are two things that you should know about learning and using EVA. First, there are just a few basic concepts, which you can learn in an hour or less. Second, you can use and benefit from EVA without applying the entire set of capabilities. The basic application of EVA is an easy and practical way to monitor and evaluate project performance. So I offer here a stripped-down version of an EVA (Earned Value Analysis) primer.

The entire EVA practice essentially consists of about six key measurement values. We actually use these values in the planning and tracking of a project, even though we often don't give them names or structure.

Establishing a Baseline

If we are going to evaluate project performance by measuring cost and schedule variance, then we have to have a *baseline* to measure against. So the first two values that we use actually show up in the project plan before we track progress. First, there is the *BAC (Bud-*

get at Completion), which is a value that we assign to a task or any part of the project. The most common budgets are based on cost, but in place of an actual dollar value, it can also be a labor value (such as planned hours) or any other value that provides a weight factor for the task. For example, if you are tracking spent time rather than actual money expenditures, you can set the BAC values based on the labor estimates for the tasks.

The second plan value is the BCWS *(Budgeted Cost of Work Scheduled)*. The BCWS is the weighted value of the task at a specific point in time during its planned execution. For instance, if a task with a budget of $5,000 were scheduled to be executed between February 15 and March 15, the BCWS on March 1 would be $2,500 (50% of the BAC). The BCWS on March 15 is $5,000. We'll use the BCWS to determine the schedule variance.

The PMI Exposure Draft for EVM offers alternative (more sensible) terms for three basic EVA nomenclature items. For example, it suggests PV (Planned Value) as an alternative for BCWS. In addition, it substitutes EV (Earned Value) for the traditional term "Budgeted Cost of Work Performed" (BCWP), and AC (Actual Cost) for the traditional term "Actual Cost of Work Performed" (ACWP).

For readers who are new to the earned value concepts, I feel that it is easier to work with the newer terms. Therefore, in this chapter, we will use the following:

PV = Planned Value = BCWS = Budgeted Cost of Work Scheduled

EV = Earned Value = BCWP = Budgeted Cost of Work Performed

AC = Actual Cost = ACWP = Actual Cost of Work Performed

Calculating Earned Value

The next two values are created when we track the project. Both of these are periodic values. That is, they relate to a specific date during the life of the project (as does the PV). The key component of the entire EVA process is the BCWP (*Budgeted Cost of Work Performed*). Does this term confuse you? Then we will call it the *"Earned Value" (EV)*, which is what it is.

Computation of EV couldn't be more elementary. It is the percent complete (%C) of a task times the budget (BAC). If on March 1, our $5,000 task is declared to be 40% complete, then the EV is $2,000. How simple can it get? EV = %C × BAC. 40% × $5,000 = $2,000. Stating this once more, *the earned value is the percent complete times the budget*.

If you're using resource hours instead of costs, the process is the same. If the BAC is 200 hours and the percent complete is 40%, then the EV is 80 hours.

The second tracking item is actual cost. In EVA-land, it is called ACWP (*Actual Cost of Work Performed*). We'll be calling it AC. If as of March 1 our subject task has accumulated $2,400 in costs, then the AC is $2,400. Still simple, right?

The Four Basic Measurements

Reviewing what we have learned thus far, there are four basic measurements. As part of the plan, we have the item budget (BAC) and the planned value of the work to be performed at a specified time (PV). As part of the tracking, we add the earned value (EV) and the actual cost to date (AC). With these measurements, we can evaluate project performance using variance and trend analysis. *It all comes down to Cost Variance and Schedule Variance*.

Measuring Cost Performance: Cost Variance and Cost Performance Index

For cost performance evaluation, we need only two pieces of data: earned value and the actual cost. We use these data to compute the cost variance. The CV (*Cost Variance*) is the earned value minus the actual cost. The calculation is: EV − AC = CV. Using our example, it is 2,000 − 2,400 = −400.

Again, although we use the term *cost,* it also works with labor hours (or any other weight factor). If the EV is 80 hours and the AC is 96 hours, the CV is –16.

It is actually more useful to express this variance as a fraction. The *CPI (Cost Performance Index)* is the EV *divided* by the AC, or 2,000/2,400 = 0.8333. We are looking for a CPI that is 1.000 or greater, so this 0.8333 signifies subpar cost performance. We spent $2,400 to do $2,000 worth of work (or 96 hours to do 80 hours of work).

Measuring Schedule Performance: Schedule Variance and Schedule Performance Index

The process is similar for computing the schedule variance. The *SV (Schedule Variance)* is the earned value minus the planned value. The calculation is: EV – PV = SV. Using our example, it is 2,000 – 2,500 = –500.

Again, the more useful expression is the *SPI (Schedule Performance Index)*, which is EV *divided* by PV. Here, our SPI is 2,000/2,500 = 0.800. Looking at the SPI, we can easily see that we are behind schedule. The SPI indicates that we are executing the work at a rate of 80% of the planned rate.

That's essentially all that there is to this whole EVA mystique. Table 3.6-1 provides a quick review.

You Don't Have to Do Both CV and SV

Let's make it even simpler. Let's say that you are not tracking actual costs or actual hours. Obviously, you cannot compute the cost variance. But that doesn't stop you from tracking the progress and computing the schedule variance. All that you need is a plan, as represented by the BAC and PV, and the periodic tracking of the percentage complete, expressed as the EV. With these data, you can determine the SV and the SPI.

TABLE 3.6-1. A Glossary of EVA Terms

Term	Explanation
BAC (Budget at Completion)	The budget
BCWS (Budgeted Cost of Work Scheduled) (a.k.a. PV)	Planned accomplishment (at any point in time)
BCWP (Budgeted Cost of Work Performed) (a.k.a. EV)	Earned value or accomplishment value (at any point of time)
ACWP (Actual Cost of Work Performed) (a.k.a. AC)	Actual cost to date
SV (Schedule Variance)	Difference between planned accomplishment and EV
CV (Cost Variance)	Difference between actual cost and EV
SPI (Schedule Performance Index)	Earned value divided by planned value
CPI (Cost Performance Index)	Earned value divided by actual cost

A similar option applies to cost. You don't even have to have a baseline plan to process cost variances. What you must have is (1) a budget (or weight factor), (2) a measurement of percent complete (which is used to determine the EV [EV = %C × budget]), and (3) the actual cost (AC). You just need to compare what you spent to the value of what you accomplished.

A Common Cost Measurement Mistake

There is a common mistake made in traditional cost performance analysis (non-EVA) where the actual cost is compared to the planned cost. This is fundamentally wrong. Just look at our example. Following this flawed practice, the accountants might report that the cost performance is favorable (spent $2,400 against the plan of $2,500). However, only $2,000 of work has actually been accomplished. The ugly truth is that the item is both behind schedule and over budget. Without earned value, there is no valid performance analysis.

Trends Are the Most Revealing

A report of a negative CV or SV should easily get our attention but may not always be a matter of great concern. What should sound the alarm is a continuing negative value or a CV or SV that is moving in the wrong direction. That's why I like to use the CPI and SPI. I plot these values against a time line (Figure 3.6-1). If the values are below 1.0 and fail to move back to this par value, then corrective action is indicated (or we acknowledge that the targets won't be met).

Summarize to Any Level

Although the data can be collected at the task level of detail, analysis is usually performed at a higher level. This is why it is so important to be able to summarize the data. We usually use a WBS to define the summarization hierarchy.

In the practical application of EVA, we roll up the data to a reasonable higher level of detail. When there are areas of unsatisfactory

FIGURE 3.6-1 SPI Trend Plot

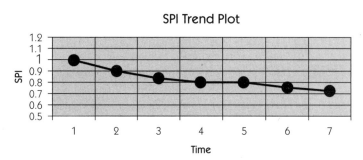

SV or CV, we can drill down to the details of the suspect area to pinpoint the cause.

Segregate by Any Classification

Most project management software supports EVA for multiple WBSs. The WBS and other task coding can also be used to segregate the data by any interest area. For instance, we can evaluate performance by location, performing craft, responsible manager, cost accounts, or any other classification that has been defined to the system.

We can roll up by classification and then drill down in the poorly performing areas. This supports a management-by-exception approach. By identifying areas that are outside the performance targets, we can focus on finding causes and correcting such nonperforming areas. This permits us to apply resources where they will do the most good.

EVA: The Easy Way

That's it for a quick overview of earned value. Just these few measurements, processed within a structured and consistent policy, can deliver significant benefits, even in a limited application of EVA capabilities.

Almost all critical path method software has this EVA capability built in. You enter the basic planning and tracking data, and all calculations and reporting are already programmed and available. If you are already entering such data, the EVA process takes no further effort.[3]

EVA and PPM

A key component of PPM is improved management of the project pipeline. That is, we strive to review the performance of active projects against several criteria with the objective of considering termination of those projects that no longer support the conditions on which approval was granted. An essential capability for such performance reviews is the process of EVA. The ability to monitor schedule and cost variances in a consistent, structured manner provides key data for performance reviews and removes personal biases from the evaluation.

PART TWO

Contributed Chapters and Case Studies

Part One covered the basic spectrum of project portfolio management (PPM). The chapters described why and how we apply PPM and covered the basics and some finer points, including processes and techniques, and how to organize and perform in a PPM environment.

Over the past decade, several pioneers in the field of PPM have documented their groundbreaking work and have developed dedicated followers. It is important that we capture that wealth of knowledge and use it to reinforce the material in Part One. Many of the disciples of the early gurus have greatly added to this cache of wisdom. Their writings too add to our growing PPM expertise.

Of equal importance is the recorded experience of the early adopters. No theory will stand the test of time until it can weather the hardships of reality. With courage and understanding, these pioneer implementers created a beachhead for others to follow. Their case studies help to validate the theory and illustrate its adoption.

Several of these gurus and pioneers have contributed to this book, and their valuable work is presented in Part Two. These chapters cover a broad spectrum of PPM. Some provide a broad-brush look at PPM, offering a different perspective of PPM from that presented in Part One but essentially validating the basic tenets. Other contributions focus on a particular aspect of PPM, providing sufficient detail to guide users to decide whether to employ such processes. Several chapters go into a great deal of detail about the entire subject of PPM, offering a comprehensive review of experiences in implementing PPM.

SECTION 4

PPM Techniques and Issues

Portfolio Planning

We initially covered PPM techniques in Part One and made special note of two very important aspects of PPM: the vital element of aligning projects with strategies and the importance of assigning value to a project to aid in the evaluation of candidate projects for the portfolio.

These are not simple topics and deserve considerable additional space. In Chapter 4.1, consultant K. C. Yelin provides a thorough and thoughtful discussion on the topic of strategies and of aligning projects with strategies. Yelin brings a special ability to provide practical guidance to help corporations solve problems and adopt new methodologies. This capability will be apparent in the two chapters that she contributed to this book.

In Chapter 4.2, consultants Ray Trotta and Christopher Gardner cover the arcane art of determining the value of a project. They remove the "value" issue from the realm of hocus-pocus to a platform with a sound footing. They introduce the basic discounted cash flow model and illustrate how that can be applied to proposed projects. A case study example illustrates the application of the model.

In addition to the general processes being used in portfolio planning, a couple of highly structured methodologies have emerged to help take some of the guesswork out of project evaluation and selection. One of these techniques, analytic hierarchy process (AHP), is a mathematical model to assist in the decision-making process. It has enjoyed wide acceptance in several application areas and is now being successfully applied to PPM. In Chapter 4.3, AHP champion Jim Devlin presents a strong and passionate case for AHP and describes how it is applied to the PPM process.

The deployment of AHP is much simpler than it sounds. Behind this seemingly mathematical model is a basic and practical decision-support process. Still, some users will find the process to be more structured than they need. We present this valuable technique as an option to be used as needed.

Another useful model, based on the work of Nobel Prize winner Harry Markowitz, is the Efficient Frontier. In Chapter 4.4, Mike Gruia shows how Markowitz's work in modern portfolio theory is applied to optimize the project portfolio. This is another mathematical-based process, and the caveat that the process is more structured than some users need applies here as well.

4.1

Linking Strategy and Project Portfolio Management

K. C. Yelin

> Strategy without tactics is the slowest route to victory.
> Tactics without strategy is the noise before defeat.
> —Sun Tzu, Chinese military strategist, c. 490 B.C.

Many organizations are accustomed to investing in the development of strategies that will drive them forward. Multiple days of leaders' and cross-functional teams' time are spent each year in off-site meetings to define or refine the organization's strategy. Participants leave the meetings with the satisfied feeling that they have raised options, hammered through them, and achieved an essential alignment among participants on the key methods that the organization will pursue to achieve its goals.

Independent of the passion exhibited during the development of strategies, the goals these strategies are intended to make happen are frequently not achieved. The inability to execute against the strategies may be related to a lack of understanding, lack of accountability, lack of resources, lack of competencies, or changes in external factors to name a few. The assumption that a "can-do" attitude alone can be counted on to deliver on complex and interdependent strategies is naive; it ignores issues of cross-functional resource allocation and competing priorities that cause drag on the organization. At the end of a measurement period, if goals are not achieved, blame for lack of results is meted out, and the cycle begins again. Over time, belief in the organization's ability to develop effective strategies and achieve goals lessens. Funding sources retreat, and when the economy is good, talented associates who want to contribute to a successful organization leave.

An explicit rigor is necessary to execute against strategy effectively. Project portfolio management is the process, projects are the vehicles, and project management is the discipline that can bridge the gap between strategy and the realization of its related goals.

What Is Strategy?

Strategy is a word we use frequently. It is a member of that stock collection of organizational jargon that includes words such as *goal*, *objective*, *plan*, and *team*. The words are used so often that we assume they have a common meaning to everyone in the organization. But assumptions about the meaning of words have caused wars, so there is high value to validate exactly how your organization is defining what it means by *strategy*.

Here are a few of the most commonly referenced definitions of strategy:[1]

> "Strategy is the framework that guides those choices that determine the nature and direction of an organization."
> —Benjamin Tregoe and John Zimmerman,
>   *Top Management Strategy*

> "Strategy answers the questions: What should the organization be doing? What are the ends we seek and how should we achieve them?"
> —George Steiner, *Strategic Planning*

> "Competitive strategy is a combination of the ends (goals) for which the firm is striving and the means (policies) by which it is seeking to get there."
> —Michael Porter, *Competitive Strategy*

As you can see, there is no single, definitive definition of *strategy*. In truth, it doesn't matter which words you use to define it; what is key is that all members of an organization have a clearly articulated and shared understanding of the elements below. When you have each of the following items, consider that you have a set of strategies:

- A position or mission comprising a set of products, services, customers, markets, geographies, channels, technologies (ends)
- A set of quantifiable goals (ends)
- Overarching approaches by which you will achieve the ends (means)
- Specific plans to apply those means and resources to achieve the ends (project portfolio management)

In visualizing the link between strategy and the project portfolio in Figure 4.1-1, we will assign the term *strategy* to the element of means or approach that will be used to accomplish the ends.

Assuming that leadership has identified the mission, goals, and strategies, the critical next level of detail is identification of specific projects that will carry out the strategies. These projects become candidates for inclusion in the organization's project portfolio. This map may be referred to as the strategic plan. When you follow it from right to left, it describes exactly what you will do to deliver on each strategy, which should result in achieving the goals and mission of the organization. Applying effective project management process, a fifth level of detail, is added to the plan. Each project candidate is defined in greater detail outlining outcomes, resource requirements, and potential time lines and accountabilities. The more explicit the plan is, the higher is the probability that the goals will be achieved. Figure 4.1-2 provides a snapshot of sample goals with links to strategies and potential projects.

FIGURE 4.1-1 Strategic Linkage in Project Portfolio

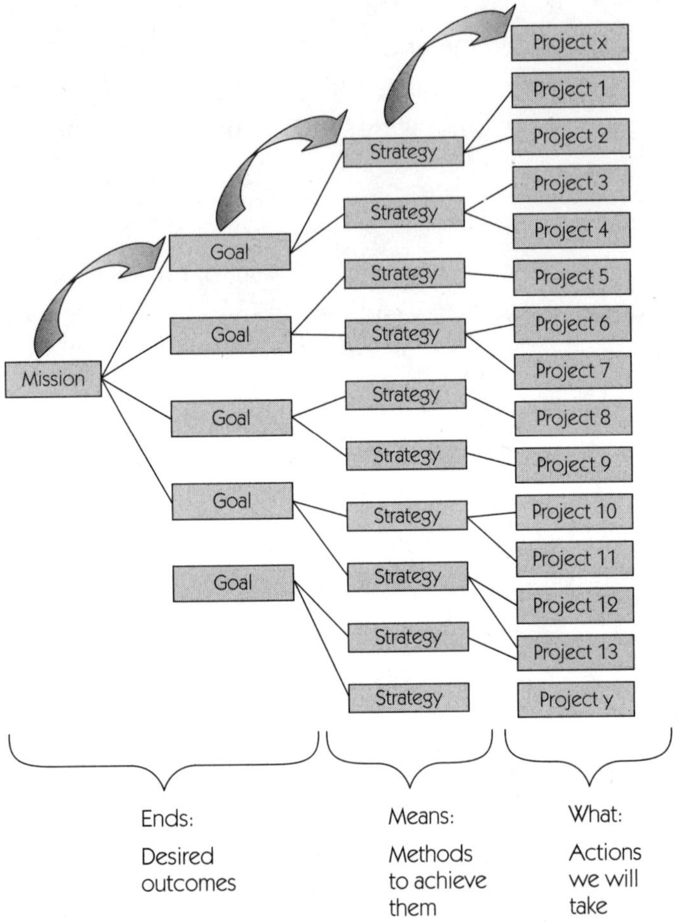

Ends:
Desired
outcomes

Means:
Methods
to achieve
them

What:
Actions
we will
take

© 1997 ICS Group.

Rating the Degree of Linkage Between Projects and Strategy

Just because a project supports a strategy does not guarantee it a pass into the project portfolio. The project is still competing with other candidates for the limited resources of the organization. As such, it needs to go through the organization's standard project portfolio

FIGURE 4.1-2 Sample Strategy Elements

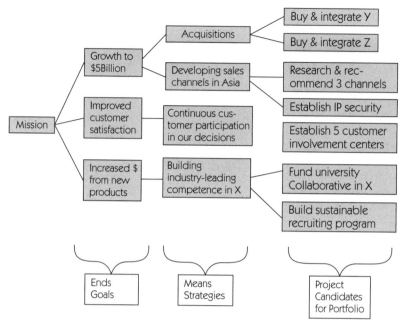

evaluation process. Among the criteria that projects will be evaluated against is the degree of impact the project has on the organization's strategies. Let's look at one way to evaluate against the criteria of strategy impact.

Assume that an organization has the following four strategies:

- Build brand value.
- Invest in core technologies.
- Build organizational effectiveness.
- Revitalize quality.

Exhibit 4.1-1 displays how each project candidate is rated for the degree of impact it has on each of the strategies. The sum of the individual strategy impact ratings provides an overall project strategy value score. This score is integrated with a project's ratings on other

EXHIBIT 4.1-1 Evaluating the Degree of Linkage and Criticality to the Strategies

PROJECT CANDIDATE EVALUATION PROCESS

Scoring:

9 = Strong alignment and/or high impact

3 = Moderate alignment and/or impact

1 = Limited alignment and/or impact

0 = No relationship

100 = Compliance project necessary for us to stay in business (compliance trumps all other evaluation criteria)

| PROJECT CANDIDATES | Strategic Alignment/Impact | | | | TOTAL STRATEGY IMPACT SCORE | Compliance — Is this a compliance project essential for us to stay open? Score yes as 100 points. | Risk — What is the probability of successfully implementing this project? 9 = High, 1 = Low | OVERALL PROJECT SCORE | NPV — What is the Net Present Value of this project to our organization? |
	Does this project build brand value?	Is this an investment in core technologies?	Does this project build organizational effectiveness?	Does this project support quality revitalization?					
Installation of plant testing equipment	1	0	0	9	10	100	3	113	$ 100,000
Develop and launch product line for seniors	9	3	0	0	12	0	3	15	$5,000,000
Marketing campaign linking products to health and safety	9	0	0	0	9	0	3	12	$ 400,000
Implement new product development process that will shorten average time by 20 percent	0	3	3	1	7	0	3	10	$
Close Plant X, transfer production to Plant Y	0	0	0	0	0	0	9	9	$3,500,000
Launch internet sales channel	1	0	0	0	1	0	3	4	$1,000,000
Build plant in China and related marketing plan for produced goods	1	0	0	0	1	0	3	4	$9,000,000

evaluation criteria, such as net present value or risk. Such a total project score is often used to do the initial prioritization of project candidates.

Some organizations employ intricate quantitative analyses to assess which projects rate highest on the portfolio admissions test. But it is not always the highest-scoring projects that make it to the portfolio. That is because the ultimate decisions of which projects will be resourced and executed are made by executives, who are human beings. The executive investment management team uses information from the evaluation process as input to their decisions, which may be made based on experience, environmental conditions, and "feel," along with healthy debate and compromise among competing programs. It is during these debates that the scope of some proposed strategies may narrow or even be discarded.

The project evaluation criteria and their degree of detail are most effective when they meet the needs and style of those who make the ultimate decisions regarding which projects will enter the portfolio. In one leading consumer products company in whose process I participated, the CEO alone made the selection of which projects would enter the portfolio and be executed. With minimal evaluation data presented to him, he made the decision in five minutes. He knew his company's strategies inside out, and to him the decisions were straightforward. In another firm, decisions were made by a group of functional vice presidents who required detailed quantitative analysis and six weeks to make portfolio decisions every quarter. Although each decision-making group had different needs and styles, both made excellent choices. Explicitly defining the linkages and dependencies that strategies have on specific projects is key to ensuring delivering on the strategies that the organization is counting on. How you communicate that linkage is tailored to the needs of those who will use the information.

Certain critical data must be made explicit and communicated to all decision makers. One is the capacity of the organization to absorb and deliver on each project (see Figure 4.1-3). Without that, organizations will attempt to launch every strategy-related project along with other "staying in business" operational projects in the

FIGURE 4.1-3 Reconciliation of Project Demand Against the Organization's Capacity to Deliver Before Commitment of Projects to the Portfolio

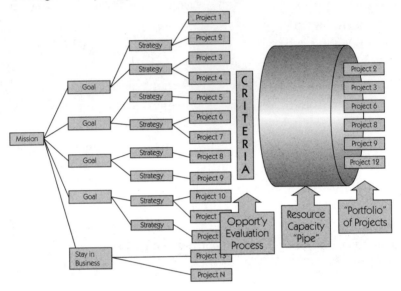

© 1997 ICS Group.

portfolio. Perhaps the greatest risk to an organization's ability to deliver on its strategies, goals, and mission is committing to more projects than it can possibly deliver. When this occurs, critical projects fail later in the cycle. An executive's fiduciary responsibility is to resource critical projects or to narrow the scope of the strategies.

Making Strategy Explicit

So far we have assumed that strategies exist for the organization. What if they do not? Do we abandon the notion of evaluating project candidates for their degree of contribution to strategies? The risk with discarding such an evaluation is embodied in the German proverb, "What's the use of running if you are on the wrong road?"

Stop and find the right road. Although this presents a challenge, you can find a map that will help you.

In every organization, a strategy does exist whether or not one is articulated. Decisions made by executives are based on some criteria or strategy; to find it, follow the money. Where is the organization spending its money? What programs are funded? What skills are being bought? Once you have analyzed such actions and identified trends, reverse-engineer them to tease out common underlying criteria or a strategy that drove them. After recording your theories, hold dialogues with decision makers to validate and refine the theories. Gain concurrence from leadership to use these as strategic criteria in the project candidate evaluation process.

PPM as a Surrogate for Strategic Planning

The definition of *strategy* looks amazingly like all of the elements necessary in project portfolio management. If your organization does not do strategic planning today, instituting project portfolio management will enable the discipline and process that defines the strategic process. If your organization does do strategy work today, integrating project portfolio management with it is a natural extension to strengthen it and increase rate of strategy realization.

In 1982, **K. C. Yelin** founded ICS Group, a management consulting firm that works with Fortune 100 market leaders to improve business execution. She was the president of ICS Group through 1999 and is the author of that firm's project portfolio management model and project leadership process. She has served on the faculty of the University of Connecticut Graduate School of Business Administration. She currently heads Yelin Associates based in Scottsdale, Arizona, and is an adviser to the project portfolio management practice at ICS Group.

4.2

How to Determine the Value of a Project

Ray Trotta, Christopher Gardner

How much influence will a proposed information technology (IT) project have on your company's share price? It's impossible to say exactly, but the technique presented in this chapter can help you get an approximate answer that is close enough. It's what's known as a discounted cash flow model, and it sizes up the value today of a proposed project: how much the project is expected to bring in for the company in revenues over the lifetime of its use minus its total cost over time, including any taxes paid on benefits to the company from the project. This technique, used for decades to evaluate all kinds of business assets, is now being applied to IT.

The technique asks a relatively straightforward question: What would the money I'm expecting over the life of the project be worth to me if I had it all right now? Of course, money you're expecting in the future isn't the same thing as money in the bank right now; inflation will eat away at its value over time, and money you risk is worth less than money you have in hand. The future benefits of an expensive grid computing project are significantly less assured than the benefits from a faster Web page server, and projects taken on by early adopters are typically riskier than those cautiously embarked on by technology laggards.

Calculating the Value of the Future Cash Flow

What to do? Determine the value of the future cash flow from the project by taking into account both the time and risk involved in going forward with the project, and then translate that discounted cash flow into a potential change in the share price. The formula for the calculations is in Figure 4.2-1.

Benefits

In the framework of this model, consider the benefits (item 1 in Figure 4.2-1) of an IT project to include all of its potential sources of cash, such as sales from a Web site or reductions in the cost of labor. Other examples might include increased productivity that allows you to avoid hiring additional call center employees. Accurately calculating a project's benefit stream involves getting a sense of who your potential customers—both internal and external—are and how effective the technology you're using is likely to be over time. And remember that while the benefit stream of an IT initiative is finite, sometimes it is quite short and sometimes very long.

Total Cost of Ownership

Next, size up a project's total cost of ownership (item 2 in the figure)—investment costs as well as operating costs—throughout its lifetime. The investment costs include the development and infrastructure costs as well as all associated non-IT expenses, such as

FIGURE 4.2-1 A Basic Equation for Calculating the Value of a Project

$$\frac{\text{Benefits (1)} - \text{TCO (2)} - \text{Taxes (3)}}{R^T \text{ (4)}} = \text{Value (5)}$$

costs associated with taking a system live and the cost of reengineering business processes to accommodate the technology initiative. The operating costs include what you have to spend to keep a project up and running. Labor costs will no doubt be incurred in both categories, and don't forget to include so-called exit costs—expenses associated with phasing out a system or a piece of hardware.

Taxes

Taxes (item 3 in the figure) must be paid on the difference between a project's benefits and its total cost of ownership, and these payments can be sizeable—indeed, they can make or break a project financially in some cases. Therefore, it's important to know what the taxes will be before you begin. To calculate the tax bite, subtract the total cost of a project from the benefits expected. That provides a figure for the project's likely gross earnings. Multiply gross earnings by the tax rate. Then factor in annual tax deductions that can help minimize the tax bite, such as depreciation and amortization. The total tax is the difference between the tax on gross earnings and the tax benefit.

Time and Risk

The key to this valuation method is that you must adjust the cash flow you expect from the project in the future for both time and risk (item 4 in the figure) in order to be able to analyze what it's worth to you right now. The time factor is straightforward: thanks to inflation and opportunity costs, money you receive in the future isn't worth as much as money in your pocket now.

The risk factor is a bit more complicated. Certainly every investment entails some risk, but some are riskier than others. The goal here is to assess just how risky the project you're considering is, and then to adjust the cash flow you're expecting from the project for that risk. The effect of the calculation, when put in present terms, is to discount the cash you're expecting in the future.

The risk factor referred to, called the *annual discount rate*, is an adjustment you make to compensate yourself for taking a risk. If you feel the risk of the project is high, then you may assign a discount rate of 50 percent or more on the total value of the project. That's a rate that venture capitalists commonly use when assessing start-up investments. If your risk is low, you may assign a discount rate of 10 percent—about the rate you would assume if you bought a building to house your corporate offices. The further out in time a project's useful life has to run, the larger the discount must be, since the risk compounds. Your company's chief financial officer can help you determine the appropriate discount rate based on your company's cost of capital—the minimum return needed to compensate a company for making an investment in new corporate assets—and other corporate investments.

Value

The value (item 5 in the figure) of an IT project can be found by adding up all annual cash flows after adjusting those sums to take into account time and risk. The resulting number shows how much new net cash you can expect to get from the project—and thus the project's value to the bottom line.

Finally, dividing this figure by the number of the company's outstanding shares calculates an equivalent change in the price per share. If that number is positive, you can safely assume that the IT project will increase the value of the business and that the business should proceed with the project. If the value is negative—in other words, it drains value—then the project should be halted.

Running the Numbers

Calculating the actual discounted cash flows from the project involves doing a separate calculation for each year in the life of the project. Here we use year 3 in Table 4.2-1 as an example:

1. Subtract the operating costs from the benefits to get the gross earnings: $3,500,000 – $610,000 = $2,890,000.

TABLE 4.2-1. Example of Present Value Calculations

	Year 1	Year 2	Year 3	Year 4	Total
Benefits	$0	$850,000	$3,500,000	$7,400,000	
Operating costs	$610,000	$610,000	$610,000	$610,000	
Gross earnings	–$610,000	$240,000	$2,890,000	$6,790,000	
Investment costs	$1,200,000				
Taxes	–$291,200	–$19,200	$828,800	$2,076,800	
Cash flow	–$1,518,800	$259,200	$2,061,200	$4,713,200	
Discount rate @ 20%	1.2	1.44	1.73	2.07	
Present value	–$1,265,667	$180,000	$1,191,445	$2,276,908	$2,382,686

2. Calculate the taxes on this amount: 32% × $2,890,000 = $924,800.

3. Adjust for the year 3 tax benefit of depreciating your investment costs over four years: 32% × ($1,200,000 ÷ 4 years) = $96,000.

4. Subtract the tax benefit from the taxes to get the total tax for year 3: $924,800 − $96,000 = $828,800.

5. Subtract the investment costs and the total tax from the gross earnings to get the cash flow from the operation: $2,890,000 − $828,800 − $0 = $2,061,200.

6. Apply the formula for the adjustment for risk and time $(1 + r)t$, where r is the annual discount rate and t is the time in years: $(1 + .20)^3 = 1.73$.

7. The cash flow from operations is divided by the adjustment to get the net present value of the cash flow for that year: $2,061,200/1.73 = $1,191,445.

8. Doing this for each year in the project's life cycle provides the total net present value of the project's cash flows, or $2,382,686: −$1,265,667 + $180,000 + $1,191,445 + $2,276,908 = $2,382,686.

9. Finally, divide that figure by the 23.5 million outstanding shares: $2,382,686/23,500,000 = 10¢ per share.

It is estimated that the project will lift share price by ten cents a share. And, since the company's shares are selling for ten dollars, that's a 1 percent increase over its current value.

Case Illustration

Amalgamated Widgets, a fictitious manufacturing company with $500 million in annual revenues, was under pressure from its shareholders and from Wall Street to increase its profitability. One possibility top management considered was to install an online procurement system to cut purchasing costs for just about everything the company buys, from raw materials for its widgets to such commoditized items as safety helmets, work gloves, and office supplies, on which the company spends about $225 million a year. There has been a lot of hype surrounding e-purchasing, and the company's executives, ordinarily a pretty conservative bunch, were uneasy about making a significant investment in a new—and, in their minds, unproven—technology. So they asked their CIO and CFO a simple question: How much actual value might such a system bring to Amalgamated's shareholders?

To answer that question, Amalgamated's CIO and CFO began by estimating the life of such an online purchasing system to be about four years, given the rapid advance of such information technology. In addition, Amalgamated's new system would not be up and running for a year because of the time it would take to build and install the system, train the company's purchasing employees, connect the system to suppliers, and educate them in its use.

BENEFITS

The goal of the system was to boost Amalgamated's ability to drive higher discounts on bulk purchases. Although the company spends about $225 million on such buys, in reality, the team estimated, it would save just 3 to 5 percent of the total spent using the system, significantly lower than the amount estimated by Amalgamated's potential IT vendors, who assumed 100 percent adoption by both employees and suppliers.

On the upside, the system would give Amalgamated new data about its buying patterns, which would give it more negotiating leverage over its suppliers. However, the savings wouldn't start until Amalgamated could cut new purchasing contracts, so there would be a lag in realizing the benefits. The result: Amalgamated felt it would realize no savings in the first year, $850,000 in year 2, $3.5 million in year 3, and $7.4 million in year 4.

TOTAL COST OF OWNERSHIP

Amalgamated decided to outsource the system to an application service provider (ASP), a move it felt would minimize the investment costs for the system to $1.2 million. The ASP quoted the operating costs at about $610,000 per year, a sure figure since the contract was written so that the ASP had to assume all other costs, including any incurred after year 4, such as exit and migration costs.

TAXES

Amalgamated's corporate tax rate is 32 percent of earnings, and the company can take a tax break of approximately $96,000 each year of the life of the project from the noncash charges generated from its investment costs. This assumes that Amalgamated spreads out the deduction it can take for the investment costs evenly over the four years.

TIME AND RISK

The cash flows Amalgamated's team expected from the system were adjusted using a discount rate of 20 percent based on a 10 percent benchmark (cost of capital) plus a 10 percent premium reflecting their analysis of the project's risk. The premium was selected because the history has been that only one in two IT projects at Amalgamated results in a return. The major risk: Would Amalgamated's employees and suppliers adopt the new system?

VALUE

Amalgamated's team calculated the value of the proposed e-procurement system by adding up the discounted cash flows for each year of the project, for a total of $2,382,686. With

23.5 million shares outstanding, the figure represented an increase of ten cents per share or a 1 percent increase on a single share price of ten dollars. Management therefore decided to approve this project.

Ray Trotta, a partner and cofounder of iValue, an IT strategy firm based in New York, teaches, speaks, and consults on technology and finance topics. Ray recently published *Translating Strategy into Shareholder Value: A Companywide Approach to Value Creation* (2003). He is also a member of the graduate school faculty of the Walter E. Heller College of Business Administration at Roosevelt University.

Christopher Gardner is a partner and cofounder of iValue and the author of *The Valuation of Information Technology: A Guide for Strategy Development, Valuation and Financial Planning* (2000).

4.3

Using the Analytic Hierarchy Process to Improve Enterprise Project Portfolio Management

James Devlin

The analytic hierarchy process (AHP) is a powerful and flexible methodology that improves project portfolio management (PPM) decisions in both commercial and government settings. Using AHP helps decision makers to think clearly about complex portfolio decisions, reach consensus on project priorities, and measure portfolio performance. Combined with advanced optimization techniques, the AHP can help a team ensure they are allocating their scarce resources to the best portfolio of projects possible. For nearly thirty years, decision makers around the globe have successfully relied on the AHP for important decisions. Over the past decade, with advances in software and hardware technology, the AHP has become an increasingly desirable methodology for ensuring optimal portfolio alignment and value and ensuring that the organizational culture survives through the process.

Background on the AHP

The AHP methodology was invented by Thomas L. Saaty in the 1970s. He published his original work on the theory in 1980 while

I thank the consulting team of Expert Choice for their valuable comments and improvements on this chapter. The screen captures in this chapter are from the Expert Choice Resource Aligner product, developed by Ernest H. Forman of Expert Choice.

teaching at the Wharton School of Business.[1] Saaty developed the methodology to address a need for improved and more intuitive decision-making processes where multiple objectives, criteria, and alternatives existed and where the interests of multiple stakeholders were involved. In his research, he discovered that the human mind is innately capable of making difficult decisions when those decisions are properly structured and measured in a way that simplifies comparison. He designed the AHP to leverage the brain's intuitiveness, in conjunction with both qualitative and quantitative information, to yield more accurate priorities and better decisions.

The validity of the AHP methodology is based in large part on its widespread appeal, ease of use, and the reasonableness of its outcomes.[2] Since the 1970s, corporate and government leaders and academicians have successfully used the AHP in many thousands of important decisions on resource allocation, strategic planning, risk assessment, project portfolio selection and analysis, and vendor selection. The methodology is perhaps the most widely used decision-making methodology in existence.

Fundamentals of the AHP Methodology

Knowing that the AHP is widely accepted in government, commercial, and academic settings is important; appreciating the theoretical underpinnings of the methodology illuminates why. Essentially the AHP is a set of characteristics, steps, and axioms that together yield an elegant and reasonable approach to making difficult decisions. The AHP methodology has three major process steps:

1. *Structure.* Complex decisions require that decision makers properly analyze and structure the benefits, costs, scenarios, and risks associated with the decision. By breaking down the decision problem into its component parts and structuring them hierarchically into homogeneous clusters, decision makers can reach agreement on the nature of the problem and minimize miscommunication and complexity.

2. *Measure*. Once the hierarchy of objectives or criteria is structured, decision makers prioritize the objectives using a simple paired comparison measurement system to determine their relative importance. When comparing all possible paired comparisons in each cluster in the hierarchy (a process known as redundant paired comparison), it has been shown that decision makers can produce ratio-scale priorities. Paired comparison judgments may also be used on the alternatives (the projects or programs) of the model, as well as ratio-based rating scales, step functions, and utility curves.

3. *Synthesize*. Once the decision makers have completed their measurements, they calculate and combine the results to determine the priorities, a process known as synthesis. This process fuses together the qualitative judgment from the various decision makers with the quantitative data and other information about the projects or alternatives. Decision makers then iterate to ensure the priorities make sense and perform sensitivity analysis to consider what-if scenarios.

Underpinning these major process steps are four straightforward axioms, or assumptions:[3]

- *Homogeneity:* When comparing objectives, criteria, or alternatives, it is essential to compare elements that are relatively homogeneous; otherwise, errors in judgment can occur.

- *Reciprocals:* Paired comparison judgments yield reciprocal judgments. "Thus for example, if one stone is judged to be five times heavier than another, then the other is automatically one fifth as heavy as the first because it participated in making the first judgment."[4]

- *Hierarchic composition:* Elements at higher levels in the hierarchy are independent of lower levels in the hierarchy.

- *Expectations:* This final axiom indicates that a decision maker's reasonable beliefs should be adequately reflected in the outcomes. In addition, all relevant objectives or criteria should be included in the analysis.

Understanding these axioms and the methodology through which they are applied helps to appreciate their applicability to portfolio management decision making.

Applying the AHP to Project Portfolio Management

The above discussion focused on the theoretical underpinnings and validity of the AHP methodology. Consider now the case for applying the AHP to PPM decision making. PPM is, as Dye and Pennypacker note, a "significant factor in long-term strategic success of project oriented organizations. . . . At its best, it is concerned with the role of top management and key decision makers in creating purposeful project investments and in formulating and implementing goals and objectives."[5]

Numerous writers have documented the value of applying the AHP methodology to project portfolio prioritization, selection, and management.[6] Although their writing is primarily focused on the selection and analysis component of PPM, additional benefit arises from measuring project performance as well. There are three main types of PPM where the AHP can and has uniquely delivered value: IT project portfolios, new product development portfolios,[7] and application development portfolios. This chapter provides a general focus on PPM, outlining principles and best practices that have been successfully applied to these and other project portfolio types.

The PPM Challenge Today

Organizations today are often quite good at managing individual projects or reasonable numbers of projects. Challenges arise, however, when project numbers increase, become more complex, and must compete in an environment with constrained resources. Project management organizations (PMOs) have arisen within many commercial and government organizations to serve as project and portfolio process owners, financial stewards, and centers of expertise. Specifically, the following challenges are often commonly recognized:

- Increasing numbers of potential projects in which to invest
- Difficulty aligning projects and portfolios with organizational objectives
- Difficulty achieving consensus among competing stakeholders regarding project priorities
- Inadequate measurement methodologies to determine project benefits, costs, and risks
- An overemphasis on project execution management, without due diligence on project portfolio selection and alignment
- More complex and challenging project constraints, including budgets, personnel, risk, time, and compliance

A recent study by the Kellogg School of Management indicated, "An estimated 68% of corporate IT projects are neither on time nor on budget, and they don't deliver the originally stated business goals."[8] While this research focused on IT projects, often the largest portion of projects in an organization's portfolio in both dollars and volume, it is clear that corporations are challenged with managing project portfolios and aligning them with organizational objectives. Importantly, organizations must have a sound methodology that facilitates picking project winners and dropping losers, while building consensus and buy-in in the process, if their PPM efforts are to succeed.

How the AHP Enhances PPM

The AHP enhances PPM throughout all phases of the portfolio management process. Although there are different approaches, we look at a typical PPM engagement supported by the AHP methodology.

Step 1: Project Portfolio Governance

The AHP methodology supports and enhances PPM governance by enabling leadership to clearly establish and communicate organizational objectives, allocate resources responsibly, and measure performance accurately. In fact, a recent book on IT governance by Peter Weill and Jeanne Ross notes that good governance requires active design and involvement from senior executives, requiring them to take the lead in allocating resources and supporting the overall process.[9]

In the wake of recent corporate scandals, investors and regulators are scrutinizing both corporate and government leaders to ensure their organizations are in compliance. C-level leaders play an important role in ensuring that the organization is protected from mismanagement or negligence and that its efforts are delivering value. This concern for governance and stewardship of scarce resources is critically important to the organization's PPM processes. Since projects constitute a significant and increasing percentage of an organization's resources, sound fiscal management and decision making in the PPM process are essential to organizational success.

In an AHP implementation of PPM, an organization typically starts by:

- Establishing a proper governance structure
- Ensuring the right stakeholders are involved in the right steps in the process
- Undertaking a project or business case inventory to understand the extent of the resource demand and the types of investments in the portfolio

On the first point, establishing the proper governance structure is critical to PPM success. Matt Light, a Gartner analyst, has provided the following best practice governance structure for an organization's PPM process:[10]

- Investment council: Provides oversight; prioritizes and selects initiatives; typically includes the COO, CIO, CFO, strategic planning, and perhaps the CEO
- Business sponsor: The business executive responsible for and requesting approval for an initiative

- Portfolio manager: Manages the portfolio and keeps other stakeholders informed in their decisions
- Program management office: The competency center that coordinates all programs and projects
- Program manager: The person responsible for managing a program
- Project manager: The person responsible for managing a single project

Note that the PMO is typically the process owner for PPM implementations, and it is there that the primary knowledge of the AHP methodology must reside. The AHP underpins and supports portfolio governance process by enabling leadership to clearly establish organizational objectives, communicate priorities, allocate resources responsibly, and measure performance accurately.

Step 2: Project Portfolio Strategic Alignment

Once a governance structure is established, decision makers are able to focus on the objectives of the business and portfolio. The PMO typically gathers the relevant decision makers, often C-level personnel (for example, the CIO and CFO, senior vice presidents, and senior business unit leaders), to brainstorm, define, and structure their objectives into a hierarchy. (The terms *objective, criteria,* and *attribute* are often interchanged in the literature of decision making. For this chapter, the term *objective* will be used because it expresses intentionality and more directly identifies the purpose sought. Moreover, experience indicates that organizations that focus on the accomplishment of objectives are more likely to do just that.) This step is often the most challenging because it requires leaders to collaborate about the nature of the problem or decision. They must consider all objectives for the business or portfolio and ultimately align the portfolio objectives as best as possible with overall corporate objectives. Figure 4.3-1 outlines the objectives of a group of leaders focused on prioritizing an IT project portfolio.

FIGURE 4.3-1 Sample IT Portfolio Brainstorming Output

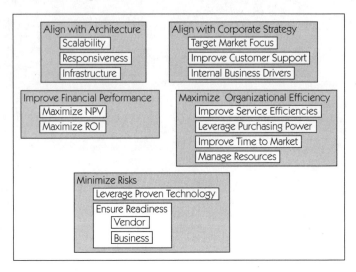

Best practice objectives hierarchies often include objectives in the organization's strategic plan, followed by clarifying subobjectives. Many organizations also choose to structure their objectives hierarchies along the lines of the balanced scorecard.[11] Different groups of leaders establish and prioritize their objectives differently, depending on their purpose and the current state of their organizations.

After structuring, decision makers prioritize the relative importance of their objectives using an intuitive paired comparison approach. This approach, fundamental to the AHP process, helps decision makers produce priorities that are proportionate to one another—what is known as ratio scale priorities. Proportionality cannot be achieved by simply assigning weights to the objectives or criteria, a common mistake that is prone to produce inaccurate or meaningless results. Rather, decision makers are encouraged to think clearly about the relative importance of successive pairs of objectives using a comparative verbal scale that ranges from Equal to Extreme or a comparative numerical scale from 1 through 9. (On the verbal comparative scale, Equal indicates that the two objectives being compared are of equal importance to the parent objective, and Extreme indicates that one is extremely more important—nearly an order of magnitude more important—than the other with respect to the parent objective. On the numerical comparative scale, a 1 indicates the two objectives are equally important with respect to the parent, and a 9 indicates that one objective is nine times more important with respect to the parent. Graphical scales representing proportionality are also frequently used.)

For example, the question being asked of the decision makers in Figures 4.3-2 and 4.3-3 is, "Which is more important and by how much, Align with Corporate Strategy or Improve Financial Performance, with respect to Optimizing the IT Portfolio to Improve Corporate Performance?"[12] Decision makers then enter a judgment through wireless keypads, on software (AHP specific, Internet portal, or spreadsheet) or on a paper-based survey, that best reflects their knowledge, position, and expertise. (Software can greatly facilitate the implementation of the methodology. Although it is possible to perform basic AHP calculations in a spreadsheet application like Microsoft Excel, there are off-the-shelf packages, such as Expert Choice, that can greatly simplify collection, calculation and display of priorities.) Importantly, decision makers should consider the pairwise judgment in the light of their position in the organization and the strategic direction of the organization at the time of measurement.

After the first judgment, the decision makers repeat the pairwise judgment process through all possible combinations of pairs. (The

FIGURE 4.3-2 John's Individual Pairwise Comparison Judgment

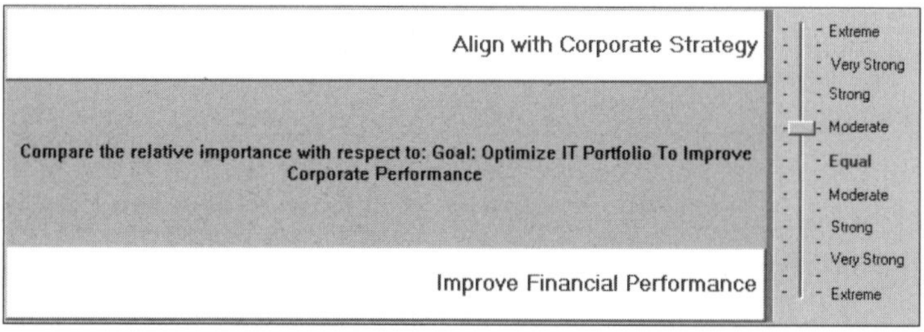

FIGURE 4.3-3 Example Pairwise Comparison with
Multiple Stakeholders

	Goal: Optimize IT Portfolio To Improve Corporate Performance										
Align with Corporate Strategy						**Improve Financial Performance**					
				▼							

	John S.	X	V	S	M	E	M	S	V	X	▲	☐ **Goal: Optimize**
Verbal	Sandra H.	X	V	S	M	E	M	S	V	X		⊞ ■ **Align with**
	Eilleen W.	X	V	S	M	E	M	S	V	X		
Graphical	John T.	X	V	S	M	E	M	S	V	X		⊞ ■ **Improve Fi**
	Alfredo S.	X	V	S	M	E	M	S	V	X		⊞ ■ **Maximize O**
	Roy A.	X	V	S	M	E	M	S	V	X		
Poll	Rajiv S.	X	V	S	M	E	M	S	V	X	▼	⊞ ■ **Minimize R** ▼
	Ammit H.	X	V	S	M	E	M	S	V	X	▼	◀ ▶

1 = Equal	3 = Moderate	5 = Strong	7 = Very Strong	9 = Extreme

formula for calculating the number of judgments in a cluster of objectives is $N(N - 1)/2$.) (Both eigenvector and eigenvalue calculation methods are taught in most engineering and higher math courses. Off-the-shelf software packages can perform these calculations automatically, so that decision makers can focus on their decisions rather than getting bogged down with math.) They then calculate their priorities using the eigenvector calculations of the AHP process. They also check for inconsistency using the eigenvalue calculations of the AHP process. They need to verify that their priorities make sense to them. If the priorities do not make sense, they should review and adjust their pairwise judgments using an iterative process.

The collaborative nature of the AHP prioritization process cannot be understated. Because of its structuring capability and straightforward measurement system, the AHP simplifies communication about priorities. By representing all relevant stakeholder positions, each person contributes to the process. Although they may not exactly agree with every result, they will agree the process was equitable and that their voice was heard, greatly building organizational consensus and buy-in in the process. Portfolio management without buy-in often fails when it comes time to implement the selected portfolio.

The AHP has a distinct advantage over other measurement methodologies because it provides decision makers with an ability to derive accurate ratio-scale priorities for both quantitative and qualitative factors through the paired comparison process. The AHP also allows decision makers to measure the inconsistency of their judgments. For example, if one said that A is greater than B and B greater than C, then A logically should be greater than C. However, human beings are not always logical. The inconsistency measure of the AHP can help decision makers to better understand the reliability and validity of their judgments, yet it does not require them to be perfectly consistent. Indeed, one could be perfectly, consistently wrong in one's decisions! Each decision maker must agree to the priorities they have established and to the process used to reach them (Figure 4.3-4).

Step 3: Project Portfolio Evaluation

Having clear direction from leadership about the strategic priorities of the organization, the PMO typically coordinates with subject matter experts and middle managers, among others, to align the projects or investments with the strategic objectives. These stakeholders can use paired comparison, verbal rating scales, or utility curves to assess how well the different projects contribute to the different objectives in the hierarchy. (While paired comparison is

FIGURE 4.3-4 Example of Top-Level Objective Priorities

more accurate than rating scales, due to the redundancy of measurement, it can become cumbersome when more than nine alternatives are considered due to the large number of possible pairs that would be necessary to measure.) Using wireless keypads, an Internet portal, or paper-based surveys, decision makers typically measure individual project performance using a rating scale such as the one in Figure 4.3-5. The scale should be developed with the stakeholder team, and its priorities should be produced using pairwise comparison judgments to ensure the intensities are ratio scale and meaningful to those using it.

Aside from measuring qualitative judgment, the AHP also leverages quantitative data. Financial objectives like return on investment (ROI) and net present value (NPV), or specific quantitative metrics on sales figures or performance, can be measured using utility curves or step functions.

Once the team has completed its judgments and ratings, the PMO calculates the results to review and confirm the project priorities. This important process, known as synthesis, provides critical insight into the collaborative communication of priorities the portfolio team produced. Figure 4.3-6 provides an example of the types of views a team might receive once synthesizing the input.

The team then conducts sensitivity analysis to validate that the priorities are reasonable and to consider alternative scenarios. Sensitivity analysis is a powerful process that allows decision makers to ask what-if types of questions. It is valid only because the priorities

FIGURE 4.3-5 A Project Rating Scale

Intensity Name	Priority
Excellent	1.000
Very Good	.722
Good	.442
Marginal	.323
Poor	.104
None	.000

FIGURE 4.3-6 Example of Project Priorities

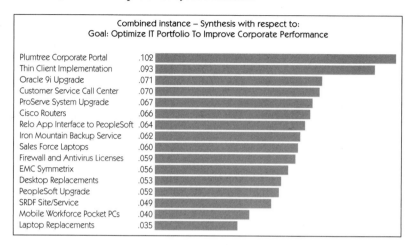

produced in the AHP are ratio scale, making them proportionate. Thus, if the team decides to consider an alternative scenario in which an objective is more heavily weighted than originally derived, they can simply adjust the priorities of the objectives to see how the alternative's priorities compensate (see Figure 4.3-7).

Thus, the PMO leverages the AHP methodology to facilitate communication from the top down (leadership communicating strategic objective priorities to staff) and from the bottom up (staff communicating project priorities to leadership), synthesizing the results to reach acceptable priorities to all members of the team.

Determining accurate project priorities (benefits) is essential to effective allocation of resources. Without accurate priority numbers for the projects, the process of allocating resources is futile because the presumed project benefits will be misleading. The project priorities of an AHP-based prioritization process reflect integrated benefit numbers and are thus more accurate than typical measurement approaches. That is, they incorporate the leadership's values, experts' judgments, and financial and other quantitative metrics. The more highly a project is rated, the more tightly it aligns with organizational objectives, making it more beneficial.

FIGURE 4.3-7 Example of a Dynamic Sensitivity Screen

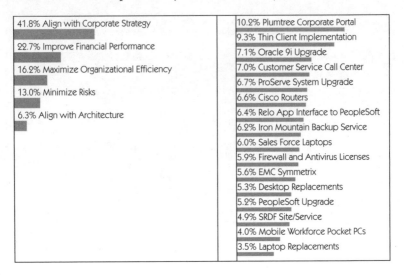

Traditional portfolio management methodologies in many cases use outdated prioritization methodologies. One such approach requires that evaluators use measurement scales that range from 1 to 5 or from 0 to 10 to score projects. Although this methodology is typical of many gate-based approaches, it suffers from the inappropriate use of numbers. The noted scales, 1 to 5 and 0 to 10, are most frequently interpreted as ordinals, or at best as intervals, and convey no information about the proportionality of the judgments being made. Moreover, it is inappropriate to perform any mathematical calculations on ordinal measures, even addition, because these numbers are not meant for calculation. (An ordinal scale is a set of numbers that is invariant under monotone increasing transformations. No mathematical operations can meaningfully be applied to ordinal measures.) Thus, use of these scales will produce results that are at best approximations and at worst misleading.

Ratio scale measures are necessary to determine the contributions of a project to organizational objectives and to allocate resources meaningfully. AHP, through its ability to facilitate redundant pairwise *relative* comparisons, overcomes the shortcomings of the 1 to 5 and 0 to 10 scales and allows decision makers to derive ratio scale priorities. Psychologists have long known that humans are much more capable of making relative than absolute judgments. The use of redundancy in the pairwise measurement process permits better accuracy and allows measurement of the consistency of a decision maker's judgments, an important point overlooked in traditional measurement systems. An optimal alignment of projects and allocation of resources requires both ratio scale measures of benefit as well as a methodology to select the combination of projects that maximizes the total benefit while adhering to constraints.

Step 4: Project Portfolio Optimization and Balancing

Having prioritized the projects with accurate benefit numbers, the evaluation team can now allocate resources to the portfolio. Rather than simply sort on the benefit number, a much more effective and efficient approach is to optimize the portfolio. To achieve the best utilization of resources, the AHP has been successfully combined with optimization and constraint modeling techniques to ensure maximum efficiency in the portfolio.[13]

Using linear integer optimization, it is possible to leverage the priorities from the projects (the integrated project benefit numbers) to solve for the optimal combination of projects that maximizes total portfolio benefit while staying within portfolio constraints. This technique is superior to sorting on a benefit number (or NPV or benefit-to-cost ratio) and funding from the top until monies expire because it will produce at least the same or higher total portfolio benefit. It can also consider multiple constraints such as budgetary constraints, human resource constraints, dependencies between projects, funding pools, time periods, project risks, and groups of projects. When this is done properly, decision makers can produce an Efficient Frontier portfolio that identifies the best bang for the buck at multiple potential portfolio funding levels (Figure 4.3-8).

At each potential funding level on the curve, billions, or even trillions or more, of potential combinations of projects can be

FIGURE 4.3-8 Example of an Efficient Frontier Graph

Alternatives		7,650	8,550	9,450	10,350	11,250	12,150	13,050	14,850	16,650	18,450
Benefit %		28.6%	35.9%	42.4%	45.9%	52.3%	54.5%	60.9%	65.7%	65.9%	70.7%
Cost		7,370	8,350	9,340	9,695	10,685	11,795	12,785	14,455	14,455	17,895
A7	Relo App Int	FUNDED	FUNDED	FUNDED	FUNDED	FUNDED	FUNDED	FUNDED	FUNDED	FUNDED	FUNDED
A2	Cisco Router		FUNDED	FUNDED	FUNDED	FUNDED	FUNDED	FUNDED	FUNDED	FUNDED	FUNDED
A16	Customer Se		FUNDED	FUNDED	FUNDED	FUNDED	FUNDED	FUNDED	FUNDED	FUNDED	FUNDED
A12	Desktop Rep										
A3	EMC Symme	FUNDED	FUNDED	FUNDED	FUNDED	FUNDED	FUNDED	FUNDED	FUNDED	FUNDED	FUNDED
A11	Firewall and	FUNDED	FUNDED	FUNDED	FUNDED	FUNDED	FUNDED	FUNDED	FUNDED	FUNDED	FUNDED
A4	Iron Mountai										
A10	Laptop Repl										
A14	Mobile Work	FUNDED	FUNDED	FUNDED	FUNDED	FUNDED	FUNDED	FUNDED	FUNDED	FUNDED	FUNDED
A8	Oracle 9i Up								FUNDED		FUNDED
A6	PeopleSoft							FUNDED	FUNDED	FUNDED	FUNDED
A1	Plumtree Co	FUNDED	FUNDED	FUNDED	FUNDED	FUNDED	FUNDED	FUNDED	FUNDED	FUNDED	FUNDED
A15	ProServe Sy	FUNDED	FUNDED	FUNDED	FUNDED	FUNDED	FUNDED	FUNDED	FUNDED	FUNDED	FUNDED
A13	Sales Force										
A5	SRDF Site/S						FUNDED	FUNDED	FUNDED	FUNDED	FUNDED
A9	Thin Client						FUNDED	FUNDED	FUNDED	FUNDED	FUNDED

Efficient Frontier

Data points (Cost): 7,650 · 8,550 · 9,450 · 10,350 · 11,250 · 12,150 · 13,050 · 14,850 · 16,650 · 18,450

Vertical axis: Percent (0–100). Horizontal axis: Cost (0–21,000).

checked to find the best combination that yields the maximum total benefit in the portfolio (the y, or left, axis) while staying with the constraints on the portfolio. (Due to the large number of possible combinations, software optimization is necessary for this effort.)

In addition to the optimization, balancing is another core concept that improves portfolio effectiveness. Since the projects in a portfolio often pertain to different aspects of the business (for example, run the business, grow the business, and transform the business or utility, enhancement, frontier), it is often necessary to ensure that the organization allocates its funding adequately across all relevant areas, or pools. To that end, having an ability to optimize across multiple different types resource areas is essential to meeting diverse allocation needs that the portfolio management environment requires.

Combined, the AHP and optimization yield synergistic benefits for an organization's PPM efforts and ensure that the project portfolio continues to align with and reflect organization objectives.

Importantly, this entire process is under full control of the management team implementing the solution. Decision makers may get nervous at first reference to optimization, yet they will soon see its benefits when they are allowed to account for realistic, often political, constraints that organizations face daily. By incorporating "must fund" and "must not fund" constraints, leaders retain control over the portfolio while ensuring that they are attaining the most value in the portfolio given those constraints.

Combined, the AHP and optimization yield synergistic benefits for an organization's PPM efforts and ensure that the project portfolio continues to align with and reflect organization's (and leadership's) objectives.

Step 5: Project Portfolio Risk Assessment and Forecasting

Another dimension to consider is whether or how to include measures of project risk. The AHP has been successfully used to assess business risk and project risk, among other types of risk. Within

PPM, the AHP is uniquely able to leverage expertise from diverse decision makers regarding the risks and probabilities of success associated with a project. Using the same structuring and measuring methodology described above, decision makers can construct a hierarchy of risk objectives or categories, essentially a risk scorecard or risk breakdown structure,[14] against which they can measure project risk, severity of impact, and likelihood of occurrence. Common risk areas are schedule risk, scope risk, budget risk, and compliance risk, among others. This process typically leverages expert judgment using rating scales with words like *Extreme Risk*, *High Risk*, *Moderate Risk*, *Low Risk*, and *Little-to-No Risk*. The decision makers must perform paired comparison on the words to determine their relative priorities, a distinct advantage over using linear rating scales. In addition, decision makers can leverage historical data, if available, in conjunction with judgments to forecast probabilities.

With project risks or probabilities of success (the inverse of risk) in hand, decision makers can now discount the project benefits with the probability of success to arrive at a risk-weighted project priority number or benefit. The discounted benefit thus is a more realistic assessment of expected value that a project is likely to deliver.

Determining accurate project risks extends the meaningfulness of the AHP prioritization effort in that it now considers realistic constraints and failures the project might encounter in implementation. While the approach is straightforward, PMOs should first focus on optimizing their portfolios based on accurate benefit numbers, saving risk-discounting practices for future iterations of the process when the organization has more maturity with the methodology.

Step 6: Project Portfolio Execution Management

With the selected portfolio in hand, the PMO is now able to execute on the projects to see them through to completion. Various portfolio and project management software products are available on the market. (Example project portfolio management products are Artemis, Business Engine, Mercury Interactive, Microsoft Project, Niku Clarity, PlanView, Primavera Team Play, ProSight, and UMT.) These products typically serve as a central repository for project information, task management, resource utilization, and various other crucial project management activities.

The execution process is a dynamic and crucial component of overall project success. It will continue to be relevant to the organization's needs only if the projects executed are aligned with the organization's objectives. A rolling portfolio planning, execution, and measurement effort will continuously ensure the relevance of the portfolio (discussed in more detail below).

Step 7: Project Portfolio Performance Measurement

Now that the best portfolio of projects has been selected and implemented, it is important to monitor project and portfolio performance to ensure they deliver the expected value. To accomplish this, the AHP methodology facilitates performance measurement of the projects against their objectives. As project and program managers update project performance metrics, the updates can be imported into an AHP-based performance dashboard to display project and portfolio performance in an intuitive way. Again, the AHP methodology here ensures that the priorities on the objectives and the performance measures are accurate and reflect a consensus of all necessary stakeholders.

Rolling Portfolio Forecasting and Alignment Process

Although this process has been presented as discrete steps, a best practice approach to implementing an AHP-based PPM process is to consider a rolling portfolio. Depending on the type of portfolio, it is fruitful to create a standard biweekly, monthly, or quarterly meeting to reassess the portfolio on an ongoing basis. During these portfolio "refresh" meetings, decision makers consider the performance of the current project portfolio in conjunction with new projects in the pipeline to determine the new portfolio. Ideally, the portfolio undergoes regular refreshing and balancing in which it is tweaked and more tightly aligned with organizational objectives. This process entails reconsideration of sunk costs on the projects already begun, and it will certainly result in holding, continuing, or killing projects that are currently in the portfolio.

Projects that are already in the portfolio should have a fair and balanced consideration when compared competitively with newly proposed projects. Since sunk costs on the existing projects are unrecoverable, they no longer count against the project and thus should not penalize it. This approach helps to ensure that projects already in place are not unfairly compared to new projects being considered. It also recognizes that the future investment in ongoing projects is likely to be less than for new projects and that killing ongoing projects that are meeting their original business plans but may not be as competitive as newly proposed projects may kill morale.

Conclusion: AHP's Value to PPM

With such a strong presence in management decision making, what makes the AHP so appealing for portfolio managers today? In short, the methodology is relatively simple, very flexible, and extremely powerful. The methodology is valuable for multiobjective decision making in general and for PPM specifically. The AHP shows considerable advantages for organizations challenged with complex portfolio decisions involving long (or even short) lists of projects, constrained resources, multiple stakeholders, multiple objectives, and compliance challenges. Adopting the AHP combined with advanced optimization can deliver immediate value to an organization's PPM efforts, primarily through the methodology's inherent ability to:

- Structure complex portfolio challenges.
- Measure benefits, costs, and risks on ratio scales.
- Leverage and synthesize data, information, and judgments from multiple stakeholders.

- Conduct sensitivity analysis with what-if scenarios.
- Generate and examine an efficient frontier of optimum portfolios over varying budget amounts.
- Measure and improve portfolio performance.
- Pick project winners and losers quickly and effectively.

In sum, organizations that adopt the AHP as the measurement method of choice for their PPM efforts can expect improved portfolio alignment, better stakeholder buy-ins, and stronger organizational confidence in portfolio decisions.

James Devlin is vice president of professional services for Expert Choice. During the past three years, he has helped senior leaders from America Online, Sovereign Bank, the Mayo Clinic, the Office of the Secretary of Defense, the Federal Aviation Administration, and the Bureau of Alcohol Tobacco and Firearms, among other organizations, to make complex portfolio, risk, and governance decisions. He is working on his doctorate in knowledge management at the George Washington University.

4.4

The Efficient Frontier Technique for Analyzing Project Portfolio Management

Mike Gruia

> Forty percent of information technology investments fail to deliver their intended results. Recent estimates indicate that $2.3 trillion is spent on projects in the United States.

Constrained by finite budgets, staff, and other resources, companies are continually faced with the issue of deciding where to invest money and effort to deliver the most value to the business. With millions of dollars in project investments at companies each year, it makes sense to treat these significant investment decisions in a manner similar to how a fund manager determines a portfolio of stocks.

What does an *optimized* portfolio really mean? How optimized are your project portfolio investments? Most IT portfolios fail to employ even the most basic optimization techniques in favor of simpler methods. This chapter asks the C-level executives to consider a readily available and easy-to-use methodology for portfolio performance optimization. It offers a first guide to treating portfolio optimization as an economic computation.

This approach draws on concepts from economics, particularly Harry Markowitz's Nobel Prize–winning Efficient Frontier and Modern Portfolio theory. Although the Efficient Frontier uses a few advanced portfolio optimization programs, it should not be seen merely as a computing procedure but as an economist's way of thinking about investing in projects.

Why the Efficient Frontier Matters

Research suggests that in the United States, 40 percent of information technology investments fail to deliver their intended results.[1] Recent estimates indicate that $2.3 trillion is spent on projects in the United States, yet the Meta Group suggests that:

- 84 percent of companies either do not conduct business cases for any of their IT projects or perform them only on select, key projects.
- 89 percent of companies are flying blind, with virtually no metrics in place except for finance.
- 84 percent of companies are unable to adjust and realign their budgets with business needs more than once or twice a year.

The result? Close to $1 trillion in underperforming investments. Not only is the spending huge, but it is typically poorly managed in a fragmented manner, using project-focused rather than portfolio-focused methods. The majority of companies simply do not employ a portfolio management strategy.

Move All Project Portfolios on to the Efficient Frontier

Companies make capital investments to exploit opportunities and create value, so any opportunity to save money and create value is clear and sensible. However, using only the net present value approach to make investment selections is not sufficient or plausible for portfolio-level decisions. This understanding leads us to modern portfolio economics and the adaptation of a powerful investment theory tool, the Efficient Frontier.

Every field has its own language and its own way of thinking. While physicists talk about motion, forces, and energy, they learn and analyze nature using the language of mathematics. Portfolio management is no different. When the ideas of portfolio management are expressed in economic and mathematical terms, they are easier to understand and verify. Most economic models are built using the tools of mathematics. *Efficient Frontiers, alignment, resource scarcity, capacity, waste:* these terms are part of the portfolio management language.

The Efficient Frontier is a fundamental scientific method that is extremely effective in visually summarizing the information required to understand all of the portfolio possibilities, the cost trade-offs, and the factors that affect the efficiency of the portfolio. Furthermore, this method allows stakeholders to organize, explore, search, and select the optimum portfolio.

The Efficient Frontier answers three key portfolio management questions:

- What are the best possibilities of projects that an organization can implement given the available budget and organizational capabilities?
- Are we getting the best from our potential portfolio of projects? If not, why are we not getting the most from our investment portfolios?
- Are we overinvesting in IT?

These are the same questions usually asked by chief executive officers, chief operating officers, and chief financial officers. With analysts and the board increasingly challenging the CEO to translate investments into bottom-line results, it is natural that he or she may question the value of IT and the soundness of the decision making involved in selecting where to invest. This leaves the chief information officer and his team under scrutiny, challenged to justify the value and method of IT investment decisions.

The Efficient Frontier helps managers and executives from the IT and the business sides of an organization understand the trade-offs between portfolio value and cost. It is an applied economics method that shows how companies manage their scarce resources. Specifically it will help in understanding the following:

- The *concepts of scarcity* and its consequences
- The *concept of value and cost* and its graphical presentation
- The *concepts of and relationships between value, cost, and current operating practices*
- *Breaking the constraints* and its influence on the Efficient Frontier

Applying the Efficient Frontier to Portfolio Selection

The Efficient Frontier curve shows all of the best possible combinations of project portfolios and the value that can be created with available capital resources in an unconstrained mode. In the example in Figure 4.4-1, the cumulative business value or discounted cash flows are on the vertical axis and available budgets are on the horizontal axis. The vertical value measures the value of the opportunity based on the impact and alignment with business drivers.

As we move from left to right, the quantity of cost increases while the value increases. This illustrates an important point: when a company is employing all available resources, it faces a trade-off. The only way it can have more value is by using capital.

Any point above the Efficient Frontier is not possible. The company can select a portfolio of projects on or under the Efficient Frontier. Portfolios along the curve are said to be efficient because the company is getting the maximum value from the available budget. Points under the Efficient Frontier curve represent inefficient portfolios. Many reasons cause a portfolio to be under the curve, including forcing in too many low-value projects or a significant mismatch between supply and demand of skill competencies, leaving the portfolio

FIGURE 4.4-1 Efficient Frontier Curve

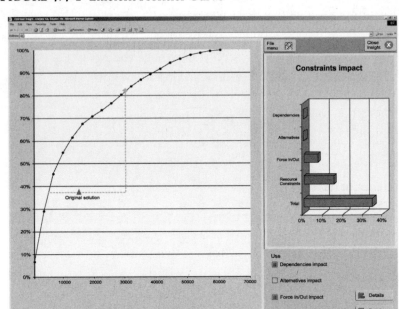

to yield less than it could have from the available budget. This brings us to an important lesson: any factor that moves the portfolio's position away from the Efficient Frontier should be challenged.

Another important outcome from Efficient Frontier modeling is the opportunity cost. The Efficient Frontier shows the opportunity cost of investing an additional dollar versus the additional value received. When the company is discovering the most valuable projects for the investment—those with the highest value/cost ratios—the Efficient Frontier is quite steep (for example, when the company plotted in Figure 4.4-1 uses $15 million, which is 21 percent of the budget, and gets 70 percent of the possible value). In contrast, when there are very few valuable projects left—those with the worst value-to-cost relations—the

> The Efficient Frontier allows us to understand the value that is destroyed by each constraint (for example, labor demand versus supply, lack of efficient alternatives, or lack of consensus).

Efficient Frontier curve is quite flat (for example, when the company plotted in Figure 4.4-1 invests from $35 million until $70 million, 50 percent of the budget, yields only an additional 15 percent of the possible value). So we see in this case that investing the first 21 percent of the available budget on the projects with the highest value-to-cost ratio provides 70 percent of the possible business value, whereas spending the last 50 percent of the available budget on projects with a lower value-to-cost ratio can only deliver an additional 15 percent of value.

Conclusion

The Efficient Frontier simplifies a complex portfolio management problem to highlight and clarify some basic questions: scarcity, efficiency, trade-offs, opportunity cost, and the value of breaking the constraints. It offers a simple way of thinking about investment decisions, discovering ways to increase the efficiency of portfolio investments, and avoiding investment in regions of diminishing returns.

Experience shows that organizations that have used Efficient Frontier principles together with accurate portfolio valuation are able to reduce waste or increase value creation opportunity by 20 percent to 40 percent.

Both the business and IT sides of an organization should get comfortable with Efficient Frontier thinking and analysis. The most important purpose of this chapter is to look at the economic ways of thinking that are applied to portfolio management. I have covered a balanced approach to applying the model based on both theoretical foundations and practical applications. Because of the mathematical foundation of the Efficient Frontier model, experience shows that this approach, together with a set of tools, is required to help you maximize the value of your investment immediately.

Of course, the Efficient Frontier is just one critical part of a successful portfolio management program. Keep in mind that the key prerequisites for success in using it are the ability to translate business strategy into business drivers, rank and weight the drivers, identify the quantifiable impact that the projects will have on the business drivers, and derive the potential value created by the projects. At that point, you can use the Efficient Frontier framework to further understand and remove constraints and to optimize labor supply and demand.

This rational approach helps to break the traditional wall between the IT and business sides and improves the way people interact with one another and make decisions.

Mike Gruia is a cofounder and president of United Management Technologies. He spearheaded the creation of the modern portfolio prioritization and optimization framework and governance approach, which is being used by leading Fortune 1000 firms worldwide. He holds B.S. and M.S. degrees in industrial and systems engineering and a P.E. in operations research from Columbia University.

SECTION FIVE

PPM Techniques and Issues

Organizing and Implementing

All the best methods in the world will not help if these methods are not properly implemented and supported in an organization that has been groomed to work with them. How we organize to implement and practice PPM is paramount to its success. Fostering a culture that is supportive of PPM and developing an enlightened and supportive executive are essential stepping-stones to making PPM work. The three chapters in this section provide exceptional guidance to this end.

In Chapter 5.1, Cliff Cohen and Randy Englund make a case for PPM. They present thirty-four typical excuses and complaints and respond with solutions, benefits, and implementation advice. If you have a selling job to do (most people will), this chapter will provide you with the ammunition to convert your stalwart opposition.

In Chapter 5.2, K. C. Yelin discusses the role of the executive. Indeed, PPM is a set of processes aimed specifically at the executive level. Although executives are normally charged with strategic and business management, they often fail to provide the leadership and guidance needed in this area. Yelin clarifies this essential role and paves the way for executive leadership and support.

As soon as we raise the subject of PPM, an immediate question is, "Where does the project management office fit in?" Although there is not a single correct answer to this question, defining this fit is critical to PPM success. In every PPM implementation, the project management office (PMO) will have a significant role. But the PMO does not own the PPM because there are others involved in governance. In Chapter 5.3, Matt Light discusses the role of the PMO and IT governance.

5.1

Making the Case for Project Portfolio Management

Clifford B. Cohen, Randall L. Englund

In today's business environment, it is important to realize maximum value for the money spent. Given the ever increasing proportion of spending related to projects, many organizations have begun to realize that maximum value cannot be achieved without doing the right projects, at the right time, and in the right way. While many of these organizations have made great strides in applying good project management practice to execute projects successfully, the question of how to ensure that projects are optimally selected, prioritized, and resourced is only beginning to gain widespread interest. For those who attempt to address this question, the answer is increasingly to apply formalized PPM.

Establishing formal PPM provides a framework within which better decisions can be made and results in numerous related benefits to the organization. Nevertheless, it inevitably involves implementing significant changes that can be met with initial resistance. To overcome this resistance, an organization must recognize that the success of any process change effort depends on the ability of staff to understand the reasons for change and their willingness to support it. In short, staff will support change more easily when it is designed to solve real and urgent problems that they both well understand and have personally experienced. Therefore, when making the case for PPM, it has become critical to identify how PPM can solve these problems in order to encourage acceptance of it and the positive change it requires.

To identify problems, it is necessary to understand what the problems are, interpret them correctly, and provide effective responses to the issues raised. One way to do this is to listen carefully to what employees are saying about their environment and to document and analyze what is heard in a manner that clearly demonstrates how PPM can address the issues expressed and provide both expected and unanticipated benefits. Once applied, this approach of making the case for PPM by identifying how it can solve real problems that staff members face becomes not only intuitive but extremely effective. When aided by the use of a formal framework for communicating the benefits of PPM, sensitivity to staff concerns can encourage passionate support of the change effort and thereby help to revitalize a project environment. It can make clear the value proposition of PPM for all stakeholders in a way that resonates at all levels within the organization.

This chapter presents a suggested framework for documenting, analyzing, and responding to project and resource related issues. All examples are based in the information systems (IS) project environment and are provided primarily as talking points that can be used to illustrate the potential benefits of PPM during the buy-in process. It is advised that when communicating these benefits to stakeholders, emphasize that a successful project effort depends on both effective portfolio management and the application of good project management discipline. Although activities consistent with sound portfolio management are described, the techniques of implementing formal portfolio and project management practices are outside the scope of this chapter. However, the suggested activities can easily be integrated into existing methodologies and can be readily applied to non-IS areas as well.

The approach taken and the problem statements captured derive from our own personal experience. The outline for the process comes from the Graham/Englund model.[1] Each of the following statements represents an opportunity by the authors to address the

types of concerns that can exist in organizations and how these concerns might be alleviated through the implementation of PPM.
Working within the framework we describe enables PPM advocates
to learn from their colleagues about how to make the case and win
their support.

Framework Description

To make the case for PPM, it is necessary to demonstrate how PPM
can address real and immediate problems in the project environment. This is best accomplished in the following ways:

- Soliciting the input of coworkers to isolate known problems
  (obtaining statements)
- Considering the sources of input (identifying who says)
- Correctly analyzing feedback based on the sources and
  natures of problems (making interpretations)
- Developing potential solutions
- Outlining business- and resource-related benefits accruing
  from implementation of suggested solutions
- Identifying PPM specific action items designed to realize
  solutions and benefits (specifying how implemented)
- Documenting and communicating findings to achieve PPM
  acceptance

The intent is to capture as close as possible the voice of the
customer by using people's actual words. In this way, they recognize
their words or thoughts and are ready to listen to the response. The
response needs to speak the language of the receiver (that is, speak
upper management talk to upper managers and project talk to
team members) so very little translation is required to understand
the message. Basically, the goal is to apply fundamental fixes to
how the organization addresses these problems and how people
think about them.

Following are fifteen examples of how the framework can be used to organize information and develop operating principles. Additional material is then provided that can benefit from similar analysis. Readers may use these examples as raw material when making the case for PPM in their organizations. In presenting this information to senior management, heed the advice of Neal Whitten, who states that when seeking the support of senior management, it is necessary to describe the problem in as few words as possible, provide a suggested solution to the problem with backup solutions if needed, and communicate specifically how senior management can help. The proposed framework supports this approach by isolating problems that impede organizational efficiency, identifying meaningful solutions, and specifying action items that can be supported in various ways by senior management.

Statements, Interpretations, and Solutions

We begin with fifteen common arguments for avoiding involvement and support for PPM. For each statement, we discuss the source of the argument, our interpretation of the complaint, and the solutions and benefits.

Statement 1

"I'm overloaded with too much going on."

Who Says. Any staff member.

Interpretation. The staff member has too many projects.

Solution. Indicates a need to reduce the number of projects happening at one time.

Benefit. When the number of projects is reduced, project quality and performance increase as attention focuses on doing the right things. In addition, extra capacity is created for attending to emergencies or engaging in creative thought. Staff are afforded more control over allocation of their time.

How Implemented

- Make reduction to a critical few projects a subtext to all discussions within the PPM process.
- Confirm that the PPM governing body truly cares about the welfare of its project managers and believes that reducing the number of projects increases productivity.

Statement 2

"I'm not sure how projects are approved or prioritized, or if the decisions are sound and the projects doable." "The squeaky wheel sure gets the grease around here. Some managers on the business side are really good at getting to the front of the line. I'm not even asked what I think. We'll see if they get my support when they come around asking for resources."

Who Says. The functional manager.

Interpretation. The functional manager is resentful because she or he perceives the project selection process as unfair. Lack of visibility and a due diligent, clearly defined, and communicated process for managing the project portfolio has caused the functional manager to doubt the decisions that are made. For both reasons, the functional manager intends to resist the decision or resort to playing politics in an effort to compete.

Solution. Remove the mystery surrounding how projects are selected, prioritized, and resourced. Avoid playing favorites or breaking the agreed rules. Staff members may still disagree with a decision, but they won't complain about "backroom deals."

Benefit. The portfolio process and plan of record (POR) become an open book, with ready access to the names of the governance council members, the business goals they are chartered to meet, the criteria they use, and the process tools that are applied to prioritize and approve projects. An escalation process, available to all, assesses urgent situations to determine a project's relative importance to business goals. A clear path exists for anyone to enter this process, as well as determine what is going on. This process lessens the perceived impact of politics that happen behind closed doors, increasing the likelihood of project success.

How Implemented

- Apply a systematic approach to portfolio management.
- Support and reinforce business and enterprise initiatives.
- Strive to communicate the process to all staff.
- Avoid playing favorites or breaking the agreed rules.
- Enforce PPM decisions in all functional areas.
- Integrate functional managers into the process as a fundamental element (especially during resourcing exercises).
- Ensure that all key areas within scope are represented in the governance team at a high enough level to prevent lack of buy-in and strengthen enforcement.
- Encourage open communication on areas of potential conflict.
- Reward interdepartmental cooperation.

Statement 3

"Project scope keeps expanding, pushing out the expected completion date."

Who Says. Any staff member.

Interpretation. A project manager might make this statement out of fear that delivering this bad news will reflect badly on his abilities. He may also be frustrated with his inability to control the scope creep. A manager may make this statement out of frustration because he has just learned that a project will slip and there was no forewarning. Both will perceive the project as out of control. The manager may intend to micromanage in an attempt to regain control. The project manager may be planning to disassociate himself from an "unsuccessful" project. Recriminations and project failure are just around the corner.

Solution. Remove the stigma associated with project redefinition. Scope creep is fine as long as it delivers business benefit and is transparently reconciled with competing resource requirements in the organization. Ensure that unnecessary scope creep does not occur by applying the 80/20 rule within a centralized, authoritative decision-making body. Operate on the premise that meeting truly important deliverables and getting projects done, rather than continually delaying delivery to achieve a product that is "more perfect," is the best way to obtain resources for other projects.

Benefit. Project staff will know that project redefinition will be discussed in a rational manner and a timely fashion, and without recrimination. This will encourage openness and commitment to objectives and support the identification of solutions to project issues that benefit the evolved needs of the business.

How Implemented

- Discuss current project status at all governance council meetings.
- The oversight governing body should monitor and question if scope changes are necessary, knowing that subsequent delays can affect resource allocation to other projects.

- Consider all factors when evaluating the possibility of scope creep.
- Consistently apply the PPM process to new work as you would to a new project.
- Know when something is good enough.
- Communicate policy on project redefinition and encourage staff to raise issues when they become known.

Statement 4

"We made this commitment to the client and must fulfill it."

Who Says. The project manager.

Interpretation. Someone has challenged the project's validity (rightly or wrongly) or attempted to add scope to the project based on new information. In the absence of formal oversight of such requests, the project manager has decided to defend the project. She probably feels that she is judged based on whether she delivers on time, on budget, on spec, and within quality constraints. This dynamic occurs in organizations that haven't learned that project execution is subordinate to project relevance. Organizations that become fixated on technique will frequently fall prey to this miscalculation. In such circumstances, project managers quickly learn that career growth depends on blind devotion to the above parameters, regardless of whether the business truly benefits from the work or the client was justified or reasonable in her original demands. Meeting one's commitments is laudable only when the commitments make sense. Several problems can be deduced from this statement:

- Demands and resulting commitments were made in a vacuum.
- The client's needs have not been previously challenged.

- No formal process exists to evaluate whether changes in scope or requests for project termination are valid and support the business.
- The project manager has no way to save face when challenged.

Expect serious amounts of money to be expended before the project fails due to lack of relevance to the business.

Solution. Remove the stigma associated with project redefinition by emphasizing and communicating the importance of considering the business benefit of proposed changes over traditional and rigid measures of project success. Raise the visibility of the decision-making process by holding regular portfolio management meetings to review project status and discuss issues, and communicate meeting outcomes in a timely fashion. Enable broad-based input and buy-in by ensuring that all projects are vetted by a centralized and empowered governance body with the capability to see the larger picture, assess organizational capacity, and support ongoing initiatives before making commitments.

Benefit. A more agile and adaptive organization results because the organization is able to constantly reevaluate its needs and adjust quickly in order to save resources. Staff support course changes because they recognize the underlying business rationales. Issues are aired and resolved before they become severe and staff feel the need to engage in "hiding behaviors." Clients are not allowed to become too powerful, to the extent that their wishes are never challenged.

How Implemented

- Emphasize and communicate the importance of considering the business benefit of proposed changes over traditional and rigid measures of project success.

- Hold regular portfolio management meetings to review project status and discuss issues. Then communicate meeting outcomes in a timely fashion.

- Ensure that all projects are vetted by a centralized and empowered governance body with the capability to see the larger picture, assess organizational capacity, and support ongoing initiatives before making commitments.

Statement 5

"This project is a must-do."

Who Says. The client.

Interpretation. This is the sincere belief of a client who has decided (often unilaterally) that his project must take precedence over other projects. The client has gotten away with this before and often is willing to threaten "taking his project elsewhere" if he doesn't get what he wants (all for the better good of the business, of course). In some cases, the client may be too close to the concept, believing that not to do the project would severely disrupt the organization. The client may be right in this assumption.

Solution. Says who? All projects are assessed for their ability to meet strategic goals, which can then be articulated versus arguing, "Because I say so." Whether due to a raw exercise of power, lack of perspective, or a justified assumption that is difficult to articulate, the answer is the same: do the right thing for the right reasons. This can be accomplished through the establishment of an empowered governance body with the ability to push back on or validate (as appropriate) project requests. The governance body must apply scientific methods when evaluating projects while also allowing intuitive expressions, so that the results are defensible and intuitive to system owners.

Benefit. The results are better communication and higher motivation to do the work (or not do the work). Discussion at the governing body level about these projects helps to parse out unnecessary elements, so that only true must-do's are undertaken. System owners who have succeeded in advocating for their projects through the proper channels will appreciate knowing that their ideas have been validated by the larger organization. This will encourage future buy-in.

How Implemented

- Obtain high-level sponsorship in key areas for PPM efforts to signal that rogue initiatives—even those championed by influential managers—will not be tolerated.

- Integrate agreed evaluation criteria into PPM activities so that clients own the results.

- As a further means of encouraging acceptance, apply the "commonsense test" through subjective discussion of issues even after objective conclusions have been reached.

- Ensure that all discussion is transparent and well communicated in order to prevent charges of operating behind closed doors and to raise the awareness of clients concerning organizational needs.

Statement 6

"This is an upper manager's pet project."

Who Says. Any staff member.

Interpretation. When a staff member says this, it is confirmation of lack of objective oversight of project selection and prioritization. The staff member means to convey that an effort is sacrosanct simply because an influential manager has adopted it. The sense of futility and cynicism that this breeds is evident in the statement. The staff member may also use this to steamroll others into providing resources. The pernicious effects of allowing such a situation to stand are hard to underestimate: power within the organization is based on alignment with influential sponsors and projects of sometimes questionable value. Staff members will not show loyalty to such a system because it is neither fair nor based on mutually recognized principles.

Solution. The solution to this situation is similar to that for statement 5 ("This project is a must-do"). The fundamental fix is to remove inappropriate influence from the organization by redirecting decision making to an empowered governance body that vets all project ideas against strategic objectives and can push back as a group instead of individually.

Benefit. The PPM governing body will act as a balancing mechanism, which cuts down on pet projects over time.

How Implemented

- Follow suggestions outlined elsewhere in this chapter for creating a PPM governing body.

Statement 7

"Project requirements are unclear."

Who Says. Any staff member; a PPM governing council member.

Interpretation. This is typically heard in environments lacking methodology. Usually a PPM governing council member will say this out of frustration when asked to approve a project lacking clarity. A staff member may say this when asked to execute a project that hasn't been properly documented.

Solution. Enforce the application of methodology and due diligence through a PPM governing body. If a project doesn't provide requested documentation to satisfy the review needs of the PPM governing body, it can be delayed, outplanned, or rejected. Requirements must be documented in a project charter, requirements specification, or other document that identifies uncertainties and the potential benefits that justify proceeding to review by the governing body.

Benefit. Implementing an effective project submittal process helps people and projects improve the quality of requirements. Clear requirements lead to projects getting done according to plan and enable effective selection of high-value projects.

How Implemented

- Enforce the application of methodology and due diligence through the PPM governing body.
- Communicate that if a project does not provide requested documentation to satisfy the review needs of the PPM governing body, it can be delayed, outplanned, or rejected.
- Ensure that project justifications identify uncertainties that exist and the potential benefits that justify proceeding.

Statement 8

"This project requires more resources. What do I do now?"

Who Says. The project manager.

Interpretation. The project manager may be concerned that once she's gone to the well for resources, no further accommodation will be possible even if the project's scope has changed, usually because no mechanism exists for reevaluating resourcing needs and redeploying as appropriate.

Solution. Integrate resource planning and management into the PPM process as a fundamental element. Include ongoing project status updates in all PPM meetings, coupled with discussion around possible responses to project changes (for example, get more resources, downscale, extend, postpone, cancel). Establish a formal PPM process based on best practice.

Benefit. Help is available. Scope creep is prevented through better definition of high-level requirements up front to satisfy the requirements of the PPM governing body. Underresourcing is avoided by concentrating on limiting the project mix to the "critical few" (a basic tenet of PPM). Because resources are not overtaxed, there is greater capacity and flexibility in the organization to accommodate temporarily increased needs. Since initial project resource planning is part of the PPM process, more accurate resourcing estimates mitigate surprises later. PPM raises project issues to the fore and provides a means of efficiently and quickly responding to project changes. The PPM governing body can push back on the cause of the problem (scope creep) and thus remove the resourcing issue as a factor.

How Implemented

- Track resourcing needs at the project skill set level to identify deficits and availability before projects are finally approved. There are many techniques for doing this.

- Ensure that each PPM meeting includes a segment to cover ongoing project status and issues.

- Structure the PPM process to require good definition of projects prior to review, focus on and approve only the critical few projects, and effectively address typical project issues (such as scope creep).

Statement 9

"This deadline is unrealistic."

Who Says. Any staff member.

Interpretation. When a staff member says this, it means that person was not included in the planning of the project. Assumptions were made and inadequate schedule estimating was done (if such estimating occurred at all). An external event is probably driving the scope and choice of an end date. This statement can become commonplace in organizations that engage solely in projects that are by nature difficult to estimate, such as research projects. Although such projects belong in the portfolio, too many of them can use up resources that could be delivering tangible and immediate value to the organization. Any number of aberrant responses can occur in response to this situation—for example, project team members avoid or prematurely leave the project (ensuring failure), or dedicated team members heroically resolve to do "whatever it takes" to make the project succeed (causing burnout, demoralization, and quality problems). Expect the client to be disappointed with the inevitable results.

Solution. There is an immutable fact of systems development: a truly accurate estimate of duration is not possible prior to completion of design. Before this, a reasonably accurate estimate is possible following the requirements stage using various estimating techniques available to project managers. The PPM governing body can adopt the position that the facts of a project should dictate its duration and outline the options that exist when hard deadlines are unavoidable (for example, allow compromises in scope or quality). The PPM governing body can sanction responsible project estimation by not requiring commitments prior to completion of design and by encouraging the use of effective estimating techniques. The governing body can also ensure the selection of a proper mix of open-ended and well-bounded projects. The PPM governing body can establish metrics tracking of planned versus actual delivery data to confirm the effectiveness of estimating techniques.

Benefit. Deadlines will be met because they are based on accurate estimating. Predictable delivery of tactical initiatives will be balanced with more open-ended initiatives having long-term promise. Morale will increase because those charged with executing projects are able to provide input into the estimation process. The unconstructive behaviors noted will be avoided.

How Implemented

- Solicit PPM support for (1) responsible estimating, (2) project redefinition procedures, (3) metrics tracking of delivery-related information, and (4) a balanced mix of projects.

Statement 10

"We have no sponsor."

Who Says. The project manager.

Interpretation. No sponsor has been assigned to a project, or the project has failed to attract a sponsor. Lack of sponsorship is a primary factor in project failure.

Solution. The PPM governing body has the dual responsibility of assigning funding and sponsors to approved projects and rejecting or outplanning projects not deserving of sponsors in the short term. All projects are required to have a sponsor in order to get funded, indicating a strong commitment to the projects from upper management. This helps focus on important rather than simply urgent projects, because more thought occurs before initiating projects.

Benefit. No project is allowed to progress without a sponsor, thus improving the chances of success. No project proposal that does not fit strategically is allowed to become a project. Resources are saved; projects bring value to the organization.

How Implemented

- Ensure that the PPM governing body has the dual responsibility of assigning funding and sponsors to approved projects and rejecting or outplanning projects that will not be immediately pursued.
- Ensure that one sponsor, not multiple sponsors or a group, is assigned to each project.

Statement 11

"How can we make decisions with incomplete information?"

Who Says. A PPM governing body member.

Interpretation. PPM governing body members typically need three things in order to commit to a result:

- They need to agree on the criteria that will be used to rank, select, and prioritize projects.
- They need to have clear descriptive information about the projects (for example, the business case, a system description, a project manager).
- They need to have a mechanism for applying criteria to create project rankings.

The criteria should be top down in nature, deriving from high-level performance goals in the organization. The descriptive information should be thorough, listing key stakeholders and other pertinent data that allow the PPM governing body members to understand the nature of the project. The ranking mechanism should be statistically sound and defensible and include an opportunity for open conversation that provides a forum for expression of the collective experience of the group. No forward progress can occur until these needs are satisfied.

Solution. The governing body and its sponsors are chartered to make top-down decisions about what the organization should do to meet strategic objectives. If the information is incomplete, make and document assumptions in order to move ahead. Then reconcile this plan with bottom-up data. Some projects achieve in- or out-plan status fairly clearly, while more complete information or fine-tuning may be required on a few questionable projects. Then engage in dialogue or request more information. The governing body, collectively rather than individually, moves ahead to make informed decisions with the information available. Track all decisions and supporting information in a PPM database and appropriate reporting formats. Use the database for scoring projects.

Benefit. The quality of dialogue improves because a forum exists for it to happen in a disciplined manner. People learn that they know more than they thought they did and keep learning better ways to improve business and project performance. The governing body realizes also that they need not do detailed allocation of skill sets across projects. Their role is to perform higher-level project selection, while line managers assign people to projects. Through better understanding of projects, the governing body is able to defend its decisions.

How Implemented

- Identify high-level criteria through interviews with the governing body and its sponsors.
- Identify pertinent descriptive information through interviews with project managers and business representatives.
- Create a tracking system that captures and reports both of the above areas of information.
- Develop and apply a process that integrates all data and includes free-form discussion to create a prioritized list of projects.

Statement 12

"This meeting was informative."

Who Says. A PPM governing body member.

Interpretation. This will be the sentiment of PPM governing body members who are operating in an environment having the elements described throughout this chapter.

Solution. Implement suggestions as outlined throughout this chapter.

Benefit. It will become apparent to those involved that well-structured PPM results in more effective meetings that achieve stated results and elicit greater involvement in the process.

How Implemented

- Implement suggestions as outlined throughout this chapter.

Statement 13

"This work-work balance is too much." "Inefficiencies cause us to miss, or fail to take advantage of, opportunities."

Who Says. Any staff member.

Interpretation. The goal of PPM is to identify the critical few projects that most benefit the organization and to make their successful execution possible. Without PPM, staff will become overwhelmed, and key work will not get done. When staff say this, they have concluded that they are spinning their wheels and don't understand the purpose of their work. This statement is a symptom of overload—the multitasking penalty. This leads to burnout and lack of commitment, with predictable results.

Solution. Doing fewer projects at a time allows the completion of more projects over time. By designing a portfolio that matches the resources and projects, focused work gets the right projects completed and includes allocation of time to pursue creative opportunities. The portfolio process increases the apparent capacity of an organization to accomplish more. In short, use the PPM techniques described in this chapter to allow staff to focus more fully on key initiatives.

Benefit. The organization will achieve a sustainable work-life balance, higher morale, increased productivity, reduced burnout, and lower costs. A realistic portfolio provides a complete solution to all stakeholders by doing only the most important projects that satisfy everybody's goals instead of attempting all possible projects.

How Implemented

- Use the PPM techniques described in this chapter to allow staff to focus more fully on key initiatives.

Statement 14

"Portfolio management should be simpler."

Who Says. Any staff member.

Interpretation. People often avoid change, and implementation of responsible portfolio management is a big change for many staff who have not previously had to account for how they execute projects. A staff member may complain that PPM is too difficult in order to avoid accountability or out of fear that critical work will not get done in a timely fashion.

Solution. Simplify as much as possible, recognizing that a number of assumptions can be made about the complex interrelationships that exist in order to make progress. With PPM, however, multi-variant criteria and analysis yield superior results to single-variable decision making. It is possible to combine simplicity with multivariant techniques to achieve a more balanced portfolio. Organizations that implement this approach rank among the highest performing. Integrating qualitative and quantitative data improves the probability of success, since it entails the consideration of both subtle and supporting factors that are important to project work. Make the case for how PPM can improve the lives of all staff by creating an orderly and aligned project environment. Minimize frustration by streamlining procedures wherever possible based on the input of other groups having PPM experience. Communicate the rationales behind the core procedures that must be implemented. Enlist the support of the PPM governing body in communicating the importance of activities, and allow PPM procedures to work by removing unrealistic deadlines whenever possible.

Benefit. A more balanced portfolio and greater project success are achieved through application of multivariant techniques and by integrating qualitative and quantitative data in the decision making process. Resistance to new procedures is mitigated by addressing deadline pressures, streamlining procedures, and stating the value proposition for PPM. Staff accountability and effectiveness are increased by remaining committed to core PPM principles designed to ensure project success.

How Implemented

- Keep the process simple enough so that everybody understands it; hide complexity whenever possible.
- Apply multivariant criteria and analysis to the decision-making process.
- Outline the positive benefits of PPM processes during training and in communications.

- Identify ways to streamline procedures.
- Consult with groups having PPM experience.
- Stand firm on core PPM processes that cannot be compromised. Use the PPM governing body to resolve queries and concerns regarding PPM activities.
- Enlist the support of the PPM governing body in communicating the importance of activities, and allow PPM procedures to work by removing unrealistic deadlines whenever possible.

Statement 15

"IS projects are not integrated with and don't seem to support business needs. They don't talk to the business. It's as if IS is only interested in playing with new technology or preventing me from solving my information needs for myself!" "IS resources and technologies aren't fully targeted at high-value initiatives tied to business goals and objectives."

Who Says.   Business staff.

Interpretation.   The business representative believes this to be the case. If this observation is true, only PPM will correct the problem. If this observation is more a matter of perception and not fact, only PPM will demonstrate the true degree of disconnect and convince the business representative that the right work is being done for the right reasons.

Solution.   The goal of portfolio management is to eliminate the trivial many projects and focus on the critical few that align with organizational strategy. The selection process should require clearly defined objectives from the business and ensure that the right projects flow through the pipeline to meet these needs. Use PPM to formalize the truth of IS effectiveness. Require the business to own the results of project selection, so that decisions not to pursue projects are not blamed on IS but rather are considered the positive results of a sound process.

Benefit. IS-business relationships are strengthened by creating an agreed-on forum for project discussion and a joint process that all parties own. Technology is made subordinate to business imperatives. Business representatives begin to understand the importance of architectural initiatives and standards (previously viewed as "playing with technology") and the challenges that IS organizations face in executing projects.

How Implemented

- Apply the PPM techniques described in this chapter to ensure shared understanding of challenges in the organization and responses to these challenges.

More Statements and General Comments

We continue here with several additional examples of statements that can be analyzed and acted on using the above framework. A brief discussion of the issue follows each statement.

Statement 16

"We don't have standards or consistent processes across the organization."

Comments. Implement a prototype process that is thorough, sustainable, experientially modeled, and tailored for the company, scalable, drawn from expert sources, and involves a cross-section of key people. This systemic approach can be leveraged across the organization.

Statement 17

"All this business overhead means I won't be able to deliver my project on time."

Comments. Since this concern is often expressed before the project has started, it may go away if the process determines that the project should not be started because of higher priorities. If the project does go ahead, full staffing and fewer conflicting activities mean better progress is possible. The "overhead" process ensures that tighter requirements and scoping focus the project on bare essentials, thereby helping to determine a more realistic deadline. Greater efficiency accrues by not starting a project until all constraining and desired parameters are addressed. A project should be done right before it is done fast. The process ensures efficient execution and, more important, correct execution. When looked at in retrospect, correctly chosen and executed projects happen faster. Clients don't mind spending money or waiting for delivery; they mind spending money and waiting if the system doesn't work.

Statement 18

"My roles and responsibilities are unclear."

Comments. Along with prioritizing projects, IS and the PPM governing body clearly define their roles and responsibilities, as well as those of their sponsors. This sets the stage to do the same across all stakeholders in this process. An overriding value is for all persons to take accountability for the success of the whole. This empowers people to do the right thing for the organization. The PPM governing body is positioned to clarify and resolve any perceived differences about project responsibilities. Clearer clarity about intent and fewer projects per person allow people more control over allocation of their time and increased satisfaction about the outcomes. Understanding what projects have been approved and what roles they will play allows staff to know why they are coming to work, that their projects are a priority and why, and that their projects are supported and understood by the entire business and its leadership.

Statement 19

"How do conflicts get resolved around here?"

Comments. Open communications to the facilitator and governing body cochair, as well as structured dialogue within governing body meetings, provide paths for quicker and more satisfactory resolution of conflicts among projects. Action items are logged and monitored to ensure closure.

Statement 20

"How is this initiative evaluated?"

Comments. Metrics are available on a master list across all projects to show how the in-plan projects match the desired mix of projects to meet business goals. Staffing levels and completion dates are tracked to ensure compliance with objectives and provide more early warning of problem areas. Periodic communications with sponsors and the governing body ensure that perceived qualitative factors are also in line with expectations. More information is available across the organization to enable all stakeholders to assess their results. Forums exist to reward interdepartmental cooperation.

Statement 21

"What does this process [PPM] have to do with budgeting?"

Comments. The portfolio process can ultimately drive the budgeting process for allocating resources to projects. More accurate information about project work helps guide the process by indicating where adjustments are needed. Enlightened companies reconcile both top-down and bottom-up information about what projects should be done and what the realistic capacity of the organization is to do those projects. Rather than measuring everything possible, they design just a few key metrics about when projects pass thresholds, achieve goals, or incur variances, and they put great effort into ensuring that full budgets support the stated goals that lead to stakeholder and shareholder value. They preserve the core values and strengths within the organization by fully funding projects that were selected based on sound criteria; they also stimulate progress by allocating a portion of the portfolio (and budget) to options, experiments, or research into potential areas for new development. This approach ensures a "whole product line" approach but does not undertake every possible project, only those that show the highest promise based on thorough evaluation by key experts within the company.

Statement 22

"I wish there was a way to improve the process in a manner consistent with enterprise initiatives."

Comments. The PPM governing body can play a pivotal role in ensuring that numerous organizational initiatives are integrated into project prioritization activities. By fashioning the process around these initiatives, compliance can be "baked in" and corporate goals reinforced.

Statement 23

"I spend a lot of time selling my project ideas, sometimes to no avail. Opportunities are lost while I try to figure out the system."

Comments. How many good ideas are lost and never pursued because a clearly communicated mechanism doesn't exist to ensure they are considered? Identifying a single point of contact (a PPM facilitator) to guide all staff with project ideas can help.

Statement 24

"They've tried portfolio management before. It hasn't worked."

Comments. There are a variety of reasons that PPM efforts fail, such as lack of sponsorship, infighting, limited scope, and poor communication. However, applying best practices, gaining support by communicating the value proposition, dedicating talented resources to the work, and making PPM a primary responsibility of established advocacy groups such as PMOs can mitigate the risk. Know that this journey has been traversed before and that maps and help are available in the literature, from consultants, from special interest groups, at conferences, and from professional friends.

Statement 25

"I just spent six months building a system that already exists over in [department]!"

Comments. Without general oversight of the project mix, the potential for implementation of redundant point solutions is great and presents an important risk to the organization.

Statement 26

"My project idea was rejected because it didn't make business sense. How can I gain the support of the business?"

Comments. An organization's IS department is more likely to approve a project if it knows that the project was vetted by a PPM process that it supports. Get assistance from the facilitator to identify weaknesses in the business argument or gain perspective on the larger picture within which the rejection occurred.

Statement 27

"I know I can't do all these projects. How can I push back within reason?" A variant of this is, "Some of my staff are ultra busy, and some seem to be idle. I try to smooth their workloads, but it feels as if I'm standing on shifting sands. Those shifting sands are projects coming or going with no apparent warning. I don't know who to hire or when to hire resources to alleviate the peaks."

Comments. PPM, through its application of effective resource management and reliance on cooperation across the organization, prevents the assignment of too many projects to a project manager. The project in-plan and proposed project timings are communicated whenever they are updated, eliminating surprises for functional managers who must oversee execution of the work. Inconsistent resource usage can be alleviated by applying a systematic approach to resource planning that identifies periods of overuse and underuse. Remember that the overall objective is increased throughput for the portfolio and for organizational initiatives in general, not to optimize any one resource (this is the responsibility of the functional managers).

Statement 28

"I'm not sure what initiatives are underway in my organization. People seem very busy, but I can't always figure out why."

Comments. PPM ensures full visibility of all projects and related staff activity to all business areas in the organization.

Statement 29

"Projects start with a bang, and then I never hear what happened with them. I have no idea whether they ended up being worth the investment."

Comments. A critical component of PPM governing body meetings should be the evaluation of the status of ongoing and completed projects. Greater visibility of project activity makes the tracking of metrics easier. The results of project evaluations should be communicated regularly to management.

Statement 30

"The projects we budgeted for last year bore no resemblance to the projects that actually were pursued. As a result, many of the initiatives were unfunded."

Comments. When budgets are developed, organizations frequently guess about what they will do and apply no systematic approach to forecasting the project mix. PPM governing bodies should dedicate a series of meetings each year to identifying and prioritizing current and future projects for use in budget planning.

Statement 31

"What good is portfolio management if projects are always delivered late or not at all?"

Comments. This is a valid concern. Choosing, prioritizing, and re-sourcing projects is fine, but failure to apply good project management discipline to those projects will undermine the end intent: *to support the PPM process in bringing value to the organization.* For instance, what is the value of evaluating project status if accurate performance reporting is not possible due to haphazard development and project tracking techniques? Implementing sound project management methodology is an important first step in reinforcing PPM efforts. It is important both to select the right projects and to do projects right.

Statement 32

"I'll bet some of our management has no idea what I'm doing. How can they know what value I'm adding to the organization and recognize my efforts if they don't know why I'm here?" A related statement is, "I like what I'm working on, but it's not clear to me that it adds any real value to my department or the company. I wish that I understood where my work fits in and what its importance is."

Comments. The first statement is almost always more a matter of perception than reality. Yet the visibility that PPM brings to the project selection process, the requirement of PPM governing board members to understand proposed initiatives, and the formalization of organizational support for planned work all reduce the perception that management is out of touch. The second statement is addressed through communication of the rationales underlying the selection of projects.

Statement 33

"I hear that the portfolio management process they've got over in IS is solving a lot of problems. Maybe it could work over in our business area for non-IS projects."

Comments. Congratulate yourself on knowing that the process is working! PPM, if properly structured, has the potential to benefit all project activity in the company—whether IS or solely business related. This is possible because the techniques and processes involved can be designed to be easily transferable between areas.

Statement 34

"They cut our budget today. Now our clients are going to go elsewhere with their projects."

Comments. When budgets are cut, resources may be lost, and a fear can develop of becoming irrelevant to the organization as a result. A properly empowered and enlightened PPM governing body will not blame or circumvent IS during hard times. This is because the premise of PPM is to encourage collaboration and shared problem solving while raising awareness of the value that IS brings. Thus, the usual response to budgetary pressures will likely be to continue to work with existing resources and cut projects as necessary in order to identify the critical few projects that can be jointly owned by all stakeholders.

Conclusion

Applying this framework approach to these and all other statements that come up serves to demonstrate the unique capabilities of PPM in addressing a surprisingly wide range of organizational issues. Although not a cure-all, PPM nevertheless emerges as a very powerful tool that all levels of management can use to improve processes throughout the enterprise.

The examples provided are only a partial list of the potential benefits achievable through PPM. They reflect careful preparation around a process to link each project to organizational strategic goals. They draw on active listening, true inquiry, and a commitment to developing an optimized process specifically for the organization. As in any other change management process, success is usually possible only when people have the opportunity to participate in the design, selection, and implementation of the new process. The framework provides a mechanism to ensure that this happens.

Readers are invited to use the framework to discover and document new benefits. We expect that as the list grows, organizations will realize the profound impact that PPM can have and will embrace the challenges that are a necessary part of its implementation. Making a case for project portfolio management improves immensely when structure and attitude align to support important business objectives.

Clifford B. Cohen worked for eleven years as an IT programmer, systems analyst, project manager, program manager, and project management office leader at a large pharmaceutical company. He now mentors project managers to achieve their maximum potential and consults on project management best practices using a holistic approach to controlling key project variables.

Randall L. Englund is an author, speaker, trainer, and executive consultant for Creating an Environment for Project Success. He is a partner in the advanced project management training venture MadelineLearning and a state university faculty member. Englund is a member of the Project Management Institute and a former board member for the Product Development and Management Association, where he is a certified New Product Development Professional.

5.2

The Role of Executives in Effective Project Portfolio Management

K. C. Yelin

> High office teaches decision making, not substance. [It] consumes intellectual capital; it does not create it. . . . They [executives] learn how to make decisions but not what decisions to make.
>
> —Henry A Kissinger, *White House Years*

Stating that executives need to be aligned with our portfolio management strategy seems intuitively obvious. But taking that from an intellectual statement to a behavior can be a challenge. If an alignment is not true, we soon find that new projects are being championed and interjected atop our current portfolio commitments and we are spending time defending a position rather than delivering on it. In this chapter, I address a natural and ideal role for executives in effective PPM as well as suggestions for enrolling them in it.

Decision maker is a natural role that an executive plays in the organization. It is a safe assumption that executives within the organization will have an impact on the portfolio. Whether formally or informally, executives will make decisions on portfolio content. Consider this scenario:

At Venturceuticals, John, the senior director of packaging, meets Bill, the executive vice president of product development, in the hallway. Bill greets him, "What's new in packaging these days?"

John replies, "Nothing much here, but I read a press release that states Xendram is introducing chewing gum as a delivery mechanism for their product, which is comparable to the function of our Quiletine product."

Bill reacts: "We can't let this happen. Xendram is always a half-step ahead of us. John, I want you to work on this capability for us. We will introduce it at the sales off-site in September. Get the formulation department to work on it with you. This is a top priority."

What just happened? Bill has made an on-the-spot decision to launch a project. Is this a good decision? What is the opinion of the chemists and the marketing department? How important is this relative to the goals of Venturceuticals right now? Where will the resources come from to do this project? What will be displaced in order to jump into this unplanned project? Bill's decision was made in a vacuum, and it may have been a poor one. Chances are good, however, that John will press ahead to fulfill Bill's request. We are accustomed to obeying the directives of senior executives, especially if we have no basis for challenging those directives. Did Bill think he did a good job? Bill prides himself on finding problems and fixing them. He walked away from the encounter smiling at his first accomplishment of the day, never to assess the impact of the project he just initiated.

Informal executive decisions typically increase the risk to achieving goals of PPM. "Piling on"—deciding or demanding that more projects be launched than can be resourced—results in lack of focus, a lower percentage of projects completed and related business objectives met, and employee exodus when the economy is good. Unlike the chance hallway encounter described, executives are frequent targets of those in the organization who are seeking support for a new idea or their pet initiative. When an executive approves lobbied-for projects outside the process, it redirects investment of assets to special interests not necessarily in strongest alignment or in balance with the organization's strategy. When an executive gives unilateral approval to invest in a new project, she behaviorally reinforces that PPM is hers alone, ensuring future circumventions of any PPM process.

Optimization of Executive Impact on PPM

Providing a specific role for executives in the PPM process, a role that leverages their decision-making ability, is one of the keys to effective PPM. We want to tap into that ability and direct it at the appropriate issues, at the appropriate level, in an appropriate forum that is consistent with the strategies and objectives of the enterprise.

Start with a clear structure for PPM (Figure 5.2-1). Within the structure, clearly define roles, accountabilities, sources of information, review and decision processes, and calendars. An appropriate role for executives is investment management (IM) with the scope of executive decisions on strategy, alignment, investment categories mix, funding of investments, and external implications. IM is the driver of PPM. Transparency becomes the auditor for adherence to the IM role. Broadly publicizing the IM-PPM structure, process, and all resulting decisions on an ongoing basis reinforces its application throughout the organization.

Nature of Decision Making in Organizations with Highly Effective PPM

At the top is an IM team composed of executives from across functions (Figure 5.2-2). This team establishes organizationwide allocation of assets among investment categories in line with strategy

FIGURE 5.2-1 Project Portfolio Management Processes, Responsibilities, and Cycles

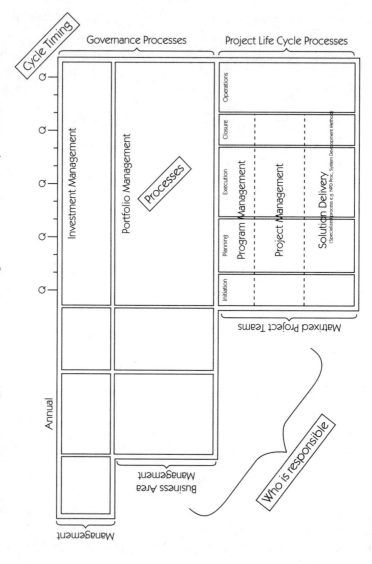

Note: This is also referred to as governance framework in project-based organizations.

Source: ©2001 ICS Group/Andrews Dimensions.

FIGURE 5.2-2 Project Portfolio Management Data and Decision Flow

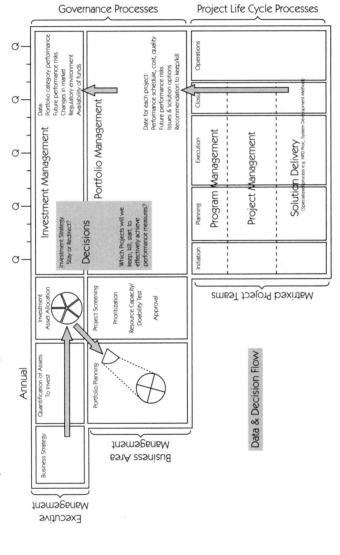

Source: ©2001 ICS Group/Andrews Dimensions.

and identifies overarching performance goals for the portfolio. Portfolio managers determine specific projects to launch, monitor, and measure. And based on performance measurements and external conditions, the IM team validates or redirects the investment strategy.

Organizations frequently have multiple portfolios. Typically a portfolio represents a category of investment or a business unit. The IM team of executives provides strategic investment direction, funding and performance requirements, and review to all portfolio managers in the enterprise.

Enrolling Executives in the Process

The processes and roles related to PPM and IM may seem foreign or tedious to executives. Yet having them understand and play their role is critical to effective PPM, so the investment of creativity and time to get them prepared reaps high returns. Look to leverage something familiar to the executives; it can speed understanding and buy-in. Assume all executives have a personal financial portfolio. Mapping the familiar financial portfolio management elements to the IM-PPM framework helped to make the characteristics of PPM much clearer. Let's explore the similarities.

Working with a financial portfolio manager, a client communicates his goals and often decides the targeted allocation of assets, for example, 40 percent in equities, 20 percent in bonds, 30 percent in real estate, and 10 percent in collectibles. The client does not select the individual investments that comprise each asset category, which is the job of the financial portfolio manager. The financial portfolio manager keeps in close contact with the client and shares the performance of the portfolio relative to the client's goals, and in the valued advisor role continues to educate and counsel the client, allaying fears of situational ups and downs, keeping the focus on the longer term. If we were to replace "financial portfolio manager" with "project portfolio manager" and "client" with "IM team," we would be describing PPM.

Applying the Three-Stage
Financial Portfolio-Client Model

When a professional financial portfolio manager begins the role of trusted advisor to a new client, the manager guides the client through three stages:

1. Buy-in to the portfolio strategy and process
2. Transition to a desired portfolio mix
3. Management of the portfolio to achieve strategy

Make a plan to gain the understanding, buy-in, and participation of the executives in the IM-PPM process by guiding them through the same three-stage process. Assume you are in the role of portfolio manager and the IM team members are your clients. Exhibit 5.2-1 contains the steps in the model. Consider how you would accomplish each of those steps as it relates to PPM.

An example of relating the executive's personal financial portfolio to the organization's project portfolio process (steps 5 to 7 in Exhibit 5.2-1) is well displayed in Figure 5.2-3, a mix of investment categories. Positioning with a value statement gets the executive's attention, for example, "Seventy percent of achieving a portfolio's goals is related to picking the right asset allocation." Show them an example of "asset allocation" in a personal financial portfolio that is likely to be similar in nature to theirs, and you will have them nodding their heads in validation. They will then be prepared to make, and have an interest in doing so, the linkage between their personal financial portfolio and the decisions they are responsible for with the organization's project portfolio.

Figure 5.2-3 contains an example of guiding executives to understand and participate in their "investment management" decision-making role relative to project portfolio management.

EXHIBIT 5.2-1 Adaptation of Financial Portfolio Client Model to Project Portfolio Executive Model

		Financial Portfolio—Client Model	Project Portfolio—Executive Model
Stage 1: Buy-in to portfolio strategy and process	1.	Understand client's overall long-term objectives	Understand organization's current strategies and goals
	2.	Understand client's current assets and how they are invested	Does IM team believe our current projects support above?
	3.	Understand client's risk tolerance	Degree of IM team willingness to change current project investments?
	4.	Understand any short-term objectives	Degree of investment in compliance projects?
	5.	Educate client on investment categories	See Figure 5.2-3. IM team selects categories.
	6.	Discuss range of potential returns on investments—and elements of measurement	Different for each category. For example, category of project development—NPV, time to market, market share, etc.
	7.	Agree on desired allocation of assets across categories	Gain IM team's agreement to ideal percentage of organization's assets to invest in categories
	8.	Communicate how we will work together—for example, monthly informational performance reports, quarterly meetings on major issues that require agreement on buying/selling, annual rebalancing of allocation, portfolio manager's full or partial discretionary authority to make day-to-day trades, fees associated with managing/administering the portfolio	Define the process and roles in IM/PPM, for example: Monthly PPM performance reports Quarterly IM/PPM review meetings Annual IM/PPM planning sessions on strategy, performance, rebalancing of portfolio mix Portfolio manager (PMM team) decides which projects are in/out Budget includes appropriate full-time support for PPM
	9.	Sign agreement on how we will work together	Have IM team sign the document that outlines above

Stage		Analogy (Investment)	Project Portfolio Application
Stage 2: Transition to portfolio mix	10.	Analyze current investments against target allocations and return measurements. Recommend new portfolio composition—specific investments to sell, hold and buy.	Do an inventory of current projects and the investments being made in them (human resources and funding). Categorize them. Share this mix with IM team, comparing to their target mix.
	11.	Gain agreement on specific new portfolio composition and the plan to transition to it.	Recommend pull of selected nonstrategic projects and investment in others. Gain agreement with IM team.
	12.	Execute the buys and sells to achieve the desired portfolio composition.	Kill projects, redeploy resources to strategic projects agreed above. Wear armor.
Stage 3: Management of portfolio to achieve strategy	13.	Portfolio manager "manages" the portfolio • Monitors investments performance • Identifies trends, research, and makes midcourse corrections • Has authority to buy and sell specific investments • Provides monthly reports to client investor	PP manager along with other key members of a portfolio's management team reviews the health and contribution of active projects. Recommend whether to keep, kill, start projects. Work with project managers to understand issues, capacity. Provide monthly report of performance and decisions to IM team.
	14.	Quarterly face-to-face client meetings: Review performance, future forecasts, risks, options for defensive or offensive opportunities. Client makes decisions based on options presented.	PM manager and IM team review performance results/project contributions, recommendations for projects for next quarter. IM team supports recommendations or provides additional insight and recommends alternative projects. IM team and PP manager decide.
	15.	Annual client meetings: Rebalance portfolio allocation targets based on cleint's current state, changes in client's overall strategy, short-term objectives and market conditions.	Did organization achieve its goals? Did the project portfolio achieve its performance targets? Rebalance PPM categories and allocation targets based on current state of the organization, changes in overall strategy, short-term objectives and market conditions.

Note: This is also referred to as governance framework in project-based organizations.

Source: ©2001 ICS Group/Andrews Dimensions.

FIGURE 5.2-3 Portfolio Investment Categories and Mix (%)

Tips:

Make linkages between executives' personal financial portfolio and the decisions they are responsible for in the organization's project portfolio. Positioning with value statements gets the executives' attention.

Personal Financial Investment Portfolio
Investment Categories and % of Assets Allocated
"Portfolio Mix"

"70% of achieving a portfolio's goals is related to picking the right asset allocation."

Money Market 10%
High Risk 5%
Real Estate 20%
Equities 55%
Fixed Income 10%

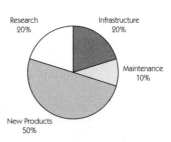

Organization Project Investment Portfolio
Invest Categories, % of Human + $ Assets Allocated
"Portfolio Mix"

"What categories would be most effective for this organization to think of in terms of investing its assets?"

"What allocation among those would support our current challenges and forward strategies?"

Research 20%
Infrastructure 20%
Maintenance 10%
New Products 50%

Sample Business Investment Categories:
Infrastructure: new or improved technology, process or facilities
Maintenance: staying in business
New Products: development and launch
Research: future possibilities

Summary

Executives have an important role in implementing effective PPM. Some points to remember are:

- The probability of achieving an organization's strategy depends on the effectiveness of its project portfolio management.
- Executive behavior and decision making are important to that effectiveness.
- An enterprise project portfolio management framework can provide clear structure, context, and information enabling executive participation and appropriate decision making.
- The investment in educating executives provides long-term returns.
- Leveraging something familiar to the executives speeds buy-in and support of framework.
- The transition to living the framework requires powerful leadership and discipline.
- Ownership and management of the PPM process is a key role to be fulfilled by one or more individuals who will hold executives accountable for their roles in the process.

In 1982, **K. C. Yelin** founded ICS Group, a management consulting firm that works with Fortune 100 market leaders to improve business execution. She was the president of ICS Group through 1999 and is the author of that firm's project portfolio management model and project leadership process. She has served on the faculty of the University of Connecticut Graduate School of Business Administration. She currently heads Yelin Associates based in Scottsdale, Arizona, and is an advisor to the project portfolio management practice at ICS Group.

5.3

Project Offices Are Key Components of IT Governance

Matt Light

> One function of a governance board is to direct and review the project office, which can provide analysis of project portfolio issues, with prioritization, remediation, and other recommendations.

Most business initiatives result in related projects being grouped into programs, many with substantial information technology (IT) components. As the project office has become a widespread organizational approach, we have noted some IS organizations struggling with their role in IT governance. Unfortunately, the experience of enterprises that have governance structures that are ill defined or dysfunctional has driven the prioritization process for projects with strong IT components into the IS organization, and even into the project office, which can be a serious error.

In some cases, the project office, often called the project management office (PMO), has performed well in this role—or at least more effectively than an absent or dysfunctional process. However, this is an approach to prioritization that is fraught with risks. Although the PMO is involved with planning and controlling strategic projects, it is charged with the tactical execution of those projects rather than specifically with strategy (including prioritization) as such.

Nevertheless, the project office can play an important support role in IT project prioritization and governance. When the delay of a key project can doom an entire initiative or when those chartered and funded are insufficient to realize the strategic initiative, a PMO can provide an early warning system, as well as recommend alternative solutions to the governance board (sometimes known as an investment council or project review board) at its regular (perhaps monthly) meetings.

With most enterprises, business units compete during annual budget periods, when conflicting priorities can be resolved at the executive level with reference to strategies driving the budget. However, during the rest of the year, conflicts involving specific resources and budget allocations will occur. Only in small enterprises can a CEO referee a majority of budget conflicts, monitor projects' progress against budget, and adjust priorities. In most other enterprises, the PMO lacks the necessary membership and neutrality to manage budget conflicts. A PMO in the IS organization may itself hoard resources for too many nonaligned pet projects. Furthermore, a project office established outside any specific functional area will lack sufficient executive authority to provide governance.

Quick, Good Decisions

Properly constituted, however, a governance board can meet regularly to track progress toward strategic objectives, make resource decisions, and resolve conflicts at the executive level when new priorities arise or when project costs become excessive or delays affect other priorities. However, making such decisions requires good, consistent information, because different business units and functional areas may have quite different ways of monitoring their work. One functional area might simply track costs against budget, without an accurate sense of progress. Often a business unit may track a project's completion percentage simply by asking the project manager for a rough estimate; others may track it against the number of planned tasks, and still others may consider only milestones on the critical path.

For a governance board to make quick, correct decisions, a best-in-class project office will provide a realistic overall picture of the project portfolio, with reporting that is standardized across the business units and functional areas. It can provide analysis and alternative recommendations prepared prior to the governance board meeting. When the governance board does make decisions, such as to cut one project's scope, add resources to another, or kill a third, the project office can communicate this critical information back to the project managers.

Coordinating the PMO with the Governance Board

A normal process by which the project office supports the governance board is to handle scheduling logistics, report circulation, and contribute agenda items. It submits a project portfolio status report before the meeting to all governance board members. Typically the report delineates the programs or sets of peer projects, sometimes in the form of bubble charts, along with a dashboard report, with the project office gathering and loading data into its PPM tool of choice, through which it manages the repository of project data. Updated schedules or progress reports are sifted through for details to highlight. These may include descriptions of events and variances, bottlenecks, trends, and delivery assessments for the upcoming month and quarter.

When there are important problems or opportunities, analysis and recommendations should be provided, complete with dissenting opinions. Less significant problems or opportunities, as well as measures taken since the last meeting by the project office, may be listed, with additional analysis or backup provided on request. Backup should include data on project risks, costs, and progress.

The project office administers the project request process, except for "lite" forms of a "virtual" project office, without dedicated staff. Normally this is the conduit for the project chartering template by which important prioritization information concerning business goals, customer impact, competitive drivers, initial cost and benefit analysis, and so forth is gathered. It provides this template to the managers proposing projects, often requiring a vice-president-level signature to do so. For newly proposed projects, the PMO may prepare a what-if analysis for the governance board.

Bottom Line

Coordination of and cooperation between a governance board and a project office should be established so that an enterprise can more easily make rapid adjustments to the project portfolio, for example, to take quick advantage of opportunities or to cancel some projects and reassign bottleneck resources to speed up others. Prioritization ranking can be revisited with less political friction. A project office can do little of this by itself for long, and a governance board comprising executive management will often find monthly meetings to be too long, ill prepared, and unproductive without the support data, analysis, and alternative recommendations an effective project office can provide.

Matt Light is a research director in Gartner Research, where he advises on applications development and project and process management. He has more than twenty years of industry experience. Prior to joining Gartner, he worked as a project manager and in various development and research management roles both as a software entrepreneur and at the Federal Reserve Bank of San Francisco. In addition, he previously directed project change processes in the project office of an electrical subcontractor and managed Auerbach Publishers' line of manufacturing automation and integration journals and reference books. He holds a B.A. from the University of Connecticut, an M.A. from San Francisco State University, and an M.B.A. in information systems from Sacred Heart University, Fairfield, Connecticut.

SECTION SIX

PPM Applications

Information Technology

There is almost an overwhelming volume of material on PPM. For a fairly young area of practice, PPM has gotten a very high level of attention, especially in two application areas: information technology and new product development. Indeed, there is a similarity in these two disciplines in that both are striving to get the maximum benefits from a limited investment.

Certainly IT has received extensive (and embarrassing) notoriety for failures. Failure to deliver on time. Failure to deliver within budget. In fact, failure to deliver at all. So it is not surprising that anything that might improve on this distressed state will catch the attention of the IT community.

Many government agencies, especially those responsible for promoting improved efficiencies and performance in IT, have been at the forefront of embracing PPM as a potential solution to the IT performance deficiencies. In the United States, the Government Accountability Office (GAO) and the Office of Management and Budget (OMB) have been very active. It has been a characteristic of these types of agencies to survey both the public and the private sectors for best practices. As a sample of the research that has been conducted in this area, Chapter 6.1 is a reprint of a report published by the Federal CIO Council on best practices in PPM for IT.

IT governance is (or should be) undergoing substantial change. This case is brought to us by David Hurwitz, who says, "IT must adopt a structured, transparent, consistent and defensible invest-ment planning methodology. If not, it will continue to be whip-sawed by executive politics, flavors of the day, and reactionary blowback. Plus, it will never get credit for the considerable cost and effort entailed in simply keeping the lights on." In Chapter 6.2, Hurwitz offers an extensive discussion and prescription on the back-bone of IT management and governance. The practice of PPM as part of this paradigm shift is presented as the structure for survival of IT in the current environment.

6.1

A Summary of First Practices and Lessons Learned in Information Technology Portfolio Management

Federal CIO Council, Best Practices Committee

Part I: Introduction—$52 Billion Is a Lot of Money

Let's start this report here. . . .

For FY 2003, the President has requested $52 billion for investments in information technology. Any way you look at it, $52 billion is a lot of money.

What Is the Problem?

Federal direction, policy, and guidance as well as the best efforts of government oversight and technical review organizations have brought a portion of much-needed control in IT planning and spending. However, significant improvements are still needed as we plan on how we spend this $52 billion investment.

Determining what to invest in, how much to invest, and then taking action to maximize the value of the return on our investment tends to be a bit more difficult. Why?

The complete document, with appendixes, may be found at http://www.cio.gov/index.cfm?function=specdoc&id=329.

First, according to Mark Forman, OMB's associate director for IT and e-government, "Many agencies fail to transform their process for IT management using the portfolio management process because they don't have change management in place before starting. IT will not solve management problems—re-engineering processes will. Agencies have to train their people to address the cultural issues. They need to ask if their process is a simple process. A change management plan is needed. This is where senior management vision and direction is sorely needed in agencies."

Second, the selection criteria for IT spending vary greatly between and within government agencies. People use different requirements, goals and objectives, preferences, tolerances for risk and uncertainty, levels of acceptance of quality, and bases of knowledge and understanding to make spending decisions.

Third, people who are buying and spending IT money often are not aware of what other people are buying and spending. Without a broader perspective, many will not make investment decisions based on the common good. This reduces the chance that the next dollar of IT spending will generate the best possible benefits. Is there a solution at hand?

Is There a Solution at Hand?

Yes. Thankfully, there is. Recognizing there are many IT buyers and spenders operating under different "drivers" within the federal government is a good first step. The next step is to make people aware of and embrace the concept of portfolio management within their organizations.

What Is Portfolio Management?

There is a lot of history behind portfolio management, and much of it is well worth the time and effort to review. The following brief history provides a starting focus point for the main purpose of this document: to provide you with lessons learned and insights from leading IT portfolio management practitioners.

A Brief Historical Overview of Portfolio Management. 1952—
The management of information technology projects, according to
portfolio management tenets, owes its origins to modern portfolio
theory (MPT). MPT first was described by Harry Markowitz in his
seminal paper entitled, "Portfolio Selection," which appeared in the
Journal of Finance.

In brief, MPT describes how, for a given risk level, there is a specific mix of investments that will achieve an optimal return. Of
course, a critical assumption here is that the investors know what
they are seeking—typically more, less, or the same level of performance or some other measurable objective.

Interestingly enough, thirty-eight years later in 1990, Markowitz shared a Nobel Prize with Merton Miller and William Sharpe
for what has become the dominant approach used to manage risk
and return within financial markets.

Fast forward to . . .

1981—In light of the increasing use and criticality of IT to business operations and success, F. Warren McFarlan applied MPT to
the management of IT. McFarlan prepared an article published in
the *Harvard Business Review* entitled, "Portfolio Approach to Information Systems." In his article, Professor McFarlan suggested that
managers employ a risk-based approach to the selection and management of IT projects. By explicitly understanding the nature of
the risks, managers can allocate their resources appropriately to mitigate the risk or can delay taking other risks in order to keep the
overall risk at a manageable level.

A broader use of the ideas of portfolio management began to
develop in the mid-1990s.

1994—GAO's report entitled, *Improving Mission Performance
Through Strategic Information Management: Learning from Leading Organizations*, described a private sector organization that used a portfolio investment process to select, control, and evaluate information
systems projects. The organization defined and applied an explicit
set of decision criteria that addressed the benefits, costs, and risks associated with a number of competing investment opportunities.

The organization believed that use of the portfolio process helped it to determine the best mix of projects and the right level of investment to make in each of them. One important outcome was to achieve a better balance between the investments it made in ongoing maintenance expenditures versus strategic initiatives.

1998—GAO continued to promote IT portfolio management in its report entitled, *Executive Guide: Measuring Performance and Demonstrating Results of Information Technology Investments.* According to many, the report is a runaway best-seller. It describes *portfolio management and analysis* as one of four strategic enterprise objectives.

Also in the same year, John Thorp published "The Information Paradox," which described portfolio management as one of three fundamental components of "benefits realization." Thorp provided case studies in which portfolio management was used to manage risk and maximize return along a number of dimensions. His risk dimensions included technology as well as organizational capability. He also addressed the advantages to be gained by evaluating projects in light of the other projects being considered. Thorp went on to describe the rudimentary steps to creating a portfolio.

Present—More recently, both GAO and OMB explicitly included IT portfolio management as central elements of good IT investment management. GAO's IT Investment Management Framework places portfolio management at the center of its model of investment management. While strong investment decision making provides a foundation to maximize returns, it is only when IT investments (all funds being committed to IT programs, projects, and systems for the benefit of the agency) are managed as a portfolio can an optimal return even be approached.

OMB's revision of Circular A-130 in 2000 also referred to portfolio management as a critical aspect of capital planning and specified its use in the process. OMB noted that "the portfolio will provide information demonstrating the impact of alternative IT investment strategies and funding levels, identify opportunities for sharing resources, and consider the Agency's inventory of information resources."

What Should We Take Away from the History of Portfolio Management? At its core, portfolio management describes the processes, practices, and specific activities to select IT investments. Portfolio management makes use of continuous and consistent evaluation, prioritization, budget considerations, and finally selection for the greatest value and contribution to the strategic interests of the organization.

Through portfolio management, the organization can explicitly assess the trade-offs among competing investment opportunities in terms of their benefits, costs, and risks. Investment decisions can then be made based on a better understanding of what will be gained or lost through the inclusion or exclusion of certain investments.

In the simplest and most practical terms, portfolio management is about the five following items:

1. *Defining goals and objectives*—clearly articulate what the portfolio is expected to achieve.
2. *Understanding, accepting, and making trade-offs*—determine how much to invest in one thing as opposed to something else.
3. *Identifying, eliminating, minimizing, and diversifying risk*—select a mix of investments that will avoid undue risk, will not exceed acceptable risk tolerance levels, and will spread risks across projects and initiatives to minimize adverse impacts.
4. *Monitoring portfolio performance*—understand the progress that the portfolio is making toward the achievement of the goals and objectives.
5. *Achieving a desired objective*—have the confidence that the desired outcome will likely be achieved given the aggregate of investments that are made.

As Lester Diamond, assistant director of IT at GAO, notes, "If you have strong portfolio management, you can explain trade-offs better; explain why you chose projects; lay out your portfolio of investments; and describe risks and how you plan to manage them.

The Hill is especially concerned about results and hates to see dollars going down the tube."

At this point, it is probably a good idea to shed a bit of light on what portfolio management is not.

It is not about doing a series of project-specific calculations and analyses, such as return on investment, benefit-cost analysis, net present value, payback period, rate of return (internal or otherwise), and then adjusting them all to account for risk. Nor is it about earned value or activity-based costing. These practices are important; however, they are project specific.

Portfolio management is not collecting after-the-fact information on IT projects to produce a report that the organization hopes will satisfy some organizational reporting requirement.

That is probably enough for the definition of portfolio management. Hopefully, you get the idea.

The Law Says That We Have to Do Portfolio Management— But Why Do We Need and Want to Do It?

With regard to the law, there is the Clinger-Cohen Act. Enough said.

However, whether you are a government official, manager, or member of the staff (government workers or contractor support), there are other compelling reasons to formulate, manage, and maintain IT portfolios.

Above all else, we need and want to do portfolio management because it will help us to determine an acceptable mix of IT products and services to buy. It will help us figure out how much to spend on those IT products and services. Lastly, it will help us to better employ IT to achieve our mission goals, performance objectives, and to support and enable business operations.

Of course, we also need to recognize that IT is not the only item we are buying to support mission and business purposes. The IT portfolio is part of an organization's broader portfolio of investments, which includes a wide variety of human and capital assets.

Whereas the IT portfolio contemplates trade-offs among IT initiatives, an organization's broader portfolio considers trade-offs among investments in all "factors of production," including workforce, buildings, equipment, as well as IT.

For an organization's chief information officer (CIO), having a working and effective process to formulate, manage, and maintain an IT portfolio is absolutely critical. Without it, the CIO cannot properly support, substantiate, and fully justify investments in IT against investments in other things.

For other organization officials, such as the chief financial officer (CFO), procurement executive, and office and program managers, IT portfolio management is no less important. They all need to have visibility into how and where IT funds are being spent and whether their IT investments are contributing to the achievement of mission, program, and business goals and operations. Indeed, since a great number of IT investments are viewed as potential workforce and performance multipliers, the importance of a sound IT portfolio cannot be overstated.

How to Initiate or Improve Portfolio Management Within Your Organization

Start with the lessons learned and insights presented in this report. Like our contributors, you also may want to start slowly.

Think about the types of IT projects and investments your organization is making. Instead of trying to grapple with the formulation, management, and maintenance of a portfolio for your entire organization, try focusing on one aspect of it. Think about starting with a specific business area or function such as:

- Mission or program area (you will probably want to pick a specific business area)
- Security
- Infrastructure

- Research and development
- Administrative support
- Nonsystem development

Over time, you can add new portfolios until you have captured all of your IT investments. Employing this type of an approach can facilitate trade-off analyses across different portfolios. For example, later in this report, we will discuss an organization that was able to determine the need for additional investments in their infrastructure efforts to keep pace with and adequately support their mission, program, and business operations.

Other organizations interviewed for this report noted a legacy of rather excessive and unnecessarily redundant spending on IT infrastructure. The leading organizations we spoke to use portfolio management and their IT capital planning and investment control process to make adjustments to their infrastructure spending.

Another thing you can do to get started down the right path is to contact the federal CIO Council for advice and assistance. Let them know what you are trying to accomplish and the issues and challenges that you are facing, and they will point you toward the organizations and people who can help.

Part II: Lessons Learned and Insights

Lesson 1: Understand the differences and the relationship between portfolio management and project management and manage each one accordingly.

An IT portfolio comprises a set or collection of initiatives or projects. Project management is an ongoing process that focuses on the extent to which a specific initiative establishes, maintains, and achieves its intended objectives within cost, schedule, technical, and performance baselines.

Portfolio management focuses attention at a more aggregate level. Its primary objective is to identify, select, finance, monitor, and maintain the appropriate mix of projects and initiatives necessary to achieve organizational goals and objectives.

Portfolio management involves the consideration of the aggregate costs, risks, and returns of all projects within the portfolio, as well as the various trade-offs among them. Of course, the portfolio manager also is concerned about the "health" and well-being of each project that is included within the organization's IT portfolio. After all, portfolio decisions, such as whether to fund a new project or continue to finance an ongoing one, are based on information provided at the project level.

Case Examples: Offer Training on Key Topics. The Department of Housing and Urban Development (HUD) has established a fairly comprehensive training program for its IT portfolio and project managers that clearly distinguishes the roles, responsibilities, and activities to be performed by each. The training is readily available and portable to other federal organizations. The Department of Agriculture (USDA) has adopted, tailored, and implemented it to support their IT portfolio and project management activities.

Lesson 2: Gain and sustain the commitment of agency officials and senior managers to make informed IT investment decision at an enterprise level and to uphold them.

The successful management of your IT portfolio requires strong leaders who recognize and understand the value of IT to the organization and the benefits that accrue from an IT portfolio management approach. Each of the public and private sector entities interviewed indicated that their organization provided executive leadership to the portfolio management process. The level of executive leadership most often tied to the clearly defined governance process was the chief executive officer (CEO) or agency head. These leaders would participate in decisions for large or high-impact capital investments.

Within the federal government, Mark Forman at OMB reminds us that "the Clinger-Cohen Act specifically mandates senior executive involvement in Agency IT decision making. The Clinger-Cohen Act directed a regulation to be crafted by the Secretary or Deputy Secretary laying out portfolio management and [capital planning and investment control]."

Portfolio management requires a business and an enterprise-wide perspective. However, IT investment decisions must be made both at the project level and the portfolio level. Senior government officials, portfolio and project managers, and other decision makers must routinely ask two sets of questions.

First, at the project level, is there sufficient confidence that new or ongoing activities that seek funding will achieve their intended objectives within reasonable and acceptable cost, schedule, technical, and performance parameters?

Second, at the portfolio level, given an acceptable response to the first question, is the investment in one project or a mix of projects desirable relative to another project or mix of projects?

Having received answers to these questions, the organization's senior officials, portfolio and project managers, and other decision makers then must use the information to determine the size, scope, and composition of the IT investment portfolio. The conditions under which the portfolio can be changed must be clearly defined and communicated. Proposed changes to the portfolio should be reviewed and approved by an appropriate decision-making authority, such as an investment review board, and considered from an organization-wide perspective.

Case Examples: Cultural Changes. The interviewees described a shift in culture, process, and responsibility (for identifying and delivering business value) from the IT organization to the business end user. Further, a senior executive representing the business function normally participates on cross-functional teams or boards.

The Office of Personnel Management (OPM), a relatively small government organization with a limited portfolio, noted its size allows for easy access to key executives, making portfolio management easier for them than for some larger organizations.

Ingram Micro describes this fundamental change within their company philosophy: "We are moving from a centralized IT organization focused with a technology driven IT portfolio to a business capability driven IT portfolio."

In making this shift, Ingram Micro moved the responsibility for identifying needs, justifying investments, approving technical solutions, and delivering business value from the CIO to regional vice presidents and corporate-level business end users.

Similar shifts from the IT organization to business owners, for aligning investment proposals with strategic agendas, were addressed in several government enterprises including the Customs Service and Bureau of Land Management (BLM), as well as in private sector companies such as EDS and SRA.

At GE Global eXchange Services, IT decisions are the responsibility of the business units and sponsors. The sponsor, as the functional leader, is required to present the business case for the requirement as well as fund, justify, and review the project.

Lesson 3: Establish and maintain an enterprise architecture to support and substantiate IT investment decisions.

Many of the leading IT portfolio managers and decision makers interviewed noted a strong reliance on their organization's enterprise architecture (EA) to provide a better understanding of IT investment opportunities and impacts.

More specifically, in several instances such as at HUD, the Department of Labor (DOL), and the Department of Education (DoED), the EA provided IT portfolio managers and investment decision makers with a useful framework to assess opportunities within and across the organization's mission areas and business lines. The EA also is being used to help formulate and target investments to improve data and information management and sharing, application development and deployment, and the ongoing operation and maintenance of the organization's technology infrastructure.

Since many federal organizations are now just beginning to define their EAs, a useful "first practice" mentioned by several government and private organizations is to develop an inventory of existing systems and current or planned IT projects.

Case Examples: The Enterprise Architecture. EDS is a strong proponent of EA and believes that it is "vitally important to the portfolio process." They stated that an architecture must be in place before investment decisions can be made in a factored way. They also believe that the organization must understand how each part of the organization operates, so that it can determine what each investment contributes to the organization.

Ingram Micro is also moving toward an EA to help manage their IT portfolio. Like EDS, Ingram Micro developed a baseline of its assets and capabilities ("as-is" architecture) as the first critical step. From there they are gaining an understanding of the current portfolio, details of their processes, and systems required in order to develop a road map for future investments.

Within the federal government, HUD relies heavily on its EA as a major component of its portfolio management process. The EA is integrated with HUD's capital planning process and is used to identify performance gaps, redundancies, and opportunities. Based on EA analyses, gaps are identified and initiatives are proposed to improve business processes. After each portfolio review, the EA is updated to reflect the enterprise's most current "to-be" state.

BLM is another government enterprise relying on its EA to guide future IT investments. BLM's EA consists of a technical architecture that is "owned" by the CIO and a business architecture, which is a set of sophisticated process models, jointly "owned" by the assistant directors, CFO, and CIO. Under the CIO, a manager titled the enterprise architect is responsible for maintaining the Bureau's EA.

BLM manages all investments to be consistent with the EA, and all investments must be compliant with the EA to receive funding. To ensure this compliance and eliminate system duplication, BLM established the System Coordination Office (SCO), whose role is to review and approve all proposals before they are presented to BLM's National Information Technology Investment Board for funding consideration.

Case Examples: The Inventory of Systems and IT Projects. The Defense Logistics Agency (DLA), among other organizations, began by inventorying investments to understand its baseline. This allowed the agency to understand how much it was investing in legacy systems and how to reduce that investment. Government and industry alike strive to reduce dollars tied to operations or backbone infrastructure projects in order to reallocate funds to strategic or constituent serving projects.

According to GE Global eXchange Services, the inventory also clearly shows areas of duplication or redundancy. The reduction of projects or systems allows for cost savings.

AXA/Equitable cited a similar need to not only understand its inventory of systems, but what those systems were delivering for the organization as the basis for its portfolio management process.

Lesson 4: Integrate IT portfolio management with the organization's planning and budgeting policies, processes, and practices.

Most leading organizations manage and maintain their IT portfolios by leveraging their strategic planning, budgeting, acquisition and procurement, and IT capital planning and investment control processes. This helps provide the necessary governance and incentive structure to ensure that portfolio management is integrated throughout the organization. This ensures the stages and steps used to formulate, manage, and maintain the IT portfolio are consistent and repeatable.

Case Examples: Integration. Large private organizations such as GE Global eXchange Services, Oracle, and Lockheed Martin noted that having a governance structure that is well documented, effectively communicated, and understood throughout the organization is critical in implementing portfolio management.

To varying degrees of success and maturity, HUD, DOL, DoEd, and the Department of Treasury have integrated their portfolio management, IT capital planning and investment control, and budget formulation and execution processes.

Lesson 5: Clearly define and communicate the goals and objectives to be served by the IT portfolio and the criteria and conditions for portfolio selection.

The performance of your IT portfolio affects a wide range of customers and stakeholders within and outside of your organization. Most of the top IT portfolio managers who contributed to this report stressed the following "needs":

- Adequately define and broadly communicate the goals and objectives of the IT portfolio.

- Clearly articulate the organization's and management's expectations about the type of benefits being sought and the rates of returns to be achieved.

- Identify and define the type of risks that can affect the performance of the IT portfolio, what the organization is doing to avoid and address risk, and its tolerance for ongoing exposure.

- Establish, achieve consensus, and consistently apply a set of criteria that will be used to select among competing IT projects and initiatives.

Case Examples: Goals and Objectives. Private sector organizations including Oracle, Lockheed, and GE Global eXchange Services indicated that a short payback period was a key criterion for investment selection.

EDS, GE Global eXchange Services, and Oracle focus heavily on evaluating cost reductions in the payback model. The payback period is often linked to the economic environment as well as competitive pressures within their respective industry.

At EDS, achieving value is key. This is measured by cost savings, cycle-time improvements, faster time-to-market, and enhanced ability to focus on core competencies through innovative use of IT.

In alignment with the business case evaluation, BLM's National Information Technology Investment Board selects investments based on a number of criteria. These include support to BLM's core business functions, improving work processes to reduce cost and improve effectiveness, return on investment (ROI), consistency with bureau enterprise architecture/strategic alignment, and project risk strategy.

Within Oracle's global network and database, portfolio decisions are based on current, standardized information. Redundancy is eliminated, and the needs of all organizational units are considered together, with a primary goal of reducing operating costs. In addition, Oracle expects new projects to be in production within six months.

GE Global eXchange Services uses criteria such as payback, cost/benefit, risk, and savings to operations. Because of the dynamics of its industry, the changing nature of IT, and the business environment, GE Global eXchange Services looks favorably on investments with shorter payback periods.

At Lockheed Martin, IT investments must meet the goal of modernizing the IT infrastructure while reducing costs. Key elements of the select decision include payback, risk (and mitigation plan), interoperability, link to shared services, and project duration.

At HUD, scoring criteria are used in such major categories as: addresses a material weakness found in GAO or Office of Inspector General audits, mission support, project management capability, feasibility of implementation, enterprise architecture, and support of principals' priorities (HUD senior executive priorities). Each major category has a series of subcriteria to fully assess how well an initiative meets the criteria.

USDA uses criteria for scoring investments including contributions to mission, risk, ROI, security, and architecture. Criteria vary based on the phase of the investment. Investments under development are scored based on cost, risk, schedule, and performance goals, as well as security and architecture. Once an investment is implemented, performance measurement shifts toward ROI and contribution to meeting mission goals. USDA reviews criteria after each investment review cycle and modifies the criteria to ensure they continue to meet business needs.

Lesson 6: Acquire and utilize portfolio, project management, decision support, and collaborative methodologies and tools.

The formulation of the organization's IT portfolio is a highly complex undertaking. Leading IT portfolio managers utilize a variety of automated tools to help them formulate, manage, and maintain their organizations' IT portfolios.

There are comprehensive IT investment management tools available, including the federal government's own IT Investment Portfolio System (I-TIPS), several other systems developed by government organizations, and a few commercially available investment management products. These tools vary dramatically in the range of portfolio management and support capabilities they provide.

For a more detailed discussion of the tools that are available and in use across the federal government, please refer to the *Smart Practices in Capital Planning Guide*, prepared by the CIO Council Committee on Capital Planning and IT Management with the support of members of the Industry Advisory Council (IAC). (Please note that since the CIO Council's restructuring, the Capital Planning and IT Management Committee has become a community of practice under the Best Practices Committee.)

Case Examples: Methodologies and Tools. MITRE uses the London School of Economics Equity Model for prioritization and selection of investments that align with corporate need. The selection process generates a ranked list of prioritized investments and expectations, which helps drive the process to joint agreement on the value, risks, and costs of the proposed investment portfolio.

AXA uses an analytical hierarchical process (AHP) model called STRAT Frames from United Management Technologies to weight the objectives. Each functional group executive vice president uses the weighted objectives to prioritize their projects. These senior managers present their "wish list" of potential projects with the expected impact.

The first filter is the correlation of contribution to achieving objectives. Each executive vice president separately describes their projects using specific impact ratings of extreme, strong, moderate, low, and none. Their impact assessments also use cost benefit analysis, net present value, payback period, and internal rate of return.

The second consideration or "filter" is the dependence on IT and what the need for spending in this area would be. The third filter is IT cost. And the fourth and final filter is accomplished by loading each business area's allocation for IT into the model. The model then lists the recommended optimized portfolio.

As part of a pilot program, AXA/Equitable Financial uses the ProSight tool to display summary-level assessments of project health across three dimensions: risk, value, and investment size. Data is provided by the project owner, made available to executive vice presidents and staff, and is tracked throughout the year. Future enhancements will include using data extractors to obtain data from existing systems.

EDS uses Metis software to create its enterprise architecture-modeling environment. The model visually presents the strategic alignment of IT assets, which can be queried down to an operational level. It is used at EDS for strategic alignment and funding, delivery operations, enterprise process models, and application portfolios.

HUD uses I-TIPS, the Enterprise Architecture Management System (EAMS), and Expert Choice to help formulate, manage, and maintain its IT portfolio.

Going into the annual IT portfolio selection process, HUD senior management uses the Expert Choice decision support tool to set portfolio selection priorities. Following the development of priorities and selection criteria weighting factors, HUD's CIO developed an initiative scoring methodology that translated strategic priorities and weights into IT project ratings and rankings. These rankings reflect the mission priorities and weights set by the department's senior executives. The Expert Choice tool is then used again to optimize a portfolio that mirrors the strategic priorities and congressional appropriation. By using the Expert Choice methodology in its IT portfolio management process, HUD is able to quickly adjust to external drivers and oversight decisions.

Some organizations are using applied information economics techniques, and others are employing the balanced scorecard method. These approaches provide their users with a highly structured, systematic, consistent, and repeatable method to help them better understand the value and risks associated with competing and complementary IT investment opportunities. Automated portfolio management tools, such as ProSight and I-TIPS, are able to support and present information resulting from these approaches.

Lesson 7: Routinely collect and analyze data and information to assess portfolio performance and make adjustments, as necessary.

The top IT portfolio managers interviewed for this report widely agreed on the need to continuously monitor portfolio performance and to establish the organization and management capacity to propose, analyze, and make modifications and adjustments to the portfolio in a timely manner. They also noted that good portfolio management requires careful attention to an organization's strategic, tactical, and operational functions.

At the strategic level, the IT portfolio manager must ensure that the mix of investments and associated funding levels is consistent with the organization's mission; program; business goals, objectives, and priorities; as well as the many institutional drivers that govern and direct agency actions, such as statutory, legislative, and regulatory requirements.

According to Mark Forman of OMB, "Agencies should seek to better understand the impact of legislative drivers. The natural tendency and primary focus of those in Congress is to serve the needs of their constituents. Members of Congress want programs that deliver results."

Dave McClure of GAO believes that "executives need to know where money is being spent, what it is being spent on, and what the value is to the agency. For executives, basic information is the key. Although it's the responsibility of the CIO to communicate across the agency, executives need to understand they have the responsibility to approve/own major IT initiatives that affect their business area. Executive ownership, participation, and accountability are often missing."

At the tactical and operational level, the IT portfolio manager is concerned that the projects and initiatives that comprise the portfolio are performing, either alone or in some combination, in a satisfactory manner. Portfolio management is combined with IT capital planning and investment control to enable managers to make adjustments to the portfolio's size, scope, schedule composition, and pace of funding.

Several leading federal organizations and a number of private companies that contributed to this report noted that they periodically conduct assessments of the overall IT portfolio as well as each individual project. Such assessments are conducted on a quarterly or semiannual basis, or as dictated by changing business conditions and constraints.

According to Gopal Kapur, president of the Center for Project Management, organizations should focus their IT portfolio assessments and control meetings on critical project vital signs. Examples of these vital signs include the sponsor's commitment and time, status of the critical path, milestone hit rate, deliverables hit rate, actual cost versus estimated cost, actual resources versus planned resources, and high-probability, high-impact events. Using a red, yellow, or green report card approach, as well as defined metrics, an organization can establish a consistent method for determining if projects are having an adverse impact on the IT portfolio, are failing and need to be shut down.

Specific criteria and data to be collected and analyzed may include the following:

- Standard financial measures, such as return on investment, cost-benefit analysis, earned value (focusing on actuals versus plan, where available), increased profitability, cost avoidance, or payback. Every organization participating in the interviews includes one or more of these financial measures.
- Strategic alignment (defined as mission support), also included by almost all organizations.
- Client (customer) impact, as defined in performance measures.
- Technology impact (as measured by contribution to, or impact on, some form of defined technology architecture).
- Initial project and (in some cases) operations and schedules, as noted by almost all organizations.
- Risks, risk avoidance (and sometimes risk mitigation specifics), as noted by almost all participants.
- Basic project management techniques and measures.

And, finally, data sources and data collection mechanisms also are important. Many organizations interviewed prefer to extract information from existing systems; sources include accounting, financial, and project management systems.

Case Examples: Data Gathering. HUD conducts quarterly IT "control reviews" to ensure that its portfolio and projects continue to meet requirements, support mission and business goals and objectives, and are progressing in accordance with planned cost, schedule, and technical baselines. The control review is used to determine whether any modification or adjustment to the portfolio is necessary.

For example, during one of its control reviews, HUD's portfolio managers discovered the organization was spending much more on new systems and much less on infrastructure than best practice organizations. This finding was supported by the increasing difficulty the infrastructure was having supporting its system load. The HUD CIO then mapped a three-year path to a best practices portfolio profile: specific percentages of the IT budget were set for each category for each of the following three years.

In addition, HUD has integrated its accounting system data with its investment portfolio data to improve the quality of portfolio management. From a control standpoint, project managers at HUD receive a monthly accounting report showing obligated, committed, and expended funds as well as unbilled costs. Schedule is tracked on major milestones and deliverables. Earned value is used to gauge project performance at quarterly control reviews.

At AXA/Equitable, updates on the status of individual projects are collected from individual project managers rather than from independent or automated sources. Both approaches have their proponents, but other factors to consider in this area are the level of effort, opportunity cost to collect the data, timeliness, availability, refresh frequency, and objectivity.

Some organizations gather portfolio management data purely from internal sources, while others look outside, collecting information and feedback from customers, employees, or other external sources. Externally collected measures, where used, are often tied to performance metrics programs. To date, much more progress appears to have been made in defining evaluation criteria and performance measurement data than in building and integrating the collection systems to furnish it.

The CIO at EDS believes that "facts and data set you free." To ensure the portfolio maintains its expected value throughout its life, continuous data collection and performance monitoring is necessary.

The metrics are collected and displayed in the "Service Excellence Dashboard," which displays the rates and ranks of services.

Customers rate services too. There is a common understanding of where the data comes from, so there is no debate about that.

Case Examples: Analyze Data. At EDS, investment decisions are made in a factored way with decision making supported by tools such as Metis. Metis software is used to create an enterprise architecture modeling environment. It visually depicts the strategic alignment of IT assets and allows for the debate of weights and value critical to portfolio management.

The use of ProSight at AXA/Equitable allows management to display summary-level assessments of project health across three dimensions: risk, value, and investment size. Data is provided to executive vice presidents and staff and is tracked throughout the year. Future enhancements will include using data extractors to obtain data from existing systems.

Many federal agencies use I-TIPS as the information repository for IT initiatives. A key advantage in using a tool (with data that is continually updated) is continuous management visibility into current performance results of each investment as well as the portfolio.

The CIO at Customs stated that using this "project health" knowledge helps Customs prioritize projects and determine whether certain projects should be accelerated, modified, or terminated.

A key to effective portfolio management at GE Global eXchange Services is a central repository of all IT projects and systems. The objective in each of these cases is to quickly access and see if there are any redundancies or overlapping projects. The CIO must have a centralized repository to gain a strong understanding of the corporate portfolio and be open to leveraging resources and ideas across business functions.

Other examples of enterprises in the public sector embracing this activity include BLM, where specific factors, including the contribution the investment is expected to make to the agency's mission and strategic plan, are required in each business case. It is then used in ranking and rating criteria to evaluate investment.

Likewise, DOL captures and documents strategic alignment in I-TIPS and uses this data as part of their investment-ranking criteria.

At Oracle, a guiding principle has been to shed capital assets to reduce costs and gain competitive advantage, particularly as it applies to the IT portfolio. They achieve this by consolidating, simplifying, standardizing, and centralizing. They offer incentives to unit managers to move them to use centralized, logically single-point solutions and by providing financial disincentives to using alternatives.

Lesson 8: Carefully consider the internal and external customers and stakeholders of the organization's IT portfolio.

During a recent interview for this report, Norm Lorentz, OMB's chief technology officer, stated that "agencies should not underestimate the need to understand [their] customers and constituents. What is demanded by [their] customers must be kept in mind. Frequently, government agencies spend more time doing business with itself, when it needs to be more citizen centered."

With regard to the members of Congress, Dave McClure of GAO contends that "the Hill tends to view [portfolio management] from an 'approval of spending motive.' Appropriators, like all budgeting officials, must carefully balance competing priorities and demands within a given funding limit. Thus, compromise and adjustments are made through this process. GAO and agencies need to discuss with their appropriations staff the trade-offs that need to be made."

Agencies can invoke good decision-making processes by maintaining their focus on justifying the value of their IT portfolio by major initiatives. This can be accomplished by communicating mission impact in terms of reliable outcome metrics.

The role of the business program cannot be ignored. After all, many of the portfolio components exist to support their operations and in turn support the mission of the organization.

Well-managed organizations effectively involve the business programs, encouraging them to own the portfolio management decisions and account for investment performance. In fact, OMB stresses that business managers actually own the portfolio. Norm Lorentz states that "the business manager owns the outcomes and must review progress. They should participate with other business owners to identify cross-functional opportunities to leverage efforts across the enterprise and portfolio. They should also share lessons learned."

Changing Viewpoints with the Use of Tools. Yet bringing business program staff in and having them assume a more corporate view is difficult. According to GAO's Dave McClure, it is difficult to take the business unit hat off and put the corporate hat on.

Even private businesses have a hard time taking the corporate view instead of their own business unit view. This is a cultural issue that people have to go through. To improve business program participation, Dave McClure advises a combination of informal and formal processes. Participants "need to have more dialogue to understand each other's business needs. The CIO can be a broker on the totality of needs and opportunity and pain scale."

Another approach is to ask business program personnel to utilize evaluation tools—scoring techniques, analytical tools, ranking, and other clear criteria. They need to understand how these criteria are used across the organization to measure IT needs.

Identify Stakeholders. Expanding business involvement in portfolio management often includes the following:

- Recognizing that the business programs are critical stakeholders, and improving that relationship throughout the life cycle
- Establishing service-level agreements that are tied to accountability (rewards and punishments)
- Shifting the responsibilities to the business programs and involving them on key decision-making groups

In many organizations, mechanisms are in place to enable the creation, participation, and buy-in of stakeholder coalitions. These mechanisms are essential to ensure that the decision-making process is more inclusive and representative. By getting stakeholder buy-in early in the portfolio management process, it is easier to ensure consistent practices and acceptance of decisions across an organization. Stakeholder participation and buy-in can also provide sustainability to portfolio management processes when there are changes in leadership.

Stakeholder coalitions have been built in many different ways depending on the organization, the process, and the issue at hand. By including representatives from each major organizational component who are responsible for prioritizing the many competing initiatives being proposed across the organization, all perspectives are included. The approach, combined with the objectivity brought to the process by using predefined criteria and a decision support system, ensures that everyone has a stake in the process and the process is fair.

Similarly, the membership of the top decision-making body comprises senior executives from across the enterprise. All major projects, or those requiring a funding source, must be voted upon and approved by this decision making body. The value of getting stakeholder participation at this senior level is that this body works toward supporting the organization's overall mission and priorities rather than parochial interests.

Case Examples: A Good Mix of Stakeholders Enhances PM Success Rate. From our interviews, we noted that stakeholders should at least include a financial, a technical, and an operations executive. At USDA, key stakeholders in the portfolio management arena include both political appointees and career executives.

At DOL, for example, the CIO's Office created key partnerships with the Office of Budget, the CFO, the Procurement Office, Office of the Secretary, and other internal decision makers in advance of their IT capital planning and investment control process.

DOL enhanced these partnerships with "CIO outreach support" to assist agencies with all facets of the new processes in their own environment.

HUD also used this outreach approach to support business units in their business case preparation. According to the deputy CIO for IT reform, "We worked with them rather than hammering them." HUD also helped business executives understand how portfolio management serves them by helping them solve problems, and in so doing, they became advocates.

In some cases, support from the business units in decentralized organizations provided the high-level support across the board support.

At AXA/Equitable Financial, for example, while the CEO was the driving force, the governance committee included the functional executive vice presidents and relied heavily on their strategies for their own business units. In general, a consensus of stakeholders at this level would know where there is a real need for a change. They are able to lay the groundwork for constructive collaboration, ensure communication, and have easy access to all levels of the organization. It is at this executive second level that the change process really gains the needed support and momentum to make the change successful.

At EDS, IT investment decisions are now based on inputs from the process owners in the business units. The process and culture have advanced enough that there can be real discussions of value. In the past, decisions were sometimes reopened. Failing projects were allowed to resurge after program decisions had already been made. In fact, it was common practice for the debate to begin after the decision had been made. This is no longer the case. When the discussion period ends and a decision is made, the focus is now on moving forward.

At USDA, key stakeholders in the portfolio management arena include both political appointees and career executives. This mix of players provides understanding and responsiveness to administrative priorities and legislative requirements, while ensuring that portfolio management processes continue during changes in leadership. Involvement and support from career executives has provided a measure of sustainability that would not otherwise be possible.

Lesson 9: Pay very close attention to the interorganizational aspects of the organization's IT portfolio.

Indeed, Lesson 9 speaks to the heart of the government-wide effort to maintain a more customer-centric focus. Accomplishing this will help to "unify and simplify" government functions, processes, and activities, including the IT resources that support them.

In addition, the national imperative to ensure homeland security has helped to garner attention to the federal IT portfolio from many populations. The general public, the administration, Congress, government agencies, as well as private organizations realize they must work together to better coordinate their activities and share information for the public good.

Three very important governmentwide initiatives, the Homeland Security Program, the ongoing Quicksilver effort, and the Office of Management and Budget's work to establish a federal enterprise architecture, very clearly demonstrate the shift away from narrowly focused and agency-specific efforts and activities.

Instead, we are in the midst of a transformational shift toward a heightened and, very hopefully, a sustained focus on the mission, functions, programs, and people that government supports and serves across all federal agencies. In addition, greater coordination and integration between federal, state, local, and foreign governments as well as the public and private industry has gained importance.

In the terms of e-government, these interfaces have been popularly described as the Government-to-Citizen (G2C), Government-to-Government (G2G), Government-to-Business (G2B), and Internal Efficiency and Effectiveness (IEE) interactions, exchanges, and transactions.

With clear direction and helpful guidance from their oversight and review organizations (such as OMB, GAO, the Federal CIO Council, and others), the leading federal IT portfolio management organizations are rapidly expanding their view of the work they do in relation to the work of others. This allows them to more carefully consider the broader impacts of the investments they are making in information technology.

The new and highest-level goals for IT portfolio management are being shaped and defined in government-wide terms. Consequently, they are goals that each and every federal organization will need to adopt. These goals, which are to be pursued and achieved on a government-wide basis, include the following:

- Ensure that there is a business case for all investments in IT.
- Clearly identify and understand the benefits and impacts of IT projects.
- Eliminate unnecessary redundancy in IT projects and initiatives.
- Consolidate IT activities wherever it makes sense to do so.
- Promote the sharing of information and supporting IT resources to support mission and business operations across organizational lines.

Case Examples: Cross-Agency Collaboration.   Perhaps the most significant example of this lesson in practice is the OMB Quicksilver effort. Quicksilver centers on the formulation and execution of a portfolio of twenty-four projects to address and provide support and solutions to many of the government's common mission and business functions. The interorganizational nature of this effort is reflected in the composition of each Quicksilver project team, which includes representatives from many federal organizations.

In the aftermath of the tragic and horrific terrorist events of September 11, the administration, Congress, and federal agencies are identifying cross-organizational mission and business areas that support homeland security, including border protection and first response. The organizations with responsibilities in these areas have been directed to work together to develop an integrated approach that will ensure adequate and appropriate levels of information and resource sharing. It is likely these efforts will rely on the formulation and implementation of a common architecture and associated portfolio of projects and initiatives.

The OMB Quicksilver initiative also can serve as a model for federal organizations with IT projects that do not have interfaces, exchanges, or transactions with other entities. Instead, the organization will look within itself and across its mission and business areas to identify areas for collaboration and shared investments. The USDA is contemplating this approach.

The Department of the Interior, Customs, the Internal Revenue Service, and other organizations involved in major transformation efforts are keenly aware of the interorganizational aspects of their IT portfolios. These organizations are working with their customers and stakeholders to establish IT portfolios. These portfolios will fully support their business activities across organizational lines and provide for the integration of IT systems and services necessary to support their interfaces, exchanges, and transactions.

And OMB's recent and ongoing effort to establish a federal enterprise architecture will, among other things, provide a common business model that agencies will be able to use to identify additional opportunities to engage in interorganizational efforts. These efforts will transform government operations and help to achieve significant gains in effectiveness and efficiency.

Part III: Conclusion and Next Steps

In performing the interviews and preparing the results for our previous CIO Council/IAC document, *Smart Practices in Capital Planning,* we noted that many private and public organizations had developed relatively sound IT investment management practices. To a large extent, these practices focused on the selection of viable and valuable IT projects and initiatives.

Conclusions

In addition to the lessons presented in this report, there also are several general conclusions or observations that were drawn from the many interviews that were conducted:

- The selection of sound IT investments is a requirement. However, effective portfolio management also requires extensive and ongoing management and maintenance.

- The move from investment management to portfolio management occurs on a continuum. Organizations generally develop and focus on ways to manage investments first, then begin to look at the bigger picture of how a collection of investments contributes toward the achievement of business objectives.

- Good portfolio management practices develop over time. None of the organizations that provided input to this report have implemented what can be called a complete portfolio management program. Instead, they have identified, developed, and implemented key and core components—many of which have been described throughout this report.

- Assistance is readily available. Both OMB and GAO are helping federal organizations make the transition from the management of individual investments to the management of their entire portfolio. Several leading organizations have looked to consultants for assistance, and have also done a good job in sharing lessons learned and best practices with their colleagues at other agencies.

- Within the private sector, many firms are adopting and adapting portfolio management practices on their own and with the assistance of consultants.

- A variety of tools exist to help an organization develop and further mature its portfolio management processes. Inventory tools, architecture repositories, and decision support software can assist in trade-off analysis. These types of tools have been widely cited as key enablers and critical success factors for effective portfolio management.

Recommended Next Steps

This report provides at a summary level the lessons learned and insights gained from interviews with representatives of several government and private organizations.

During the interviews, much important and useful information was collected around each of the lessons learned. Over the next several months, the Best Practices Committee plans to prepare a series of more in-depth Portfolio Management Practice Papers. Some of the topics to be addressed will include:

- Methodologies and tools to formulate, manage, and maintain IT portfolios
- Management of portfolio risk
- Organizational roles and responsibilities for effective portfolio management
- Portfolio management within a federated organization
- Use of subportfolios to improve investment control
- Integration of portfolio management capital planning and investment control, budget formulation and execution, and procurement and acquisition processes

Appendix

Acronyms

BLM	Bureau of Land Management
CCA	Clinger-Cohen Act
CEO	Chief executive officer
CFO	Chief financial officer

CIO	Chief information officer
CPIC	Capital Planning and Investment Control
Customs	U.S. Customs Service
DLA	Defense Logistics Agency
DOL	U.S. Department of Labor
EDS	Electronic Data Systems
GAO	General Accounting Office
GEGXS	GE Global eXchange Services
HUD	U.S. Department of Housing and Urban Development
IAC	Industry Advisory Council
IT	Information technology
ITIB	Information Technology Investment Board
ITIM	IT investment management
I-TIPS	Information technology portfolio management system
OMB	Office of Management and Budget
OPM	Office of Personnel Management
ROI	Return on investment
SCO	System Coordination Office
USDA	U.S. Department of Agriculture

6.2

The Backbone System of IT Management and Governance

IT Management and Governance 101

David Hurwitz

Information technology (IT) organizations and the executives who lead them find themselves in the most challenging of times. After a period of relatively liberal spending, IT organizations are finding (often dramatically) reduced budgets, while expectations for contribution remain undiminished.

This chapter describes why IT is in this current state of challenge, what is really different about the management and governance of IT (it's not the technology), how each of four subsystems—portfolio management, enterprise project management, resource planning, and financial management—serve a vital role in the solution, and what new management and governance structures are required.

The Challenge and Opportunity of Twenty-First-Century IT Leadership

IT organizations and the executives who lead them find themselves in the most challenging of times. IT, so long perceived as a natural engine of progress, emerged from the recent spending bubble caught between a rock and a hard place: its budget has been reduced, often dramatically, while expectations for its contribution remain undiminished.

Where Else Is Enterprise Portfolio Management Applied?

IT management and governance is not the only application of enterprise portfolio management (EPM). It can be applied to any area of the enterprise where specialized resources work on a portfolio of projects and initiatives. However, aside from IT, EPM is most commonly applied to the management of new product development in engineering and R&D, known as product development planning and management, and to the management of professional services, known as professional services automation (PSA).

Moving beyond this paradox requires a fresh approach to IT management and governance—one that facilitates partnership between IT leaders and fellow operating executives and that delivers tactical execution at a level of excellence rarely seen in the past. Today's world-class IT operations must remain in alignment with the strategic priorities of the enterprise, must deliver promised results with control and predictability, and must transparently report costs, progress, and problems in time to act on them.

Achieving this is a challenge because IT management and governance has always been a uniquely difficult operation to evaluate. Even those who understand its technical minutiae often have trouble objectively judging the quality of results delivered by the chief information officer (CIO).

As it happens, IT is different from other operational departments—not because of the technical underpinnings of servers, networks, and applications but because IT provides the infrastructure for every other department, almost all of which is critical, though only some provides differentiation for the enterprise. Whether or not it is organized on a shared-services model, IT must accommodate the competing demands of departmental heads, business unit chieftains, board-level strategic priorities, and budgetary constraints.

These must be met while rationalizing the typical set of accumulated systems from twenty years of mergers and reorganizations. This web of competing priorities makes for both a strategic planning nightmare and a profusion of programs, initiatives, and projects, the likes of which is not seen anywhere else in the enterprise. To top off this twenty-first-century management challenge, the specialized resources necessary to mobilize modern IT are expensive or scattered, or both.

The CIO's current challenge is somewhat comparable to that faced by manufacturing twenty years ago. The parallel rise of electronics—assembled from thousands of small, expensive, and rapidly obsolescing piece parts—and Japanese just-in-time production methods forced manufacturing executives to reengineer processes and adopt new classes of operational management systems. IT will do the same. The reengineering will come from the savvy use of outsourcing (more about this later), Web services, and utility computing. Of equal importance, new management and governance systems are required.

The Rise of Portfolio Management

IT must adopt a structured, transparent, consistent, and defensible investment planning methodology. If not, it will continue to be whipsawed by executive politics, flavors of the day, and reactionary blowback. Plus, it will never get credit for the considerable cost and effort entailed in simply keeping the lights on.

The Origins of Portfolio Management

In looking for a proven investment planning methodology, one might look to the literal originator of the term. Anyone who has attended even a single retirement planning session has a passing familiarity with portfolio management, the core management structure of financial planning. Portfolio management is based on asset allocation models, where a portfolio is viewed as a pie that can be divided—and analyzed—by any of several attributes. These analytic attributes— goals, risk levels, costs, and forecast returns—also serve as planning buckets. For instance, if the goals within a financial portfolio are growth, income, and capital preservation, then the first decision becomes how much of the overall portfolio to allocate to growth, how much to income, and how much to capital preservation. Only subsequently do decisions come into play as to which financial instruments in each category to sell, retain, or buy. These tactical decisions are much easier to make when constrained by their relatively minor role in the overall asset allocation model. For example, deciding which large capitalization financial services stock to buy is a relatively easy decision to make when such investments as a group comprise only 8 percent of the portfolio.

Business Investment Planning

Now consider the asset allocation model as applied to business investment planning, specifically within IT. Here the set of goals might be revenue growth, cost reduction, regulatory mandate, and business continuation. Simply answering how much of the overall IT capital and operating budget should be allocated to each of these is an executive-level question of considerable depth, requiring evaluation of strategic priorities, planning horizons, capital allocation, criteria, and so on. As with financial portfolio planning, the evaluation of specific assets and projects within each category occurs only after the determination of how much to invest in each category. And portfolio analysis doesn't stop with goal alignment. The portfolio must also be analyzed by a variety of other criteria, including risk, strategic alignment, and expected return, among others.

Contrast the asset allocation model with how IT planning is often done: individual projects, systems, and initiatives are approved or rejected in the abstract, with little analysis performed or considered as to their impact on the portfolio as a whole. It is bottom-up, in contrast to classical strategic management, which is top-down. It is no wonder that the results appear, and often are, chaotic.

While an asset allocation model can point the way to the future, it first requires a high-level yet current portfolio inventory, no small matter in a large IT shop. An IT portfolio inventory sufficient for planning purposes need not be exhaustive. Rather, it should characterize at a macro level everything that must be considered when drawing up the IT portfolio plan: applications, physical assets, projects (ideally grouped into programs or initiatives), infrastructure assets (such as networks and bandwidth), and resources (internal, contracted, and outsourced). These classes of portfolio items are what give rise to various forms of portfolio management, such as application, asset, and project portfolio management, all of which are related.

Initial IT portfolio inventories often reveal copious and expensive redundancies, such as an insurance company with eleven billing systems, a manufacturer with four accounts payable AP systems, and a financial services provider with seven customer portals. Portfolio management projects often stop at this point, however, as the new visibility of these redundancies triggers a system or asset rationalization program that can be expected to save millions of dollars all by itself.

But the march of progress never stops. New projects are always knocking at the door. Examples include a fast-growing division with a major new business initiative that must be enabled, another division that is being spun off, yet another that is being acquired. IT will be called on to respond, for none of these can succeed without it. No one, least of all the CIO, wants IT to be the roadblock to strategic imperatives. And so implementing portfolio management gets pushed to the following year, or maybe the year after that.

To make sure savings are realized, respond effectively to dynamic circumstances, and keep IT aligned with the business, a system is required: a portfolio management system. Such a system provides comprehensive IT portfolio modeling and macro inventorying, analysis (by goal, risk, status, budget, expected return, and so forth), and scenario planning. Importantly, the portfolio management system must seamlessly link to the systems that drive controlled delivery of the tactical programs that are derived from the investment planning process. Otherwise the strategy may become undone by poor execution.

Taking the Next Step: IT Governance

Given this portfolio management framework, IT is in a position to engage with executive stakeholders in an IT governance process. This often takes the form of an IT governance committee (sometimes called the IT steering committee), which functions like a board of directors, first deliberating and ultimately approving budgetary parameters, such as how much portfolio investment to direct toward cost reduction programs, for example.

Every IT governance committee must address which parts of the portfolio to outsource. In some cases, the determination will be that all of IT should be outsourced and in other cases that none should be outsourced. More common is the determination that specific assets should be outsourced: levels of infrastructure, areas of development or support, or specific systems. Determining the right mix, and then crafting transition programs to the proposed portfolio, is a challenge perfectly suited for portfolio management.

Opportunity management—requests for significant new systems and projects—should also be processed through portfolio impact assessments, with the request sponsors self-assessing how the proposal will score in terms of goal, risk, status, and so forth. This works best if an "IT suggestion box" can be deployed as a Web-based work flow, allowing self-assessment right at the source of an idea, then funneling ideas from every corner of the enterprise through a structured review and escalation process.

In short, IT governance is, first and foremost, the structured executive oversight of IT investment to ensure alignment with strategic priorities. The framework provided by the portfolio management module of an IT management and governance (IT-MG) system significantly increases the likelihood of the IT organization's achieving the defined goals that emerge from the governance process.

Winning Strategy Depends on Successful Tactics

Leaders, and the strategies they launch, are often undone by poor tactical execution. It happens several times during a single basketball game. Just watch the coach's pained expressions. It happens to philharmonic conductors, generals, and most certainly to managers and executives. The best strategy in the world—complete with compelling mission, proper budgeting, appropriate resource assignments, and visible executive sponsorship—will end up as a failure if the tactical programs required to execute it aren't well managed.

Nowhere else is the role of tactical execution more critical than in IT, with its unusually large numbers of projects, cross-functional delivery and sponsorship arrangements, and role as a corporate change agent. This last function shouldn't be overlooked since most successful IT projects change work processes and routines throughout the enterprise. Sometimes it is a small change, like upgrading the e-mail system, and sometimes it is a big change, like implementing a new AP system. And some might consider a small change like the e-mail upgrade a big change, thus highlighting the challenge of the change agent.

Tactical execution used to focus simply on project management. To this technique many world-class IT organizations are placing increasing weight on process management to address those business challenges that are perpetual, unlike projects that have beginnings, middles, and ends. Examples of IT-MG organizational processes are idea and opportunity management, phase-gated processes, and after-action feedback assessments.

However, project management across the panoply of IT programs remains a core competency. Gantt charts, critical path analysis, task tracking, time capture, and estimates to completions are all as central today as ever before. The challenge for large organizations is to optimize execution at more than just the individual project level. This is because project managers can be successful as individuals while programs stumble, strategies crumble, or the organization as a whole fails.

Therefore, tactical management systems must scale from the management of individual projects up to the management of programs that are full of projects, and then ultimately up to the management of asset allocation criteria that are supported by multiple projects, programs and initiatives (see Table 6.2-1).

TABLE 6.2-1 Sample Enterprise Project Map Linked to Portfolio Management

Portfolio Criteria	Cost Reduction		Regulatory Compliance	
	Data Center Consolidation	System Consolidation	Sarbanes-Oxley	Privacy
Programs				
Projects	Memphis into Erie	Evaluate each AP system	Map Section 404 exposure points	Develop customer privacy policy
	Paris into London	Develop a superset AP system	Implement new Section 404 controls	Conduct gap analysis against policy
	Hong Kong into Singapore	Migrate users to the super-AP		Close the gap

Enterprise project management is not done at the desktop computer level. Detailed planning is often done at this level. But enterprise project management requires an enterprise system, one that is broadly and easily accessible, consistent, coordinated, secure, and designed for the needs of large organizations.

In addition, an enterprise project management system must go beyond task planning and status tracking. It should richly support the collaboration requirements of project teams (threaded discussions, document management, and the like) because they are usually cross-functional (and therefore not used to working with one another), often geographically dispersed, and occasionally operating in more than one language, given the prevalence of offshore development.

Critically, just as the portfolio management module described in the previous section must seamlessly link to the enterprise project management module, so too is the corollary true: tactical transactions and activity must seamlessly bubble up to portfolio management. In this way, not only line managers will know what's really going on but also senior and executive-level management.

People Are the Most Important IT Assets

IT organizations are populated with specialists, such as process analysts, database analysts, trainers, network managers, and software engineers. Many of these specialized resources are in-house contractors or outsourced staff. Achievement of high utilization rates depends on enterprise-wide visibility of resource usage and availability, ease of requisitioning and assignment, and, especially, sophisticated planning capabilities. Many schedules are undone when key resources don't free up when project plans assumed they would. This often happens when shared resources are simultaneously assumed to be available by more than one project manager. The reverse—underutilization of resources—is also possible and especially galling in today's lean operating environments.

The digital assets in the portfolio—hardware, software and systems—are specified, designed, deployed, and maintained by people (the human assets). Thus, the truism that people are the most important assets is especially valid in knowledge- and process-based organizations like IT. Beyond the ability to deliver, staffing costs remain one of the largest IT spending areas. Thus, proactive and adept resource planning remains one of the core competencies of world-class IT management.

Financial Accountability Drives Good Governance

Departmental and business unit heads know that IT systems underlie nearly all business initiatives. Yet they tend to undervalue or overuse IT unless it hits expense budgets, hence, the surging popularity of charge backs and IT cost allocations. These internal billing mechanisms force budgetary owners in the business to account for the costs, and therefore the value, of their IT systems. One by-product of this IT financial consciousness is that internal customers become naturally engaged with the overall IT governance process: how IT priorities are set and how those priorities affect their initiatives become topics of great importance to them.

Detailed and correctly allocated financial management of IT initiatives is a management challenge that has historically been difficult to address. Aside from the emergence of charge backs, American companies have found that reporting for compliance with the SOP 98–1 standard has also emerged as a driver for the need to track labor and costs on IT projects accurately. This U.S. accounting standard alone, which allows for the capitalization of costs expended in the latter stages of a project, can lead to major reductions in reported expense levels.

Thus, accurate time, status, and expense tracking are now as important to finance as they have always been to the project and program manager. However, capturing the transactions to support this level of reporting, backing up the transactional flow with proper project accounting, and then posting the resulting entries to the general ledger require a financial management module that is tightly integrated with the core project and process management modules. By enabling charge backs and SOP 98–1 reporting for capitalization, IT financial management systems drive widespread support for proper IT governance.

IT Management and Governance: The Backbone System for World-Class IT

The information backbone of an enterprise comprises various systems of record. Examples include accounting, procurement, inventory control, and customer support. Just as these are the backbone systems of the business units, so is an IT-MG system the backbone for world-class IT returns.

The IT-MG system's seamless melding of portfolio management with project and process management is a compelling marriage of the strategic to the tactical: a structured investment allocation decision framework that drives, and is informed by, a system for precise tactical execution. Add to this mix the vital supporting functions of resource planning and project-based financial management, and the result is the comprehensive system needed for IT control and visibility.

IT governance is a hot topic today for good reason. IT continues to be very expensive, more than occasionally frustrating, and at least as important as ever before. Thus, control and visibility are required, which means proper governance. Satisfying these requirements in large IT shops, even those that have outsourced large chunks of their portfolios, requires a proper backbone system. The rise of IT-MG systems is therefore perfectly timed for IT today. With such a system, CIOs can more effectively step up to the same level of management capabilities as their peers on the executive committee. Just as manufacturing emerged stronger and more nimble after meeting the challenge of electronics and just-in-time delivery, so will IT emerge as more controlled, predictable, transparent, and valuable to the success of the enterprise.

David Hurwitz is responsible for Niku's outbound marketing strategies and programs. He has nearly twenty years of experience in enterprise application management and marketing and has played key roles in a number of Silicon Valley companies. Most recently, he was vice president of marketing and strategy at Perfect Commerce, an innovative provider of strategic sourcing and enterprise supply management software.

SECTION SEVEN

PPM Applications

─────────

New Product Development

I have noted that the two most significant application areas for PPM are information technology and new product development (NPD). In the NPD area, there is one standout expert who has earned the title of guru. Indeed, it is virtually impossible to read anything on the application of PPM to NPD without a reference to Robert G. Cooper. Thanks to Cooper's generosity, you will not have to locate the Cooper references. He has written two chapters for this book that cover the core of his groundbreaking work.

Cooper is the author of the Stage-Gate® concept and techniques, which provide structure, order, and control to the entire NPD process.[1] Stage-Gate is a valuable tool for developing ideas into projects and maintaining the portfolio pipeline. It is a highly structured yet practical method of managing a project through its life cycle, ensuring that (from proposal to launch), the project is viable and in support of the organization's strategies and objectives. I first mentioned Stage-Gate in Chapter 2.2 and promised a more detailed treatment of the subject. In Chapter 7.1, we get the details from the developer of the concept. In Chapter 7.2, Cooper continues his thorough and perceptive exploration of portfolio management for product innovation. This chapter provides complete guidance for implementing a set of processes to support the evaluation, prioritization, and selection of projects for the portfolio.

There are significant and obvious reasons that PPM is a natural for NPD. In NPD, we are dealing with investment, innovation, opportunity, limited resources, and risk. Whether we evaluate these elements properly, employing a structured, repeatable methodology, can determine the success or failure of an enterprise. It's that important.

7.1

A Stage-Gate® Idea-to-Launch Framework for Driving New Products to Market

Robert G. Cooper

New products are critical for the survival and prosperity of the modern corporation. New products launched in the previous three years now account for about 40 percent of companies' sales revenues and are seen as a major instrument of company growth. Innovation is no longer an optional investment, according to a recent executive survey: almost half of senior executives rate innovation as "very critical" to their future business success.[1]

The term *new product* is defined as anything that the organization offers to its marketplace for use or consumption and is new to the selling organization—that is, something it had not previously sold or made. This definition includes tangible goods as well as service products.

Product innovation is not so easy, however. Indeed, new products fail at an alarming rate (about one in ten new product concepts

This chapter is taken from two books by the author: *Product Leadership: Pathways to Profitable Innovation*, 2nd edition (Reading, Mass.: Perseus Books, 2005), and *Winning at New Products: Accelerating the Process from Idea to Launch*, 3rd ed. (Reading, Mass: Perseus Books, 2001). It also draws on other writings by the author: "Doing It Right—Winning with New Products," *Ivey Business Journal*, July-Aug. 2000, pp. 54–60; "Stage-Gate New Product Development Processes: A Game Plan from Idea to Launch," in E. Verzuh (ed.), *The Portable MBA in Project Management* (New York: Wiley, 2003); and even earlier publications such as "Stage-Gate Systems: A New Tool for Managing New Products," *Business Horizons*, 1990, 33(3).

Stage-Gate® is a registered trademark of Product Development Institute, Inc.

succeeds); 44 percent of new product projects fail to meet their profit objectives, and 49 percent are launched late to market.[2] Thus, many senior managers seek ways to improve their new product success, profitability, and speed to market and to build best practices into their product innovation methodology.

A Stage-Gate® framework is one solution that many leading companies have adopted to drive new product projects to market quickly and effectively.[3] The analogy of a North American football game helps to explain the concept. Imagine a football team without a game plan. The coach urges his players to "go out there and play hard . . . play to win." These are wonderful words of encouragement, but without a playbook or game plan, there's likely to be chaos on the football field.

A Stage-Gate new product process or idea-to-launch framework is simply a playbook or game plan to guide new product projects from beginning to end. In this chapter, we look at what a Stage-Gate framework is and then at ten best practices that top-performing businesses have built into their frameworks or playbooks. The chapter also provides the details of a best-in-class Stage-Gate idea-to-launch framework via a walk through the process. And the chapter ends with a look at how Stage-Gate methods have been applied to other types of development projects and some tips on how to implement Stage-Gate.

Necessary for Effective Product Development

Almost every top-performing company has implemented a Stage-Gate framework to drive new product projects through to commercialization, according to the American Productivity and Quality Center (APQC) benchmarking study on product innovation management best practices.[4] A solid idea-to-launch process is the strongest best practice observed among the sample of businesses and was embraced by virtually every top-performing business in the study. The Product Development and Management Association's (PDMA) best practices study concurs: "Nearly 60 percent of the firms surveyed use some form of Stage-Gate process."[5]

Stage-Gate methods work. According to the PDMA best practices study, "The Best [companies] are more likely to use some type of formal NPD process than the rest. They are more likely to have moved from simpler Stage-Gate processes to more sophisticated facilitated or third-generation processes."[6] And the APQC benchmarking study found that many of the practices that businesses had embedded within their idea-to-launch process have a very strong positive impact on performance: they separate the best performers from the rest.

Structure of the Stage-Gate® Framework

The Stage-Gate new product approach is a conceptual and operational model for moving a new product project from idea to launch. Stage-Gate methods break the innovation process into a predetermined set of stages, each stage consisting of a set of prescribed, cross-functional, and parallel activities (Figure 7.1-1). The entrance to each stage is a gate, which controls the process and serves as the

FIGURE 7.1-1 Overview of the Stage-Gate Idea-to-Launch Framework

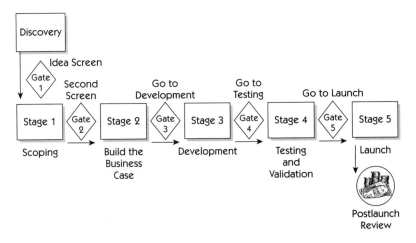

Source: R. G. Cooper, *Winning at New Products: Accelerating the Process from Idea to Launch*, 3rd ed. (Reading, Mass.: Perseus Books, 2001).

quality control and go/kill checkpoints. This stage-and-gate format leads to the name *Stage-Gate process*.

The Stage-Gate method is based on the experiences, suggestions, and observations of a large number of managers and firms and on my own and others' research in the field. In short, it is a game plan or playbook based on how winning project teams and winning business consistently win the game. Since this method first appeared in print, it has been implemented in whole or in part in hundreds of leading firms worldwide, many of which have provided an excellent laboratory setting to refine and improve the process.[7]

The Stages

Stages are where the action occurs. They are analogous to the plays in a North American football game. The players on the project team undertake key tasks in order to gather information needed to advance the project to the next gate or decision point.

The stages are defined by the activities within them, and there is usually a fairly standard or prescribed list of actions for each stage. Specifying the activities within a stage amounts to answering the questions:

- What does management need to know at the end of this stage in order to make an informed decision to move forward?
- Therefore, what actions are required in order to get this information?

For example, in Stage 2, Build the Business Case, a number of key actions may be required to deliver a solid business case, for example, undertaking voice-of-customer research, doing a competitive analysis, defining the product, and doing a source-of-supply assessment. These required or prescribed actions are mapped out within each stage of the Stage-Gate framework.

Stages include best practices. It's not just enough to map out a process that contains only current practices; there's no improvement in simply doing that. Later in this chapter, the success drivers, which must be built into each stage, are outlined.

Stages are also cross-functional. There is no R&D or marketing stage. Rather, each stage consists of a set of parallel activities undertaken by people from different functional areas within the firm, working together as a team and led by a project team leader. And these actions within each stage occur rapidly and in parallel—a rugby approach.

In order to manage risk using the Stage-Gate method, the parallel activities in each stage must be designed to gather vital information—technical, market, financial, operations—in order to drive down both the technical and business risks of the project. Each stage costs more than the preceding one, so that the game plan is based on incremental commitments. As uncertainties decrease, expenditures are allowed to mount. Risk is managed.

From Idea to Launch: An Overview

The general flow of the typical Stage-Gate model is shown pictorially in Figure 7.1-1. Here the key stages are:

- **Discovery:** Prework designed to discover opportunities and generate new product ideas.
- **Scoping:** A quick, preliminary investigation and scoping of the project. This stage provides inexpensive information, based largely on desk research, to enable the field of projects to be narrowed before Stage 2.
- **Build the Business Case:** A much more detailed investigation involving primary research, both market and technical, leading to a business case. This is where the bulk of the vital homework is done and most of the market studies are carried out. These result in a business case: the product definition, the project justification, and a project plan.
- **Development:** The actual detailed design and development of the new product, along with some product testing work.

The deliverable at the end of Stage 3 development is an alpha-tested or lab-tested product. Full production and market launch plans are also developed in this potentially lengthy stage.

- **Testing and Validation:** Tests or trials in the marketplace, lab, and plant to verify and validate the proposed new product and its marketing and production/operations: field trials or beta tests, test market or trial sell, and operations trials.

- **Launch:** Commercialization—the beginning of full operations or production, marketing, and selling. Here the market launch, production/operations, distribution, quality assurance, and postlaunch monitoring plans are executed.

At first glance, this overview portrays the stages as relatively simple steps in a logical process. But don't be fooled: this is only a high-level view of a generic process, that is, the concept of the process. In a real company process, drilling down into the details of each stage reveals a much more sophisticated and complex set of activities: a detailed list of activities within a stage, the how-to's of each activity, best practices that the project team ought to consider, and even the required deliverables from each activity in that stage (for example, in the format of templates). In short, the drill-down provides a detailed and operational playbook for the project team—everything they need to know and do in order to complete that stage of the process and project successfully.

The Gates

Preceding each stage is an entry gate or a go/kill decision point. The gates are the scrums or huddles on the rugby or football field. They are the points during the game where the team converges and all new information is brought together. Effective gates are central to the success of a fast-paced new product process:

- Gates serve as quality control checkpoints. Is this project being executed in a quality fashion?

- Gates also serve as go/kill and prioritization decision points. They provide the funnels where mediocre projects are culled out at each successive gate.

- Gates are where the action plan for the next stage is decided, along with resource commitments.

Gate meetings are usually staffed by senior managers from different functions—the gatekeepers—who own the resources required by the project leader and team for the next stage.

Gates Format.   Gates have a common format (Figure 7.1-2):

- A set of required *deliverables*: What the project leader and team must bring to the gate decision point (such as the results of a set of completed activities). These deliverables are visible, are based on a standard menu for each gate, and are decided at the output of the previous gate. Management's expectations for project teams are thus made very clear.

- *Criteria* against which the project is judged in order to make the go/kill and prioritization decisions.

- Defined *outputs*: for example, a decision (go/kill/hold/recycle), an approved action plan for the next stage (complete with people required, money and person-days committed, and an agreed time line), and a list of deliverables and date for the next gate.

FIGURE 7.1-2 Common Format of Gates

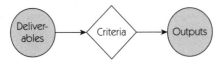

Types of Gate Criteria. Each gate has it own list of criteria for use
by the gatekeepers. There are three types of gate criteria:

- Readiness-Check: These are yes/no questions that check
  whether the key tasks have been completed, and that all
  deliverables are in place for that gate—in effect, a quality
  check. A no answer can signal a recycle to the previous
  stage: the project is not ready to move on. Checklists are
  the usual format for these readiness items—for example:

  Is the product definition complete? Yes ☐   No ☐

  Fact based? Signed off by project team? Yes ☐   No ☐

- Must-Meet: These are yes/no or "knock-out" questions
  that include the minimum criteria that a project must meet
  in order to move forward. A single no signals a kill decision.
  Again, checklists are the usual format for must-meet items—
  for example:

  Is the project within our business's mandate? Yes ☐   No ☐

  Does the project meet our policies on values and ethics?
  Yes ☐   No ☐

  Is the project technically feasible (better than 50 percent)?
  Yes ☐   No ☐

- Should-Meet: These are highly desirable project characteristics (so a no on one question won't kill the project). They are
  used to distinguish between superb projects and the minimally
  acceptable ones. These should-meet items are typically in a
  scorecard format (see Chapter 7.2). And the resulting project
  attractiveness score is used to make go/kill decisions and also
  to help prioritize projects at gates.

Using the Gate Criteria. Gate criteria are designed to be used by
the leadership team at the gate meeting. After the project is presented and debated, each criterion is discussed. The readiness-
check and must-meet questions are displayed on a video projector
and debated openly by the gatekeepers. A single consensus no is
enough to kill or recycle the project.

The should-meet questions are best handled on a physical score-card. These criteria are scored by the gatekeepers independently of each other at the gate meeting (paper and pen or computer-assisted scoring). Scores are tallied and displayed (for example, on a video projector) and the differences debated. A consensus go/kill and prioritization decision is reached, and if go, the action plan is approved and resources committed to the project team.

Building In Best Practices: The Key Success Drivers

A number of best practices must be built into the idea-to-launch framework in order to yield superlative results. Many insights have been gained over the years into what makes for successful product innovation. The challenge now is to take all of these lessons learned and integrate them into the Stage-Gate playbook.

Sharper Focus, Better Project Prioritization

Most businesses' new product efforts suffer from a lack of focus: too many projects and not enough resources to execute them well.[8] Adequate resources are a principal driver of businesses' new product performance, but a lack of resources plagues too many development efforts.[9] Sometimes this lack is simply that management has not devoted the needed people and money to the company's new product effort. But often this resource problem stems from trying to do too many projects with a limited set of resources—that is, from a lack of focus, the result of inadequate project evaluations. The root cause of this lack of focus is management's failure to set priorities and make tough go/kill decisions. In short, the gates are weak.

The need is for a new product funnel rather than tunnel. A new product funnel builds in tough go/kill decision points in the form of gates; the poor projects are weeded out; scarce resources are directed toward the truly deserving projects; and more focus is the result (Figure 7.1-3). The expectation is that a certain percentage of projects will be killed at each gate, especially at the earlier ones

FIGURE 7.1-3 A Funnel Leading to a
Tunnel to Weed Out Poor Projects Early

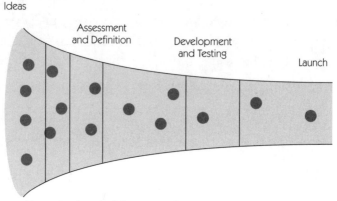

Ideas and projects should be successively screened or culled out at each gate,
leaving only the best projects in the pipeline—a funneling approach. Once into
Development, most of the poor projects have been weeded out, so the funnel
begins to resemble a tunnel.

(gates 1, 2, and 3 in Figure 7.1-1). These gates are thus the bailout
points where the question is, "Are you still in the game?" They are
the quality control checkpoints in the new product process and
check the quality, merit, and progress of the project.

Products with Competitive Advantage: Differentiated Products, Unique Benefits, Superior Value for the Customer

Top-performing businesses build in product superiority at every opportunity, and they look for the "wow!" factor. This is one key to
new product success, yet all too often, when redesigning their new
product processes, too many firms fall into the trap of repeating current, often faulty practices. There's no attempt to seek truly superior products, and so the results are predicable: more ho-hum, tired,
vanilla products that don't make much money.

Here's how to drive the quest for product advantage:

- Ensure that at least some of the criteria at every gate focus
  on product superiority. Questions such as, "Does the product

have at least one element of competitive advantage?" "Does it offer the user new or different benefits?" and "Is it excellent value for money for the user?" become vital questions to rate and rank potential projects.

- Require that certain key customer actions designed to deliver product superiority be included in each stage of the process. Examples are given in the "strong market orientation" item below.

- Demand that project teams deliver evidence of product superiority to gate reviews, and make product superiority an important deliverable and issue at such gate meetings.

Exemplary Quality of Execution

A common theme throughout the Stage-Gate process is the emphasis on quality of execution: doing it right the first time. The argument that the proponents of Total Quality Management make is this: The definition of quality is precise: It means meeting all the requirements all the time. It is based on the principle that all work is a process. It focuses on improving business processes to eliminate errors.[10] The concept is perfectly logical and essentially simple, and the same logic can be applied to new product development.

A quality-of-execution crisis exists, however, in the product innovation process. Figure 7.1-4 shows assessments of sample activities from idea generation through to the postlaunch review. Note how poorly most are executed (the gray bars). For example, only 19 percent of businesses undertake effective idea generation, only 18 percent do a first-rate job on the market research, and only 26 percent do business case development well.[11] Note also how much better the top-performing businesses execute these activities (the black versus white bars). For example, 57 percent of top-performing businesses do excellent market research in new product projects; by contrast, only 23 percent of poor performers do excellent market research. Similar differences are noted for most of the activities in the figure.

FIGURE 7.1.4 Quality of Execution of Key Activities: Impact on Performance

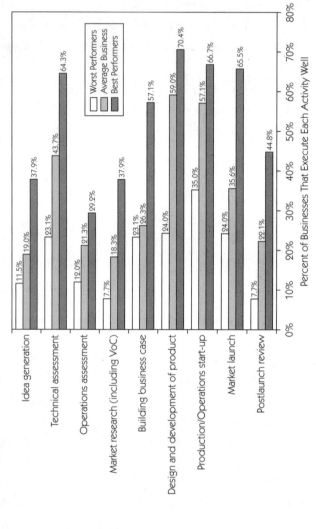

Note: This shows that 19 percent of businesses do an excellent job on idea generation. This is a key but weak activity. Note that 37.9 percent of best performers (and only 11.5 percent of poor performers) handle idea generation proficiently.

Source: American Productivity and Quality Center, *New Product Development Best Practices Study: What Distinguishes the Top Performers* (Houston: American Productivity and Quality Center, 2002).

Clearly there is a need for a more systematic and quality approach to the way firms conceive, develop, and launch new products. The way to deal with the quality-of-execution problem is to visualize product innovation as a process and apply process management and quality management techniques to this process. Note that any process in business can be managed, and managed with a view to quality. Get the details of the process right, practice discipline to the process, and the result will be a high-quality output.

A Strong Market Orientation with Voice-of-Customer Inputs

If positive new product performance is the goal, then a market orientation (executing the key marketing activities in a quality fashion) must be built into the new product process as a matter of routine rather than by exception. Marketing inputs must play a decisive role from the beginning to the end of the project. Here are six best-practice marketing actions that should be built into an idea-to-launch process:

- Customer-focused ideation to gain insights into customer problems
- Preliminary market assessment in the very early phases of the new product project to assess the market opportunity
- Voice-of-customer research to identify unmet or unarticulated needs, that is, what the winning new product must be and do
- Competitive product analysis, that is, figuring out what competitors' strategy is and how to beat them
- Value-in-use analysis to determine the economic value of the product to the customer or user
- Concept and *protocept* tests, preference tests and trial sells, that is, constant iterations with customers from Stage 1 through to launch using a series of build-test-and-redo loops or spirals

In order for these marketing actions to be undertaken proficiently, adequate marketing resources must available to project teams; often these are noticeably absent on project teams. Note that much more marketing and sales resources and people are available to new product project teams in top-performing businesses according to the APQC study.[12]

Better Up-Front Homework and Sharp, Early, and Stable Product Definition

New product success or failure is largely decided in the first few plays of the game—in those crucial steps and tasks that precede the actual development of the product. The up-front homework defines the product and builds the business case for development. The ideal new product process ensures that these early stages are carried out and that the product is fully defined before the project is allowed to become a full-fledged development project.

The need for solid upfront homework parallels the case for a stronger market orientation. Top performers ensure that the new product process does indeed include solid homework (Stages 1 and 2 in Figure 7.1-1) and stable, fact-based product definition. For example, they build in a product definition check point at Gate 3 in the process. And they halt projects if the homework and product definition aren't in place.

A True Cross-Functional Team Approach

The new product process is cross-functional: it requires the inputs and active participation of players from many different functions in the organization. The multifunctional nature of innovation coupled with the desire for parallel processing means that a cross-functional team approach is mandatory. It has these essential ingredients:

- A cross-functional team with committed players from the different functional areas

- A defined team captain or leader, championing the entire project from beginning to end and with formal authority (co-opting authority from the functional heads)

- A fluid team structure, with new members joining or dropped as work requirements demand

- A small core group of responsible and committed team players from beginning to end

- Most important, a team that is accountable for the entire project's end results (not just team members responsible for their part of the project)

A Fast-Paced Game Plan via Parallel Processing

These new product teams face a dilemma. On the one hand, they are urged by senior management to compress the cycle time: that is, to shorten the elapsed time from idea to launch. On the other hand, they are urged to improve the effectiveness of product development: cut down the failure rate: to do it right, which suggests a more thorough, longer process.

Parallel processing is one solution to the need for a complete and quality process, yet one that meets the time pressures of today's fast-paced business world. Traditionally, new product projects have been managed using a series approach: one task strung out after another in sequence. The analogy is that of a relay race, with each department running with the project for its 100-meter lap. Phrases such as "handoff" or "passing the project on," and even "dropping the ball" or "throwing it over the wall," are common in this relay race approach to new products.

In marked contrast to the relay race or sequential approach, with parallel processing many activities are undertaken concurrently rather than in series. The appropriate analogy is that of a rugby match rather than a relay race.[13] A team (not a single runner) appears on the field. A scrum or huddle ensues, after which the ball emerges. Players run down the field in parallel with much interaction, constantly passing the ball laterally. After 25 meters or so, the players converge for another scrum, huddle, or gate review, followed by another stage of activities.

With parallel processing, the game is far more intense than a relay race and more work gets done in an elapsed time period: three or four activities are done simultaneously and by different members on the project team. Second, there is less chance that an activity or task will be overlooked or handled poorly because of lack of time: the activity is done in parallel, not in series, and hence does not extend the total elapsed project time. Moreover, the activities are designed to feed each other (the metaphor of the ball being passed back and forth across the field). And finally, the entire new product process becomes cross-functional and multidisciplinary. The whole team—marketing, R&D, engineering, sales, manufacturing—is on the field together, participates actively in each play, and takes part in every gate review or scrum.

An Efficient Process with Time Wasters Removed

The idea-to-launch framework must be built for speed. This means eliminating all the time wasters and work that add no value in the current new product process. Go through the process end to end and look at every required procedure, form to be filled out, or paperwork that must completed. There's probably a lot of unnecessary work that does not add any value to anyone. If it does not add value, get rid of it. And look at every committee that must sit and review projects or facets of projects. Again, if they're not really needed, get rid of them.

A Dynamic, Flexible, and Scalable Process

The idea-to-launch framework must be flexible and dynamic, responsive to changing conditions and varying circumstance of projects. It cannot be a rigid, lockstep process. Smart companies have built maneuvers into their processes in the interest of flexibility and speed:

- Ask the project team to map out the best path forward for their project, using the standard process as a guide, but not every stage activity or gate deliverable is mandatory.

- Permit combining gates and collapsing stages, or even going back to a previous gate or stage (see Stage-Gate Express later in this chapter).

- Move long-lead-time items forward (for example, instead of awaiting a specific gate approval to order production equipment, certain long-lead-time items can be ordered in advance as long as the risk is recognized).

- Allow overlapping stages. A project team can begin the next stage before the entrance gate even occurs (although taking this practice too far can lead to chaos).

- Use self-managed gates, where the project team makes its own gate decisions rather than wait for senior management to call a meeting.

- Allow fuzzy gates or conditional gates, where projects can be moved ahead conditional on certain future events or future information.[14]

In addition, recognize that not all development projects are the same size and risk. Lower-risk projects do not need all the activities and stages that higher-risk ones do.

Performance Metrics in Place

The idea-to-launch framework must feature solid performance metrics, so that senior management can assess how well new product development and the process is working, and, most important, so that project teams are held accountable for results. According to the APQC study, putting metrics in place is indeed a best practice with a strong positive impact, a distinguishing feature of top-performing businesses.[15]

How does one establish new product performance metrics? For individual new product projects, success metrics often include:

- First-year sales (versus the sales forecast in the business case at Gate 3)
- Product profitability (for example, NPV) versus that forecast in the business case
- On-time performance: actual versus promised launch date[16]

Top performers build in a postlaunch review point twelve to eighteen months after launch, as in Figure 7.1-1, where these metrics are used to gauge the ultimate success of the project. Here the project's actual results are assessed versus those results promised back when the project was approved at Gate 3. In addition, sales, profits, and on-time performance results for individual projects can be aggregated or averaged to yield performance metrics for the business's entire new product effort.

A Walk Through the Stage-Gate Framework: Idea to Launch

Now that the key success drivers have been identified, let's have a more detailed look at the Stage-Gate framework—what's involved at each stage and gate. Let's do a walk-through of the model, stage by stage, as in Figure 7.1-1.

Discovery Stage

Ideas are the feedstock or trigger to the process, and they make or break the process. Don't expect a superb new product process to overcome a shortage of good new product ideas. The need for great ideas coupled with high attrition rate of ideas means that the idea generation stage is pivotal: the goal is great ideas and lots of them!

Many companies consider ideation so important that they handle this as a formal stage in the process, called Discovery. They build in a defined, proactive idea generation and capture system (Figure 7.1-5). Ideas are fed to a focal person, who then gets a decision at

FIGURE 7.1-5 A System for Idea Capture and Handling

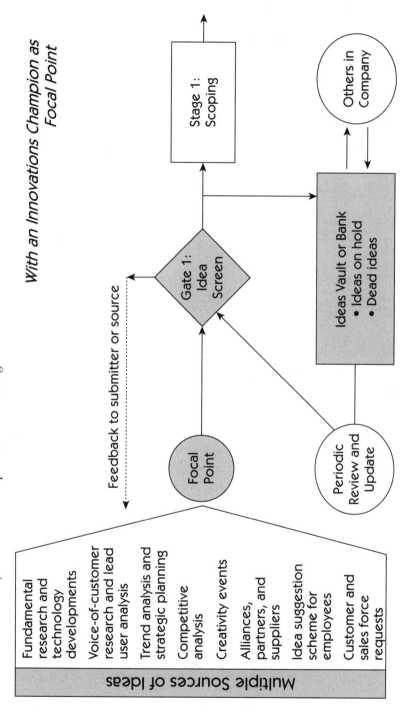

With an Innovations Champion as Focal Point

Gate 1. Go or kill ideas are archived in an idea vault, while teams are assigned go ideas to move forward into Stage 1.

Many activities can be built into the Discovery stage in order to stimulate the creation of great new product ideas. Such activities include undertaking fundamental but directed technical research, seeking new technological possibilities, working with lead or innovative users[17] or undertaking product value analysis with customers,[18] using voice-of-customer research to capture unarticulated needs and customer problems,[19] competitive analysis and reverse-brainstorming competitive products, installing an idea suggestion scheme to stimulate ideas from your own employees, and using your strategic planning exercise to uncover disruptions, gaps and opportunities in the marketplace.

Gate 1: Idea Screen

Idea screening is the first decision to commit resources to the project. The project is born at this point. If the decision is go, the project moves into the scoping or preliminary investigation stage. Thus, Gate 1 signals a preliminary but tentative commitment to the project: a flickering green light.

Gate 1 is a "gentle screen" and amounts to subjecting the project to a handful of key must-meet and should-meet criteria. Finan-

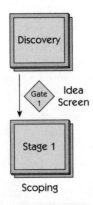

cial criteria are typically not part of this first screen, since relatively little reliable financial data is available here. A checklist for the must-meet criteria and a scorecard or scoring model (point count rating scales) for the should-meet criteria are used to help focus the discussion and rank projects in this early screen.

Stage 1: Scoping

This first and inexpensive homework stage has the objective of determining the project's technical and marketplace merits. Stage 1 is a quick scoping of the project, involving desk research or detective work; little or no primary research is done here. Stage 1 is often done in less than one calendar month's elapsed time and five to ten person-days' work effort.

A preliminary market assessment is one facet of Stage 1 and involves a variety of relatively inexpensive activities: an Internet search; a library search; contacts with key users, distributors, and salespeople; a survey of competitors' Web pages or literature; focus groups; and even a quick concept test with a handful of potential users. The purpose is to determine market size, market potential, and likely market acceptance and also to begin to shape the product concept.

Concurrently a preliminary technical assessment is carried out, involving a quick and preliminary in-house appraisal of the proposed product. The purpose is to assess development and manufacturing routes (or source of supply), technical and manufacturing/operations feasibility, possible times and costs to execute, and technical, legal, and regulatory risks and roadblocks.

Stage 1 thus provides for the gathering of both market and technical information, at a low cost and in a short time, to enable a cursory and first-pass financial and business analysis as input to Gate 2. Because of the limited effort and depending on the size of the project, very often Stage 1 can be handled by a team of a few people, usually from marketing and from a technical group.

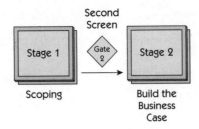

Gate 2: Second Screen

The project next proceeds to a second and somewhat more rigorous screen at Gate 2. This gate is essentially a repeat of Gate 1: the project is reevaluated in the light of the new information obtained in Stage 1. If the decision is go at this point, the project moves into a heavier spending stage.

At Gate 2, the project is subjected to a list of readiness check questions and also a set of must-meet and should-meet criteria similar to those used at Gate 1. Here additional should-meet criteria may be considered, dealing with sales force and customer reaction to the proposed product and potential legal, technical, and regulatory "killer variables," the result of new data gathered during Stage 1. Again, a checklist and scoring model facilitate this gate decision. The financial return is assessed at Gate 2, but only by a quick and simple financial calculation (for example, the payback period).

Stage 2: Build the Business Case

The business case is constructed in Stage 2, a detailed investigation stage that clearly defines the product and verifies the attractiveness of the project prior to heavy spending. It is also the critical homework stage, which is so often weakly handled.

Stage 2 sees voice-of-customer research undertaken to determine the customer's needs, wants, and preferences, that is, to help define a superior, differentiated, and winning new product. Competitive analysis is also a part of this stage. Another market activity is concept testing. A representation of the proposed new product is presented to potential customers, their reactions are gauged, and the likely customer acceptance of the new product is determined.

A detailed technical appraisal at Stage 2 focuses on the technical feasibility of the project. That is, the customer needs and "wish list" are translated into a technically and economically feasible solution on paper. This translation might even involve some preliminary design or laboratory work, but it should not be construed as a full-fledged development project. A manufacturing (or operations) appraisal is often a part of building the business case, where issues of manufacturability, source of supply, costs to manufacture, and investment required are investigated. If appropriate, detailed legal, patent, and regulatory assessment work is undertaken in order to remove risks and map out the required actions.

Finally, a detailed business and financial analysis is conducted as part of the justification facet of the business case. The financial analysis typically involves a net present value (NPV) calculation, complete with sensitivity analysis to look at possible downside risks.

The result of Stage 2 is a business case for the project: the product definition, a key to success, is agreed to, and a thorough project justification and detailed project plan are developed.

Stage 2 involves considerably more effort than Stage 1 and requires the inputs from a variety of sources. Stage 2 is best handled by a team consisting of cross-functional members, the core group of the eventual project team.

Gate 3: Go to Development

This is the final gate prior to the development stage, the last point at which the project can be killed before entering heavy spending. Once past Gate 3, financial commitments are substantial. In effect, Gate 3 means "go to a heavy spend." Gate 3 also yields a sign-off of the product and project definition. Because of the substantial resource commitments here, Gate 3 is usually staffed by the leadership team of the business for major projects.

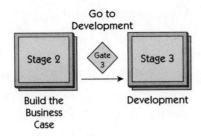

This Gate 3 evaluation involves a review of each of the activities in Stage 2, checking that the activities were undertaken, the quality of execution was sound, and the results were positive. Next, Gate 3 subjects the project once again to the set of readiness-check, must-meet, and should-meet criteria similar to those used at Gate 2. Finally, because a heavy spending commitment is the result of a go decision at Gate 3, the results of the financial analysis are an important part of this screen.

If the decision is go, Gate 3 sees commitment to the product definition and agreement on the project plan that charts the path forward. The development plan and the preliminary operations and market launch plans are reviewed and approved at this gate. The full project team—an empowered, cross-functional team headed by a leader with authority—is designated.

Stage 3: Development

Stage 3 witnesses the implementation of the development plan and the physical development of the product. Lab tests, in-house tests, or alpha tests ensure that the product meets requirements under controlled conditions. Also, the production, operations, or source-of-supply process is mapped out.

For lengthy projects, numerous milestones and periodic project reviews are built into the development plan. These are not gates per se: go/kill decisions are not made here. Rather, these milestone check points provide for project control and management. Extensive in-house testing, alpha tests, or lab testing usually occurs at this stage as well. The deliverable at the end of Stage 3 is a lab-tested or alpha prototype of the product.

The emphasis in Stage 3 is on technical work, but marketing and operations activities also proceed in parallel. For example, market analysis and customer feedback work continue concurrently with the technical development, with constant customer opinion sought on the product as it takes shape during development. These activities are back-and-forth or iterative, with each development result (for example, rapid prototype, working model, first prototype) taken to the customer for assessment and feedback: spiral or iterative development. Meanwhile, detailed test plans, market launch plans, and production or operations plans, including production facilities requirements, are developed. An updated financial analysis is prepared, while regulatory, legal, and patent issues are resolved.

Gate 4: Go to Testing

This postdevelopment gate is a check on the progress and the continued attractiveness of the product and project. Development work is reviewed and checked, ensuring that the work has been completed in a quality fashion and that the developed product is consistent with the original definition specified at Gate 3.

This gate also revisits the economic question using a revised financial analysis based on new and more accurate data. The test or validation plans for the next stage are approved for immediate implementation, and the detailed market launch and operations plans are reviewed for probable future execution.

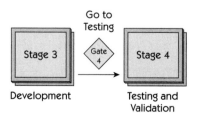

Stage 4: Testing and Validation

This stage tests and validates the entire viability of the project: the product itself, the production process, customer acceptance, and the economics of the project. It also begins extensive external validation of the product and project. A number of activities are undertaken at Stage 4:

- In-house product tests: Extended lab tests or alpha tests to check on product quality and product performance under controlled or lab conditions

- User, preference, or field trials of the product: To verify that the product functions under actual use conditions and also to gauge potential customers' reactions to the product and establish purchase intent

- Trial, limited, or pilot production/operations: To test, debug, and prove the production or operations process and to determine more precise production costs and throughputs

- Pretest market, test market, or trial sell: To gauge customer reaction, measure the effectiveness of the launch plan, and determine expected market share and revenues

- Revised business and financial analysis: To check on the continued business and economic viability of the project, based on new and more accurate revenue and cost data

Sometimes Stage 4 yields negative results, and it's back to Stage 3.

Gate 5: Go to Launch

This final gate opens the door to full commercialization: market launch and full production or operations start-up. It is the final point at which the project can still be killed. This gate focuses on the quality of the activities in the testing and validation stage and their results. Criteria for passing the gate focus largely on the expected financial return, the project's readiness for launch, and the

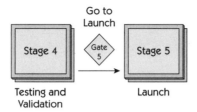

appropriateness of the launch and operations start-up plans. The operations and market launch plans are reviewed and approved for implementation in Stage 5.

Stage 5: Launch

This final stage involves implementing both the market launch plan and the production or operations plan. Production equipment is acquired, installed and commissioned (sometimes this is done earlier in Stage 4, as part of the Stage 4 production trials); the logistics pipeline is filled; and selling begins. Barring any unforeseen events, it should be clear sailing for the new product—another new product winner!

Postlaunch Review

Two postlaunch reviews are typical. The first, an interim review, occurs about two to four months after launch, when initial launch results are available. Here, a postaudit is done while the details of the project are still fresh in team members' minds. This postaudit assesses the project's strengths and weaknesses, identifies what can be learned from the project, and provides key learnings on how to do the next project even better. In addition, interim commercial results (initial sales and production costs, for example) are reviewed, and needed course corrections are made.

The final review is held once the project is stable and commercial results are known, typically twelve to eighteen months into market. Here the project team is disbanded, and the product becomes a

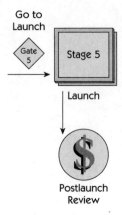

"regular product" in the firm's product line. This is also the point where the project and product's performance is reviewed. The latest data on revenues, costs, expenditures, profits, and timing is compared to projections made at Gates 3 and 5 to gauge performance. Project team accountability is a central issue here: Did the team deliver the results it promised or forecast? This review marks the end of the project. Note that the project team and leader remain responsible for the success of the project through this postlaunch period, right up to the point of the postlaunch review.

Stage-Gate Express for Lower-Risk Projects

Stage-Gate frameworks are scalable, with different versions to handle different types of projects. The full-fledged Stage-Gate model in Figure 7.1-1 is designed for larger, higher-risk new product projects with much at stake and many unknowns. But many projects are much smaller than this. They include product modifications, extensions, improvements, simple sales requests, and single-customer projects. Forcing such smaller projects through the full five-stage model only creates frustration, unneeded work, and the impression of added bureaucracy, a sure way to cause people to circumvent an otherwise excellent framework.

When the project risk is low, use an abbreviated version of Stage-Gate: the three-stage Stage-Gate Express framework in Figure 7.1-6.[20] Here's how the three-stage version works:

- Stages 1 and 2 in Figure 7.1-1 are combined into a single "homework" stage. The usual Stage 1 activities are then merged with Stage 2 tasks. In lower-risk projects, often much of the needed information is readily available, and so the work effort required for the homework phase in Stage-Gate Express is considerably less than in the full five-stage process.

- Stage 3 (Development) is merged with Stage 4 (Testing and Validation) in Figure 7.1-1. The project team reviews the activities normally undertaken in Stages 3 and 4 and decides which are relevant to the smaller project and which should be omitted or abbreviated.

- Because stages are combined, Gates 2 and 4 are eliminated (often the project team conducts a "self-check" or "self-managed gate" prior to moving ahead).

The result is a fast-track process suitable to facilitate product development for low-risk projects.

Stage-Gate for Technology and Platform Developments

Technology development or technology platform projects promise to open up new strategic opportunities to the business.[21] A limited number of businesses that engage in such innovative developments have successfully employed a different type of Stage-Gate process to drive these special projects through to fruition. ExxonMobil Chemicals has even published a synopsis of its special process to handle the company's technology projects.[22]

FIGURE 7.1-6 Stage-Gate Express: A Three-Stage Version for Lower-Risk Projects

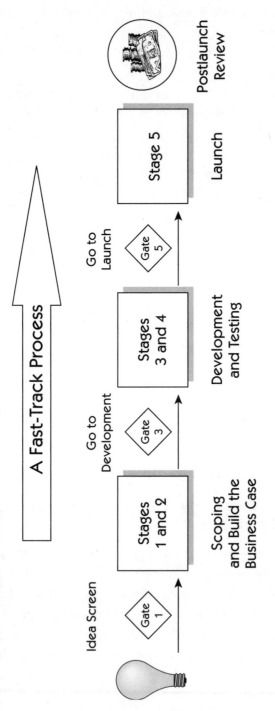

Stage-Gate® Express is for lower-risk, simpler projects: line extensions, product improvements, product modifications. A two-stage version can be used for single and simple customer requests.

Source: R. G. Cooper, *Winning at New Products: Accelerating the Process from Idea to Launch*, 3rd ed. (Reading, Mass.: Perseus Books, 2001).

First, here are some definitions:

- Technology development (TD) projects are those where the deliverable is new knowledge and a technological capability (also called "science projects" and "fundamental" or "basic research projects"). This new capability or new knowledge may spawn a number of specific new product projects (and thus may overlap with the notion of a platform project—a technology platform). When the TD project begins, there may be no specific new product (or new manufacturing process) well defined. Rather, the scientist initiates some experiments with the hope of finding some technical possibilities and discoveries that might yield ideas for commercial products or processes.

- Disruptive technologies and radical innovations yield projects that are a special subcategory of technology developments What is a disruptive technology? Most new technologies result in improved performance, which can come from incremental innovations or from those that are more radical in character. Most technological advances in industry are sustaining, but "occasionally disruptive technologies emerge: innovations that result in worse performance, at least in the near term."[23] These innovations may be inferior to the existing technology when measured on traditional performance metrics, but they bring a new performance dimension or a new value proposition to the market. For example, the first digital cameras produced a poorer picture (lower resolution) than traditional 35mm film cameras and were considered inferior products by most camera users. But for a handful of users, most notably those who wanted the picture in digital format so that they could modify or electronically transmit the photo, such as real estate agents, there was new value in the digital camera.

- Platform projects are defined in the PDMA handbook to be "design and components that are shared by a set of products in a product family. From this platform, numerous derivatives can be designed."[24] Thus, Chrysler's engine transmission from its K-car was a platform that spawned other vehicles, including the famous Chrysler minivan.

The notion of platforms has since been broadened to include technological capabilities. For example, ExxonMobil's Metallocene platform is simply a catalyst that has yielded an entirely new generation of polymers. Thus, a platform is like an oil drilling platform in the ocean, which you invest heavily in. From this platform, you can drill many holes relatively quickly and at low cost. Thus, the platform establishes the capability, and this capability spawns many new product projects much more quickly and cost-effectively than starting from scratch each time. A platform project could be based on a new technology or a technology development (above) and is called a *technology platform project*.

The main difference between these and a typical new product project, for which Stage-Gate in Figure 7.1-1 is designed, is that technology and platform developments are often much broader, more vaguely defined, and more difficult to predict at the outset than is the typical new product project. For example, in a technology development project designed to ultimately yield new products, it may take months of technical research before it's even clear what might be technically possible. So undertaking a market analysis in Stage 1 in Figure 7.1-1 and detailed market studies in Stage 2 makes little sense because the product hasn't even been defined or characterized. And the criteria for project selection are clearly different here than they are for a very tangible, well-defined new product project simply because so little is known about the commercial possibilities early in the life of such projects.

Stage-Gate-TD

The methodology for handling such technology platform and technology developments is shown in Figure 7.1-7. The method is called *Stage-Gate-TD*, where "TD" stands for "technology development." The top part of the schematic shows the three stages of the process:

1. Scoping: A relatively inexpensive stage involving literature search, secondary research, and detective work. Its purpose is to lay the foundation and define the scope of the project.

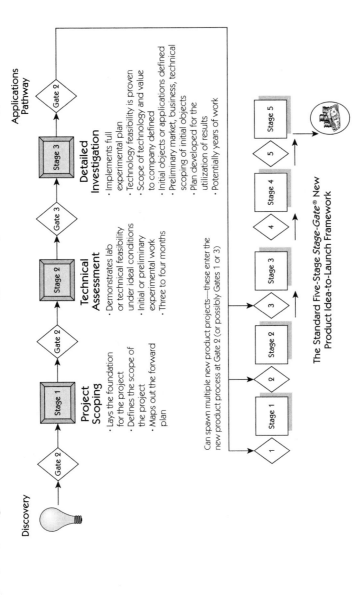

Discovery

Gate 2

Project Scoping
· Lays the foundation for the project
· Defines the scope of the project
· Maps out the forward plan

Gate 2

Technical Assessment
· Demonstrates lab or technical feasibility under ideal conditions
· Initial or preliminary experimental work
· Three to four months

Gate 3

Detailed Investigation
· Implements full experimental plan
· Technology feasibility is proven
· Scope of technology and value to company defined
· Initial objects or applications defined
· Preliminary market, business, technical scoping of initial objects
· Plan developed for the utilization of results
· Potentially years of work

Applications Pathway

Gate 2

Can spawn multiple new product projects—these enter the new product process at Gate 2 (or possibly Gates 1 or 3)

The Standard Five-Stage *Stage-Gate*® New Product Idea-to-Launch Framework

Source: R. G. Cooper, *Winning at New Products: Accelerating the Process from Idea to Launch*, 3rd ed. (Reading, Mass.: Perseus Books, 2001).

2. Technical assessment: A more extensive stage designed to demonstrate technical feasibility—in other words, that something is worth pursuing further.

3. Detailed investigation: The full experimental effort to take the technology to the point where you can start working on specific new product projects or perhaps on a new manufacturing process. During this stage, commercial possibilities (for example, some possible new products) are identified and defined, and preliminary market and business analyses are conducted on each.

The Applications Pathway gate is where senior management meets to decide what do with this new technology or capability. Very often, multiple new product projects are defined, which then enter the standard five-stage Stage-Gate framework (across the bottom of Figure 7.1-7) at Gate 1, 2, or 3, depending on how far along and how defined the project already is.

The TD gates are similar to those in the traditional Stage-Gate framework, except that the gatekeepers usually include a strong contingent of technology people, as well as senior people from key businesses within the corporation, that is, businesses where this new technology will eventually be commercialized. Readiness-check, must-meet and should-meet questions (in the form of a scorecard) are used to focus the discussions and make more effective go/kill decisions, but the specific criteria are different from those in the gates of a regular process in Figure 7.1-1.[25]

Some Tips on Implementing Stage-Gate

Designing and successfully implementing a Stage-Gate framework is no small task. When it is done well, the rewards are significant: faster to market by about 30 percent, higher success rates, and more projects on time and on target.

To achieve these enviable results, an investment is required. Let's assume that the business's leadership team has decided to move forward and implement a Stage-Gate framework for new products (or perhaps for technology developments). Step 1 is preparatory (see Figure 7.1-8 for a step-by-step approach to implementing a Stage-Gate framework). First, establish a cross-functional, cross-business task force with strong leadership and executive sponsors in place. Next, find out what's working and what needs fixing in the current product development methods: conduct an audit of the current process; do some retrospective reviews of recent past projects to find out how well or poorly they were handled; hold some town hall meetings to better understand the problems and challenges faced by product developers in the organization; and do some internal and external benchmarking (including a solid literature search).[26] Most firms get some outside help and expertise so that they don't repeat many of the same mistakes that slowed other businesses down in their efforts to adopt a Stage-Gate framework.

FIGURE 7.1-8 Key Steps in Implementing
a Stage-Gate New Product Framework

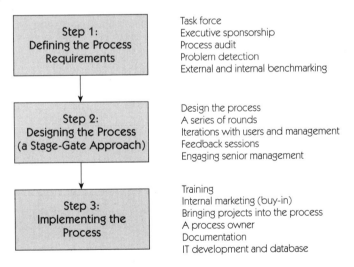

Source: R. G. Cooper, *Winning at New Products: Accelerating the Process from Idea to Launch*, 3rd ed. (Reading, Mass.: Perseus Books, 2001).

Step 2 is the physical design of the Stage-Gate framework (Figure 7.1-8). This step usually proceeds in a series of off-site meetings, whereby the task force crafts the process stage-by-stage and gate-by-gate. Note that multiple iterations of the process are developed, and each should be tested with the user community within the business. Often what the task force thought was an excellent model receives anything but rave reviews from the potential user group. So seek feedback many times in an iterative design effort, and build the feedback into the proposed Stage-Gate framework. Some task forces shorten this step considerably by purchasing an off-the-shelf version of Stage-Gate such as SG-Navigator™.[27]

The final step, implementation, is by far the most difficult and time-intensive. Figure 7.1-8 lists the many activities that firms undertake when implementing Stage-Gate. The challenge here is to get people in the organization, from senior executives on down, to understand, support, and live the process. Here are the key actions:

- Assign a process manager to shepherd the process and its implementation. This person and position is key. No process, no matter how clever, ever implemented itself.

- Train everyone from the gatekeepers through to junior technicians. Although the newly developed process may seem simple to the task force that designed it, the process is quite foreign to everyone else in the company. Don't underestimate the communication and training job required here.

- Get existing projects into the process fast. Don't sit around for months waiting for new projects to enter Gate 1. Instead, shoe-horn existing projects into the new process right away. Better yet, as soon as the task force starts designing the process (Step 2 in Figure 7.1-8), start piloting some existing projects.

- Develop user-friendly documentation, and put an IT support system in place. IT helps users adopt, use, and embrace the process quickly (there are many solid IT support tools around, such as the Accolade™ and SG-Navigator™ decision support systems).[28]

Doing It Right

Product innovation is one of the most important endeavors of the modern corporation. The message from both Wall Street and Main Street is "innovate or die!" Customers as well as shareholders seek a steady stream of innovative new products. Customers want innovative products because they demand value for money, and shareholders seek the organic and profitable growth that innovations provide. Without a systematic new product process, however, the product innovation effort often is a shambles—a chaotic, hit-and-miss affair. The Stage-Gate framework is an enabler or guide, building in best practices and ensuring that key activities and decisions are done better and faster. But Stage-Gate is considerably more complex than the simple diagram in Figure 7.1-1 suggests; there are many intricacies in the details—both the "what's" and the "how-to's." And implementing the process is also a major challenge. Many leading companies nevertheless have taken the necessary step and designed and implemented a world-class idea-to-launch Stage-Gate framework, and the results have been positive: better, faster and more profitable new product developments.

Robert G. Cooper is professor of marketing at the School of Business, McMaster University in Ontario, Canada, and ISBM Distinguished Research Fellow at Penn State University's Smeal College of Business Administration. He is the father and developer of the Stage-Gate process, now widely used around the world to drive new products to market. He is a prolific researcher and thought leader in the field of product innovation management, with more than ninety articles in leading journals on new product management and six books.

7.2

Portfolio Management for Product Innovation

Robert G. Cooper

Much like a stock market portfolio manager, senior executives who manage to optimize their R&D investments will win in the long run.[1] Management in successful businesses in product innovation focuses resources on the right arenas, select winning new product projects, and strive for the ideal balance and mix of projects. That is what portfolio management is all about: resource allocation and investment decisions to achieve the business's new product objectives.

Portfolio Management Defined

Portfolio management is formally defined as a dynamic decision process, whereby a business's list of active new product (and development) projects is constantly updated and revised. In this process, new projects are evaluated, selected, and prioritized; existing projects may be accelerated, killed, or deprioritized; and resources are allocated and reallocated to ac-

This chapter is based on R. G. Cooper, *Product Leadership: Pathways to Profitable Innovation*, 2nd ed. (Reading, Mass.: Perseus Books, 2005); R. G. Cooper, S. J. Edgett, and E. J. Kleinschmidt, *Portfolio Management for New Products*, 2nd ed. (Reading, Mass: Perseus Books, 2002); and R. G. Cooper, *Winning at New Products: Accelerating the Process from Idea to Launch*, 3rd ed. (Reading, Mass: Perseus Books, 2001).

tive projects. The portfolio decision process is characterized by uncertain and changing information, dynamic opportunities, multiple goals and strategic considerations, interdependence among projects, and multiple decision makers and locations.[2]

The portfolio decision process encompasses or overlaps a number of decision-making processes within the business, including periodic reviews of the total portfolio of all projects (looking at all projects holistically and against each other), making go/kill decisions on individual projects on an ongoing basis, and developing a new product strategy for the business, complete with strategic resource allocation decisions.

New product portfolio management sounds like a fairly mechanistic exercise of decision making and resource allocation. But there are many unique facets of the problem that make it perhaps the most challenging decision making faced by the modern corporation in business today:

- New product portfolio management deals with future events and opportunities; thus, much of the information required to make project selection decisions is at best uncertain and at worst very unreliable.

- The decision environment is a highly dynamic one. The status of and prospects for projects in the portfolio are ever changing as markets change and new information becomes available.

- Projects in the portfolio are at different stages of completion, yet all projects compete against each other for resources, so comparisons must be made between projects with different amounts and quality of information.

- Resources to be allocated across projects are limited. A decision to fund one project may mean that resources must be taken away from another, and resource transfers between projects are not totally seamless.

The Importance of Portfolio Management

Portfolio management and the prioritization of new product projects is a critical management task. Roussel, Saad, and Erickson claim in their widely read book that "portfolio analysis and planning will grow to become the powerful tool that business portfolio planning became in the 1970s and 1980s."[3]

Here's why portfolio management, that is, the ability to pick the right projects and make the right investments, is vital to winning the product innovation war.

First, a successful product innovation effort is fundamental to business success. This logically translates into portfolio management: the ability to select today's projects that will become tomorrow's new product winners.

Second, new product development is the manifestation of the business's strategy. One of the most important ways of implementing strategy is through the new products one develops. If the business's new product initiatives are wrong—the wrong projects or the wrong balance—then it fails at implementing its business strategy.

Third, portfolio management is about resource allocation. In a business world preoccupied with value to the shareholder and doing more with less, technology and marketing resources are simply too scarce to allocate to the wrong projects. The consequences of poor portfolio management are evident: scarce resources are squandered on the wrong projects, and as a result, the truly deserving ones are starved.

Specific reasons for the importance of portfolio management, cited by managers in a survey of 205 firms and derived from a best practices portfolio study, are set out in Exhibit 7.2-1.[4]

There are essentially three main goals that an effective portfolio management system should achieve. Management should set its sights on at least some of these goals (according to benchmarking results, very few companies achieve all three):

EXHIBIT 7.2-1 Key Reasons That Portfolio Management
Is a Vital Management Task

1. Financial—to maximize return, maximize R&D productivity, and achieve financial goals.

2. To maintain the competitive position of the business—to increase sales and market share.

3. To properly and efficiently allocate scarce resources.

4. To forge the link between project selection and business strategy. The portfolio is the expression of strategy; it must support the strategy.

5. To achieve focus—not doing too many projects for the limited resources available and providing resources for the great projects.

6. To achieve balance—the right balance between long- and short-term projects, and high-risk and low-risk ones, consistent with the business's goals.

7. To better communicate priorities within the organization vertically and horizontally.

8. To provide better objectivity in project selection and weed out bad projects.

Source: R. G. Cooper, S. J. Edgett, and E. J. Kleinschmidt, "New Product Portfolio Management: Practices and Performance," *Journal of Product Innovation Management,* 1999, *16,* 333–351; and R. G. Cooper, S. J. Edgett, and E. J. Kleinschmidt, "Portfolio Management for New Product Development: Results of an Industry Practices Study," *R&D Management,* 2001, *31,* 361–380.

- *To ensure strategic alignment.* The main goal here is to ensure that regardless of all other considerations, the final portfolio of projects truly reflects the business's strategy: that all projects are on strategy, support the strategy, or are critical components of the strategy; and that the breakdown of spending across projects, areas, markets is directly tied to the business strategy (for example, to areas of strategic focus that management has previously delineated).

- *To maximize the value of the portfolio.* Here the goal is to allocate resources so as to maximize the value of the portfolio for a given spending level. That is, one selects projects so as to maximize the sum of the values or commercial worths of all active projects in the pipeline in terms of some business objective, such as NPV (net present value), EVA (earned value analysis), return on investment, likelihood of success, or some other strategic objective).

- *To seek the right balance of projects.* The goal of seeking the right balance flows logically from the first goal, strategic alignment. Here the principal concern is to achieve the desired balance of projects in terms of a number of parameters—for example, the right balance in terms of long-term projects versus short-term ones or high-risk versus lower-risk projects and across various markets, technologies, product categories, and project types (for example, new products, improvements, cost reductions, maintenance and fixes, and fundamental research).

Although the focus here is on portfolio management for new products, because technology resources used in new products are also required for other types of projects, portfolio management also includes process developments, extensions and modifications, cost reduction projects, platform developments, and even fundamental research projects.

Strategic Portfolio Management

Portfolio management and resource allocation can be treated as a hierarchical process, with two levels of decision making. This hierarchical approach simplifies the decision challenge somewhat (see Figure 7.2-1):[5]

- **Level 1: Strategic portfolio management.** Strategic portfolio decisions answer the question, "Directionally, where should the business spend its new product development resources (people and funds)?" How should resources be split across projects types, markets,

FIGURE 7.2-1   The Portfolio Management System and Its Elements: The Two Levels of Decision Making

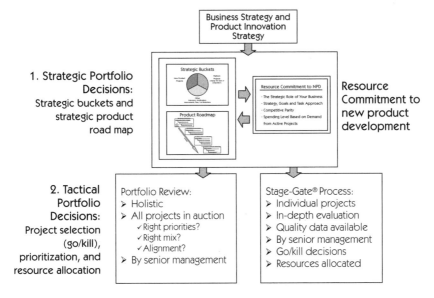

Source: R. G. Cooper, *Product Leadership: Pathways to Profitable Innovation*, 2nd ed. (Reading, Mass: Perseus Books, 2005).

technologies, or product categories? And on what major initiatives or new platforms should the business concentrate its resources? Establishing strategic buckets and defining strategic product road maps are effective tools.

• **Level 2: Tactical portfolio decisions (individual project selection).** Tactical portfolio decisions focus on individual projects but obviously follow from the strategic decisions. They address the question, "What specific new product projects should the business undertake?" Such decisions are shown at the bottom part of Figure 7.2-1.

The Strategic Product Road Map

The product road map is a strategically driven resource allocation method (middle right part of Figure 7.2-1). This top-down approach is designed to ensure that the list of projects (at least the major ones) contributes to or is essential for the realization of the business's strategy and goals.[6] A strategic product road map is an effective way to map out this series of assaults in an attack plan.

A road map is simply management's view of how to get where they want to go or to achieve their desired objective.[7] The strategic road map is a useful tool that helps senior management ensure that the capabilities to achieve their objective are in place when needed. There are different types of road maps: the product road map and the technology road map.

Let's use a military analogy. The term *strategy* was first used in a military context, and much of what we know about strategy comes from the military field. You are a five-star general and are at war. You have clearly specified goals: presumably to win the war or achieve certain ends. You may have identified certain key strategic arenas—fronts, major battlefields, or arenas on a map—where you hope to attack and win. But as you chart your strategy, you see that there are some key assaults or initiatives along the way—individual battles that you must fight in order to see your strategy succeed.

Now let's translate this into a new product context:

- **Goals:** What goals your business has, including specific new product goals. For example, what percentage of your business's growth over the next three years will come from new products?

- **Arenas, fronts, and major battlefields:** These are the strategic arenas defined in your business and new product strategy. Which markets, technologies, and product types does the business plan to attack? Where will it focus its development efforts?

- **Deployment:** How many troops will the business place on each battlefield or front (or strategic buckets, later in this chapter)?

- **Assaults and initiatives:** The major developments that you must undertake in order to implement your strategy: the major new product, technology, or platform developments, that is, your strategic road map.

Your strategic product road map defines the business's major new product and platform developments along a time line, establishes place marks for these major initiatives, and tentatively commits or reserves resources for them. An example is in Figure 7.2-2 for an equipment manufacturer. Here the product road map not only maps out the various major product introductions and their timing; it also defines the platforms and platform extensions needed to develop these new products.[8]

The technology road map is derived from the product road map but also specifies how you will get there. That is, it lays out the technologies and technological competencies that are needed in order

FIGURE 7.2-2 Strategic Product Road Map: New Platforms and Major Products

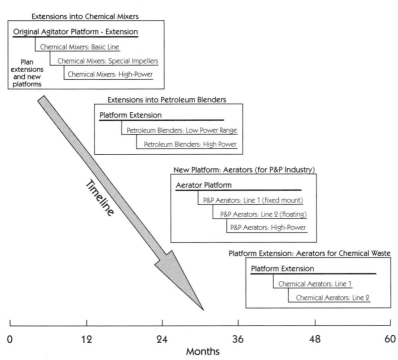

Source: Based on work in M. H. Meyer and A. P. Lehnerd, *The Power of Platforms* (New York: Free Press, 1997).

to implement (develop and source) the products and platforms in the product road map. The technology road map is a logical extension of the product road map and is closely linked to it. Indeed, at Lucent Technologies, the two are combined into a product-technology road map as a tool to help management link business strategy, product plans, and technology development.[9]

Most often, the specification of projects on the product road map is left fairly general and high level. For example, designations such as "a low-carb beer for the Atkins diet market" or "ceramic-coated tooling for the aerospace industry" or "low-power petroleum blenders" are often the way these projects are shown on the product road map time line. That is, place marks for projects yet to be defined are the norm. The road map is meant to be directional and strategic, but not provide detailed product and project definitions. As each project progresses through the idea-to-launch process, however (the Stage-Gate® process in Chapter 7.1), increasingly the project and product becomes specified and defined.

Developing the Strategic Product Road Map

The development of a product road map flows logically from the product innovation strategy. Delineating the major initiatives required as part of the product road map is a multifaceted task:

- *Strategic assessment.* Sometimes the mere specification of a strategic arena as top priority leads logically to a list of those products and projects that are necessary to enter and be successful in that arena. For example, a major health products company identified "wound care" as a priority strategic arena (the company already sold a few products in this health care sector but was a minor player). However, once "wound care" was made top priority, the specific products the company needed to be a force in this sector became evident, and the development programs to generate these products fell into a logical sequence in a product road map.
- *Portfolio review of existing products.* Here, one takes a hard look at the business's current product offerings and decides which

are tired and should be pruned and which should be replaced. Forecasts of products' life cycles often reveal the need and timing for replacement products or perhaps even a new platform. In addition, gaps in the product line are identified. In this way, place marks are inserted in the product road map for these required developments. Such an exercise is undertaken periodically in order to keep the product line fresh, current, and complete.

• *Competitive analysis.* Where are the business's products and product lines relative to those of its competitors? Here one assesses competitors' current and probable future offerings and where they have advantage, and then assesses the gaps. This exercise often points to the need for new products either immediately or in the foreseeable future.

• *Technology trend assessment.* Here one forecasts technology and what new technologies, and hence new platform developments, will be required and their timing. For example, each new cell phone technology signals a host of development projects within cell phone manufacturing firms and also within service providers.

• *Market trends assessment.* This is a forecasting exercise and looks at major market trends and shifts. In this exercise, often one is able to pinpoint specific initiatives that must be undertaken in response to these evident trends; for example, in the food business, "the development of a line of nutriceutical 'good-for-you' foods."

Strategic Buckets

A second strategic resource allocation approach is strategic buckets, which can be used alongside or instead of the product road map. When translating the business's strategy into strategic portfolio decisions (the middle left part of Figure 7.2-1), a major challenge is spending breakdown or deployment. Where does senior management wish to spend its resources when it comes to product innovation: on what types of projects and in what product, market, or technology areas? And how much do they wish to spend in each area?

The strategic buckets model operates from the simple principle that implementing strategy equates to spending money on specific projects. (Note that "resources" includes dollars as well as people time; hence, resource or money allocation is for both fiscal expenditures and person-months allocation.) Thus, operationalizing strategy really means setting spending targets.

The method begins with the business's strategy and requires senior management to make forced choices along each of several dimensions—choices about how they wish to allocate their scarce resources. This enables the creation of "envelopes of resources" or "buckets." Existing projects are categorized into buckets; then senior management determines whether actual spending is consistent with desired spending for each bucket. Finally, projects are prioritized within buckets to arrive at the ultimate portfolio of projects— one that mirrors management's strategy for the business.

A rather simple breakdown is used at Honeywell: the Mercedes Benz star method of allocating resources (Figure 7.2-3). The leadership team of the business begins with the business's strategy and uses the Mercedes emblem (the three-point star) to help divide up the resources. There are three buckets:

- Platform development projects, which promise to yield major breakthroughs and new technology platforms
- New product developments
- Others, which include extensions, modifications, product improvements, and cost reductions

Management divides the R&D funds into these three buckets. Next, the projects are sorted into each of the three buckets; management then ranks projects against each other within each bucket. In effect, three separate portfolios of projects are created and managed, and the spending breakdown across buckets and project types mirrors strategic priorities.

What dimensions should be used in the strategic buckets splits? One leading R&D planning executive identified them as "whatever dimensions the leadership team of the business find most relevant

FIGURE 7.2-3 Strategic Buckets: The Mercedes Benz
Star Method of Portfolio Management

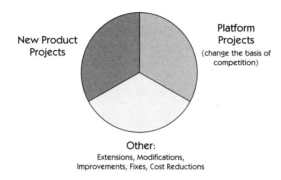

New Product
Projects

Platform
Projects
(change the basis of
competition)

Other:
Extensions, Modifications,
Improvements, Fixes, Cost Reductions

The business's strategy dictates the split of resources into buckets;
projects are rank ordered within buckets, but using different criteria
within each bucket.

Source: R. G. Cooper, S. J. Edgett, and E. J. Kleinschmidt, *Portfolio Management for New Products,* 2nd ed. (Reading, Mass.: Perseus Book, 2002).

to describe their own strategy." In other businesses, such as ITT Industries, the dimensions used in each business unit are prescribed. ITT uses two dimensions: project types and business areas. And Honeywell uses only the single-dimension project types as in Figure 7.2-3. Some common dimensions to consider are:

- *Strategic goals:* Management splits resources across the specified strategic goals. For example, what percentage will be spent on defending the base? On diversifying? On extending the base?
- *Across arenas:* The most obvious spending split is across the strategic arenas defined in the business strategy (arenas are generally product, market, or technology areas where the business wishes to focus its new product efforts). That is, once management has defined the arenas of strategic focus and the priorities of each, they then move to deployment and decide how many resources each arena or battlefield should receive (see Figure 7.2-4, left).
- *Product lines:* Resources are split across product lines: For example, how much to spend on product line A? On product line B?

On C? A plot of product line locations on the product life cycle curve is used to help determine this split.

- *Types of projects:* Decisions or splits can be made in terms of the types of projects (as in Figures 7.2-3 or 7.2-4, right).

As an example, given its aggressive product innovation strategic stance, EXFO Engineering (a manufacturer of fiber-optic test equipment) targets 65 percent of R&D spending to genuine new products, another 10 percent to platform developments and research (technology development for the future), and the final 25 percent to incrementals (the "supportfolio," that is, product modifications, fixes, and improvements).[10]

- *Technologies or technology platforms:* Spending splits can be made across technology types (for example, base, key, pacing, and embryonic technologies) or across specific technology platforms.

- *Familiarity matrix:* What should be the split of resources to different types of markets and different technology types in terms of their familiarity to the business? Some companies use the popular familiarity matrix (technology newness versus market newness) to help split resources (see Figure 7.2-5).[11]

- *Geography:* What proportion of resources should be spent on projects aimed largely at North America? At Latin America? At Europe? At Asia-Pacific? Or globally?

FIGURE 7.2-4 Deciding the Spending Splits: Strategic Buckets by Strategic Arena and Product Type

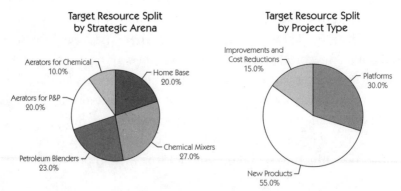

FIGURE 7.2-5 Familiarity Matrix Bubble Diagram: Resources Split Across Market and Technology Newness Categories

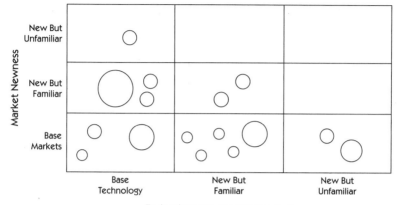

Note: Projects are shown as bubbles, with bubble size denoting the resources being spent on each project.

Source: Reported for Bayer in Cooper, Edgett, and Kleinschmidt, *Portfolio Management for New Products.*

- *By stage or phase of development:* Some businesses distinguish between early-stage projects and projects in development and beyond. Two buckets are created: one for development projects and the other for early-stage projects. One division at GTE allocates seed corn money to a separate bucket for early-stage projects.

The Optimal Split in Project Types

A major strategic question is, "What's the best mix or balance of development projects—for example, incremental developments versus true innovations?" Certainly, a business's new product strategy ideally should be reflected in the breakdown of types of product developments it undertakes—that is, where the funds are invested. In addition, breakdowns of new products and projects by type are a predictor of the business's new product development performance. For example, too much emphasis on short-term small projects might point to an underachieving business. Table 7.2-1 shows the breakdown results from the APQC benchmarking study. Incremental product changes is the dominant category, representing 32.7 percent of all projects on average. Next are new products to the business, accounting for 24.2 percent of projects. Then are major product revisions, making up 21.9 percent of projects. There is an even balance among projects across these three most popular categories. And on average, fairly noninnovative products—incrementals, revisions, and promotional developments—together account for about 64 percent of projects. By contrast, new-to-the-world products—true innovations—represent a minority of development projects (10.2 percent).

TABLE 7.2-1. Breakdown of Projects by Project Types: Best versus Worst

	Average Business	Best Performers	Worst Performers
Promotional developments and package changes	9.45%	5.89%	12.31%
Incremental product improvements and changes	32.74	28.21	40.42
Major product revisions	21.97	25.00	19.15
New to the business products	24.16	24.11	20.00
New to the world products	10.23	15.89	7.42

Note: Columns do not add up to 100 percent due to a small percentage of other types of products.

Sources: R. G. Cooper, S. J. Edgett, and E. J. Kleinschmidt, *Best Practices in Product Innovation: What Distinguishes Top Performers* (Product Development Institute, 2003) [www.prod-dev.com]; R. G. Cooper, S. J. Edgett, and E. J. Kleinschmidt, *New Product Development Best Practices Study: What Distinguishes the Top Performers* (Houston: American Productivity and Quality Center, 2002) [www.apqc.org].

Do the best performers adopt a different mix of project types, and is there an optimal portfolio of project types? Consider how the average business compares to the best- and worst-performing businesses in Table 7.2-1. What is noteworthy is the shift toward much more innovative and bolder projects as one moves from worst to best performers. For example, more than half (53 percent) of worst businesses' projects are the small, incremental ones—promotional or package changes or incremental product improvements and changes. By contrast, just over one-third (34 percent) of best performers' projects are these small, incremental ones. Top performers take on a higher proportion of larger, more innovative projects: 40 percent of best performers' projects are either new to the business or true innovations (new to the world). By contrast, only 27 percent of worst performers' projects are these bolder projects. Best performers undertake twice as large a proportion of true innovations (new-to-the-world products) than do worst performers: 15 percent of their projects are true innovations (versus 7 percent).

Tactical Decisions: Picking the Right Development Projects

Tactical portfolio decisions focus on projects and address the questions: What specific new product and development projects should the business undertake? What are their relative priorities? And what resources should be allocated to each? These tactical decisions are shown at the bottom part of Figure 7.1-1.

To make effective tactical decisions, two project selection processes should be installed (gates and portfolio review), both working in harmony, as in Figure 7.1-1 (bottom).

Project decisions are made at *gates* (bottom right of Figure 7.1-1). Embedded within the idea-to-launch new product framework are go/kill decision points called gates (see Stage-Gate® in Chapter 7.1). Gates provide an in-depth review of individual projects, and render go/kill, prioritization, and resource allocation decisions; hence, gates must be part of the portfolio management system.

Many companies already have a gating process in place and confuse that with a comprehensive portfolio management system. Doing the right projects is more than simply individual project selection at gate meetings; it's about the entire mix of projects and new product or technology investments that the business makes. Project selection deals only with the fingers: go/kill decisions are made on individual projects, each judged individually and on its own merits. Portfolio management deals with the fist: it is holistic and looks at the entire set of project investments together.

The second decision process is the periodic *portfolio review* (bottom left of Figure 7.1-1). Senior management meets perhaps two to four times per year to review the portfolio of all projects. Here, senior management also makes go/kill and prioritization decisions, where all projects are considered on the table together, and all or some could be up for auction. Key issues and questions are:

- Are all projects strategically aligned (fit the business's strategy)?
- Does management have the right priorities among projects?
- Are there some projects on the active list that should be killed or perhaps accelerated?
- Is there the right balance of projects? The right mix?
- Are there enough resources to do all these projects?
- Is there sufficiency? If one does these projects, will the business achieve its stated business goals?

Both decision processes, gating and portfolio reviews, are needed. Note that the gates are project specific and provide a thorough review of each project in depth and in real time. By contrast, portfolio reviews are holistic: they look at all projects together, but in much less detail on each project. In some businesses, if the gates are working, not too many decisions or major corrective actions are required at the portfolio review. Some companies indicate that they don't even look at individual projects at the portfolio review, but consider projects only in aggregate. But in other businesses, the majority of decisions are made at these quarterly or semiannual portfolio reviews.

Tools to Use for Effective Gates and Portfolio Reviews

Within these gates and portfolio reviews, a number of tools can be used to help achieve portfolio goals: maximize the portfolio's value, achieve the right balance and mix or projects, and ensure strategic alignment yet not overload the development pipeline.[12]

Maximizing the Value of the Portfolio

The methods used to achieve this goal range from financial tools to balanced scorecard models. Each has its strengths and weaknesses. The end result of each is a rank-ordered or prioritized list of "go" and "hold" projects, with the projects at the top of the list scoring highest in terms of achieving the desired objectives: the portfolio's value in terms of that objective is thus maximized.

Rank Projects Using Their Economic Value or Net Present Value.
The simplest approach is merely to calculate the NPV (net present value) of each project on a spreadsheet. Most businesses already require the NPV and a financial spreadsheet as part of the project's business case, so the NPV number is already available for each project.

The NPV, a proxy for the economic value of the project to the business, can be used in two ways. First, go/kill decisions at gates are based on NPV. Project teams should use the minimum acceptable financial return or hurdle rate (as a percentage) for projects of this risk level as the discount rate when calculating their projects' NPVs. If the NPV is positive, the project clears the hurdle rate. So NPV is a key input to go/kill decision at gates. A best practice here is for the business's finance department to develop a standardized spreadsheet for this calculation so all project teams produce a consistently calculated NPV. Also, the finance people should develop a table of risk-adjusted discount rates for project teams to use for different risk levels of projects: low risk (such as a cost reduction project) to high risk (a genuine new product, first of its kind).

Second, at portfolio reviews, all projects are ranked according to their NPVs. The go projects are those that are at the top of the list. One continues to add projects down the list until resources run out. The result is a prioritized list of projects, which logically should maximize the NPV of the portfolio. In the example in Table 7.2-2, the top four projects are Foxtrot, Beta, Echo, and Alpha, but there is a resource limit of $15 million in the development budget. Thus, only two projects are go: Foxtrot and Beta (they consume almost all of the $15 million budget). The value of the portfolio is $115 million from these two projects.

This method is fine in theory, but there are some problems. The NPV method assumes that financial projections are accurate for development projects (they usually are not); it assumes that only financial goals are important, for example, that strategic considerations are irrelevant; it ignores probabilities of success and risk (except by using risk-adjusted discount rates); and it fails to deal with constrained resources, that is, the desire to maximize the value for a limited resource commitment, or getting the most bang for the limited buck. A final objection is more subtle: the fact that NPV assumes an all-or-nothing investment decision, whereas in new product projects, the decision process is an incremental one, more like buying a series of options on a project.[13]

This NPV method has a number of attractive features, however. First, it requires the project team to submit a financial assessment of the project. That means they must do some research, make some fact-based projections, and think through the commercial implications of the project before development begins. Second, a discounted cash flow method is used, which is the correct way to value investments, as opposed to EBIT (earnings before interest and taxes), ROI (return on investment), or payback period. Finally, all monetary amounts are discounted to today (not just to launch date), thereby appropriately penalizing projects that are years away from launch.

Rank Projects Using the Productivity Index Based on the NPV.
Here's an important modification to the NPV ranking approach that recognizes that resources are limited. The problem is that

TABLE 7.2-2. Using NPV to Rank and Prioritize Projects

Project	PV (present value of future earnings)	Development Cost	Commercialization Cost	NPV (net present value)	Ranking Based on NPV	Decision
Alpha	30	3	5	22	4	Hold
Beta	64	5	2	57	2	Go
Gamma	9	2	1	6	5	Hold
Delta	3	1	0.5	1.5	6	Hold
Echo	50	5	3	42	3	Hold
Foxtrot	66	10	2	58	1	Go

Note: All figures are in millions of dollars

some projects (for example, Foxtrot and Beta in Table 7.2-2) are great projects and have huge NPVs, but they consume many resources, thus making it impossible to do other less attractive but far less resource-intensive projects. Other projects, although having lower NPVs, are quite efficient: they can be done using relatively few resources. How does one decide?

Simple. The goal is to maximize the bang for buck, and the way to do this is to take the ratio of what one is trying to maximize (in this case, the NPV) divided by the constraining resource (the R&D dollars required). (This decision rule of rank order according to the ratio of what one is trying to maximize divided by the constraining resource seems to be an effective one. Simulations with a number of sets of projects show that this decision rule works very well, truly giving "maximum bang for buck.") One may choose to use R&D people or work-months or the total dollar cost remaining in the project (or even capital funds) as the constraining resource. This bang-for-buck ratio or "productivity index" is shown in column 4 in Table 7.2-3: Productivity index = NPV of the project/Total resources remaining to be spent on the project.

Now it's time to re-sort the list of projects. But first consider the constraint: the R&D spending constraint is $15 million for new products in this business (the resources required to do all the projects in Table 7.2-3 adds up to $26 million). To select the go projects, one simply reorders the project list, ranking projects according to the productivity index (this reordering is shown in Table 7.2-3). Then one goes down the list until out of resources. Note that column 6 shows the cumulative resource expenditure. One runs out of resources (that is, hits the $15 million limit) after project Alpha.

The point to note here is that introducing the notion of constrained resources, which every business has, dramatically changes the ranking of projects. Compare the ranked list in Table 7.2-2 with that in Table 7.2-3. Note that Foxtrot, the number one project in Exhibit 2.7, drops off the list entirely using the productivity index in Exhibit 2.8; the resulting portfolio contains more projects; and its overall economic value is higher.

TABLE 7.2-3 Ranking Projects According to the NPV-Based Productivity Index

Project	NPV	Development Cost	Productivity Index = NPV/ Development Cost	Sum of Development Costs
Beta	57	5	11.4	5
Echo	42	5	8.4	10
Alpha	22	3	7.3	13
				Limit reached
Foxtrot	58	10	5.8	23
Gamma	6	2	3.0	25
Delta	1.5	1	1.5	26

Note: The Productivity Index is used to rank projects until out of resources. The horizontal line shows the limit: the $15 million in development costs is reached. Go projects are now Beta, Echo, and Alpha. Foxtrot drops off the list. The value of the portfolio is NPV = $121M from these three projects.

This NPV productivity index method yields benefits in addition to those inherent in the straight NPV approach above. By introducing the productivity index ratio, the method favors those projects that are almost completed and have little cost remaining in them (the denominator is small, hence the productivity index is high). And the method deals with resource constraints, yielding the best set of projects for a given budget or resource limit.

Introduce Risk by Using Expected Commercial Value. This method seeks to maximize the commercial value of the portfolio, subject to certain budget constraints, but introduces the notion of risks and probabilities. The expected commercial value (ECV) method determines the probability-adjusted value of each project to the corporation, namely, its expected commercial value. The calculation of the ECV, based on a decision tree analysis, considers the future stream of earnings from the project, the probabilities of both commercial success and technical success, along with both commercialization costs and development costs (see Figure 7.2-6 for the calculation and definition of terms). Because the method treats new product development investment decisions in a series of stages, the solution a close proxy for options pricing theory or real options.

The ECV can be used at gate meetings as an input to the go/kill decision, much like the NPV, except risk and probabilities are built in. For portfolio reviews, in order to arrive at a prioritized list of projects, what resources are scarce or limiting are identified, much like the NPV productivity index example above. Then the productivity index ratio is computed: what one is trying to maximize (the ECV) divided by the constraining resource. Projects are rank-ordered according to this new productivity index until the resource limit is reached. Projects at the top of the list are go, and those at the bottom (beyond the resource limit) are placed on hold. The method thus ensures the greatest bang for the buck—that the ECV is maximized for a given resources limit.

This ECV model has a number of attractive additional features. It includes probabilities and risk, which are inherent in any new

FIGURE 7.2-6 Determining the Expected Commercial Value of a Project

A model of a two-stage investment decision process. First, invest $D in development, which may yield a technical success with probability P_T. Then invest $C in commercialization, which may result in a commercial success with proability P_{CS}. If successful, the project yields an income stream whose present value is $PV. More sophisticated versions of this model entail more stages than the two shown here and an array of possible outcomes from each stage.

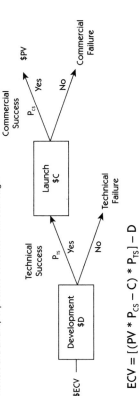

$$ECV = [(PV * P_{CS} - C) * P_{TS}] - D$$

$ECV = Expected commercial value of the project

P_{TS} = Probability of technical success

P_{CS} = Probability of commercial success (given technical success)

D = Development costs remaining in the project

C = Commercialization (launch) costs

PV = Net present value of project's future earnings (discounted to today)

Source: Cooper, Edgett, and Kleinschmidt, Portfolio Management for New Products.

product project; it recognizes that the go/kill decision process is an incremental one (the notion of purchasing options, a stage-wise decision process); and it deals with the issue of constrained resources and attempts to maximize the value of the portfolio in the light of this constraint.

Use a Simulation Financial Model for Major Projects. Another way to introduce risk and probabilities is the use of a computer-based Monte Carlo simulation model, such as @Risk. Here's how these models are used. Instead of merely imputing a point estimate for each financial variable in the spreadsheet, such as year 1 sales, year 2 sales, and so on, one inputs three estimates for each variable: a best case, a worst case, and a likely case. A probability curve (much like a bell-shaped curve) is drawn through each set of estimates. So each financial estimate (sales, costs, investment, and others) has a probability distribution.

The model begins by calculating multiple scenarios of possible financial outcomes, all based on the probability distributions. Tens of thousands of scenarios are quickly generated by the computer, each yielding a financial outcome such as the NPV. The distribution of the NPVs generated in these thousands of scenarios becomes the profit distribution—an expected NPV as well as a probability distribution of NPVs.

One can use the NPV and its distribution to help make the go/kill decision at gates, much as in the method for ranking projects using their economic value or NPV; take the expected NPV and divide by the costs remaining in the project; and rank the projects according to this probability-adjusted NPV, much as in ranking projects using the productivity index based on the NPV.

These simulation models, such as @Risk, are commercially available and relatively easy to use. But there are a few quirks or assumptions in the model that cause problems. For example, the model fails to deal with the options notion of a new product project, and it permits the generation of all-but-impossible scenarios.

Nonetheless, it's a solid method and particularly appropriate for projects that involve large capital expenditures and where probability distributions of input variables can be estimated.

Score Projects Using a Balanced Scorecard Approach. Scoring models or balanced scorecards are based on the premise that a more balanced approach to project selection is desirable—that not everything can be reduced to a single NPV or ECV metric. Thus, a variety of criteria are used to rate the project. These criteria are based on research into what makes new product projects successful, and hence are proven proxies for success and profitability.

In a scorecard system, each senior manager rates the project on a number of criteria on 1–5 or 0–10 scales. Typical criteria include:

- Strategic alignment
- Product and competitive advantage
- Market attractiveness
- Ability to leverage core competencies
- Technical feasibility
- Reward versus risk

The scores from the various senior managers at the gate review are tallied and combined, and the project attractiveness score is computed: the weighted or unweighted addition of the item ratings. This attractiveness score is the basis for making the go/kill decision at gates, and can also be used to develop a rank-ordered list of projects for portfolio reviews. A sample scoring model for well-defined new product projects is shown in Exhibit 7.2-2. (Different scorecards with different criteria should be used for different types of projects: one scorecard for simple projects such as line extensions and modifications; another scorecard for true new products, as in Exhibit 7.2-2; and yet another scorecard for major platform projects.)

EXHIBIT 7.2-2 A Typical Balanced Scorecard for New Product Project Selection

Factor 1: Strategic Fit and Importance

- Alignment of project with our business's strategy
- Importance of project to the strategy
- Impact on the business

Factor 2: Product and Competitive Advantage

- Product delivers unique customer or user benefits
- Product offers customer/user excellent value for money
- Competitive rationale for project
- Positive customer/user feedback on product concept (concept test results)

Factor 3: Market Attractiveness

- Market size
- Market growth and future potential
- Margins earned by players in this market
- Competitiveness—how tough and intense competition is

Factor 4: Core Competencies Leverage

- Project leverages our core competencies and strengths in:
  Technology
  Production/operations
  Marketing
  Distribution/sales force

Factor 5: Technical Feasibility

- Size of technical gap
- Familiarity of technology to our business
- Newness of technology (base to embryonic)
- Technical complexity
- Technical results to date (proof of concept?)

Factor 6: Financial Reward versus Risk

- Size of financial opportunity
- Financial return (NPV, ECV)
- Productivity index
- Certainty of financial estimates
- Level of risk and ability to address risks

- Projects are scored by the gatekeepers (senior management) at the gate meeting using these six factors on a scorecard (0–10 scales).
- The scores are tallied, averaged across the evaluators, and displayed for discussion.
- The project attractiveness score (PAS) is the weighted or unweighted addition of the scores, taken out of 100.
- A PAS score of 60/100 is usually required for a go decision.

Sources: R. G. Cooper, *Product Leadership: Pathways to Profitable Innovation*, 2nd ed. (Reading, Mass.: Perseus Books, 2005); R. G. Cooper, S. J. Edgett, and E. J. Kleinschmidt, *Portfolio Management for New Products*, 2nd ed. (Reading, Mass.: Perseus Books, 2002).

Scoring models generally are praised in spite of their limited popularity. Research into project selection methods reveals that scoring models produce a strategically aligned portfolio and one that reflects the business's spending priorities; they yield effective and efficient decisions better than the financial tools outlined above; and they result in a portfolio of high-value projects.[14]

Seeking the Right Balance of Projects

A major portfolio goal is a balanced portfolio: a balanced set of development projects in terms of a number of key parameters. The analogy is that of an investment fund, where the fund manager seeks balance in terms of high-risk versus blue-chip stocks and balance across industries and geographies in order to arrive at an optimum investment portfolio.

Visual charts effectively display balance in new product project portfolios. These visual representations include portfolio maps or bubble diagrams (see the example in Figure 7.2-7), an adaptation of the four-quadrant BCG (stars, cash cows, dogs, and wildcats) diagrams that have seen service since the 1970s as strategy models, as well as more traditional pie charts and histograms.

A casual review of portfolio bubble diagrams will lead some readers to observe that "these new models are nothing more than the old strategy bubble diagrams of the 1970s!" *Not so.* Recall that the BCG strategy model and others like it (such as the McKinsey-GE model) plot business units on a "market attractiveness" versus "business position" grid. Note that the unit of analysis is the business unit: an existing business whose performance, strengths, and weaknesses are all known. By contrast, today's new product portfolio bubble diagrams, which may appear similar, plot individual new product projects—that is, future businesses, or what might be. As for the dimensions of the grid, here too the "market attractiveness" versus "business position" dimensions used for existing business units may not be as appropriate for new product possibilities, so other dimensions or axes are extensively used.

What are some of the parameters that should be plotted on these portfolio diagrams in order to seek balance? Different pundits recommend various parameters and lists and even suggest the best plots to use.

Risk-Reward Bubble Diagrams. The most popular bubble diagram is the risk-return chart (see Figure 7.2-7). About 44 percent of businesses with a systematic portfolio management scheme in place use this bubble diagram or one like it.[15] Here, one axis is some measure of the reward to the company and the other is a success probability.

One approach is to use a qualitative estimate of reward, ranging from "modest" to "excellent."[16] The argument here is that too heavy an emphasis on financial analysis can do serious damage, notably in the early stages of a project. The other axis is the probability of overall success (probability of commercial success times probability of technical success).

In contrast, other firms rely on very quantitative and financial gauges of reward, namely, the probability-adjusted NPV of the project.[17] Here the probability of technical success is the vertical axis, as probability of commercial success has already been built into the NPV calculation.

A sample bubble diagram is shown in Figure 7.2-7 for a business unit of a major chemical company. Here the size of each bubble shows the annual resources committed to each project (dollars per year; it could also be people or work-months allocated to the project). The four quadrants of the portfolio model are:

- *Pearls* (upper-left quadrant): These are the potential star products: projects with a high likelihood of success and that are also expected to yield a very high reward. Most businesses desire more of these. There are two such Pearl projects, and one of them has been allocated considerable resources (denoted by the sizes of the circles).

- *Oysters* (lower-left quadrant): These are the long-shot projects: those with a high expected payoff but with low likelihoods of

FIGURE 7.2-7 A Risk-Reward Bubble Diagram

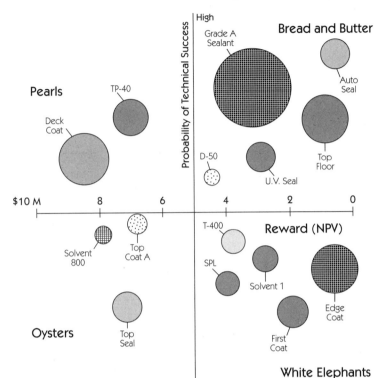

Note: Projects are plotted as bubbles, with bubble size denoting the resources committed to each project. The shading or cross-hatching shows the product line that each project is associated with.

Source: Cooper, Edgett, and Kleinschmidt, *Portfolio Management for New Products.*

technical success. They are the projects where technical breakthroughs will pave the way for solid payoffs. There are three of these; none is receiving many resources.

- *Bread and Butter* (upper-right quadrant): These are small, simple projects with a high likelihood of success but low reward. They include the many fixes, extensions, modifications, and updating projects of which most companies have too many. More than 50 percent of spending is going to these projects.

- *White Elephants* (lower-right quadrant): These are the low-probability and low-reward projects. Every business has a few white elephants; they inevitably are difficult to kill, but this company has far too many. One-third of the projects and about 25 percent of spending fall in this quadrant.

Given that this chemical business is in a specialty area and a star business seeking rapid growth, a quick review of the portfolio map in Figure 7.2-7 reveals many problems. There are too many White Elephant projects (it's time to do some serious project pruning), too much money spent on Bread and Butter low-value projects, not enough Pearls, and heavily underresourced Oysters.

One feature of this bubble diagram model is that it forces senior management to deal with the resource issue. Given finite resources, the sum of the areas of the circles must be a constant. That is, if one adds one project to the diagram, another must be subtracted; alternatively, one can shrink the size of several circles. The elegance here is that the model forces management to consider the resource implications of adding one more project to the list: some other projects must pay the price.

Also shown in this bubble diagram is the product line that each project is associated with (the shading or cross-hatching). A final breakdown is timing, indicated by color (not shown in the black-and-white figure). Thus, this apparently simple risk-reward diagram shows a lot more than risk and profitability data. It also conveys resource allocation, timing, and spending breakdowns across product lines.

Bubble Diagrams That Capture Newness to the Firm. Two key dimensions that senior managers should consider when mapping their development portfolio are:

- Market newness—how new or "step-out" the markets are for projects underway
- Technology newness—how new the development and manufacturing technology is to the business

Both dimensions are proxies for risk and aggressiveness.[18] Here, development projects are plotted on these two axes in order to help management view the current portfolio and whether it has the right balance and mix of step-out versus close-to-home projects (similar to the newness diagram in Figure 7.2-5). Again, circle sizes denote resources allocated to each project. This is the second most popular bubble diagram used for NPD portfolio management by industry.

Traditional Charts to Display Resource Breakdowns. There are numerous other parameters, dimensions, or variables across which one might wish to seek a balance of projects. As a result, there is an endless variety of histograms and pie charts that help to portray portfolio balance—for example:

• Resource breakdown by project types is a vital concern. What is the spending on genuine new products versus product renewals (improvements and replacements), or product extensions, or product maintenance, or cost reductions and process improvements? And what should it be? Pie charts effectively capture the spending split across project types—actual versus desired splits, shown in italics in Figure 7.2-8. Pie charts that show the resource breakdown by project types are a particularly useful sanity check when the business has already established strategic buckets. Now one can compare the current resource split (the "what is") to the target split ("what should be") as defined by strategic buckets, as in Figure 7.2-8. Note in this figure that the market sector splits are almost on target, but the project types are too heavily weighted toward cost reductions and fixes.

• Markets, products, and technologies provide another set of dimensions across which managers seek balance. The question is: Does the business have the appropriate split in R&D spending across its various product lines? Or across the markets or market segments in which it operates (see Figure 7.2-8)? Or across the technologies it possesses? Pie charts are again appropriate for capturing and displaying these types of data. And once again, these pie charts

FIGURE 7.2-8 Pie Charts: Actual versus Targeted Resource Allocation in the Portfolio

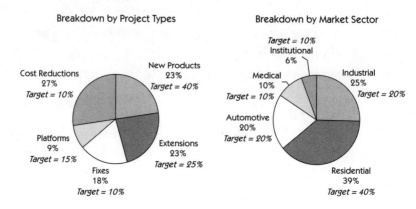

Note: The targets are shown in italics, and the pie chart slices show expenditure breakdowns to date.

close the loop on the strategic buckets exercise, revealing the "what is" versus the "what should be."

• Timing is a key issue in the quest for balance. One does not wish to invest strictly in short-term projects or totally in long-term ones. Another timing goal is for a steady stream of new product launches spread out over the quarters, that is, constant "new news" and no sudden logjam of product launches all in one quarter. A histogram captures the issue of timing and portrays the distribution of resources to specific projects according to quarters or years of launch.

• Another timing issue is *cash flow.* Here the desire is to balance projects in such a way that cash inflows are reasonably balanced with cash outflows in the business. Some companies produce a timing histogram that portrays the total cash flow per year from all projects in the portfolio over the next three to five years.

Popularity and Effectiveness of Portfolio Methods

Which methods are the most popular, and which work the best? In practice, not surprisingly, the financial methods dominate portfolio management, according to a portfolio best practices study.[19] Financial methods include various profitability and return metrics, such as NPV, ECV, ROI, EV, or payback period—metrics that are used to rate, rank-order, and ultimately select projects. A total of 77.3 percent of businesses use such a financial approach in portfolio management (see Figure 7.2-9). For 40.4 percent of businesses, this is the dominant method.

Other methods are also quite popular:

- *Strategic approaches:* Letting the strategy dictate the portfolio is a popular approach and includes strategic buckets, product road mapping, and other strategically driven methods. A total of 64.8 percent of businesses use a strategic approach; for 26.6 percent of businesses, this is the dominant method.

- *Bubble diagrams or portfolio maps:* Slightly more than 40 percent of businesses use portfolio maps, but only 8.3 percent use this

FIGURE 7.2-9 Popularity of Portfolio Methods

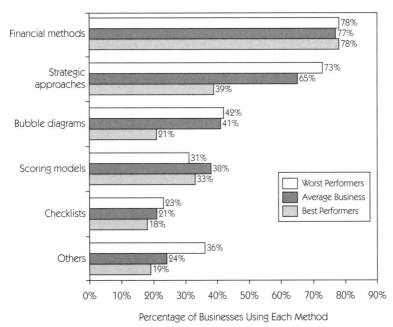

Source: Cooper, Edgett, and Kleinschmidt, *Portfolio Management for New Products.*

as their dominant method. The most popular map is the risk-versus-reward map in Figure 7.2-7, but many variants of bubble diagrams are used.

- *Scoring or scorecard models:* Scaled ratings are obtained by using scorecards at gates and are added to yield a project attractiveness score. These models are used by 37.9 percent of businesses; in 18.3 percent, this is the dominant decision method.

- *Checklists:* Projects are evaluated on a set of yes-no questions. Each project must achieve either all yes answers or a certain number of yes answers to proceed. The number of yes answers is used to make go/kill and/or prioritization (ranking) decisions. Only 17.5 percent of businesses use checklists, and in only 2.7 percent is this the dominant method.

Popularity does not necessarily equate to effectiveness, however. When the performance of businesses' portfolios was rated on six metrics in our study, those businesses that relied heavily on financial tools as the dominant portfolio selection model fared the worst. Financial tools yield an unbalanced portfolio of lower-value projects and projects that lack strategic alignment. By contrast, strategic methods produce a strategically aligned and balanced portfolio. And scorecard models appear best for selecting high-value projects and also yield a balanced portfolio. Finally, businesses using bubble diagrams obtain a balanced and strategic aligned portfolio.

It is ironic that the most rigorous techniques—the various financial tools—yield the worst results, not so much because the methods are flawed but simply because reliable financial data are often missing at the very point in a project where the key project selection decisions are made. Often, reliable financial data (expected sales, pricing, margins, and costs) are difficult to estimate in many cases because the project team simply has not done its homework. As one executive exclaimed as he referred to his business's sophisticated financial model being applied to projects with very soft data, "We're trying to measure a soft banana with a micrometer." In other cases, an overzealous project leader makes highly optimistic projections in order to secure support for his project.

Implementing a Systematic Portfolio Management Process

Having a portfolio management approach in place seems to be more important than the details of which tools and metrics one chooses. Any portfolio system seems to be better than no system at all. The research shows clearly that businesses that feature a systematic portfolio management process, regardless of the specific approach, outperform the rest (Figure 7.2-10).[20] Top-performing businesses in product development have implemented a systematic portfolio

FIGURE 7.2-10 Impact of Portfolio Management Practices on Performance

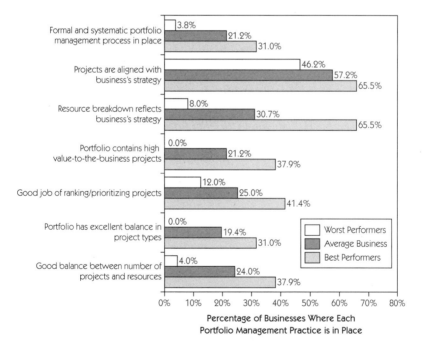

Reads: 21.2% of businesses have a systematic portfolio management process in place (meaning that 79% do not!). Best performers are better here, with 31.0% having such a system, while only 3.8% of poor performers do.

Sources: Cooper, Edgett, and Kleinschmidt, *Best Practices in Product Development,* and Cooper, Edgett, and Kleinschmidt, *New Product Development Best Practices Study.*

management approach; they have achieved strategic alignment of projects with their innovation strategy; they prioritize and rank their projects effectively so that their portfolios contain high value-to-the-corporation projects; and they seek and achieve the right balance and mix of projects. Portfolio management pays off.

Robert G. Cooper is professor of marketing at the School of Business, McMaster University in Ontario, Canada, and ISBM Distinguished Research Fellow at Penn State University's Smeal College of Business Administration. He is the father and developer of the Stage-Gate™ process, now widely used around the world to drive new products to market. He is a prolific researcher and thought leader in the field of product innovation management, with more than ninety articles in leading journals on new product management and six books.

SECTION EIGHT

Applications

PPM for Theory of Constraint Advocates

In this section, we offer a little bonus. In Chapter 8.1 on the application of theory of constraints (TOC) to project portfolio management, Larry Leach includes an overview of TOC and critical chain project management (CCPM) as he advocates these practices as an alternative to conventional project management approaches.

In the project management community, there is a significant and growing cadre of advocates of theory of constraints and critical chain project management, which are philosophies and methodologies developed by Eliyahu M. Goldratt. The followers of TOC and CCPM have approached near cult status, often summarily rejecting conventional project management practices while forwarding their praise of TOC and CCPM.

Although we must question abandoning traditional practices outright, we can find some very wise and useable advice in this alternative approach. A primary focus of TOC is to recognize and exploit bottlenecks (constraints). Certainly this makes a lot of sense for PPM. This focus is critical to the activity of project prioritization and selection. The project selection process must fully consider constraints to the project throughput, whether people, manufacturing capacity, or other limitations.

Furthermore, TOC practitioners stress the value of keeping resources applied to single projects and getting the projects done as soon as possible (as opposed to a multiproject application). Recent feedback from early implementers of PPM has indicated that doing fewer projects at a time will often result in getting more projects done in the long run.

We are indebted to Larry Leach for preparing this chapter. For the benefit of those who are not up to speed on TOC, he starts with an overview of TOC and CCPM, including his arguments as to the advantages of these techniques over conventional approaches. He then demonstrates how TOC thinking is applied to PPM.

What is indeed interesting is that despite the claim of difference from conventional thinking, the principles of TOC application to PPM essentially support the same key tenets that appear elsewhere in this book. Perhaps there is a slightly different slant and an emphasis on terms that have been favored by the TOC community. Nevertheless, we see the same list of key principles:

- Expected project value should be modified by estimated risk.
- Range of risk is a measurable factor that should be matched against the risk culture.
- Project selection should consider active as well as pending projects.
- When considering active projects, the valuation data should be updated.
- Termination (or delay) of active projects should be considered an option.

The message is to recognize that PPM is equally applicable to advocates of TOC/CCPM as to the traditional project management community.

8.1

Applying the Theory of Constraints to Project Portfolio Management

Larry Leach

This chapter describes an approach to apply the theory of constraints (TOC) to project portfolio management. It adds to the knowledge of the critical chain method of project management[1] and the synthesis of critical chain with the Project Management Body of Knowledge (PMBOK™), called critical chain project management (CCPM).[2] Although the critical chain method brings improvements to several areas of the PMBOK™, it does not address many of the processes necessary for project success. TOC tools and thinking can add value to these other processes, including project portfolio selection and management.

The first two parts of the chapter describe the TOC and CCPM, which form the basis for TOC portfolio selection and management. CCPM development focused on managing projects to achieve the results faster, assuming that they were the right projects. Although development did focus on managing portfolios of projects, TOC portfolio management also assumed the right set of projects. The final part of this chapter extends that thinking to project portfolio selection.

The Theory of Constraints

The theory of constraints provides a simple way to understand a complex system.

TOC Principles

The starting hypothesis of TOC is that any system must have a constraint that limits its output. If there were no constraint, system output would either rise indefinitely or go to zero. Therefore, a constraint limits any system with a nonzero output. Figure 8.1-1 shows that limiting the flow through any of the arrows can limit the total output of the system. The downward-pointing arrow identifies the system constraint. Sometimes it helps to think of the constraint in physical systems as a bottleneck, a constriction limiting flow through the system, as when a highway narrows down from three lanes to two. All organizations have a constraint that limits their ability to deliver projects. TOC provides a way to discover and use that constraint to improve the overall system throughput.

In *What Is This Thing Called Theory of Constraints*, Goldratt (1990) states, "Before we can deal with the improvement of any section of a system, we must first define the system's global goal; and the measurements that will enable us to judge the impact of any subsystem and any local decision, on this global goal."[3]

W. Edwards Deming noted in *The New Economics for Industry*, "We learned that optimization is a process of orchestrating the efforts of all components toward achievement of the stated aim."[4]

TOC poses the theory that for any value chain (at any time), only one constraint limits throughput. This is easier to see for a single project, where a project plan can have only one longest path (or, if more than one, they must be exactly the same length). The constraint may not be evident for a portfolio of projects. Even for a sin-

FIGURE 8.1-1 TOC Limits the Output of a System by a Constraint

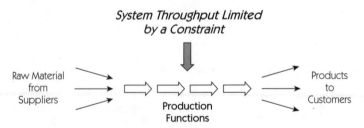

System Throughput Limited by a Constraint

Raw Material from Suppliers

Production Functions

Products to Customers

gle project, the constraint (longest path) often seems to shift due to fluctuations in project activity performance. But at any time (with rare exception), only one path controls the actual time to complete the project.

Business accounting systems trace back to the turn of the twentieth century and aside from automation have changed little. (This is about twice the history of modern project management systems.) Their development includes assumptions (no longer listed) about the design of business enterprises. One significant assumption, for example, is to treat people as expenses rather than assets. Another is to treat work in progress as an asset rather than an expense.

At the turn of the twentieth century, big business (which defined cost accounting) consisted primarily of large production plants with very large capital investments, for example, resource industries, steel, railroads, and, a little later, automobile manufacturing. The large production plants cause large fixed cost. At that time, things were tough for labor: labor was a variable cost. It was mostly applied to unskilled jobs and therefore plentiful and easy to replace. Consequently, it was easy to vary the workforce with demand.

Today the skilled workforce is much less variable, and the traditional fixed costs are much less fixed. The concept of allocating costs to labor or products always requires many assumptions. These assumptions, often long forgotten, influence the business decisions made using the cost accounting practices.

TOC considers the focus on present accounting systems as cost world thinking, because it operates on the assumption that product cost is the primary way to understand value and make business decisions. Cost world thinking requires the allocation of many expenses to products through elaborate product cost schemes, such as activity-based costing. These schemes are full of assumptions and often lead to erroneous understanding and decisions.

TOC applies throughput world thinking, which focuses on flow and rests on three definitions:

> *Throughput(T)*: All of the money you make from selling
>   your product (revenue minus raw material cost).

Inventory (Investment)(I): All of the money you have tied up in fixed assets to enable the throughput. A primary difference between TOC and conventional cost accounting is that TOC combines fixed assets (often called investment) and work-in-progress inventory into one category. This can cause confusion when we consider return on investment for a project. To align better with conventional terminology, this chapter will use the word *investment* for all of the money spent on a project.

Operating Expense (OE): All of the money spent to produce the throughput.

Major accounting authorities around the world have endorsed the TOC method, but TOC accounting has yet to cross the chasm into common terminology.

Throughput thinking focuses all decisions on the goal of the company: to make money now and in the future. All decisions and measures relate to the global goal. For example, in the cost world, managers measure operating efficiencies of local workstations. Financial people count inventory as a company asset. If they do not need workers to produce product for customer need, then they produce product for inventory, increasing efficiency to make themselves and their local plant look good. Unfortunately, the plant does not make money on inventory. Inventory costs money to make (raw materials) and to store, so it hurts cash flow and reduces disposable cash at the plant. Present accounting systems count inventory as a good thing (an asset), but it is bad for business. Earned value extends this thinking to projects, claiming value has been earned based on the estimated cost for work items. In reality, most projects are worth nothing (or have a negative value due to potential project terminations costs) until the project is complete and in operation.

An effective way to evaluate the meaning of the dilemma facing managers is to apply one of the thinking process tools invented by Goldratt: the evaporating cloud. Figure 8.1-2 illustrates the throughput world/cost world evaporating cloud. Block A represents

FIGURE 8.1-2 The Throughput World/Cost World Evaporating Cloud Exposes the Manager's Dilemma

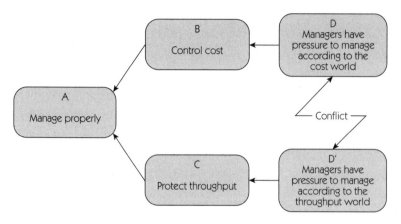

a common objective all managers share. Blocks B and C are requirements to achieve the objective. You read the cloud, "In order to manage properly, managers must control cost." You read the lower branch, "In order to manage properly, we must protect throughput." So far so good.

Focus on throughput requires understanding and controlling the whole system to optimize throughput. The most important effect of throughput world thinking is that it requires focus on throughput as the much preferred path to system improvement. Looking at how **T**, **I**, and **OE** affect net profit and return on investment leads to an immediate conclusion that **T** is the most important variable. Improvements in throughput are unbounded, while improvements in **OE** and **I** are limited (from the present value to zero).

Cost world thinking leads to a piecemeal view of each part of the production system. Costs add algebraically. The cost world leads to focus on **OE**. You can reduce **OE** in any part of the system, and the sum of the **OE** reductions adds up. This thinking leads to entity D, with the logic, "In order to control cost, managers have pressure to manage according to the cost world." Some ask, "Why hasn't everyone adopted throughput accounting and thinking?" TOC experts answer, "Inertia."

I have witnessed and read about many alleged cost savings improvements projects that purport to save cost through piecemeal cost reductions, including saving money by reducing parts of people. Of course, one can only reduce whole people, not parts, so it is no surprise that such proposals fail to achieve the intended return on the investment. One interesting example I reviewed recently was a several million dollar project performed by a company wishing to reduce printing and mailing cost. The idea was to make electronic forms accessible to many agencies throughout the country over the Internet versus purchasing them centrally and mailing them to the agencies. The project completed successfully in that it produced the electronic forms. There were even some who appreciated having the electronic forms available. However, there was no return on the investment, or, more correctly said, the return was negative. The cost to have forms printed centrally was usually a fraction of a cent per page. The cost of mailing was not saved because some material still had to be mailed to the agencies, and the additional forms not mailed did not reduce mailing expense or warehouse and printing expense. Worse, printing the forms in the field cost from ten to thirteen cents a page. This is one typical story, by no means exceptional.

Throughput reasoning extends to the conclusion that *a system operating with each step at optimum efficiency cannot be an efficient system*. Most people intuitively believe that operating each part of a system at maximum efficiency causes the system to operate at maximum efficiency. You can see that an optimum system has to feed the bottleneck at its capacity and process the downstream parts at the bottleneck's average processing rate. This means that, on average, every nonbottleneck process must operate at lower efficiency than the bottleneck in order to have reserve capacity to make up for fluctuations.

This understanding is a major reason that TOC is able to make such an immediate impact once people understand it. Managers design and operate most current systems without the critical understanding of TOC. They work to cut costs everywhere, including the capacity of the constraint (because they have not identified it). They work to improve efficiency everywhere, including workstations upstream of the constraint that may cause the constraint to work on things that do not translate to short-term throughput. Once they understand the theory, identify the constraint, and improve its throughput, the system throughput increases immediately.

Five Focusing Steps

TOC applies five focusing steps as a process to get the most out of a system in terms of the system goal. Figure 8.1-3 summarizes these steps.

FIGURE 8.1-3 The TOC Five Focusing Steps

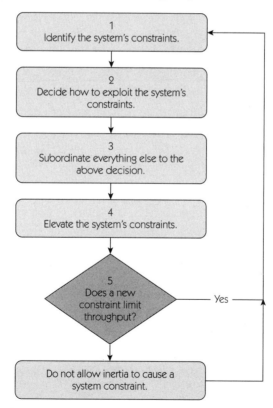

IDENTIFY the System's Constraints. In order to improve the system in terms of the goal, you have to identify what is holding it back. You have to answer, "What to change?" The system's constraint is like a weakest link of a chain; no matter what we do to improve other links in the chain, the chain does not become stronger until you improve the strength of the weakest link. It is evident that you have to find the weakest link before you can improve it.

In a project management system, the weakest link can be anywhere: in the project management process, company management policies, or any of the supply chains, work procedures, the measurement system, or communication. Since a project does not have physical form until it is well under way, the constraint is often not evident. Systems theory describes why and how symptoms may occur a long time after the actions that caused them.[5] You also know that the symptoms may appear somewhere other than the cause, through cause-effect chains. Therefore, study of why projects have gone wrong may not identify the actual cause of the symptoms.

TOC identifies the constraint of a nonproduction system as a core conflict. Like any other constraint, the core conflict is the primary cause of the reasons that the system is not performing better. It is the root cause of one or more undesirable effects in the system. In order to eliminate these undesirable effects, you have to identify the core conflict first.

Decide How to EXPLOIT the System's Constraint. Exploiting the system constraint is getting the most out of the weakest link of the chain. There are usually a number of ways to do this. For example, in a production facility, one way to improve throughput of the production system is to change the way the system puts things through the bottleneck (constraint). It must ensure that policies maximize using the constraint in terms of the goal. For example, ensuring the quality of parts entering the bottleneck prevents the bottleneck from wasting time on defective parts. The schedule ensures that products with the closest delivery date complete first.

For a nonproduction system, you have to decide how to eliminate the core conflict and ensure that you change the necessary parts of the system so that the natural cause-and-effect chains that result from your changes will achieve the desired effects you want.

SUBORDINATE *Everything Else to the Above Decision.* This is the key to focusing your effort. While subordinating, you may find many assumptions that seem to inhibit doing the right thing. Since project management has been in existence for over forty years with little change, isn't it likely that there are some assumptions, policies, or artificial constraints that do not work well anymore? Is it possible that some of the measures used to manage a project actually make it less likely to meet the goal?

ELEVATE *the System's Constraints.* *Elevate* means to add more of the constraint resource, be it people or time. It is an undesirable step, because it usually takes time to get more of a resource (people, machines, facilities) and usually requires investment. When faced with a capacity problem, this is where most managers start. You should not start here: you should exhaust the possibilities of the first three steps and the last step before you consider elevating your constraint.

If in the previous step a constraint has been broken, do not let inertia become your constraint. Go back to step 1.

Continue to Evaluate for New Constraints

As you continue to exploit or elevate the current constraint, you always eventually unearth another constraint. It may be lurking a few capacity percents above the current constraint, or you may be able to improve the system many tens of percents before you uncover the next real constraint. This is not a problem; it just provides a natural strategy to follow in improving a system: always focus on the current constraint. This is the optimum continuous improvement strategy.

TOC Thinking Process

The TOC thinking process provides a universal problem-solving approach to apply the five focusing steps to complex organizational systems. It has demonstrated substantial use in fields from corporate strategic planning to trouble-shooting complex technical problems. The thinking process answers three questions about any problem:

- What to change?
- What to change to?
- How to cause the change?

The thinking process starts with a representation of current reality: the current reality tree (CRT). The CRT is a logic diagram showing how one or at most a few root causes lead to many undesired effects in the current system. That root cause (*What to change?*) is the constraint of the overall system.

The thinking process identifies the organization direction (*What to change to?*) with a future reality tree (FRT). The FRT can guide an entire organization to achieve any desired set of objectives or solve any set of problems. It can come from the CRT or be developed to define a future direction. Dettmer provides excellent examples of applying the thinking process at the strategic level.[6] The FRT provides a way to identify the projects that you should consider for your portfolio. It also can provide a high-level relationship map between the projects.

The thinking process tools to address *How to cause the change?* are called the prerequisite tree and transition tree. These tools provide a coherent strategy and synchronized plan to implement the change. I often substitute a project plan for the TOC transition tree tool.[7]

Critical Chain Project Management

Critical chain project management (CCPM)[8] brings together the principles of TOC, Goldratt's critical chain,[9] and the PMBOK™. CCPM makes three radical assertions about project management:

- You do not have to finish each task on time to finish a project on time.

- Starting a project sooner does not mean it will finish sooner.

- Adding buffers reduces project duration and cost.

The following sections describe how CCPM accomplishes these apparent paradoxes for a single project and in a multiproject system.

Single-Project CCPM

CCPM develops a critical chain, rather than a critical path, as the primary focus of the project. The critical chain includes both logical and resource dependence. CCPM establishes the critical chain after removing resource contentions rather than before considering the resource limitations. The critical chain remains unchanged for the entire duration of the project and is the primary focus of the project manager.

Consider the little project illustrated by Figure 8.1-4. Assuming each task is estimated with each resource working 100 percent of their time on the task, how likely is it that project will finish on time? Most people quickly recognize that it is pretty unlikely because the plan calls for several resources to do two or three tasks at

FIGURE 8.1-4 An Example Critical Path Project

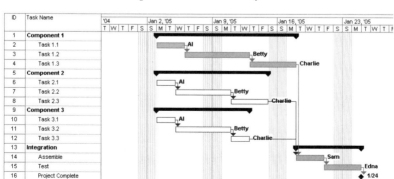

the same time, which will stretch out those tasks by at least a factor of two or three. Thus, it is unlikely the project would complete as scheduled. This is not news to the world of project management, and numerous approaches to resource leveling can resolve this problem. Figure 8.1-5 illustrates the same project after resource leveling. Note that the project due date moves to the right.

Although the resource-leveling capability exists in most project software, few project managers use it. My informal surveys at the Project Management Institute seminars I give (a large portion of the attendees are certified Project Management Professionals) indicate that only about 5 percent of project managers resource-level. My review of customer project plans indicates more severe planning problems in a large majority of cases, often using scheduling tools to draw Gantt chart pictures with no resource loading or task relationships, much less resource leveling.

Examine Figure 8.1-5 a little closer. Notice what happened to the critical path after resource leveling: every path has a gap in it. The software does not specify the algorithm used to select the particular tasks as critical, and I know that other software (including other versions of the software used) makes different choices. Since all of the paths show float after resource leveling, what should the software do?

Identifying the critical chain resolves this conflict. The critical chain is the longest path through the network after resource level-

FIGURE 8.1-5 The Resource-Leveled Critical Path Project

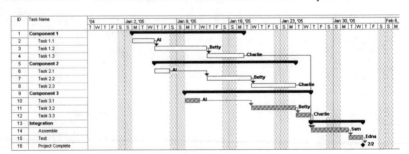

ing. The critical chain has no float or slack when identified. It usually differs from the critical path, as it can jump the task logic network. Figure 8.1-6 illustrates the critical chain for the Figure 8.1-5 network, comprising WBS 1.1, 1.2, 2.2, 3.2, 3.3, 4.1, and 4.2. Later steps in creating the complete critical chain network may introduce apparent float or slack into the network.

Figure 8.1-6 also illustrates the reduction of activity duration, and additions of buffers. Four feeding buffers are inserted as WBS FB19, FB22, FB18, FB20. The feeding buffers help ensure that both the inputs and the resources are available to start critical chain tasks. The critical chain scheduled project duration is about the same as the resource-leveled critical path, including the project buffer. You should expect completion before the end of the project buffer, and half the time before the start of the project buffer.

CCPM uses mean (roughly 50 percent) probability activity duration estimates and an aggregated project buffer to deliver the project on time. This significantly reduces the scheduled project lead time and significantly increases the probability of completing the project.

FIGURE 8.1-6 Identifying the Constraint to a Single Project:
The Critical Chain and Adding Buffers

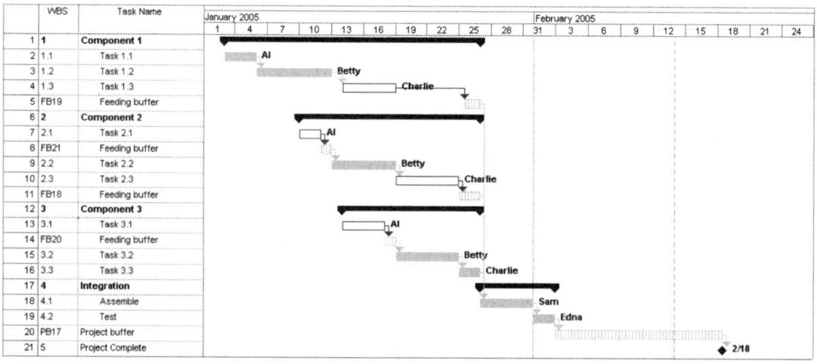

Note: The critical chain appears as the light gray bars in this graphic. They would typically be red in a color graphic.

CCPM solves the merging activity problem (the fact that an activity with multiple predecessors with finish-to-start relationships cannot start until the last predecessor completes) and the early-start, late-finish dilemma (Which way to schedule?) by the use of feeding buffers. Inserting FBs where each activity chain feeds the critical chain (including the entry to the project buffer) helps to immunize the critical chain from delay in these feeding paths. Late-starting the feeding chains against these buffers, as allowed by resource leveling, resolves the early/late start question.

Consider an activity on the critical chain that requires inputs from three tasks; one is the immediate predecessor on the critical chain and the other two on parallel network paths. If the tasks are estimated with a fifty/fifty chance of completing each task within the duration estimate, the chance of having all three is only one-eighth (probabilities multiply). The latest of the three tasks will determine the start time of the common successor task. The feeding buffers add extra time to the noncritical chain paths, moving the predecessors earlier in time so that the chance of having each of those feeder chain inputs is very high. This increases the chance of having all three predecessors, and thus the start of the successor task, back up to near fifty/fifty.

The feeding buffers (combined with the activity-dependent schedule created with establishing the critical chain) allow starting activities as late as possible, while protecting the overall project, because the feeding buffers add enough time to ensure the feeding chains are complete when needed (to a high probability). The scheduled start of the feeding chains will be later than early-start times, giving the project the maximum focus and cash flow advantages from starting later. Compare the start times of tasks 2.1 and 3.1 in Figure 8.1-6 to their start times in Figure 8.1-4 to see this effect.

CCPM uses buffer management during project execution to answer two primary questions:

For project and task managers: "Which task do I work on next?"

For the project manager, "When do I take actions to accelerate the project?"

Tracking TOC projects requires identifying when tasks start and finish and obtaining estimates on the remaining duration for tasks in work. The reason for using remaining duration rather than estimates of completion is that humans tend to overestimate the percentage complete. When called on to look forward and consider the work remaining to complete a task, more accurate estimates are obtained. Remaining duration is also the actual number needed to project completion, and estimating it directly avoids the assumptions necessary to convert a percentage complete estimate to a remaining duration estimate.

CCPM project tracking uses the estimates of remaining duration for incomplete tasks to calculate the impact of the task status, including the absorption of variation by feeding buffers, to determine how much of the project buffer has been used. Priority is placed on the tasks that cause the greatest amount of project buffer penetration. Using task priority in this way enables resources to focus on one project task at a time, thereby completing it in the minimum possible time. Tasks do not have due dates. This helps avoid having Parkinson's Law (task durations extend to use available time) or Student Syndrome (waiting to start a task until the due date is urgent) cause late task delivery. The ability to update remaining duration after tasks start also encourages using mean task duration estimates.

The mechanism to complete projects as soon as possible answers two different questions. The answer to the first question, "Which project task should I work on next?" addresses the task and resource manager's need to enable relay-racer-like task performance, avoiding bad multitasking. The answer to the second question, "When should we take action to recover schedule?" helps the project team decide when to take action to recover buffer that is being used up at too high a rate.

Figure 8.1-7 illustrates a task manager view into a CCPM project that is underway. The tasks are color coded in the task number box on the left (not visible in the graphic) to highlight the priority of the task. Red tasks (in this graphic, the first item) get the highest priority, as they are on a path that is causing significant project

FIGURE 8.1-7   Critical Chain Software Updates Tasks Using
Remaining Duration, Prioritizing Tasks to Be Worked On

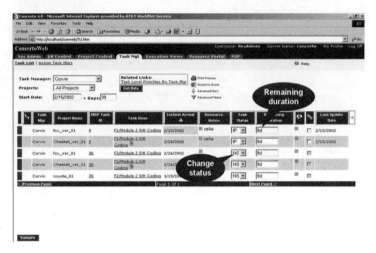

Source: Used by permission from Realization, Inc.

buffer use. The Concerto software used to generate this screen shot
is the only multiproject CCPM software that I know of that directly
provides the task level priority for the multiproject environment.

The amount of project buffer penetration also answers the second question by providing the signal to take proactive action to recover buffer (see Figure 8.1-8). If the buffer is in the yellow region
(the middle in this figure), plans are developed to recover buffer. If
the buffer penetration moves into the red region (the upper portion
in the figure), the buffer recovery actions are implemented. This approach causes the project team to focus on the tasks delaying the
project versus those that might earn the most value. Figure 8.1-8 also
shows the trend of buffer penetration, enabling anticipatory action
and easy determination of the efficacy of buffer recovery action.

Multiple-Project CCPM

The TOC process applies directly to manage projects in the multiproject environment. Consider the multiproject system illustrated
by Figure 8.1-9. Resources share their time across the three projects,

FIGURE 8.1-8 Tracking Project Progress with a Fever Chart to Signal the Project Team When to Take Action to Recover Buffer

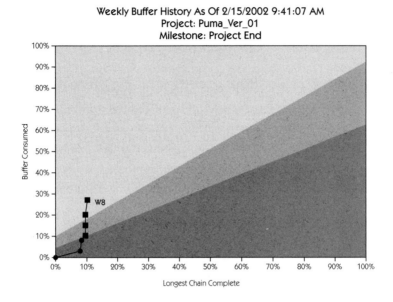

Weekly Buffer History As Of 2/15/2002 9:41:07 AM
Project: Puma_Ver_01
Milestone: Project End

FIGURE 8.1-9 A Multiproject Plan with Resources Allocated One-Third to Each Project

which causes all project tasks to take more than three times as long as they need to. Multiproject CCPM identifies the multiproject constraint as the most used resource across all of the projects and staggers the projects so resources can work 100 percent on any task they are assigned to, like the runners in a relay race. The projects are pipelined so the resources can move from project task to project task as needed to make the whole system of projects flow to the capacity of the constraint resource.

The management team first has to identify the company capacity constraint resource. This is most often a certain type of person, but may be a physical or even a policy constraint. The company constraint resource becomes the *drum* for scheduling multiple projects. This terminology comes from the TOC production methodology, where the drum sets the beat for the entire factory. Here, the drum set the beat for all of the company projects. Think of the drummer on a galleon. What happens if even one rower gets out of beat?

The project system becomes a pull system because the drum schedule determines the sequencing of projects. Management pulls projects forward in time if the drum completes project work early. Delays could affect subsequent projects when the drum is late. For this reason, projects in a multiproject environment also require buffers to protect the drum to ensure that they never starve the capacity constraint for work. CCPM schedules the projects to ensure that they are ready to use the drum resource should it become available early. CCPM staggers projects to the capacity of the drum resource, so resources can focus on one task at a time and all projects can finish sooner (see Figure 8.1-10).

Note that CCPM does not attempt to schedule all resources across all projects. The reason is that such schedules change every

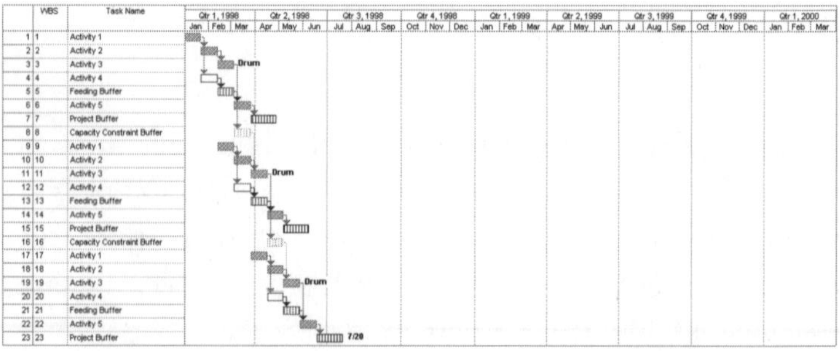

FIGURE 8.1-10 Staggering Projects to the Capacity of the Drum Resource

day as the project tasks vary. The schedule can never provide task-level start and stop dates. It is essential to determine the right task to work on based on the actual results to date. Thus, attempting to schedule into the future for all resources is meaningless. Dynamically answering the question, "Which task to work on next?" also makes it unnecessary.

Also note that synchronizing the projects to a single drum resource reduces resource contention for all resources, not just the drum resource. The example actually eliminated contention between resources for all projects because the projects are identical. Although most multiproject environments do not have identical projects, synchronizing projects to the drum usually reduces a significant amount of the resource contention in the plans, even if it does not eliminate all apparent cross-project resource contention.

The reason there will be sufficient capacity for all resources with this approach is that the drum resource is the most loaded resource across all of the projects. Leveling across projects for the most loaded resource allows sufficient time for the other resources, which have excess overall capacity, to complete their work. This does not prevent actual conflicts for any of the resources, including the drum resource. It simply ensures that there is enough time to resolve those conflicts and keep to the scheduled completion date. Buffer status provides a tool to decide which task to work on next, resolving the conflict for the resources. When they have more than one task available to work, they work on the one causing the most project buffer penetration.

TOC Portfolio Selection

We present CCPM as a practical and effective method of planning and controlling one or more projects. However, it is even more important to make sure that we are planning the right projects. This next section looks at portfolio selection, based on a TOC thinking process.

Project Identification

The first step in portfolio selection is to get an initial list of projects to select from. The TOC thinking process, or other strategic planning processes, should drive generation of this list. The main point of TOC at this level is that the projects must support the company goal and work on the company constraint. For example, if the company is a product company, strategic planning should drive projects for product development from consideration of the customer's needs and competitive strategies. The first step identified the need for projects but not necessarily the best solution to achieve the desired outcome.

Selecting the project portfolio must consider the various types of projects a company may perform. One way to categorize projects is by their customer and time urgency, as illustrated by Table 8.1-1. This categorization can be useful in a TOC approach to portfolio selection and management, as it influences the priority that will be assigned to each project.

Certain projects may have no apparent value to the company or have a value that is at best very difficult to quantify but are simply required. Type III projects are often this way. You simply have to perform the projects in order to stay in business.

The second step in portfolio selection is to create a model of each project that will enable developing the necessary information to assess the projects against the existing portfolio and other pro-

TABLE 8.1-1 Categorizing Projects by Customer and Time Urgency

	Absolute Deadline	*ASAP*
External Customer	Type I: Proposal, Event, Contract with penalties	Type II: Construction
Internal Customer	Type III: Y2K, Regulatory	Type IV: Product Development, Process Improvement

posed projects. These models should contain enough detail to understand, at a preliminary level, potential project dependencies. For example, if a company has determined that certain groups of products will share common modules (for example, as done by Microsoft and lean automobile companies), then the related projects must be linked and assessed together in portfolio development.[10]

Carrying the second step out to a level useful for portfolio development should entail consideration of broad alternative directions to achieve the outcome of the proposed projects. Often companies seize on the first solution that comes to mind at this stage and then stick with it throughout the process. This is usually a serious mistake, as the first solution that comes to mind is frequently not a good one. But once a satisfactory solution is found, there is a tendency to stop the search for better solutions. You should treat solutions posed at this stage as assumptions about the direction of the solution to enable the selection and planning process to go on, but take specific action to prevent these early solutions from getting locked in without serious review. One way to ensure this is to plan project solution direction assessments early in each new project and require serious analysis of at least several (three to five) distinctly different alternative ways to achieve the desired project outcome.

Project Selection

Once you have the information on the candidate projects, you can move on to portfolio selection. Three primary principles differentiate TOC portfolio selection from many conventional approaches:

- Recognition that there is (usually) an ongoing portfolio
- Ranking based on impact on the goal through throughput, inventory (investment), and operating expense
- Consideration of uncertainty and dependent events

The first and last points can be shared with some other approaches to portfolio selection, but often they are not addressed.

The TOC approach to ranking of projects can parallel conventional techniques, ranking according to the risk-adjusted return on investment (ROI): Risk ROI = $ROI \times (1 - R)$, where ROI = return on investment and R = risk factor, ranging from 0 (no risk) to 1 (maximum risk).

Companies often assume that ongoing projects have higher priority than new project proposals. Sometimes they make this assumption implicitly by considering only new projects for addition to the portfolio and not considering elimination of ongoing projects at the same time. This is a version of the sunk-cost fallacy, wherein people judge additional investments based on how much they have invested so far. Sunk costs are in fact sunk and should not influence decisions going forward. It is very hard for most people to decouple their thinking from what has been spent to date, but unless there could be some way to recover the sunk investment, it truly has no direct relevance for decisions regarding future investment. This means that evaluations of ongoing projects need consider only the future investment, not the investment that has already been committed.

It logically follows that you can consider project portfolio decisions one new project at a time.[11] The standard of comparison is the portfolio of ongoing projects, not the other projects proposed, coincidently, at the same time. It's okay to have a periodic process to dream up and propose new projects in a bunch. But when you do so, you should compare them to ongoing projects on the basis of remaining investment or latest estimated impact on operating expense. It is equally okay to propose new projects one at a time, at any time, and compare them to the current portfolio.

When evaluating a new project proposal against the existing portfolio, it can be important to update the return on investment calculations for the existing portfolio. One reason is that the investment calculation need only consider the estimated remaining investment to complete the project; that is, it should not include the sunk cost. In addition, often there is better information available on the range of investment and throughput impact as a project progresses.

The TOC approach to portfolio selection focuses on the goal of the organization. Project selection (including cancellation) should maximize the achievement of the goal over time. This means increasing throughput while minimizing increasing (or decreasing) inventory and operating expense. Since operating expenses are ongoing while increases in inventory (keeping in mind the TOC definition, which includes investment) are frequently transient, the impact on throughput per impact on operating expense is usually more important than the impact on investment. Thus, if one wished a simple ratio for project comparison for project ranking, TOC suggests:

$$ROI = (\Delta T - \Delta OE)/(\Delta I)$$

Where

ΔT = Probable impact on throughput

ΔOE = Probable impact on operating expense

ΔI = Probable investment increase required by the project. This includes the estimated project cost and can be negative for projects directed at reducing work in progress (WIP) inventory.

The deltas signify that each project has an incremental effect on the company throughput, operating expense, and investment.

TOC developed from understanding variation. This understanding carries into project selection. No one can predict the future exactly. All predictions involve some (usually considerable) uncertainty. The amount of this uncertainty is important to portfolio selection. Many approaches to portfolio selection consider only the mean (or some other central tendency) of the return and investment. Such approaches miss a key element of understanding variation and uncertainty. Consider the two projects illustrated in Table 8.1-2. The projects have identical estimates of the mean return and investment.

TABLE 8.1-2 Investment and Return Comparison of Two Projects with Different Risk

Project	Investment			Return		
	Minimum	Mean	Maximum	Minimum	Mean	Maximum
A	20	30	40	40	60	80
B	10	30	50	20	60	100

Would you rank one more attractive than the other? Which one? Why?

Note that based on these predictions, project B *could* have a best-case ROI of 10 (maximum return/minimum investment), while the maximum ROI of project A is only 4. On the other hand, project B could have a worst-case ROI of only 0.4 (minimum return/maximum investment); that is, it would lose money, whereas project A is predicted to at least break even in the worst case. Which you prefer can depend on many factors, including the relative size of the project compared to the financial position of your company (Can you afford the loss?) and the other projects currently in your portfolio. Substituting increase in throughput for return and increase in operating expense for investment does not materially alter the decision you have to make.

The project ranking included the impact of uncertainty or risk into a single number (ROI) for project portfolio ranking. This requires using a risk-adjusted metric. One way is to rank risk on a scale of 0 to 1, where 0 represents no risk (no uncertainty about either the investment or the return) and 1 represents a finite probability of losing your entire investment with no return.

You can estimate the risk factor a variety of ways. One way is to use a table like Table 8.1-3, estimating likely maximum and minimum impacts on throughput, operating expense, and investment. One way of estimating the risk is to compare the relative range of the variation. Table 8.1-3 illustrates an example of doing this. You can evaluate each project over a standard period of time, say five to ten years (or eight, as in the example), or you can use differing times, since ROI brings it all down to one number.

Table 8.1-3 provides a best-case and worst-case estimate for each of the elements of ROI. It then calculates the totals for the best and worst case for each element and estimates the variation (risk) for the investment and net profit. The illustrated approach uses the statistical term *s*, or standard deviation, as the measure of variation. I have assumed three standard deviations between the best- and worst-case estimates. Psychological studies evaluating people's ability to estimate reveal an overconfidence bias. That is,

TABLE 8.1-3 Project Analysis Spreadsheet for Developing the Risk-Adjusted ROI

		Project Risk-Adjusted Return on Investment								Total			
Year		1	2	3	4	5	6	7	8	Best	Worst	Average	S
Revenue	Best			3,000	3,300	3,630	3,993	4,392	4,832	23,147			
	Worst			1,500	1,575	1,654	1,736	1,823	1,914		10,203		
Raw material expense	Best			50	52	50	50	50	50	302			
	Worst			100	103	106	109	113	116		647		
Throughput	Best			2,950	3,249	3,580	3,943	4,342	4,782	22,845		16,201	
	Worst			1,400	1,472	1,548	1,627	1,711	1,798		9,556		
Operating expense	Best			50	52	53	55	56	58	323		502	
	Worst			100	105	110	116	122	126		680		
Net profit	Best			2,900	3,197	3,527	3,888	4,286	4,724	22,522		15,699	4,549
	Worst			1,300	1,367	1,437	1,511	1,589	1,671		8,876		
Investment	Best	800	600							1,400		2,200	533
	Worst	2,000	1,000								3,000		
Net return										21,122	5,876	13,499	4,580
ROI										16.1	2.0	7.1	
Risk (s/Xbar)													0.3
Risk ROI										10.6	1.3	4.7	

people tend to underestimate the range between the best and worst cases. It really does not matter much what you assume, as long as the spreadsheets you develop give the right behavior as a comparison tool between candidate projects (for example, the risk increases as the difference between best and worst case increases). You are interested in a relative ranking of projects.

Table 8.1-3 calculates risk R as the ratio of the standard deviation for the net return to the value of the net return. It calculates the standard deviation for the net return as the square root of the sum of the squares of the standard deviation of the net profit and investment. The reason is that in statistics, variances add when you add quantities. Variance is the square of the standard deviation. The main thing to understand about this is that if one of your estimates (net profit or investment) is significantly more uncertain than the other, it will dominate the risk calculated this way.

You don't have to be a statistician to use this information, but it is important to recognize that if one component of the risk is significantly larger than the other components, variation in the smaller component is even less significant than it looks. Usually the uncertainty in the project benefit is much larger than the uncertainty in the project cost. But people tend to focus on the cost because it seems more tangible and controllable.

You should use the average-risk ROI from a Table 8.1-3 calculation for each project to rank the projects for inclusion in your portfolio.

This ratio approach to risk tends to rank low-risk projects higher than high-risk projects regardless of the absolute value of potential return or loss. If your organization is risk seeking or risk averse, you may want to use a nonlinear multiplier or adjust the method of determining the risk factor.

Project Sequencing: Big Rocks First

The next step is to determine how the projects can be pipelined through your project delivery system. A given mix of projects may cause a resource to constrain the availability of your system to deliver the projects you have selected, at least adjusting the time you should plan on starting the projects. As illustrated above for multi-project TOC project management, you need to sequence the projects anyway to keep the individual project durations as short as possible. The TOC approach to sequencing projects is called *pipelining*. It creates a schedule for the drum resource (that resource which sets the beat for the whole project system) for all of the projects and then translates that back to schedules for each individual project. The master scheduler levels the work for only the drum resource across all of the projects. The work for other resources is not leveled across all projects.

There is an urban legend about a science professor who provided a demonstration to his class. He put a very large glass jar on the lab bench and put some large rocks into it. He asked the students, "Is it full?" They answered, "Yes." He then picked up a can filled with small pebbles and poured them in around the big rocks. He asked again, "Is it full?" The students, getting the idea, smiled and said, "Yes, *now* it's full." He then picked up a can with sand in it, and poured the sand in around the pebbles, and asked again, "Is it full?" The students, now a little worried, tentatively answered yes again. Finally, in the version I like best, he picked up a large bottle of beer and poured it into the jar, telling the students, "*Now* it is full. The purpose of this demonstration is to show that there is always room for beer." No, the purpose was to show that what at first appears to be a full system may not be full. The same will be true for your project delivery system as you add projects to it. You can often add more projects that do not use much of the drum resource without affecting all of the other projects.

As noted earlier, all projects are not created equally (see Table 8.1-1). Projects that you have committed to clients are, by and large, more important than internal improvement projects. Yet both types of projects may compete for the same resources within your company. One way of reconciling the priority conflict is to use the matrix presented in Table 8.1-1 for types of projects to guide placing projects in the drum schedule. First overall priority should go to projects that you have company commitments for (see Table 8.1-4).

TABLE 8.1-4 An Approach to Entering Projects into the Drum Schedule

	Date Driven	ASAP
External	Priority I: Big rocks: first access to drum	Priority II: Throughput/constraint sequence
Internal	Priority III: As necessary	Priority IV: Throughput/constraint sequence

You can fit the other projects in around them. There may also be some relatively high-priority projects that you have to do (for example, regulatory requirement, broken infrastructure, obsolete software) but don't have an identifiable ROI. Those should be priority 3 initially, but may move up to priority 2 if they can't meet need dates as priority 3.

You should then use your risk-adjusted ranking to put the projects into the drum schedule. You can use the risk-adjusted ROI as demonstrated to select the projects, or you can rerank the projects you have selected in terms of the amount of throughput (T) they will use relative to the amount of the drum resource (constraint, C) they demand, that is, the T/C ratio.

Figure 8.1-11 illustrates a TOC scheduling tool used to perform project pipelining. The Concerto software uses Microsoft Project to plan each individual project as a critical chain project and then provides an easy to use tool to insert projects into the multiproject schedule and estimate the impact on all of the projects in the system.

Net Present Value

Net present value (NPV) is a calculation tool to account for the time value of money. It applies a discount to future cash flows using an interest rate reflective of expected inflation, interest, or some

FIGURE 8.1-11 Concerto Software Pipelining
Tool for Scheduling Multiple Projects

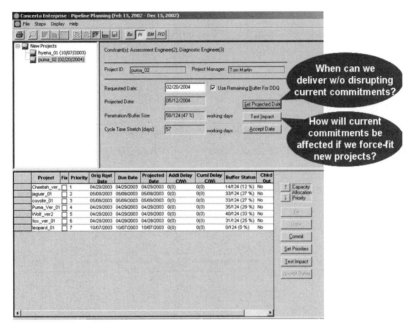

other financial rate. It affects both the positive and negative cash flows from projects. Since it treats short-term cash flows as more valuable, it favors projects with short-term returns and longer-term investments, which are usually exclusive. It doesn't directly hurt your portfolio evaluation process, but it does have the downside of conveying a degree of precision in future estimates that probably isn't justified (the mathematical elegance might inappropriately increase belief in your uncertain estimates). It also requires estimating an appropriate discount rate, a matter that adds variation to your portfolio process and is a topic that your financial people can argue about endlessly. You normally will not find great differences in the attractiveness or relative priority of projects whether you use NPV or not. Nevertheless, it is simple to program it into your project evaluation spreadsheet. Should we return to double-digit inflation and interest rates or if you have a mix of short-term and very long-term projects to rank, you might consider using NPV. Otherwise, I suggest not doing so. Be prepared for comments from your financial people if you choose not to use NPV, as they seem to appreciate the sheer beauty of the calculation and often have little understanding of uncertainty.

Special Cases

Most organizations have some level of special case considerations that make the ROI approach difficult—for example:

- Projects driven by regulatory requirements
- Performing required facility, equipment, or software upgrades due to obsolescence or growth needs
- The need to keep a product development pipeline full at several stages so as not to run out of new products in the future

Special cases can be handled by applying the TOC focusing steps and thinking process and keeping the goal of the organization in mind. Many of these issues are addressed in the other chapters in this book, and many of the solutions suggested remain viable in the context of CCPM.

TOC Portfolio Management

TOC portfolio management seeks to complete projects as soon as possible and answer management's two questions: "When are you going to be done?" and "How much is it going to cost?"

Portfolio management also requires continuous assurance that the project benefit is going to be achieved. The following demonstrates how TOC seeks to operationally answer those questions with forward-looking action decisions.

When Are You Going to Be Done? Figure 8.1-12 illustrates the primary method used by CCPM to track schedule performance on a portfolio of projects. The project tracking must be timely to aid the

FIGURE 8.1-12 Portfolio Status Chart Based on CCPM Values

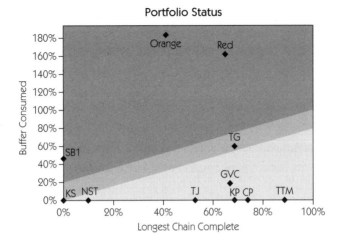

operational purposes of project management, thereby giving portfolio managers better insight into the performance of projects than
many systems. A graphic such as Figure 8.1-12 is usually accompa-
nied by a table providing the current projected completion date for
each project, compared to the scheduled completion (when the
project buffer would be 100 percent consumed). This directly answers the question asked. CCPM simplifies viewing progress on a
project portfolio, highlighting those requiring buffer recover action.

Projects that are in the light gray (lower region) are doing fine,
and require no management attention. Projects in the medium gray
(middle region) should be creating buffer recovery plans. Projects
in the dark gray (upper region) should be implementing buffer recovery plans. Note that projects with buffer penetration less than
100 percent may still be on track to complete on time. Management should drill down for projects in the upper (dark gray) region
to examine the trends and efficacy of the buffer recovery actions.

How Much Is It Going to Cost? For some types of projects, the
TOC approach clarifies that project investment cost is much less
important than previously thought. For example, the impact of

completing new product development projects as soon as possible to gain the first-to-market advantage usually far outweighs the cost to accelerate the project. However, in certain situations and for certain types of projects, cost can be important. For example, a company doing primarily fixed-price projects on contract can make or lose money based on project cost.

When project cost is important, the earned value method of comparing actual cost to estimated cost becomes necessary. The reason is that actual cost is influenced by schedule. Understanding how a project is performing on cost relative to the estimate requires removing the confounding effect of schedule because a project may appear to be over or under on cost, but may actually be ahead or behind on schedule.

For this purpose, you should use a cost buffer.[12] The cost buffer is the cost equivalent to the schedule buffers described above. There should be one cost buffer for the project. The total project estimate is the sum of the task estimates plus the cost buffer. You should estimate the cost buffer considering the cost variation of each of the project cost elements.

You can track cost buffer penetration using the same graphics presented above for schedule buffer tracking. The only difference required is to change the abscissa to represent the percentage of the task budget expended. You can use both the single-project trend version of the chart (Figure 8.1-8), and the multiproject point version (Figure 8.1-12).

You should estimate cost buffer penetration as a percentage of the cost buffer consumed. The earned value cost variance (CV) is the amount of cost buffer consumed. Using the cost buffer this way is an excellent example of combining conventional project management methods with TOC.

Schedule and cost buffer tracking sometimes give contrary indications. For example, you may be in the red on both cost and schedule. Some options to accelerate schedule may require additional expenditures. Understanding the impacts on project benefits may help you resolve such conflicts.

Ensuring Project Benefit

Although many companies do a good job of tracking performance on the schedule, cost, and scope of authorized projects, I have never seen an example of providing an equivalent level of measurement or scrutiny to project benefit. Often, once a project is started, the focus switches to the performance of the project. From a TOC perspective, this is surprising given the large impact that project benefit has on the ROI and the usual case of much greater uncertainty on project benefit than on project investment.

Periodic updating of the project risk-adjusted ROI (Table 8.1-3) provides one mechanism to ensure project benefit. Ensuring accountability for project benefit can add to focus on it.

I discussed how the TOC approach enables adding new projects to the portfolio as they arise and that when doing so, one should update the project risk-adjusted ROI to rank the projects considering only the remaining investment to complete, removing the sunk cost. This provides an opportunity to also update the benefit estimates.

Larry Leach is the president of Advanced Projects and teaches graduate-level management courses for the University of Phoenix. He has published many papers in his field and is the author of *Critical Chain Project Management* (2nd ed., 2004). Larry is certified as a Project Management Professional by the Project Management Institute, an instructor for PMI's seminar series, and a speaker at PMI conferences and for global project management training. He has master's degrees in business management and mechanical engineering.

SECTION NINE

Case Studies

We can write all we want about why and how to do project portfolio management. Perhaps the best teacher, however, is the experience of others who have gone the PPM route. The four chapters in this section present case studies with the intent of providing illustrations and insight into the implementation of the PPM processes.

We start with one of the early adopters, Crompton Corporation. I have great admiration for these brave souls who dare to take a new fork in the road well before it is marked and paved. With ten years invested in moving to PPM, Crompton Corporation has had enough time to evaluate the benefits from PPM, fine-tune the processes, and catalogue what to do and what not to do. Rebecca Seibert tells the insightful and revealing Crompton story in Chapter 9.1. The lessons to be learned from the Crompton/Seibert experience will go a long way in providing guidance into what to do and what not to do in implementing PPM. Seibert frequently mentions the guidance provided by the writings of Cooper, Edgett, and Kleinschmidt. Fortunately, much of this source material was updated and is provided in Chapters 7.1 and 7.2 by Robert Cooper.

The second case study features Hewlett-Packard. The merger of HP and Compaq in 2002 created monumental challenges, and skeptics questioned its potential value and success. Under the critical eye of the industry and the public, Don Kingsberry, director of the HP Global Program Management Office, elected to test the benefits of PPM. In Chapter 9.2, Kingsberry discusses the challenges and accomplishments of this venture as he employs PPM to ferret out redundant programs and validate alignment of projects with newly emerging strategies. We are extremely indebted to Kingsberry for sharing the proprietary PPM and program management methods and wisdom developed at HP.

Wherever structured methods are developed to address management issues, an obliging tool industry steps up to provide software to automate the processes. These vendors become partners with the early adopters to facilitate the growth and success of the technology. They are all proud to present their successes, and we include two of these in this section. Chapter 9.3 covers the application of PPM at AOL. Chapter 9.4 discusses PPM at EW Scripps. Both firms report significant benefits from their PPM applications.

9.1

Managing Your Technology Pipeline Portfolio Management Process and Its Evolution over Time

Rebecca Seibert

In 1995, the petroleum additives business at Crompton Corporation implemented a disciplined business technology portfolio management (PM) system. Designing and implementing project management was the third element of a four-element implementation plan for the petroleum additives business that included a successful implementation of a Stage-Gate® process for new product and new process development programs (NPPD),[1] training and deploying cross-functional project teams for all NPPD programs, and a front-end innovation process.[2] The goals of the PM process were textbook:[3]

- Maximize the value of the portfolio for the business and corporation.
- Achieve a balanced portfolio of short-term and long-term programs that were strategically aligned through the business.
- Effectively allocate the *right* resources on these short- and long-term programs.

This robust business portfolio management process has morphed and evolved over the past decade, changing as necessary to meet the needs of the business, the corporation, and the corporation's stakeholders. What has remained constant over this time period is the use of a portfolio management process whereby the business is able to evaluate, select, prioritize, and manage opportunities and projects in a dynamic decision-making environment. This process has been effective in meeting our business goals. Success is measured in many ways. The most significant indicator of a process that is working effectively is the fact that in a market with growth of zero to –1 percent on a worldwide basis, the Crompton petroleum additives business has grown at a rate far above this and remains a business "that will receive investment to grow."[4] Currently, the petroleum additives portfolio management process is being used as the basis for other businesses at Crompton and will be implemented at the corporate-level within a year.

This chapter does not explain how to design, implement, or maintain a portfolio management system. Rather, it is to tell a story of one business and one person's adventures in PM. It examines the basics of our PM process, tools that worked for us and some that were less effective, implementation experiences, and because the process implementation was driven from within the R&D ranks of the business, how we knew when the process had progressed from a technology-owned process to a business-owned process. This process has survived and thrived amid changes in ownership of the corporation, a merger, and several changes in personnel, including changes in the business head twice in the past ten years. It has survived because our portfolio management process has given us the ability to maximize the value of our pipeline portfolio through effective selection and management of a risk- and resource-adjusted portfolio of projects aligned to meet the business' strategic plans.

Building the Whole Business Technology Project Portfolio (The Collection of Programs)

Robert G. Cooper, Scott Edgett, and Elko Kleinschmidt define portfolio management as a dynamic decision process, whereby a business's list of development projects and new product programs are reviewed, updated, and revised on a regular basis. In this process, new products are evaluated, selected, and prioritized. Existing projects are also evaluated and may be accelerated, deprioritized, or killed. Resources are naturally allocated to active projects according to priorities set. The portfolio management process is characterized by uncertain and ever changing information, dynamic opportunities, multiple conflicting goals, strategic considerations, interdependence among projects, and multiple decision makers spread across the world. Decision making in portfolio management encompasses a number of decision-making processes within the business, including regularly scheduled portfolio reviews; analysis and decision making on the collection of projects that make up the portfolio; making go/no go decisions on individual projects on an ongoing basis; setting new product, process, and project strategy for the business; and making strategic resource allocation decisions.[5]

This is essentially how we approach portfolio management. Our business team consists of the commercial management, marketing management, and technical management players. We consider technology portfolio management to be a business process and collection of many tools that are designed to help the business team make better decisions, manage risk, and plan for the future. We work hard not to be driven by the process, but to drive the process to enable us to achieve our business strategy.

Our portfolio management system has *three critical elements* that have contributed to its successful design, implementation, and sustainability:

- It encompasses the whole innovation pipeline.
- It features senior management–level support, proactive participation, and staff proactive support and participation.
- It uses effective practices, tools, and methodology.[6]

Encompassing the Whole Innovation Pipeline

If one of the objectives of portfolio management is to ensure alignment of the technology portfolio with the business strategy, then portfolio management processes need to encompass the whole innovation pipeline, not merely focusing on the new product and new process development portion of the pipeline. Figure 9.1-1 illustrates the spectrum of activities that can occur along the innovation pipeline.

Focusing on only the NPPD piece in portfolio management and ignoring or placing less emphasis on technical service, factory service, application development of commercial products, or new concept development, for example, in balancing one's pipeline can lead to difficulties. Initially we considered only new product or new process development programs in our portfolio process. However, in the first portfolio review, we found that we were spending much of our time discussing and updating the business management team on programs that fell into the product life cycle management category. We were analyzing their importance and making portfolio prioritization decisions in reference to them rather than focusing on growth programs. Thus, we quickly revised our portfolio manage-

FIGURE 9.1-1 Innovation Pipeline Activities

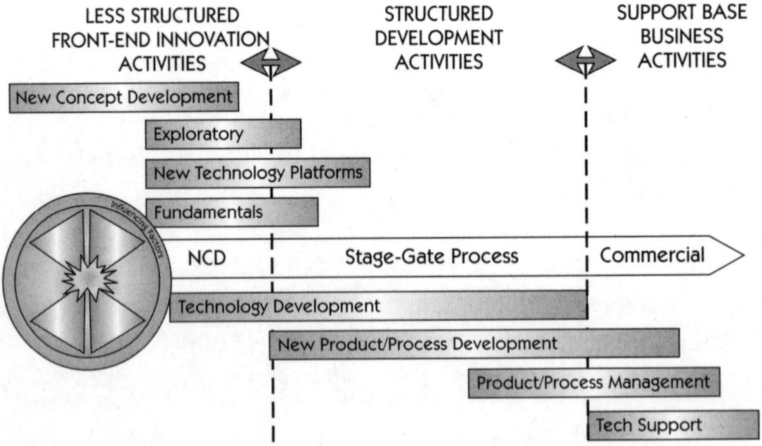

Source: P. Koen and others, "New Concept Development Model: Providing Clarity and a Common Language to the 'Fuzzy Front End' of Innovation," *Research Technology Management*, 2001, 44(2), 46–55.

ment system to accommodate all programs that technology resources would be allocated to. In my interactions with people from other companies that have an active portfolio management process, I have learned that they also have found the need to expand their process to include the whole pipeline, not just new product programs.

In addition, we revised our Stage-Gate process to include reviews of all programs, not just new product or new process programs. Companies that have excluded or ignored the key discipline of ongoing postlaunch product life cycle management in the past have found that over time, resources are not available to work on new projects.[7] Some have shifted to evaluating the portfolio in terms of buckets or categories,[8] such as support/enhancement, derivative, platform/next generation, and breakthrough.[9] Since every activity a resource spends time and money on should bring value to the corporation, it stands to reason that all activities along the innovation pipeline should be reviewed and prioritized as part of the portfolio management process. Focusing only on the middle new product development portion of the pipeline can lead to overmanagement of the middle and poor management of the front and tail ends of the pipeline. Throughput or movement of programs through the pipeline will suffer over time if management of the front end of the pipeline is neglected. Support functions such as technical service, manufacturing, and operations certainly contribute positively to the value of the corporation. They undertake projects that achieve enhancements in existing products and processes. These should be part of the managed portfolio.[10]

Senior Management Support, Proactive Participation, and Staff Support and Participation

When asked what the *one key element* of our portfolio management system is that makes it effective, my answer is, "*Senior management support and proactive participation by them and their staff.*" It's easy to say senior-level support is important; however, more than this is required. Senior management participation is essential not just in the initial implementation of any business process, but also in sustaining an effective process over time. It requires senior management's interactive and proactive participation on a consistent basis. The proactive participation of their staff is critical as well. For example, if the business managers or the marketing managers are not providing high-quality data needed to run the appropriate financial analysis or if they are not participating in the pipeline-filling activities at the front end, then the *right* programs are not necessarily chosen to enter the pipeline, individual projects fail over time due to incorrect or insufficient information, and the pipeline goals are not met. Participation and accountability of the business team are essential.

To illustrate this point, consider the first portfolio review meeting we held in 1995. The executive vice president of the division attended the entire day-long off-site meeting as his way of promoting participation and emphasizing his support of the new process. Also in attendance were the business vice presidents and their commercial and technical management staff. Although it made sense that we needed to manage our portfolio better, there was nothing natural about the first portfolio management meeting of the minds. It was clear to the technology team that a disciplined portfolio management process was long overdue. We had too many programs in our pipeline vying for resources. It was clear to the executive vice president of the division that our portfolio needed more disciplined focus on the strategy, fewer programs, and faster delivery of earnings. However, the rest of the leadership team was not convinced. Resources in technology had historically been treated as existing in strategic business unit (SBU) buckets that would not be moved between businesses. The executive vice president opened the meeting with, "These are not *your* resources or your programs. They are the corporation's resources and programs."

Our task was to take the collection of miscellaneous programs and determine which were strategically tied to business goals and how to allocate resources across them. Overallocation of R&D and marketing personnel was commonplace in our organization. As a result, project goals were rarely met in a timely basis, and goals were unrealistic. The initial activity the group participated in was designed to change their mind-set in terms of selection of programs and allocation of resources and recognition that these activities cost money. Picture eighteen technical, marketing, and operation managers sitting in a conference room at a hotel. On the table in front of them were fifty-two pieces of paper, each individually labeled with a new product or new process project name that the business was funding. Listed on each paper were the resource requirements required to complete that project as specified by each of the project leaders. Handed out to the managers were several bags of poker chips containing hundreds of poker chips labeled with each person's initials in the division—twelve chips per person in technology, marketing, or operations representing one month of a person's time per poker chip. The assignment was to allocate the poker chips to the pieces of paper, fulfilling the resource needs of each project.

The reception was less than enthusiastic. Certainly this could have been done in a spreadsheet format easily, as we do today. However, the objective was twofold: (1) to communicate that people are resources that equate to money spent by the corporation and (2) to show that our time and talents were finite. As the poker chips were distributed among the papers on the table, it became alarmingly clear to everyone in the room that there were many more projects with critical resource needs than there were poker chips to provide resources to the programs. In fact, fewer than a quarter of the programs could be resourced fully before the poker chips (people and time) ran out. It also demonstrated that there was no slack time for technical or market development personnel to investigate front-end opportunities. This exercise communicated the fact better than I could ever explain to them that we had too many programs and too few resources. It was the foundation that convinced the team that we had some tough decisions to make in terms of what programs we should resource.

Fast-forward five years to when Uniroyal Chemical Company merged with Witco Corporation. Petroleum additives was one of the businesses that benefited from this merger. Our product lines were compatible and increased the basket of goods we had available to offer customers. What did not increase appreciably was the size of the technology department. Thus, we again had a situation of too many programs and too few resources. We also had a major strategy change with the merger of the two companies. The new vice president of the petroleum additives business politely listened to my sales pitch concerning our Stage-Gate process for managing individual programs and our portfolio management system for assessing, defining, and managing the collection of programs. At the end of the presentation to him and his team, his comments were, "I like this! Let's scrap our current process, which is far too cumbersome, and use this one. It gives me the elements I am looking for to achieve our strategy for growth." It is notable that his company, prior to merger, had expended considerable resources on a different project and portfolio management process with little success. To his credit, he walked his talk and was my most supportive, proactive participant in implementing the portfolio process, maintaining it over time, and holding his team accountable for the data needed to manage the portfolio, as well as the pipeline results, in the new organization.

Innovation as a Strategy

When I introduce the topic of portfolio management, I raise the issue of why portfolio management needs senior management. Steven Wheelwright and Kim Clark, in their book *Revolutionizing Product Development*, address the timing and impact of management attention and influence.[11] In many cases, senior management does not spend enough time or dedicate appropriate resources early in the development funnel to develop concepts and strategies for creating, shaping, and selecting the right set of projects to fill the innovation pipeline for commercial success in the short and long term. Their impact early in setting vision and strategy and selecting the right programs and activities is invaluable and creates a foundation for a healthy pipeline. Regular monitoring and early risk abatement are critical and will result in a higher pipeline throughput rate, a reduction in the need for senior management involvement late in the pipeline for crisis-reduction activities, and less rework on projects.

It is well recognized that companies need to create development funnels, not tunnels. However, loading the funnel with the best projects up front requires senior management's active participation to identify and select these opportunities. Management's ability to influence a development project's outcome is high early in the development process, during the initial investigations/knowledge acquisition and concept validation/state of candidate phases. In other words, influence by senior management is best realized at the front end of the innovation pipeline, where new concept development and selection of programs occurs. Typically, however, senior management's actual activities are limited early in the innovation pipeline and increase dramatically late in the project when the program is in trouble or needs to expend significant resources in terms of money and capital. After-the-fact problem solving rather than problem-prevention planning is the focus. Proper time spent planning up front in the pipeline to select and define programs leads to a pipeline filled with well-defined projects, adequate resourcing and risk management plans, proper skill levels on the programs, and agreed-on execution plans that the team is then charged with carrying through. Once senior management understands and believes in this chart, one can begin to engage them in the activities of the shaded region and in creating a disciplined project portfolio.

Since strategic planning is conducted at the business unit level and the corporate level, technology strategies should also be integrated into the business and corporate strategies. This is a challenge for technology and business leaders, who can frequently be distracted by day-to-day issues and quarterly earning requirements. It takes time and energy to affect both levels. It requires both a short-term focus and a longer-term focus on an enterprisewide basis by both technical and commercial leaders. Technology leaders and business leaders must demonstrate strong leadership, ownership, and credibility in the portfolio management activities. For an effective, sustaining portfolio, involvement in the process at all levels of the organization is necessary. Consider one of the models we use in our process, shown in Figure 9.1-2.

FIGURE 9.1-2 From Ideas to Programs to Products and Processes

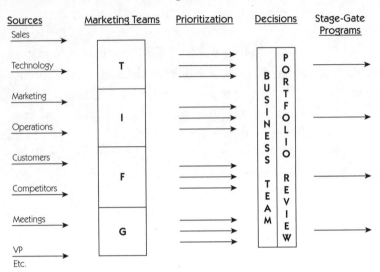

Ideas, opportunities, and program options come from many sources. The process needs to include collection of this information and then analysis of the information as a mechanism for defining programs that fit the business strategy. Cross-functional market and business teams are one mechanism for evaluating information for ideas and opportunities.

Effective Tools, Methodologies, and Practices

There are many tools and methodologies available for managing one's portfolio. These are described in books and journals and also readily available on the Internet. But the most effective tool is people: *the right set of people*.

The Right Set of People. The challenge is to find the RIGHT SET OF PEOPLE appropriately dedicated to design, implement, champion, participate in, and nurture the portfolio management system. Teamwork and being well networked in the organization are very important. I frequently recommend *The Wisdom of Teams* to people as a way to foster their understanding of the importance of a team-oriented culture.[12] A certain camaraderie exists in our business team. We operate under two mottos: "All hands on deck" and "We work hard; we play hard." "All hands on deck" means that very few handoffs occur in our team settings. The expression "that's not my job" is not in the mind-set of the business team. If we need marketing information for a specific program and the marketing manager is occupied with other duties, it is not uncommon for the technology team member, for example, to gather that information and communicate it to the team. The lines of functionality are often blurred, allowing people with the appropriate skills to be empowered to get the work done. Issues are openly discussed and often in a very animated manner. The heavyweight team is most often the structure present for program management and portfolio management.[13] Skills outweigh job titles. There is a level of respect present between the team members that allows us to share our thoughts openly. It is critical that we share our thoughts, even if it means disagreeing with "the boss." And we take the time to talk about our families, our hobbies, our exasperating teenagers, and our adorable toddlers. Understanding each others' *whole* lives and not just our work lives helps us understand each other better and enables us to communicate better as a team. Consensus decision making is desired; however, when this cannot be reached, a decision is made by the appropriate person, and the team moves forward to carry out plans to support that decision.

The Process Owner. Included in the right set of people is the process owner. This was a newly created position in our organization whose responsibilities are to create, implement, and manage the innovation pipeline through the use of project and portfolio management best practices. The design of our Stage-Gate process and our portfolio process were part of this solution, as were the shift to project management by heavyweight cross-functional teams. The design and implementation of both processes were completed with the business and technology team deeply involved in the design.

The process owner facilitated this. This position reports directly to the vice president of technology and is a member of the business leadership team. One improvement I suggest is that the position should report to the commercial side of the business, not the technology side. The characteristics of a person fulfilling this role are many. Of course, this person needs to be well versed in program management, portfolio management, and the design and implementation of business processes. However, these can be learned if there is a lack of experience in these areas. More important, the person needs to have good interpersonal skills, a focus on team-building activities, the ability to handle a diverse set of personalities, excellent facilitation skills, be well networked with the businesses and technology departments, and be optimistic. This person's job is to also seek continuous improvement in the process.

Communication. The advantage of an effective portfolio management process is the communication that occurs at all levels of the organization. Tools that enhance communication of critical pipeline issues are vital. Issues are identified and communicated so that the risk can be managed. When issues are identified on a regular basis, the team learns to make decisions together quickly and move on to other items.

In selecting the set of projects to make up the portfolio, significant communications occur. Dashboards provide snapshots in time of a program's status. Involving a cross-functional business team in the selection process results in decisions being made as a result of the communication process. Senior corporate management and technology management become aligned. The portfolio tools do not make decisions for the team. They lead to communications that result in the team's making a decision. Often it is not the decision that is the most meaningful but the exchange of information that occurs as the team systematically reviews each project for its status, deliverables, strengths, weaknesses, opportunities, and threats.

Our portfolio management system consists of regularly scheduled meetings. There are two types of portfolio meetings we schedule.

The major portfolio analysis, with review and reworking of the technology portfolio, occurs twice a year. It is generally held off-site, and the worldwide business team attends. The outcome of this *working* meeting is as follows:

- Agreement on pipeline programs, prioritization, and resource assignments.

- Agreement on strategic integration and alignment of the technology portfolio with the business strategy. This includes planning for support of existing platforms, products, services, and programs, as well as future platform planning.

- Focus on the front end, including clear identification of opportunities we are currently not resourcing but are considering for the future. This includes specific action plans to drive decision making on these opportunities in the near future.

- Management of the resources across and within projects within SBUs.

- Portfolio management process performance and improvement plans.

Although this is an ambitious list, it is accomplished because of the prework that is put together and distributed prior to the meeting.

The second type of meeting we hold are monthly meetings scheduled to coincide with the monthly business team meeting. The monthly business team meetings are held by the vice president of the business to review the business performance, identify and resolve commercial issues, perform supply and operations planning, and address portfolio opportunities. They are held on a specific day each month, and people attend on a worldwide basis either in person or by telephone. We share documents over the Internet. The portfolio portion of the meeting is scheduled in a one- to two-hour period and covers these items:

- The progress of the aggregate portfolio pipeline
- Resource consumption issues

- One or two specific program updates and issues resolution or a Stage-Gate type of review for go or no-go decisions
- Evaluate new project opportunities

The list of projects to be reviewed or gate decisions to be made are scheduled ahead of time on a six-month planning basis at the off-site portfolio working meeting. Participants at this monthly meeting can be broader, since project reviews and gate review can be on the agenda. Project teams are invited in as the team presents their gate review package and recommendations of next steps. Since decisions on one program affect all programs in the portfolio, it is a wonderful opportunity for individual project teams to see the business team at work, resolving the aggregate portfolio issues, as well as making decisions on the specific project recommendations of the project team.

Elements of the Portfolio Management System

A basic flowchart of our portfolio management process is shown in Figure 9.1-3. The boxes explain the specific steps in the process. The functions typically involved in the work of the step are noted underneath in brackets. This basic flow chart was developed internally, but in reality it is probably not unlike the basic flow chart many companies could draw to demonstrate their project management process. The value is in the quality of the execution.

Portfolio Documentation

The portfolio documentation required for consideration for optimum resourcing consist of the following elements:

1. Project-level information form
2. Project snapshot form[14]
3. Anchored scales
4. Expected commercial value financial analysis

FIGURE 9.1-3 Portfolio Management Review Process Flowchart

Petroleum Additives Division Portfolio Management Review Process

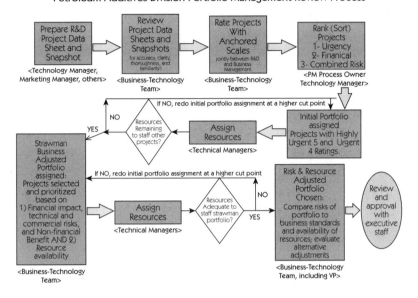

5. Design for Six Sigma or Six Sigma charter form, if appropriate[15]

6. Project plan containing milestones, critical tasks, and resource requirements

Element 1: Project-Level Information

The first step in receiving funding is to provide project-level information. This form, fondly referred to as the "9 Question Form," is known throughout the petroleum additives organization as the place to start when someone has identified an opportunity, project, or idea. The sole objective is to capture as much information as possible to allow the business team to make an initial determination as to the attractiveness of the opportunity. It has evolved from a printed piece of paper that was copied and distributed for comments and consideration to an online form that can be electronically altered by anyone with input. Many organizations have similar forms.

One business at Crompton currently implementing a portfolio management process has customized the form to capture Six Sigma or Design for Six Sigma critical to quality parameters as well. Exhibit 9.1-1 shows an example of the information that is covered. These project-level information forms can be evergreen, adding and

EXHIBIT 9.1-1 Project-Level Information Questions

Project-Level Information

- What is the objective of the project?
- Type of project (support, growth, defensive, etc.).
- Existing or proposed market.
- What technology/market deficiency are you attempting to solve?
- What is the reason for the project?
    - Performance need or improvement and customer interest when completed
    - How many/what customers have validated this need?
    - What are the critical to quality (CTQ) factors (what aspects of the product are key to the customer)?
- Approximation of potential market size, annual sales, profit, or cost savings.
- Timing and resource requirements to complete, indicating any possible trade-offs.
- Describe its fit with core capabilities and significant capital/equipment needs.
- Describe any special requirements for development that we do not currently have.
- Competitive position that will be achieved by this project.
- Urgency of the need for completion.
- Estimate of competitive impact of delay if work is not started in (1) 6 months, (2) 12 months, (3) 2 years.
- If this is a program in progress, what, if any, are the present obstacles or roadblocks?

---

amending information as needed. It is important to recognize that all the information asked for may not be available. We capture what we know and revise as more information is learned.

Element 2: Project Snapshot Form

A snapshot (see Figure 9.1-4) is a high-level form that attempts to capture the status of a project at a moment in time. This one-page format contains much of the information necessary to make fast assessments of projects. It is probably our most referenced form at all levels of the organization. It provides the basic information of the project, including name, type, business and technical objectives (high level), and spending in the left column. Financial benefits are captured in the center column. The right column contains program status, issues, short-term commitment information, and team composition. Along the bottom is gate timing status. There are columns capturing metrics for plan, current estimates, and last estimates for

FIGURE 9.1-4 Snapshot Form

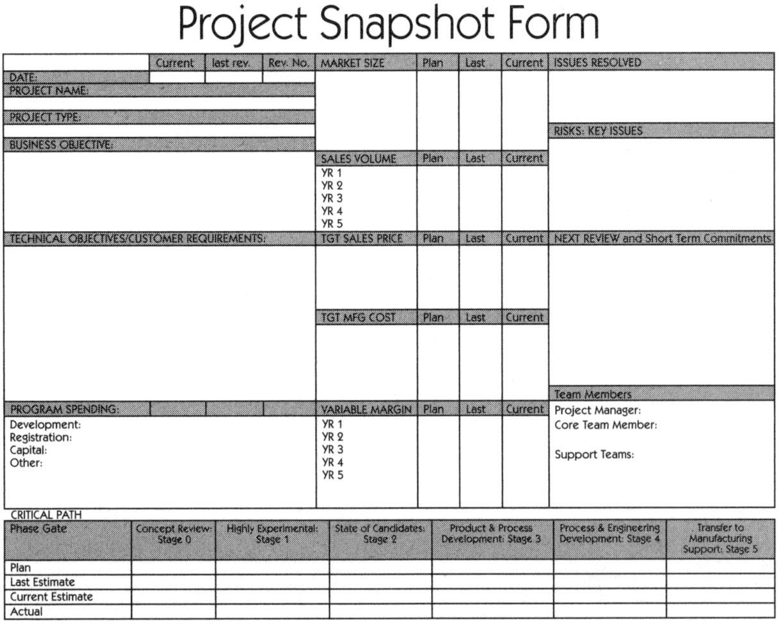

Project Snapshot Form

Current | last rev. | Rev. No. | MARKET SIZE | Plan | Last | Current | ISSUES RESOLVED

DATE:

PROJECT NAME:

PROJECT TYPE:

RISKS: KEY ISSUES

BUSINESS OBJECTIVE:

SALES VOLUME | Plan | Last | Current

YR 1
YR 2
YR 3
YR 4
YR 5

TECHNICAL OBJECTIVES/CUSTOMER REQUIREMENTS:

TGT SALES PRICE | Plan | Last | Current

NEXT REVIEW and Short Term Commitments

TGT MFG COST | Plan | Last | Current

Team Members

PROGRAM SPENDING:

Development:
Registration:
Capital:
Other:

VARIABLE MARGIN | Plan | Last | Current

YR 1
YR 2
YR 3
YR 4
YR 5

Project Manager:
Core Team Member:
Support Teams:

CRITICAL PATH

Phase Gate	Concept Review: Stage 0	Highly Experimental: Stage 1	State of Candidates: Stage 2	Product & Process Development: Stage 3	Process & Engineering Development: Stage 4	Transfer to Manufacturing Support: Stage 5
Plan						
Last Estimate						
Current Estimate						
Actual						

financials and critical path timing information. This form is ever-green and is updated as frequently as necessary but at a minimum of twice a year.

Element 3: Anchored Scales

Comparing projects is difficult in a dynamic decision-making environment. Comparing projects is sometimes akin to comparing apples and cows. They seem completely different. How does one place them on the same plane for decision making? Projects are at different stages of development. Projects are not independent of each other. The decision to fund one project takes away funds from another project. Projects do not stand still, and there is always more information to be sought. New opportunities are continually presenting themselves to the business. Our anchored scales are a communication and decision-making tool that provide the business team a process with which to evaluate projects with respect to strategic benefit, commercial and technical risk, and urgency. The numerical assessment obtained for each project allows ranking of the programs to develop a balanced portfolio.

These scales include several important factors affecting the decisions to assign resources for the budgeting process. These were developed internally to reflect our business's projects and situations that we experience most often or sought in our growth plans. Participation in the Research-on-Research Subcommittees of the Industrial Research Institute was especially helpful in the development of these scales.[16] The scales use judgmental ratings based around anchoring words and phrases designed to capture our qualitative views as easily and as reliably as possible. The scales address these areas:

- Strategic fit, including nonfinancial business benefits
- Commercial risk
- Technical risk
- Urgency (initiation and completion)
- Financial rating

The last area of financial results is a temporary fill-in for calculations related to net present value, which can take time to complete accurately, especially for programs early on in the innovation pipeline.

The value in using anchored scales is not just the numerical ranking that results. Initially, rating the projects was done on an individual basis, and then a brief meeting was held to clean up the data where discrepancies existed. However, one process improvement the team made was to anchor all projects at the same time together. The cross-functional market teams or business teams rate the projects together. Consensus must be reached on a rating. In reaching consensus, many issues found value in that they were able to unearth information that might not have surfaced otherwise. Connections between projects, markets, and outside opportunities are realized. This communication is very valuable. Discussions about the project's risk tolerance are especially valuable. The conversation threads are usually captured in a document, including follow-up action items. Use of anchored scales is easily applied to a SWOT (Strength, Weaknesses, Opportunities, Threats) analysis and a C&E (Cause and Effect) Matrix. It is also a good team-building tool. The categories of anchored scales we use to rate projects are shown in Exhibit 9.1-2.

The scales consist of a simple scoring scheme, such as 1 (low) to 5 (high), such that each number is uniquely associated with a set of key business words or phrases that are the anchors. The scales have been drafted as much as possible to accommodate and reflect the likely ranges of projects and business situations that are typical for our organization. They are easily adaptable to other businesses with different issues and are currently being used by another division at Crompton. Responses are meant to be qualitative, not quantitative. As each project is scored on a specific scale, the responses should reflect the overall positioning based around one's sense of how the project is reflected in the anchoring words and phrases.

Additional anchored scales can also be used to examine the entire portfolio to determine whether their technology portfolios are aligned with the strategy of the businesses they serve.[17]

EXHIBIT 9.1-2 Anchored Scales for Rating Projects

1. Nonfinancial Benefits

    1.1 Impact on Business

    1.2 Importance to Competitive Positioning

    1.3 Platform for Growth

    1.4 Durability of Product/Solution

2. Commercial Risk

    2.1 Marketing Risk

    2.2 Clarity of Problem Definition

    2.3 Commercial Risk of Missing Performance Targets

    2.4 Material Usage Risk

    2.5 Certainty of Market Need

    2.6 Risk of Commercial Response

3. Technical Risk

    3.1 Competencies/Skills

    3.2 Complexity of Problem

    3.3 Degree of Invention Required

    3.4 Pilot, Scale-Up, and Manufacturability (internal or tolled)

    3.5 Intellectual Property/Proprietary Position

4. Urgency

5. Expected Financial Results

Element 4: Expected Commercial Value Financial Analysis

We began using the published expected commercial value concept for evaluating financial options associated with programs entering the innovation pipeline.[18] Of note in our process are the "bang" (ECV) and the "bang for the buck" (ECV/resource limitations) financial impact evaluations. These demonstrate the financial gain to be achieved based on the degree of resourcing needed to achieve

the goal. ECV seeks to maximize the commercial value of the portfolio. It determines a basic net present value calculation and reduces or constrains it by the risk in the project and specified budget
constraints. In our modeling, technical and commercial risks constrain the calculation, along with R&D resources, required development dollars, and required capital investment necessary to
achieve the programs goals. The decision tree analysis is in Figure 9.1-5.

This method is a decision tree analysis based on future earnings,
probabilities of commercial (P_{cs}) and technical success (P_{ts}) from
anchored scales, launch $(\$C)$, and development $(\$D)$ costs. A
strategic importance rating can also be factored into the formula to
weight the ECV upward or downward depending on strategic intent. Over time it serves as an excellent discussion tool for the business and technology teams for monitoring the project's ECV and
ECV/development costs as the project moved through the pipeline.
It can be dangerous to use the ECV method solely to eliminate programs, especially when evaluating programs early in the innovation
pipeline or programs with high risk. Options analysis should be applied in these cases as another method for evaluating the opportunity. Internal rate of return and payback on capital invested are also
metrics used in the financial analysis.[19]

FIGURE 9.1-5 Decision Tree Analysis

$$ECV = [(NPV * P_{CS} - C) * P_{TS}] - D]$$

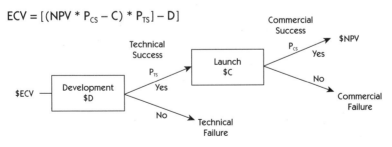

Source: Robert Cooper.

Portfolio Management Working Meetings, Reviews, and the "Black Book"

To recap a bit, we prepare and review the project data sheets for current and potential programs. These sheets cover all types of programs along the innovation pipeline. Snapshot forms are completed for programs that are currently funded or stand a reasonable chance of being funded. All projects are rated using the anchored scales. Programs rated a 5 ("most urgent") are resourced first. If resources still remain, then programs rated a 4 ("urgent") are resourced. Typically, we exhaust our resources at this point. This is the "Initial Portfolio Assigned" step in Figure 9.1-3. The programs already funded in this step, as well as the remaining other programs with enough available data, are evaluated in detail in terms of a financial analysis. The financial analysis is performed in the form of an expected commercial value calculation. High-level project plans are created for proposed programs, including resource needs and critical milestones. These are the elements that help the business team determine the "Strawman Business-Adjusted Portfolio" refered to in Figure 9.1-3. The most urgent programs are resourced, but the pipeline is also balanced for short- and long-term programs, short- and long-term financial impact, and strategic intent. This portfolio is the one that we take to the full-day working portfolio meeting. It is there that we review what is currently in the portfolio and what we are not funding and discuss where we need to be to meet our business strategy. The result at the end of the day is a risk- and resource-adjusted portfolio that is formed by comparing the risk in the portfolio to business standards and availability of resources. Several alternative portfolios are evaluted and adjustments are made until there is consensus in the resulting innovation pipeline portfolio. The last step is an executive review of the resulting risk- and resources-adjusted business technology portfolio.

Disciplined portfolio management can be difficult to maintain long term. It requires time up-front planning for what might be rather than what is. Portfolio management meetings include the elements of data collection, data analysis, and data management. Portfolio management (1) provides decisions on the collection of projects, (2) identifies urgent must-do projects, (3) seeks pipeline management, (3) seeks portfolio management, (4) feeds the Stage-Gate process, and (5) identifies critical must-do or next steps in individual programs and ideas.

The end result of our portfolio review and portfolio management working meetings that occur twice a year is known as the PM Black Book (so-called because the results, while available online, are also contained in a black three-ring binder that each member of the team receives a copy of for reference). The contents of the PM Black Book is shown in Exhibit 9.1-3.

The team knows where to locate information in the black books, and each member of the team has a favorite section that he or she tends to refer to for information on specific programs. Prior to the working portfolio meeting, a draft of this notebook is distributed to each of the members of the business team. Each member reviews the book prior to the meeting, thus allowing the team to discuss issues and plan for the future rather than reviewing data. The whole business team contributes to the information contained in the notebook and is held accountable for the information's accuracy.

The Transition to a Business-Owned Portfolio Process

This process was initially created from within the technology management ranks. The process owner is one of the managers on the technology management staff. However, the portfolio management system long ago made the transition from a *technology-driven process to a business team–owned system*. Indicators of this transition are as follows:

- Portfolio management system elements are integrated into the business leader's monthly business team meetings.
- Selected programs are reviewed every month at these business team meetings. If no gate review is scheduled, then one or two

EXHIBIT 9.1-3 Contents of the Project Management Black Book

Section 1: Executive Summary and Observations, Programs and Pipeline Charts

Section 2: Pipeline Planning:
- Plan for Scheduled Reviews
- Some Project Opportunities Not Currently Resourced, *but we are thinking about . . .*
- Projects and Ideas for Consideration

Section 3: Technology Program Updates and Risk Management
- NPPD Programs, SBB Programs, Application Development Programs
- Accomplishments, Milestones and Issues

Section 4: Technology Pipeline Analysis Dashboards
- Resource Utilization
- Risks and Rewards

Section 5: NPPD Projects (organized by project)
- Snapshot Forms
- SS/DfSS Charter Forms
- Milestone and Critical Path Charts
- ECV Analysis Spreadsheets
- Project Description Sheets

Section 6: Technical Service, Factory Service/Support Base Business Programs
- Snapshot Forms
- SS/DfSS Charter Forms
- Milestone and Critical Path Charts

programs are reviewed with the team for monitoring purposes. The level of detail depends on the issues and decisions needed to be made.

- Application development programs for existing commercial products (as opposed to new product application development, which is managed within new product categories) and operation or support base business-type programs have been added to the portfolio management working meetings. This occurred at the request of the business team.

- Twice a year, business managers and technology managers on a worldwide basis participate in the working portfolio management meetings. Attendance is mandatory.

Implementation Experiences

Portfolio management systems are a terrific approach to handling resource gridlock: too many projects, projects that never die, projects of the week, and others. Certainly Stage-Gate systems are meant to control these issues; however, portfolio management also cleans the pipeline out on a regular basis. From a budgetary point of view, using this system has enabled us to gain approval for technology development programs by demonstrating their linkage to the business strategy. Because technology requires lead time for invention prior to market introduction, it is a mechanism for avoiding late-to-market issues. This process has enabled us to defend our existing head count at budget time, as well as increase head count to support critical programs. We have been successful in gaining approval in the budget for increases in the product testing budget and toxicology/registration budgets. These two budgets have historically been difficult to increase, as they tend to be a large percentage of the R&D budget.

I have often compared designing, implementing, and maintaining a portfolio management system to climbing a mountain. Sometimes the slopes are manageable, and the climb is easy. Then the landscape changes, the clouds move in, and the climb becomes painful and labored. You slip, fall back, lose ground, and must climb up that slope again. A plateau is reached, and you catch your breath before you tackle the next steep slope. If you put a great team in place, the design and implementation may go smoothly. Eventually, however, tough decisions will need to be made, and the slope will be slippery and treacherous. Every time the team composition changes on the business and technology teams, you probably lose some ground and have to learn to climb the slope again as a team. Maintaining the portfolio management system over the long term requires the whole team to be actively engaged in continuous improvement discussions. Every portfolio meeting should close with a discussion or survey of what is working and what is not.

We learned as a business team how to perform portfolio management, not just portfolio analysis. This meant looking at commercial failures of the past and determining honestly, as a team, what went wrong, why, and what we would change for the future to avoid a repeat performance. We learned as a business team to analyze for and allocate resources within and across SBUs to maximize the value of our portfolio. We had to learn how to categorize different types of programs and make portfolio decisions relating to them and their fit with our strategy:

- Balance in short- and long-term programs
- Balance for low- and high-risk programs
- Across different project types: new products, improvements, cost reductions, expansions, early pipeline technology development, market development, and others
- Appropriate support for each SBU depending on strategy
- Support of different technologies from embryonic to pacing to base

Flexibility in portfolio management is important. The world is not monochromatic but a wonderful digital rainbow of colors. This is the environment we had to learn to make decisions in. We learned how to push as a team to make decisions on programs, especially the tough no-go decisions, recognizing that these decisions would free up resources for better opportunities. Sometimes the decision making is difficult because the team must focus on what might be rather than what is. Decisions are always being made in a dynamic environment. It is difficult to compare projects when available information is scant or constantly changing. Programs do not stand still; thus, the best we can do is present snapshots in time as a basis for our decision making and try to project reasonably into the future. Projects are at different stages of development and competing for the same resources. Projects are not independent of each other; thus, funding decisions have wide-reaching repercussions on other programs.

New opportunities are continually presenting themselves, thus changing the landscape on a continual basis. For example, we would agree on a portfolio of programs to be supported at our full-day working meeting. Inevitably, a new opportunity would soon present itself. Since no slack existed for additional unbudgeted or hot programs to be introduced, we had to be prepared to make important, fast decisions on these opportunities. This can be done at monthly business team meetings or outside the meetings, depending on the urgency. We have accepted that it is okay to react on the fly to fund a project, using email or the telephone, if the window of opportunity will be lost, as long as the necessary parties are involved in the decision making and it is clear what program we are placing on hold or reprioritizing to free up resources for this new opportunity. However, full examination and a gate decision are required at the next business team meeting. This flexibility and discipline in the process need to be continually monitored by the process owner so that abuses do not occur.

Our meetings are interactive and lively yet facilitated and orderly. At our first portfolio management meeting, we made no-go decisions on two-thirds of the programs, realigned our programs to the business strategy, restructured our development teams, and put plans in place to train the teams on project management. More recently, at our full-day working portfolio management meetings, we spent only a small portion of the day on the current pipeline. The majority of the time is spent at the front end of the innovation pipeline, looking at new concept development, and the front end of our Stage-Gate process. These are all prior to commercial development, where we are screening opportunities and focusing on technology development. The gate reviews in our Stage-Gate process are managing the later pipeline programs. This is the area where Wheelwright and Clark have said management teams need to focus.[20] When our business team progressed to these discussions as the primary focus in our portfolio meetings, it became obvious that the process had truly made the transition to a business-owned process.

What's Next

Six Sigma methodology is a corporate initiative, supported at all levels of the corporation. We have been implementing Six Sigma and Design for Six Sigma within our Stage-Gate and portfolio frameworks for about a year. These tool sets are providing an additional set of methodologies and tools to gather information and data, analyze those data, and promote decision making in our project teams, Stage-Gate activities, portfolio management activities, and front-end development activities. The metrics we use within Stage-Gate and portfolio management are easily rolled up into the Six Sigma dashboards. From a technology management perspective, we are training our teams on the various tool sets and methodologies in Design for Six Sigma. This training should strengthen our capabilities at the front end of the innovation pipeline where we need to be focusing our efforts for long-term success.

Rebecca Seibert is technology manager of a group of synthesis and formulation chemists and portfolio manager for petroleum additives at Crompton Corporation, a specialty chemical company. She holds several patents and is responsible for the creation and implementation of ideation, Stage-Gate, and portfolio management processes at Crompton. She is the company representative to the Industrial Research Institute and past chair of IRI's Process Effectiveness Network and holds advanced degrees in chemistry and business marketing strategy.

9.2

Using PPM to Ease the Hewlett-Packard–Compaq Merger

Don Kingsberry

On Labor Day, September 3, 2001, the press got wind of a planned merger between the Hewlett-Packard Company (HP) and Compaq Computer Corporation. The next day, HP formally announced its intention to merge with Compaq Computer in what would be the biggest technology merger in history. One week later, on September 11, 2001, a major terrorist attack occurred in the United States. About one month later, the families of the children of the founders of HP announced their opposition to the merger. HP management then had an uphill battle. The case wound up in a Delaware court case, which permitted the merger to go forward. After securing approval from the U.S. government and the European Union, HP management needed to win the votes of a majority of the shareholders and was ultimately successful in doing so. The merger was finally concluded, and the combined companies officially became one on May 7, 2002. A tremendous amount of planning and effort had gone in to making this merger a success. The merger planning and execution required a rigorous degree of program management and project management discipline.

There was a large challenge in defining the information technology (IT) projects required to support the new company and identifying those projects that needed to be stopped and the resources that needed to be moved to new work. At the outset of the merger,

HP established a merger integration office, and the global program management office (PMO) team had full-time resources assigned this effort.

The global PMO needed to categorize the projects to identify the most critical programs from those less important and to determine the prioritization by identifying which needed to be implemented first and to perform true portfolio management on a very large scale.

The Project Problem

Probably the best-known study of information technology project success rates was undertaken by the Standish Group, whose research showed that across industries, only 28 percent of IT projects are successful on average; 23 percent fail outright, and the remaining 49 percent are considered challenged based on the triple constraints of being on time, on budget, and as originally specified (Figure 9.2-1). Failed projects are those that are cancelled before completion. Challenged projects may be completed and operational, but they are

FIGURE 9.2-1 Project Success Rates

28%

Successful: on time and on budget as originally specified

Challenged: completed and operational, but over budget, over schedule, and/or with reduced functionality

Failed: cancelled before completion

49%

23%

□ Successful
■ Failed
□ Challenged

Source: Standish Group International, *Extreme Chaos* (West Yarmouth, Mass.: Standish Group International, 2001).

either over budget, over schedule, or delivered reduced or less than the originally specified functionality (or the failure to meet any combination of these triple constraint criteria).

Even with great success over sixty-four years of experience in business, HP is not immune to these project challenges seen throughout the IT world. With the largest technology merger in history of HP and Compaq, the new HP is a $70-plus billion company with an IT budget greater than $3 billion. The merger of two diverse cultures made it even more imperative to have a common project management language, processes, and repository of project management information.

In tough times especially, it is more important than ever before to focus on project management, and the quality of this effort is critical. The focus placed on project management discipline is really the path to IT success.

HP is now one of the fifteen largest companies in the world and we have over ten thousand IT professionals, working on over three thousand active projects all over the world at any point in time. We do use portfolio management, and for the first time in the company history, we now have all our IT projects in one common central database, a true enterprise-scale project management system.

We have also implemented a standard project management methodology based on industry standards but using our own internal best practices from HP's rich history. This standard methodology provides a way to compare programs and evaluate their potential for success.

Global Program Management Office

The implementation of the enterprise program management office at HP is called the Global PMO. In the first year after the merger, it focused on the IT organization. Leveraging off the success with IT, it has since expanded to support the other business (non-IT) organizations at HP, starting with all of HP global Operations across the company.

Global PMO is responsible for program operations, program management infrastructure, support of project portfolio management, and facilitation of communication within HP and with our customers.

Global PMO Vision

Stated at its most basic level, the vision for the PMO organization is that every program launched completes successfully:

- Successfully complete every program/project that is launched.
- Achieve competitive advantage through PMO project and knowledge management and collaboration.

Thus, the overarching principle of the Global PMO is that program and project plans accurately reflect the work people do.

Global PMO Mission

The PMO acts as a Center of Excellence for program and project management to ensure a high degree of consistency for successful implementation of projects across the organization. The Global PMO mission is to:

- Provide a best-in-class methodology to manage the organization's work
- Deliver the best portfolio of processes and tools to program teams
- Provide one state-of-the-art PMO database for:
  - ➤ Collaboration
  - ➤ Learning
  - ➤ Management visibility & reporting

- Drive employee professional success and development
- Enable effective Portfolio Management for selection, prioritization, & optimization of programs & projects

Global PMO Goals and Objectives

Global PMO has these goals and objectives:

- Project Management Expertise—Raise the level of Project Management competency/skill in the organization and company—achieve competitive advantage with an industry leading program success rate
- Consistent Methodology—Implementation of a common Methodology to manage our work—best practices to ensure repeatable success
- Enterprise Project Management System—standard database (Primavera Systems TeamPlay)—Provide employees a world-class system to enable knowledge sharing & management visibility of all work
- Improve probability that HP Programs deliver On-Time, On-Budget, and On Target
- Improve Program & Project collaboration, communications, and knowledge management for HP and our customers
- Improve the efficiency of HP Program & Project Management processes
- Improve the predictability, visibility & accessibility of HP Program/Project Plans and schedules
- Simplify the HP IT customer engagement processes
- Ensure Project partnership / sponsorship
- Increase the return on investment on HP Projects

Global PMO Charter

And this is the Global PMO charter:

- Implement and maintain critical PMO operational procedures, policies, training, and systems that enable an industry leading Program success rate
- Provide Global Program administration and leadership, which ensures that Programs and Projects are delivered on Time, on Budget, and on Target
- The PMO is a Center of Excellence for Program and Project Management to assure a high degree of consistency and control to implement successful projects across HP
- The PMO develops project evaluation metrics, implements PMI standard methodologies, and supports project reviews through Customer Driven Project Management
- The PMO provides executive portfolio management to assure project alignment with strategic business objectives

The New Language of Business Is Project Management

A key to the success of the Global PMO was the strong endorsement of HP's chief information officer at the time, Bob Napier. Bob envisioned project management as the new language of business: "I am a big, big proponent of a standardized global IT program management function or office: a common IT methodology, a common way of doing reporting, a common way of doing priorities, a common way of doing metrics. I'm a firm believer that if you can't measure it, you can't manage it. I believe that everybody who is an IT professional, at least in my organization, needs to speak the language of program management and project management. It's all about planning to win."[1] Sadly Bob Napier passed away in October 2003, but he left a lasting legacy of leadership.

Global PMO Strategies

The PMO's strategy has been to use the available, recognized industry standards where they exist and to move away from stand-alone PC-based tools for project management to a new enterprise-scale common system. The merger of multiple companies and organizations also called for moving away from different approaches to a standard methodology to manage projects more consistently. The new company called for recognition that project management is a unique skill set and required investment in specialized training.

These are the strategies:

- Utilize industry recognized standards PMI, CMM (Software Engineering Institute Capability Maturity Model).
- Use state-of-the-art system for project management with one common centralized database.
- Deliver world-class methodology incorporating both industry and internal best practices based on experiences.
- Deliver specific project management training and guidelines for users.

Global PMO Key Principles of Project Management

Many successful organizations have established a principle-driven model to help guide their employees to take the correct actions and do the right things when direct supervision isn't available and no one is watching. The U.S. Marines is an example of an organization where a set of well-known principles guides the troops in the field. The PMO also established a set of principles to help guide the work of project managers and team members:

1. Project plans accurately reflect the work our people are doing.
2. All significant IT work has a project plan, and the plan is used to manage the work.
3. All IT Projects are managed in the TeamPlay system.
4. Projects go through a formal approval process—with an identified ROI.
5. Projects are managed with an approved methodology.
6. Projects have a WBS [work breakdown structure] with key milestones and a critical path identified.
7. All Project Plans must have a saved baseline.
8. Projects should generally be planned to last no more than 1 year.
9. Project actual data (costs/hours worked) results are updated once per week.
10. Project Plans are Scheduled (updated) at least once each week.
11. All Activities/Tasks have at least 1 specific resource or a role assigned.
12. Projects have all supporting documentation (Charter, ROI, etc.) linked to the plan.
13. Projects conduct formal Phase Exit reviews at all significant transitions.
14. Projects follow HP Corporate Policies—with all the required project information, codes, & financials established
15. Lessons Learned are compiled on all projects.
16. The appropriate level of project management discipline, process, and quality is applied to each project based on its scope, cost, and impact.

Key Tools of the Global PMO

One of the main roles of any PMO is to define a standard set of key tools for the organization to use to manage its projects with consistency:

- Primavera TeamPlay—Enterprise Project Management System.

- HP Methodology—Customized methodology developed to provide a model approach to deliver all HP projects. It includes key deliverables and promotes the use of best practices that increase a project's probability of success. The methodology is integrated with the Enterprise Project Management System.

- Principles—Sixteen Key Principles of Project Management.

- Policies—A small set of three visible and straightforward statements of position with intention and direction that are aligned with principles and require mandatory adherence.

- Standards—Aligned with principles and policies and providing more details on operational processes.

- Guidelines—How-to steps for the Enterprise Project Management System, TeamPlay, and Methodology processes.

- Strategic Road Map—Plan of record (POR) defined every six months outlining the major programs for the next six-month period for each organization

- CIO Steering Review Board—PMO, financial, and enterprise architecture reviews followed by final review and program approval by the CIO

- Categorization of programs/projects (A, B, C)

- Weekly executive-level program scorecard reports

- Program health tracking metrics

- Extended PMO teams in each HP organization

- Global PMO Web site where all of these tools and training are readily available along with operational status reports

In addition, the Global PMO drives system integration of the Enterprise Project Management Systems (Primavera TeamPlay) with other key enterprise management systems to reduce data error/

redundancy (PeopleSoft interface), maximize project and program financial tracking (SAP Interface), increase administration and support productivity, and provide a 360-degree vertical and horizontal view of the enterprise's programs and projects.

There are many examples of the importance of the enterprise system and its integration with other corporate repositories. Often one of the most difficult challenges in project management is to maintain a clean, consistent resource pool. Because most organizations use stand-alone PC-based project management tools, the same resource usually will be shown on multiple project plans working over forty hours per week on each one, and therefore the data about that "duplicated" resource is completely bogus no matter how detailed the individual project plans may be. With a true enterprise-scale system and one common central resource pool, fed from the official HR system, a person is listed once and only once; the resource is not duplicated, and the planning information is therefore accurate.

PMO Focus

In summary, the PMO has concentrated on four main focus areas, each with a broad impact on the organization and many people:

Project management expertise: Raise the level of project management competency/skill in the organization and company and achieve competitive advantage with an industry-leading program success rate.

Best-in-class methodology: Implement a standard methodology to manage work using internal and industry best practices to ensure repeatable success.

State-of-the-art enterprise project management system: Implement the Enterprise Project Management System and tools to provide employees a world-class system that enables knowledge sharing and visibility of all work in one common database.

Portfolio management: Ensure business/function alignment and interlock through active reporting, tracking, and analysis of POR programs.

Project Portfolio Management at HP

We sought to optimize the investment mix between the maintenance and support work, infrastructure projects, and innovation projects that are vital in sustaining competitive advantage and building leadership. We also require project management training for all IT professionals, and we are teaching them what our former chief information officer called "the language of business today, which is not English, French, or Spanish, but Project Management."

Prior to the implementation of the Global PMO and the corporate focus on project management, HP had the following problems common to many organizations:

- No common executive-level program status reporting
- No master plan of HP programs for customers
- Some projects with no real project plans
- Some projects managed with task lists
- Some projects with real and detailed project plans
- Different and inconsistent project methodology
- Employees not trained on project management system
- Project plans not in one database
- Actual project status unknown or unavailable
- Actual project costs very difficult to assess

In addition to resolving these problems, the purpose of the Global PMO is to help answer the following general management questions:

- What is the status of projects in my area?
- Why is this project running late?

- What happens if I reassign resources?
- How many people do I need?
- How effectively are my people being used?
- What has been our performance, and where are we headed?
- Are we meeting our customer commitments?

We use return-on-investment or business case analysis on every project and have implemented a rigorous project approval process that all projects must go through. We evaluate every project along three critical dimensions: the project management effort including the plan, the financial analysis, and an architectural review to ensure it complies with our defined infrastructure and technical requirements. There are two key questions asked for every project: (1) What is the business problem we are trying to solve? (2) What is the proposed solution description?

Most projects, regardless of organization, are being done for a handful of reasons, and we have put these into general benefit categories: revenue generation, cost savings, compliance (legal or regulatory), customer satisfaction, integration (mergers), and infrastructure related.

We start with the strategy, ensuring it is aligned with the corporate business strategy. Annually each organization in the company is responsible for the development of its three-year strategic plan. Based on this plan, every six months, a tactical plan of the major programs planned for the upcoming six-month period is defined. Then tactically we try to launch the right programs from the plan of record. The governance process requires a formal approval of each individual project. The architecture then uses engineering discipline to seize elegance from complexity, and the PMO implements disciplined execution with global collaboration a state-of-the-art EPMS.

Launch the Right Programs

With today's challenging business environment, a key for success is focusing limited resources on the most important programs and projects and getting the optimal return on investment. Figure 9.2-2

FIGURE 9.2-2 Launch the Right Programs

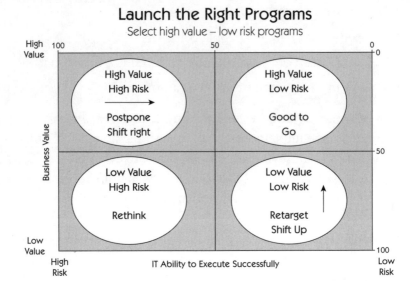

Source: R. Napier, "The Role of Governance and Program Management in the CIO Office," HP CIO Summit, New York, Apr. 2003.

shows how the Global PMO determines the right programs to launch by evaluating business value against risk. By preventing low-value/high-risk projects from ever being launched, more resources can be focused on ensuring the success of the highest value projects.

Twice a year, we develop a plan of record that sets out the major proposed programs and projects for the next six months for every group. We can then evaluate all these efforts against a set of risk criteria, which include project management risk, interlock or interdependency risk between projects, and financial risk. We then plot the results on a 2-by-2 matrix, where the vertical axis is the business value (rated low to high) and the horizontal axis is the ability to execute (rated high risk to low risk). This allows us to compare programs where we are looking for the high value-lower risk projects.

The purpose of this process is to provide a standard method, evaluation criteria, and tools to rank and evaluate the program portfolio. This process provides:

- An apple-to-apple comparative analysis view of the complete program portfolio
- An integrated view of program risk and business value across businesses and functions
- A starting point for discussions of program funding priorities and adjustments

The process has three key steps:

1. Evaluate and score each program using the evaluation criteria. In order to rank the active and planned programs for an organization, nine evaluation criteria have been defined. A template is provided for each criterion to use as a guide in scoring a program for those criteria.
2. Log each program's scores in the summary scoring worksheet, and sort programs by total score in ascending order.
3. Plot programs in the portfolio risk-to-value quadrant graph using the total benefit and total risk scores for each program.

Evaluation Criteria Descriptions

The approach is intended to create a simple and standard way to rank the business priority, integration priority, return on investment (ROI), overall readiness to launch, and the risks associated with each program. The focus is on programs that have both a high priority and a high probability of successfully achieving planned objectives.

The following benefit criteria were considered to determine a program's potential value to the business:

Business priority: Within the strategic road map or POR, each group, working with its business partners, established a priority ranking from 1 (highest) to N. Within some functions, priorities were set by domain within the group, resulting in several number 1 priorities.

Integration priority: This priority on a scale of 1 (highest) to 10 reflects the priority of the program as needed to integrate premerger systems.

Return on investment: The ROI calculator was used, and the result translated to a 1 (highest) to 10 scale. If no ROI analysis was completed, a 10 was assigned.

The following risk criteria were considered to determine program risk from multiple dimensions. All factors were rated on a 1 (highest) to 10 scale, with 1 indicating the best chance of achievement or lowest risk:

Magnitude of change risk: This considers the magnitude of change required for a program to achieve its objective. It includes the number of people affected, the degree of potential resistance to change, and the number of organizations affected.

Organization maturity risk: This considers only the impact of the merger on the sponsoring organization. No attempt is made to assess progress in resolving merger issues, and no consideration is given to organizational maturity issues other than the merger challenge.

PMO risk: This addresses the status and quality of the program plan. Industry standard program management risk factors are used with data from the PMO database. Programs with no plan in place and due to start late in the period receive a 10.

Interlock risk: This measures the degree to which a program depends on deliverables (IT or business) from outside the sponsoring business group. This is tracked within the PMO for programs beyond the scoping phase.

Business process risk: Most programs achieve business results by enabling change in specific business processes. This risk factor addresses both the degree of change required (for example, 10 percent of the process steps or 90 percent) and the complexity of the process itself (for example, supply chain processes are more complex than the hiring process).

Resource risk: This is an assessment of available skills required for a program. It focuses on resource cost, availability of the resource, and skill set required for a program/project.

Table 9.2-1 is an example of an evaluation criteria chart.

Using the data from the summary scoring worksheet, the programs are plotted in the appropriate quadrant. Figure 9.2-3 provides a comparative view of all programs or a particular group's programs based on their business value and risk.

We have developed a set of forty-two standard "health check" criteria to enable us to instantly evaluate the progress of any particular project that is underway and to understand if it is in trouble or headed for success. We look at risks, issues, critical path analysis, resource analysis, sponsorship, alignment with strategy, earned value metrics, dependencies, and many other factors with an impact on the triple constraints of project management: time, cost, and scope. We treat the project status information as a corporate asset.

Proof the Solution Works: Results and Impact

Once we passed the one-year anniversary of the largest technology merger in history, people started asking what had made this merger of HP and Compaq successful where so many other previous large technology mergers have failed. Our CEO, Carly Fiorina, unhesitatingly answered that question very well on national television: "We have managed the integration with incredible discipline and attention to detail. We've had project management discipline and program management discipline over absolutely everything that we've done." For the merger implementation, we used our EPMS to initiate and manage all the critical projects. We had about two

TABLE 9.2-1. Evaluation Criteria Chart

PMO Risk		
Planned: On-Time, On-Budget, On-Target Functionality-Green	• Project Condition Green • Well Managed—Detailed Plan	1
	• Activities/Resources Assigned • Updated with Actuals	2
	• Financials Identified • Baseline Established	3
2 of the 3 Triple Constraints at Risk-Yellow	• Project Condition Yellow • Phase vs. % Complete Issue	4
	• Methodology in Place • Past Scheduled Start	5
	• Schedule/Cost Variances • Business Requirements Issue	6
3 of 3 Triple Constraints at Risk-Red	• Project Condition Red • No Indicated Start/Resources	7
	• No % Complete • No Actuals Spent	8
	• Lacking Methodology/Tasks • No Baseline	9
No Project Plan	• No Data	10
Risk Criteria Guidelines		

Note: Green projects are funded. Yellow projects are recommended to cancel to reach a $xxxM or more reduction. Red projects are recommended to cancel if the reduction is $xxxM or less. Black projects indicate summary or other innovation project costs.

FIGURE 9.2-3 Project Selection Plot Example

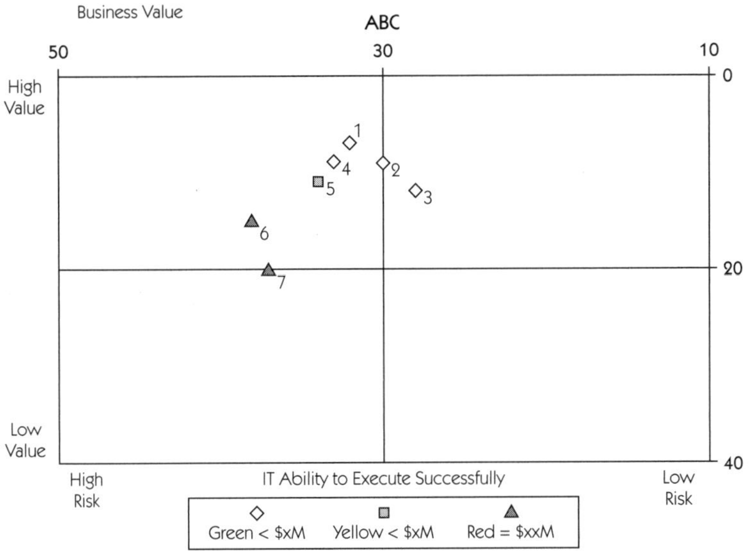

Note: Green projects are funded. Yellow projects are recommended to cancel to reach a $xxxM or more reduction. Red projects are recommended to cancel if the reduction is $xxxM or less. Black projects indicate summary or other innovation project costs.

Source: D. Kingsberry, "HP Global PMO," internal HP Global PMO Web site, June 26, 2003.

hundred critical projects that we classified as the "must starts" and about three hundred of the next-tier projects that we categorized as the "must-do" projects. All of these went through the formal approval process, and project plans for each were built immediately in our system.

An equally important effort for the PMO was stopping projects that were no longer part of our strategy. We called this list the "must stops," and there were over one hundred of these efforts identified. It was crucial to track these projects, ensure they were actually stopped, and redeploy the resources to the new critical programs. Stopping projects that are no longer germane to the company strategy is one of the important functions for any PMO and should be part of its measurement of success. Project management processes, tools, techniques, and discipline have long been well applied in the engineering and construction communities, but have not been so well applied or practiced in the IT space. HP believes the time has come for this to change.

First Hundred Days of the New HP

There was a major effort prior to the actual formal close of the merger to define a hundred-day plan for implementation during the first three months of the new company:

- Rolled out the Global PMO: Defined a common program portfolio, defined a common set of program metrics and reporting, and created common resource management capabilities
- Ramped up to over fifteen hundred active programs
- Provided a controlled halt to two hundred legacy programs in the first ninety days
- Launched the 100 highest-priority "must-start" integration programs from the "clean room plan" in the first thirty days from the merger close on May 7, 2002
- Launched the next-tier high-priority integration and innovation programs with 250 "must-do" programs in the first sixty days
- Drove a relentless one-company, one-HP communication process
- Burn the ships
  - ➤ Operated in the new model and culture
  - ➤ Stopped investments not aligned with adopt-and-go decisions
  - ➤ Reinforced and rewarded success; managed issues swiftly

Implementation Summary

- The Enterprise Project Management System Primavera Team-Play is now one of the fifty largest applications in production at HP.
- The vast majority of users like this application; it has a user satisfaction rating above 93 percent.
- Users are overwhelmingly satisfied with the application's functionality.
- Primavision, the new additional Web-based client, resource, and portfolio management system, provides another new set of capabilities in functionality and performance.
- Delivered first integrated IT plan of record (for the two combined companies)

Executive Level-Benefits

- Executive visibility of programs and projects, enabling sound management decisions on priorities and accountability for all the work
- Supported the development of the first integrated plan of record for the two combined companies
- Visibility of breakout of types of spending by the HP organization (innovation, infrastructure, support, maintenance)

Implementation Lessons Learned

- Critical to have the program management office or organization in place
- Sustained senior management support and unwavering commitment
- Small core team empowered to make decisions and take action

- Establish clear mission, goals, processes, procedures, and policies
- Start delivering operational data immediately; don't wait for systems
- Engagement, alignment, and partnership with users

Things That Went Well with the Implementation

- Pilots as a method of engagement and alignment
- Planned and timed implementation, change management, communications
- Web site containing all PMO-related information: operational reports, marketing material, user manuals, policies and instructions
- Reporting requirements can drive process and policy
- Advanced communication to users
- On-site consulting assistance when required
- Quality technical support and quick response team
- Online training
- Passion

Current Status

Following is a summary of where we are now with our practices.

Current Global PMO Metrics. Two and a half years following the merger, we have:

- 60 category A top projects identified and managed
- 137 category B projects identified and managed
- More than 3,500 active IT projects worldwide in the system

- More than 2,000 IT projects completed since the merger in May 2002
- More than 8,000 people who have completed the project management system Web-based training
- More than 56,000 total resources in the project management system resource pool

Global PMO Extended Team Meeting. The Global PMO conducts weekly meetings with the extended PMO groups. The meetings include value-rich and relevant presentations along with providing a forum for bidirectional communication. The extended team PMO managers representing each organization are then able to cascade the communications, share the content covered, and implement the appropriate process within their organizations.

IT Methodology Team Forum. A methodology core team also exists with at least one member from each organization. The team meets biweekly with various subteams meeting the alternate week. Methodology changes are reviewed by the core team and then communicated and implemented in monthly releases.

The Future. The CIO has provided this project management guidance:

- Focused investment in senior project manager training, including enabling project managers to be available for training, will continue to be a high priority.
- Creation of a job family for project managers is required to establish a professional project management career path.
- TeamPlay, the HP standard project and portfolio management system of record, is the only accepted IT project management tool.

- Project management maturity improvements are assessed through use of the project management maturity model (PMMM) and organizational project management maturity model (OPM3) program effectiveness metrics.

Integrating the "What" and the "How." The Global PMO has become integrated with the HP business processes and is part of our continuous improvement, as shown in Figure 9.2-4.

HP is now a global provider of products, technologies, solutions, and services to businesses and consumers. As a result of the merger, it has over 140,000 employees in over 170 countries, doing business in more than forty currencies and more than ten languages.

The annual revenue for the new combined companies is now approaching $80 billion. The firm has an annual research and development budget approaching $4 billion. HP is also among the ten

FIGURE 9.2-4 Accelerating a High-Performance Organization: PMO Integrating the "What" and "How"

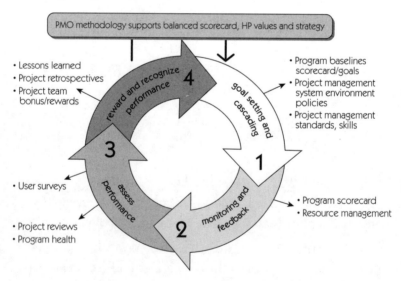

Source: D. Kingsberry, "HP Global PMO," internal HP Global PMO Web site, June 26, 2003.

largest patent holders in the world, with a total patent portfolio exceeding nineteen thousand, and the current rate of new inventions is generating approximately eleven patents per day.

The IT organization has been combined with the global operations functions of the company and is now responsible for many of the horizontal processes, including the supply chain, e-business, customer operations, and indirect procurement.

One of the most recent large-scale mergers that is also considered one of the most successful is the Exxon and Mobil merger, which promised to deliver a savings of $2 billion over a three-year period. The HP–Compaq merger by comparison was able to achieve over $3 billion in savings in just over one year.

Currently at HP, over 70 percent of the most strategic category A projects are on track to be completed on time, on scope, and on budget, a rate far exceeding the industry average for IT projects. In the first year after the merger, HP also saw a reduction in the average project duration by approximately 39 percent. The average budget for HP's category A projects exceeds $9.5 million, and 57 percent of these projects are global in nature and scope.

HP now has over thirty-six hundred employees with Project Management Professional (PMP) certification, the third largest number of PMP-certified professionals of any organization in the world today. As expected, most of these PMPs are members of HP's external-facing customer services organization, so the challenge has been to increase the number working internal to the company.

In addition to encouraging PMP certification, the organization provides access to George Washington University's School of Business master's program in project management that is delivered by ESI International. Since the merger, over 370 HP employees have received a master's certificate, and over 4,791 people have attended additional project management courses provided by ESI.

While certainly not without its challenges and resistance to change, the organization is moving forward. The future of both business and IT requires professional project management. The PMO is about providing a standard approach to methodology, metrics, priorities, risk management, reporting, communications, and governance. There is an important linkage between strategy, tactical planning, and the actual execution of the work, and this is the role the PMO helps to fulfill.

Today there are tremendous demands placed on the functions of all organizations. Many of our customers often ask us, "How do you manage the size and complexity, how do you prioritize, how do you track all the work, and how do you measure?" The answer is the PMO and the project management discipline we instill.

Don Kingsberry is the director of the Global Program Management Office for Hewlett-Packard's operations and information technology. As a member of Hewlett-Packard's global operations and information technology management teams, he is responsible for H-P's worldwide operations and management information systems program and project management and for driving competitive advantage throughout the company's e-business processes and infrastructure. He has a master's certificate in project management from the George Washington University.

9.3

Developing a PPM Capability at America Online

Rich Dougherty

America Online, Inc. (AOL), a wholly owned subsidiary of Time Warner Inc., based in Dulles, Virginia, is the world's leader in interactive services, Web brands, Internet technologies and e-commerce services.

Having grown rapidly during the 1990s, the AOL executive team recognized the need to enhance and formalize many of its project-based processes in order to sustain success and growth. This transformation initiative was branded "integrated project development" and included a number of key process enablers and capabilities, among them project portfolio management.

For AOL, PPM needed to bring the right people together at the right time to synthesize and aggregate qualitative judgments and quantitative data from cross-functional business teams to:

- Ensure the project portfolio was aligned with AOL's strategy and objectives
- Ensure the selection of high-business-value projects
- Achieve and maintain the right mix and balance of projects

Special thanks to John Sammarco with AOL and Aaron Smith with Projects@Work for their contributions to this case study.

- Promote greater accountability via fast and binding decision making

Action

In early 2002, AOL formed a team, led by John Sammarco, director of portfolio management, to define and develop portfolio management capability, which included responsibility for methodology, training, and support tools. Recognizing the importance that adoption of the initial capability would play in the long-term success of the initiative, the team established a set of guiding principles for AOL's PPM capability:

- Be academically sound and industry proven
- Be "AOLized," incorporating AOL strategy and reflecting institutionalized measures
- Leverage and reflect AOL internal collaboration
- Be within a manageable level of complexity
- Represent a quantum leap forward—but not perfection
- Meet both company-level and business-level needs
- Be absorbable within the current capability maturity
- Be successfully piloted before full rollout

While the team was developing the methodology, it concurrently assessed a number of leading support tools in the industry and decided to use Expert Choice primarily for its ability to value projects by synthesizing quantitative factors and qualitative judgments from a group of stakeholders.

In late 2003, with the methodologies, training, and support tools in place, AOL began to set up seven portfolio management teams (PMTs), each centered on a line of business. Although there was a desire to adopt the new process and tools rapidly, AOL resisted the urge to rush the implementation in favor of gradual assimilation.

This meant introducing these concepts and approaches gradually, getting quick wins, building momentum, and making sure that the changes to process were understood and embraced before taking the next step. In short, we needed to take an incremental implementation. In one example, it took six months to phase it in.

A key component of AOL's PPM capability design was to not only help teams make more justifiable decisions, but to also achieve rapid and binding decision making. To do this, AOL needed to bring all the business functions—business leadership, marketing, finance, legal, technology, and others—together on a regular basis to review, assess, and select ideas, concepts, and projects.

Equally important, AOL introduced new scoring models based on a weighted hierarchy of objectives and measures (Figure 9.3-1). The scoring model that AOL uses is similar to the model shown in Figure 9.3-1. In the left pane of the figure are the organizational objectives. Some of the objectives are financially oriented and quantifiable (for example, "Maximize NPV"), and others are qualitative (for example, "Improve Service Efficiencies"). In addition, some are more important than others, and this is reflected in the weights (for example, "Leverage Knowledge Global Weight 27.8%"), which are collaboratively derived by the PMT members. In the upper right pane of Figure 9.3-1 are the IT projects or investments that the organization is prioritizing. The numbers, or "scores," next to each project (for example, "AS/400 Replacements .061") represent the relative priority of the project in relation to the other projects. These scores are collaboratively derived by measuring the contribution of each project to each objective.

In using such a scoring model, AOL was able to expand decision-making criteria beyond revenues and earnings, aggregating and synthesizing quantitative data with qualitative judgments in real-time and in a group setting.

Using this technique, AOL was able to cross-prioritize project investments for the first time, and it accomplished this objective faster by just diving in instead of debating details. When it came to

FIGURE 9.3-1 Weighted Objective Hierarchy

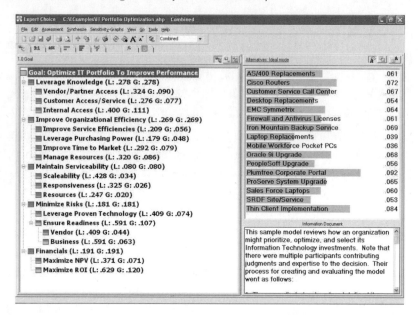

Note: This is not the actual objective hierarchy that AOL uses, but is rather a representative sample set of objectives. "L" indicates the Local weight of an objective and the "G" the Global weight of an objective. So for example, the Internal Access subobjective is 40 percent of its parent objective, Leverage Knowledge, and 11 percent of all the objectives. The weights of the subobjectives in the same cluster will always add up to one.

the use of scoring models, AOL understood the importance of getting a solid model piloted quickly, knowing that it will evolve and improve over time. We did not want to stay in committee trying to build a perfect scoring model when we recognized that our first step would constitute a quantum leap forward and that getting the collaboration started sooner rather than later would ultimately be more productive.

AOL now has seven portfolio management teams (PMTs): five centered on the major lines of business and two (the technology and corporate units PMTs) chaired by the chief technology officer and chief financial officer (CFO), respectively. The meetings of each PMT are chaired by the respective business owner. However, since the PPM process is a cross-functional one, each PMT has applicable executive representation from the marketing, finance, legal, and technology functions as well.

The seven PMTs are at various stages in their implementation, according to Sammarco, who facilitates the corporate units team. Each PMT has someone whose role is similar to Sammarco's to facilitate the entire PPM process so that the chairperson and team members can make effective decisions.

This group of facilitators convenes periodically to share best practices and discuss common challenges. The seven teams are officially tied together at the top of the organization by an investment review board (IRB) consisting of senior executives, including the chief executive officer, two vice chairs, the CFO, and other business leaders. The IRB commissions PMTs and allocates resources, while the PMTs commission project teams and allocate resources. The project teams are then accountable to the PMTs, and the PMTs are accountable to the IRB.

Although it emphasized a flexible, user-friendly approach as it rolled out the new portfolio management capabilities, the implementation team knew the processes would not initially be seen as simple due to a general unfamiliarity with PPM throughout the company. But rather than risk diluting the potential power of PPM for the sake of simplicity, the team decided to strive for a manageable level of complexity instead.

When it came to AOL's use of tools, a similar philosophy was adopted. Sammarco and the portfolio team focuses on the lower-level intricacies of building rating scales for their objectives and measures and generating their own reports, while keeping the executives focused on exercising their leadership and judgment and setting the objectives for the portfolio.

In practice, technology plays a key role in managing the complexity. After the presentation of a business case during a PMT meeting, the PMT members share their judgments using handheld transmitters, which are displayed for all by a projection system as illustrated in Figure 9.3-2. They then discuss their perspectives before finalizing their assessment. So, for example, in Figure 9.3-2, the PMT is evaluating how well the Oracle 9i Upgrade project rates with respect to the Improve Time to Market objective. Using the ratings scale (Excellent to None) toward the top of the screen capture, Marketing judges that the Oracle 9i Upgrade project makes an Excellent contribution to the Improve Time to Market objective, while Finance rates the contribution as Very Good, and so on. The application then synthesizes the input from each participant to arrive at a priority score for each project. This approach builds consensus without creating an obstacle to move forward. The Expert Choice technology, which is based on the analytic hierarchy process, provides the capability to measure a project's business value to a set of weighted objectives.

FIGURE 9.3-2 PMT Group Evaluation of Project versus Improve Time-to-Market Objective

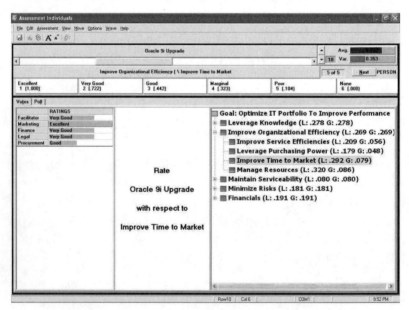

Note: This information is not actual AOL data but is rather a representative sample.

Using a scoring model based on weighted objectives allows the PMTs to modulate the portfolio to map to the strategic priorities of the business. As illustrated in Figure 9.3-3a and 3b, using dynamic sensitivity analysis functionality, the PMT can vary the weights of its objectives and view the corresponding change in the priorities of its investments. For example, in one PMT, a particular objective (as an example, see Figure 9.3-3a, Leverage Knowledge [27.8%]) was a predominant factor in the scoring model. It stood to reason that the projects that contributed strongly to that objective fared better than those that didn't (for example, in Figure 9.3-3a, Plumtree Corporate Portal was the highest-priority project). By varying the weights of the objective as shown in Figure 9.3-3b (Leverage Knowledge now has a weight of 6.5% and Improve Organizational Efficiency is now the predominant objective), the PMT can see how the priority of the projects changes (in Figure 9.3-3b, the Iron

FIGURE 9.3-3 Dynamic Sensitivity Analysis

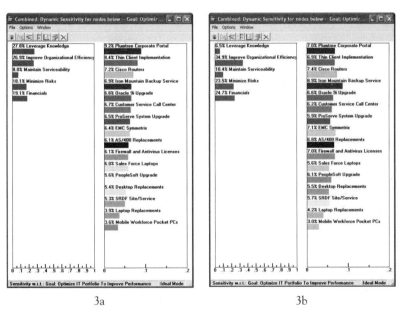

3a   3b

Note: This information is not actual AOL data but rather a representative sample.

Mountain Backup Service is now the highest-priority project, for example). At a subsequent quarterly portfolio review, it was evident to all that the portfolio was indeed aligned with the PMT's strategic objectives and that the key objective was well covered.

PMTs typically know the top few projects that they absolutely must have and that the bottom few are, at best, nice-to-have projects. Where the methodology and tool has the most benefit is to prioritize the middle—the 60 or 80 percent of should-have projects.

Results

With the new methodology and solution, the PMT was able to meet aggressive time lines for developing a cross-prioritized project list in time for the 2004 planning cycle. More important, the team was able to cut out over 80,000 hours of demand from an initial portfolio of about 200,000 hours that were requested from the business executives. This 40 percent reduction allowed the PMT to balance resource capacity versus demand without adding head count, and resulted in a project portfolio that has a greater overall return on investment.

Since the initial successes in early 2004, PMT members have been more closely examining business cases and the anticipated contribution that their proposed projects will make. As a result, some project requests have been withdrawn prior to their ever being vetted by the PMT. In addition, they have embraced the project evaluation techniques and tool to the point where they are now actively scoring projects (with handheld transmitters) after the project's business case has been presented rather than having a portfolio analyst perform that function. This has enabled the PMT to discuss their different perspectives in real time, arrive at consensus, and accept full accountability for the portfolio and its associated outcomes.

In summary, the PPM capability is helping AOL align its portfolio to its strategy and return the company to growth. These are the lessons learned:

- Keep it simple. Early success is critical. Keeping new processes simple and easy to adopt will not only produce quick
  wins but will also build invaluable momentum for the rest
  of the journey.

- Make the establishment of a solid resource management
  capability a prerequisite. A portfolio management team
  needs to understand not just which projects to initiate but
  when to initiate them in order to ensure that the necessary
  resources are available to deliver.

- Build and sustain executive support. At the end of the day,
  project portfolio management changes the way a business
  does business. Without strong advocacy from top management, whose job responsibilities will also change, a PPM
  capability that is fully integrated into the business cannot
  be achieved.

Rich Dougherty joined Expert Choice in December 2001 and currently serves as the company's chief executive officer. He has also
served as vice president of business development for Statusphere,
an Internet services software firm and vice president of sales and
marketing and a member of the executive team of FastTide. He
earned a B.A. from the University of Virginia and an M.B.A. from
the University of North Carolina in Chapel Hill.

9.4

EW Scripps

A Media Giant's Portfolio Management Solution

Vanessa McMillan

EW Scripps is a 125-year-old worldwide media conglomerate with successful ventures in print, newspaper, television, and online retail. It operates twenty-one daily newspapers, fifteen broadcast TV stations, four cable and satellite television programming networks, and a television retailing network. Scripps's brands include Home & Garden Television, Food Network, DIY—Do It Yourself Network, and Fine Living. HGTV reaches about 85 million U.S. television households, and Food Network can be seen in about 84 million households. Scripps Networks Web sites include FoodNetwork.com, HGTV.com, DIYnetwork.com, and fineliving.com. The company's programming can be seen in eighty-six countries.

The company's television retailing subsidiary, Shop at Home Network, markets a growing range of consumer goods directly to television viewers and visitors to the Shop at Home Web site (shopathometv.com). Scripps also operates Scripps Howard News Service and United Media, which is the worldwide licensing and syndication home of popular comic strips *Peanuts* and *Dilbert*.

In 2002, the already profitable enterprise chose to streamline its information technology (IT) processes by implementing an aggressive portfolio management solution under the direction of Oscar de Jongh, managing director of the project management office (PMO), Scripps Office of Technology, who recognized that the organization needed companywide process improvement across all geographical locations. Previously, EW Scripps did not have a PMO, and IT was traditionally decentralized. He saw that there was not a consistent project approval process and that IT must be centralized in order to reduce redundant work. This was before Sarbanes-Oxley (SOX) compliance pressures were even an issue. (The SOX Act Legislation of 2002 makes senior executives criminally liable for misrepresenting financial information.) He knew that a smoothly running, profitable business needed to load all initiatives into a central database for analysis.

De Jongh challenged his team to make a full-blown list of business requirements and start evaluating project portfolio management (PPM) vendors against the requirements list. The list was narrowed to seven or eight vendors, which were then rated by members of de Jongh's team according to perceived functionality. The list was further culled to three vendors. "At the end of the day, one company stood out as a company that was eager to become a partner in our success," said de Jongh. "I wasn't looking for just a software vendor."

After PlanView was selected, the software was successfully deployed and members of de Jongh's team trained. Although initially it was implemented in small environments within the corporation, the software now ties together the corporate office in Cincinnati, the company's online endeavor in Knoxville, and Shop@home in Nashville, and it was recently rolled out to the United Media office in New York.

One issue EW Scripps encountered is a very common one for organizations seeking to implement PPM: cultural change. According to de Jongh, one reason that the company has not been able to recognize a larger return on investment from the solution is that Scripps manages its cultural change very slowly, minimizing the resistance level from staff.

EW Scripps uses every function of the PPM solution: project management, resource management, investment analysis, portfolio management, and service and financial management. It is now able to manage the demand for IT work it receives from other lines of business. The solution also allows Scripps to effectively scope and prioritize projects, allocate resources, and identify priorities. Along with portfolio management, the company uses best practice automation, program management, resource utilization, and time reporting (critical to Sarbanes-Oxley requirements to make determination decisions on labor capitalization). According to de Jongh, the IT group has consistency and standards, which have allowed it to gain control of its project management environment.

One department using the software identified a redundant project for online credit card processing, saving the company $1 million and instantly justifying the investment in PPM. Shrewd investment decisions and efficiency with which IT performs work has given the entire company an advantage, according to de Jongh. "We make better decisions on investments, how we choose and allocate new technical projects and how we ultimately track performance."

De Jongh, as well as members of Scripps's executive team, also uses the executive dashboard functionality (Figure 9.4-1). They use executive analysis not only to prioritize initiatives but also to monitor the trends and health of their investments. Although de Jongh's team sometimes has limited resources, they are able to select the right work based on ROI calculations and strategic objectives. The company now makes business decisions down to the developer resource level and charges project managers to help drive those decisions using their PPM suite.

EW Scripps also uses the software to manage its Sarbanes-Oxley compliance initiatives. "The amount of money we've been able to capitalize because we have certifiable, trackable data is considerable," said de Jongh. "This alone has more than paid for our investment in PPM."

Prior to PlanView, we could capitalize $25,000 for work delivered from an external source. The limit on internal was $100,000. It was more beneficial to use a more expensive contractor than someone internal because the finance department felt strongly that an invoice from a vendor for code delivered was auditable. The de-

FIGURE 9.4-1 Executive Dashboard

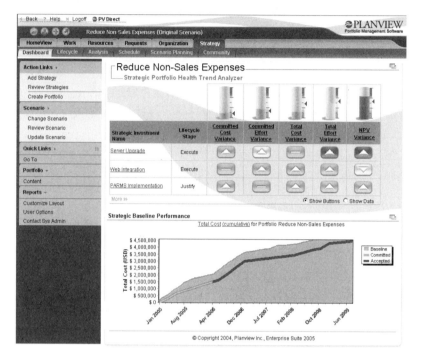

Note: The attributes are normally in color. The deep indicators are red, signifying unsatisfactory performance. The lightest buttons are green, indicating satisfactory performance. The intermediate buttons are yellow, indicating marginal, subpar performance.

partment didn't think the same could be said for the use of internal resources. "When I demonstrated the reports that the PPM software generates, they saw that we had auditable, reliable data that comes at a click of a button from PlanView," said de Jongh. "We have accountability with regard to our labor." De Jongh was then able to produce three months of data and timesheet reports to the office of the chief financial officer. "Within forty-eight hours, he had assurance the data was irrefutable and dropped our internal capitalization to $5,000."

De Jongh hopes to begin measuring performance against the baseline that's being established now. He'd like to get all resource managers to start scheduling at a more detailed level. "Right now, we have no idea what the capacity is to do things today or tomorrow. We only know yesterday and are not in a position to be planning strategically until we are measuring ourselves against a baseline."

EW Scripps continues its partnership with its PPM vendor by working very closely with PlanView in the Early Adopter program. "The better tools we have, the better we can work," said de Jongh. "Our relationship with our PPM vendor resulted in a partnership for developing new functionality for the software. "We are helping them to develop a better tool for our organization and the marketplace. It's a win-win situation for everyone involved."

Vanessa McMillan is director of marketing at PlanView, a provider of enterprise portfolio management solutions.

SECTION TEN

What Others Are Saying About PPM

The chapters in this final section are representative of what is being said about PPM by other experts on the subject. These chapters will help to solidify some of the earlier discussions; some also bring a special point of view or a special wisdom to our understanding of the world of project portfolio management.

We start with *Beyond Triple Constraints*, authored by long-time colleague Robert Graham, with coauthor Dennis Cohen. Graham has earned an international reputation for his contributions to recognizing the human side of project management. His books and papers on this subject formed the nucleus of my PM library. In Chapter 10.1, Graham and Cohen look at the elements of schedule, cost, and outcome as they are changing with time. They take us to this century, where measurements and decisions are more closely related to shareholder value.

Even before I became a fan of Graham, I was drawn to the philosophy of Rational Decision Making, as presented by Kepner-Tregoe. For close to fifty years, this firm has researched and expounded on structured methods of problem solving and decision making. This was clearly presented in Charles Kepner and Benjamin Tregoe's book, *The Rational Manager*.[1] It was a natural extension of this area of study to move into project management, and even more appropriate to move into project portfolio management since the very nature of PPM is rational decision making. Coauthors James Schlick and Andrew Longman are partners at Kepner-Tregoe and have been the developers of Kepner-Tregoe's capabilities in the PM area. In Chapter 10.2, James Schlick and Andrew Longman show how a rational decision process is a fundamental component of PPM. It will take us out of the constant crises of overextended resources working on the wrong projects.

Superb contributions to the literature on PPM are gushing out of every conceivable source. A valuable resource area is the developers of tools and systems for PPM. In Chapter 10.3, Gil Makleff provides a recipe of the best practices for PPM that teach how to implement a PPM capability.

The Project Management Institute (PMI) has a growing membership, now exceeding well over 100,000 project management practitioners. In Chapter 10.4, PMI's Knowledge and Wisdom Center sets out the basics of project portfolio management.

The excellent and concise overview in Chapter 10.5 by James Pennypacker and Patrick Sepate wraps up our coverage of PPM.

10.1

Beyond the Triple Constraints

Developing a Business Venture Approach to Project Management

Robert J. Graham, Dennis Cohen

In the future, project management will become standard management practice, the way things are done in organizations. For this to occur, however, project management practices will have to develop from the current technical orientation into a business and organizational orientation. This means that the time-honored triple constraints of outcome, cost, and schedule/duration currently used to measure technical project success will have to be expanded into broader measures of project success, such as the project's overall contribution to organizational value. This expansion of success criteria will change decision making during projects, the way projects are judged as successful, and the way that project managers are developed, measured, and rewarded. That is, it will change the entire profession of project management. This chapter begins by outlining the changes in project management that have resulted in diminishing the adequacy of the triple constraints for measuring project success. It then develops a future business venture model of project success that shows how the triple constraints (see Exhibit 10.1-1) eventually influence shareholder value and thus expand those project measurements into business system measurements. The business

The contents of this chapter appeared in the *Proceedings of the Project Management Institute Annual Seminars and Symposium*, Nashville, Tenn., Nov. 1–10, 2001. It is reprinted with the permission of PMI and the authors.

EXHIBIT 10.1-1 What Is the Triple Constraint Approach?

With the triple constraint approach you ask questions similar to those below.

Outcome. Does this new feature conform to the specification? Is it needed to achieve performance criteria? Can we get management approval for this change in time to include it in this version of the product?

Cost. How much will this new feature cost? Is there money in the budget? If not, can we get a budget increase? Can we get the increase in time to include it in this version of the product?

Schedule/Duration. How much time will this add to the schedule? Is this acceptable to upper management? If not, can we get an extension?

Normally, if the feature does not satisfy the three criteria or if extensions are not granted, then it is rejected. This approach pits project manager against upper manager and often leads to rejection of good ideas.

Source: D. J. Cohen and R. J. Graham, *The Project Manager's MBA: Translating Project Decisions into Business Success* (San Francisco: Jossey-Bass, 2000).

systems calculator that it introduces shows the effects of various project decisions on the project's eventual contribution to shareholder value (for the calculator, see www.projectmanagersmba.com).

Defining Project Success: From Triple Constraints to Shareholder Value

Project management began as a sort of counterculture movement. The original project managers worked outside the organization. In fact, they were normally outside in a trailer at a construction site in what was then a prototypical project office. Back then, the art of project management was something akin to voodoo, and the seal of the craft was the PERT chart. Project managers were measured by their ability to work within the triple constraints. Projects in the past had a bit more certainty in the outcome, as the main source of uncertainty was in the technology used to deliver that outcome. But the tables turn, and as the technology becomes more reliable, we find the definition of the project outcome becomes more illusive. A brief history of this change is given below.

The Distant Past

We look at the issues of the period in terms of outcome, cost, and schedule:

• *Outcome.* In many cases in the past, the project manager had done something similar before, so an example was available. For example, most early project management was done at construction sites. This results in reliance on clear specifications. Project practice dictated not to begin a project until detailed specifications were written. Often the specifications were made even clearer by the architect's drawings. This allowed the project manager to know most of the components of the final product when the project began.

• *Cost.* If you know what components cost and how much labor is needed, costs are much easier to estimate. This causes a reliance on the budget as project decisions were evaluated on their effect on the budget. The project manager was measured on adherence to budget. Only approved change orders were allowed, which resulted on heavy reliance on upper management for decision making.

• *Schedule.* If you know how long components take, scheduling is easier. This causes reliance on PERT and schedule techniques. Due to familiarity with similar projects, it was easier to change people on the project without affecting the schedule. The project manager was also measured on adherence to schedule. Only approved change orders were allowed, which again results in heavy reliance on upper management for decision making.

The use of the triple constraint provided metrics for upper management measurement, evaluation, and control. They knew how well the job was done when the project was over. Triple constraints also provided criteria for evaluating options for project decision-making. Thus, the triple constraints solved problems for both the project manager and upper management.

The Recent Past

As uncertainty in projects increased, the efficacy of the triple constraints decreased. With more uncertainty, the reliance on triple constraints begins to cause, not solve, problems. The first wave of increased uncertainty occurred when project management moved inside the organization and was applied to organization (customer) issues.

- *Outcome.* Fewer examples were available for internal projects, and these were not repeatable, as the customers always wanted something new. Project managers were still trained not to start without specifications. The result was to force specifications from customers who were not really certain about what they wanted. These specifications gave the illusion of certainty, but the result usually disappointed the customer.
- *Cost.* With a budget based on forced specifications, more changes were required as the project progressed. The project manager was measured on adherence to budget, so necessary project changes required further consultation with upper management, which slowed things down.
- *Schedule.* Since the schedule was based on forced specifications, it was highly affected by the many changes and decision delays.

Metrics used to evaluate projects caused suboptimization due to the myth of certainty. Relying on triple constraints caused project managers to chase after the wrong goal, satisfying constraints rather than satisfying the customer. When this occurs, something is delivered by the deadline, but it is not really what the customer wants.

Lower customer acceptance leads to lower market sales and organization profit. However, since something was delivered somewhere near the budget, the project was often considered a success, even if the project outcome was a failure. Obviously change was needed.

The Future

The next wave of increasing the uncertainty is being caused by the increasing speed of change—so-called Internet time. In extreme uncertainty, it becomes impossible to determine a fixed outcome, cost, and schedule for any project. The myth of certainty is no longer believable, so outcome, cost, and schedule become project variables rather than constraints. Guidance for decision making thus becomes the effect of the decision on economic value to the organization.

- *Outcome*. Project outcomes begin very vague and then continually change due to customer information gained from rapid prototyping. Project success is only known after the project outcome life cycle is completed, and it is heavily dependent on the project's contribution to economic value.
- *Cost*. The cost is continually changing and in need of constant review. The old concept of cost is seen as possibly irrelevant to the goal of contributing to economic value. Costs are thus seen as investments made now to increase organizational value in the future.
- *Schedule*. The schedule becomes much more externally driven and not in your control. It is based more on the market than on time needed to produce the project outcome. As cycle times are reduced, project outcome success is heavily dependent on how you begin. Thus, the fuzzy front end, the time at the beginning, becomes most important for project success. This irritates upper managers, who like to jump in at the end.

Triple constraint metrics used to evaluate projects will now cause real problems and possibly failure due to the need for changes during project. Relying on triple constraints may cause you to deliver the wrong product. Something will be delivered by the deadline, but the technology may have changed and the market may have moved on. For the future, a new metric will be needed.

The New Metric: Project Contribution to Business Results

Future project managers need a longer-term business orientation that takes into account project contribution to business results. For most business organizations, this means project contribution to business strategy and shareholder value. Fortunately, both of these can be seen as an extension of the triple constraints. What was before a set of three fixed constraints that bounded the project now becomes three variables that enable the project to achieve business results. This is achieved through a dynamic process of jointly optimizing the three project variables of cost, schedule, and outcome in the service of strategic alignment, shareholder value, and ultimately business results.

Why strategic alignment? Because certain tactical moves may be inconsistent with an overall strategy for the company. If a project engages tactically in an inconsistent direction, it may subtract from long-term business results even though it adds to economic value over the short term. For example, a project that emphasizes cost savings for a new product or service in a company that stresses customer intimacy may save money over the short term, but it will not contribute to business results over the long term. The same holds for a project that emphasizes the latest technology in a company with a strategy that emphasizes low cost, high volume, and process efficiency.[1]

Why shareholder value? Because over the long run and on average, that is the goal of a publicly owned corporation. Shareholder value is a measure of economic value added for the company as a whole. If projects do not contribute to this in some way, they represent money invested with a return below investor expectations, which will lower the stock price over time and impair the company's ability to raise capital to support its competitive advantage in the marketplace. Thus, shareholder value provides a compass for projects to maintain their direction in a stormy and turbulent environment. As things are constantly in flux, the project manager uses shareholder value as the system objective to set priorities and make decisions to guide project midcourse corrections.

How Project Decisions Relate to Shareholder Value

Here we are going to focus on project decisions related to project contribution to shareholder value. The system of variables that influence shareholder value from within the project is illustrated in Figure 10.1-1. Project contribution to shareholder value is influenced by two major factors: the combined cash flow of the project and its outcome life cycle (the project venture) and the internal charge for capital used to finance the project venture.

Capital Charge

The internal charge for the use of capital is based on the company's weighted average cost of capital (WACC). Project managers do not influence this over the short term. Over the long term, however, they can lower this by managing good projects with successful outcomes. The capital charge is influenced by the use of capital by the project venture and the WACC for the company. The use of capital by the project venture is a combination of the use of capital by the project and the use of capital by the project outcome life cycle. At this point, we can see the influence of the three project variables on this part of the business system. Project cost and project duration are a direct influence on the project's use of capital. The longer and the more expensive the project is, the higher the capital charge is. Outcome, in turn, influences the capital charge of the project outcome life cycle. Here, consideration of time to breakeven and the use of working capital become important. These financial results

FIGURE 10.1-1 Business Systems Diagram

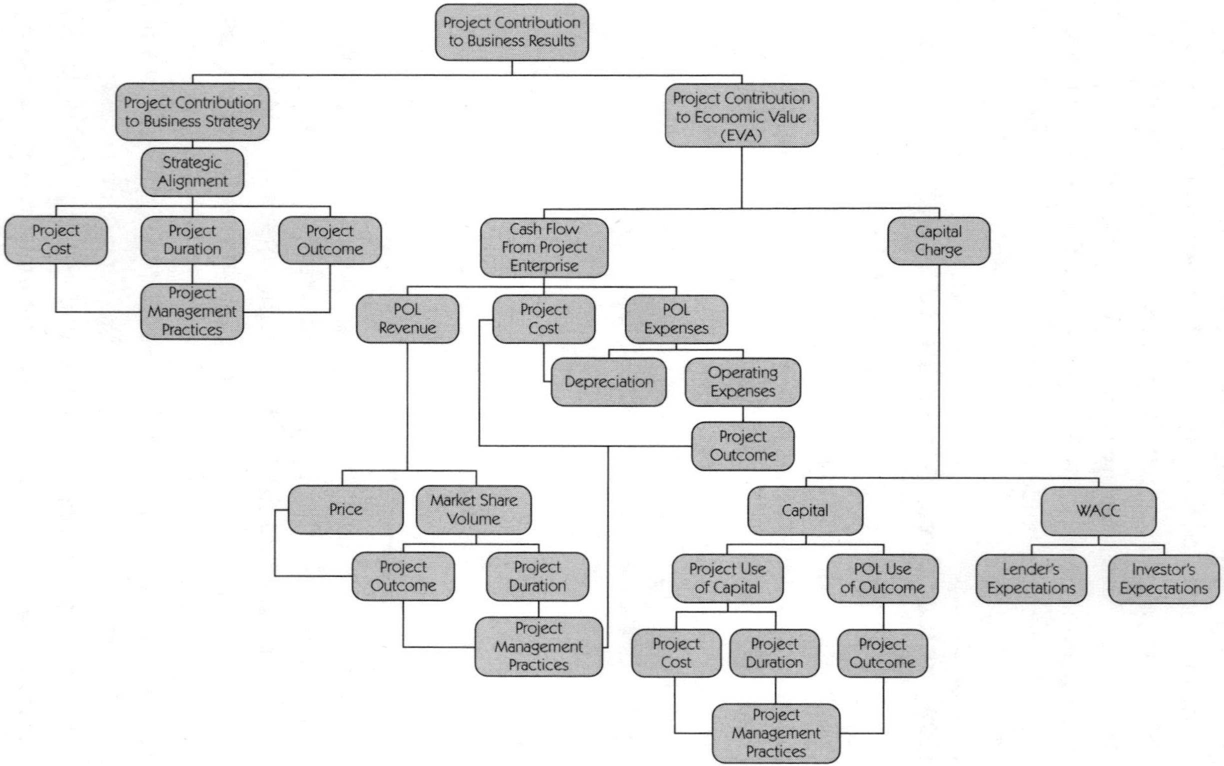

can be influenced by decisions made during the project, so the project manager and team members should understand the business implications of their decisions. For example, the decision to add a new feature may increase the project duration, which will result in an increase in the capital charge.

Cash Flow

The cost of the project, the revenues during the project outcome life cycle (POL), and the POL expenses influence the combined cash flow of the project enterprise. Project cost has a direct impact on immediate cash flow, but it also influences depreciation charges stemming from the POL. Duration and outcome influence price and market share, which determine POL revenues based on time-to-market considerations and meeting customer and end user expectations. Outcome also influences POL operating expenses that along with depreciation influence total POL expenses.

As illustrated in Figure 10.1-1, this is a fairly complex system of variables and does not lend itself to a set of recipe answers on how to maximize shareholder value. Decision making within the project is based on a sound business case that justified the project in the first place. The case is constructed to make all assumptions explicit and to explore the dynamics of the relationship in the business system of the project. This is in stark contrast to the numbers game that is often played out using a business case purely for gaining project approval. You know it well: "What numbers do I have to fill in to get this project approved?" During the project, the business case is further researched, fleshed out, and turned into a detailed business plan so that the project team can continuously check assumptions about projected results with actual results. Decisions about duration, cost, and outcome are then made in relation to how they interact with each other and how this interaction affects shareholder value. The process always involves trade-offs. For instance, we can cut the budget and eliminate features, but at what cost to customer demand and revenue from the POL? We can pull out all of the stops and spend whatever it takes to be first to market, but will the gain in market share really pay back enough to cover our additional expense? Although conventional wisdom says yes, it may not always be the case.

Business System Calculator

Because this is a fairly complex system, many people can better learn its dynamics through a hands-on approach. We have developed a calculator to allow you to experiment with different decisions in order to see how they influence shareholder value under different assumptions. We explain where to get it (at no cost) and how to use it below. We have also developed a simulation that illustrates how a portfolio of projects influences a company's shareholder value over time depending on how they are managed. This is available as part of a course to help project managers improve their business decision making in projects.

The business systems calculator is a spreadsheet program that can be downloaded from www.projectmanagersmba.com. Instructions are contained in the program, under the first tab. As input, you will use values typically contained in the business plan. This includes project cost and duration, as well as the starting price and cost, and the price and cost erosion, of the project outcome. Input concerning the market is also required. This includes an estimate of the total market volume over the POL, the time the market for the outcome will begin, and estimates of your market share for entering the market at various times. The WACC is also input. Output includes the net present value for the entire venture as well as a graphical representation of the venture's contribution to shareholder value over the life of the project. Project decisions can then be evaluated by estimating the decision's impact on any of the input variables and then calculating the resulting effect on shareholder value.[2]

Robert J. Graham, PMP, is an independent management consultant in the areas of project management and organizational change. Previously he was a senior staff member of the Management and Behavioral Sciences Center at the Wharton School, University of Pennsylvania, where he taught in the M.B.A. and Ph.D. programs and was also part of the Wharton Effective Executive program teaching project management to practicing executives. He is the author of *Project Management as If People Mattered* and coauthor of *Creating an Environment for Successful Projects* (with Randy Englund), *The Project Manager's MBA* (with Dennis Cohen), and *Creating the Project Office* (with Randy Englund and Paul Dinsmore). He has a B.S. from Miami University and an M.B.A. and Ph.D. from the University of Cincinnati.

Dennis Cohen is the founder and president of Optimal Performance Network. Before founding OPnet, he founded and led both the Management and Executive Leadership and Project Management Practice Areas for SMG. He is the coauthor of *The Project Manager's MBA* (with Robert Graham) and has delivered numerous papers on project and strategic leadership at professional conferences. Dennis has also been a Research Associate at the University of Pennsylvania's Wharton School Management and Behavioral Science Center and a Senior Fellow with the Wharton Center for Applied Research. Dennis holds a B.A. and M.A. from the University of California, Berkeley; an M.A. and Ph.D. from the University of Wisconsin; and an M.B.A. from the Wharton School of the University of Pennsylvania.

10.2

From Overload to Productivity via Systematic Decision Making

James Schlick, Andrew Longman

Overload has become a way of life as firms struggle to manage a barrage of projects in an attempt to meet increasing marketplace demands. All too often, that overload leads to project paralysis.

In one division of a large manufacturing company, a scheduled high-priority project was never actually completed. A project manager at a midsize service organization confesses he rarely meets a deadline on large projects because time-consuming, low-priority activities keep getting dumped in his lap. A pharmaceutical company lags behind the industry because there are not enough of the "right people" to complete its most critical work.

What Is Happening to These Organizations?

The scale and number of projects underway have outstripped organizations' ability to manage them. Leading business journals continue to tout projects as a way of life, but in many companies, project management effectiveness is in a precarious state. Not only projects but also business performance is jeopardized when organizations take on more projects than they can handle.

Consider the medical device industry, where time-to-market is a crucial determinant of profitability.[1] A pharmaceutical leader dominated the industry with an innovative stent for cardiac surgery.

Despite a significant advantage over smaller, slower competitors, its inability to create a systematic process for managing product development resulted in a critical loss of market share.

In a growing economy, the name of the game may not even be market share, as many e-companies have already demonstrated. The new equation is even simpler: faster, faster, faster. And whether an organization has been intentionally streamlined or weakened through fierce competition for skilled knowledge workers, the resources to get there first may be all too scant.

This means that project management is everybody's job. Designated project managers are trained in the most sophisticated software tools, but those tools are often too complex and cumbersome to use effectively. Projects are initiated at any and every level of the organization, and once initiated, they take on a life of their own. Some are started and never finished, while low-value projects sap resources from critical initiatives. Most critical, executives at the top find it difficult to view a roll-up of project activity that helps them make the tough decisions.

Perhaps more so than at any other time in business history, organizations find themselves dangerously overextended. They start multiple projects with limited resources, in flattened organizations, without common logic or language, and with no clear framework for establishing priorities.[2] These organizations need a way to balance what they want to do with what they can do in a given time frame.

Symptoms of Project Proliferation

The project proliferation disease is spreading fast. Top management wants to get a lot done, now—and others don't hesitate to throw additional "high-priority" projects into the hopper. Corporate executives may not make the connection between project glut and its depleting side effects; they only know that employee morale is low and project delivery dates are chronically late.

The wear and tear of project proliferation in an organization may be characterized by these other symptoms as well:

- Rising overhead and increasing complexity
- Slow cycle time on getting new products from idea to launch
- Uneven (start-and-stop) project activity
- Overwhelmed and overtasked project managers
- Lengthy and unproductive project review meetings
- A perpetual scarcity of project resources, with senior management time wasted in disputes between project managers and resource managers
- Frustration among project participants over the lack of project results
- Executive concerns about the organization's ability to deliver on critical new projects

A look beyond the symptoms reveals the root causes of the proliferation syndrome: an informal or inadequate process for initiating projects; unfocused or "moving-target" project priorities; and inconsistent or poorly executed project planning, resource allocation, and implementation.

The truth is that any organization's resources are limited. One way or another, only certain projects will get done. The choice is whether this happens arbitrarily or deliberately.

The Cure: Project Complexity Reduction

To build a successful financial portfolio, investors first articulate their strategic financial objectives. They weigh the relative merits of investment alternatives, characterizing the risks and benefits of each. They analyze exactly what resources are available for investment and determine how they will be allocated among alternatives. Careful measurement of the portfolio's success against the strategic yardstick is ongoing. And when returns accelerate or diminish, investors make the tough calls in order to maximize return over the long haul.

Building a project portfolio in today's organizations requires no less. A systematic method for evaluating the organization's project investments is critical. Such an approach tips the balance from the depleting effects of project proliferation to project productivity and company profit.

What might such a cure look like? In an automotive manufacturing plant, typical for its size and industry, senior executives assessed the merit of 135 projects. Project task lists, resource and staffing requirements, and other relevant information were summarized. Following a rigorous two-day decision session, where each project was evaluated against eight strategic objectives, the final "must-do" list of projects was dropped to 35. The implementation plan called for rigorous project management techniques, including monthly variance reports to the plant staff. The result? Most of the designated projects were successfully completed during the following year, leading to a jump in the division's productivity, product quality, and revenue.

Six steps are common in project portfolio initiatives:

1. *Analyze the overall project environment.* Before moving to remedy the situation, any organization needs to take a long, hard look at the status quo. Interviews and other assessment tools reveal the nature of the gap between the current approach to managing projects and a systematic portfolio approach. What is the universe of projects currently underway? What is the basis for our definition of projects: Regulatory compliance? Customer requirements? Market or product expansion? What strategic time frames are our projects intended to meet? And, most critical, what is the current process for project initiation, implementation, measurement of results, and closeout or termination? How does the environment support project-focused as opposed to function-based work?

2. *Develop project portfolio objectives.* The senior management team needs to undertake the definition of specific, strategically

linked objectives for building the project portfolio. What exactly is our project portfolio expected to accomplish? What are our strategic and operational objectives, and what are their relative merits? How will long- and short-term objectives be balanced? How will we quantify the assessment of individual projects against those objectives? And have we ensured that the appropriate people are involved in these considerations? The outcome of this process is the full commitment of senior executives to clear and commonly held objectives to guide difficult decision making.

3. *Analyze resource capacity.* It's not uncommon to find an organization that has identified fifty thousand hours of project time needed but only fifteen thousand hours of people time available to devote to project work. A reasonable assessment of the organization's available resources must go hand-in-hand with decision objectives. What resources—people, facilities, and technology—are available for project work? What functional areas do they represent, and how will that affect their allocation? An understanding of organizational project capacity is an essential precursor of balanced decision making.

4. *Gather and organize data on current and anticipated projects.* Whatever the project management methods used in various parts of the organization (which may vary widely), project data needs to be collected and reported in a consistent format for evaluation. What are the major tasks of each project, and what specific resources are required for their completion? What value will be created by the project? How do the resource requirements stack up against project capacity? What unique risks or benefits must be considered? When many projects are involved, computer spreadsheets and databases are useful tools for organizing and managing project data. The key to this effort is simplicity. This information should be documented on a single page for each project. Then all projects can be fairly evaluated (see step 5), using a consistent framework for analysis.

5. *Evaluate the project portfolio.* Based on the objectives developed and the project data collected, senior managers evaluate each project for inclusion in the portfolio going forward. The critical decisions

they are required to make, their strategic project choices, will not be easy. How do projects compare in their alignment with objectives? Which will be accelerated, delayed, or cancelled? Ultimately these decisions will redirect resources toward those critical few projects that will best advance the objectives of the organization. With the support of expert facilitation, individual members of the team will assess their personal risk tolerance, understand their contribution to the decision process, and build commitment to the portfolio plan.

6. *Implement a complexity reduction system.* The final key is the installation of a simple and sustainable management system to control project proliferation permanently. How will new and existing projects continue to be measured against objectives within a consistent framework? What project management skills and common practices will support the organization's ability to monitor the project portfolio? How will we recognize the value of our portfolio watchdogs and master project managers? How will computer systems—centralized project databases, spreadsheets, charts—make useful information available throughout the organization? Continuous portfolio management ensures that every project plays a part in helping the organization achieve its business objectives.[3]

Case Study: A Typical Patient

A mobile phone manufacturer rested (quite uncomfortably) at the bottom of its industry segment in profitability rankings. The projects in its portfolio were intended to bring new products to market quickly. Critical company resources were shared across projects, from high-level research to essential documentation for the Federal Communications Commission. Project proliferation had slowed product development and rollouts while raising the level of frustration in the company.

Analysis revealed a bevy of bottlenecks, not the least of which concerned the fast-dwindling population of a critical human resource, bench technicians. When the project leadership team reviewed upcoming project requirements with resource managers, they discovered that if they didn't fill critical positions now, many of their current projects would screech to a halt within six months.

Fortunately, this stimulated the implementation of a full-blown project portfolio management process. Many other critical resource concerns were identified, forcing the company to reprioritize projects and reallocate resources.

Within six months of instituting the project portfolio process, the organization skyrocketed from "cellar dweller" to champ. It now ranks at the top in industry profitability, having doubled the rate of new products to market.

Four Keys to Strategic Project Portfolio Management Success

The following four actions provide a framework for successful project portfolio management:

- Understand projects in a strategic context to focus resources on your critical business priorities.
- Use a systematic decision-making process to support your top team in making difficult choices.
- Monitor projects using a shared approach that incorporates proven tools and practices.
- Build antidotes to project proliferation that keep resources focused on your strategic portfolio of projects.

James D. Schlick, a partner of Kepner-Tregoe, specializes in assessing the needs of clients and designing solutions to meet those needs. He is also the principal designer of Kepner-Tregoe's project management process and workshop, Engineering the Performance System workshop, and eThink application software. He holds a bachelor of science in engineering operations from Iowa State University and a master's degree in industrial operations from Purdue University.

Andrew Longman, a partner in Kepner-Tregoe, is also director of marketing, responsible for the worldwide promotion of the company's brand and consultants. He helped design and implement eThink, Kepner-Tregoe's critical-thinking support software, and its project management software, Project Logic. He is certified by the Project Management Institute as a Project Management Professional (PMP).

10.3

The Seven Habits of Highly Effective IT Portfolio Management Implementations

Gil Makleff

Portfolio management is on its way to becoming a mainstream practice, with over 50 percent of Global 2000 companies expected to adopt portfolio management by 2004.[1] Three forces continue to drive the need for a sound methodology and proven tools for IT portfolio management:

- *Increased need for compliance and accountability.* With the Sarbanes-Oxley legislation, executives can no longer claim, "I was not aware." Portfolio management provides the rationale for large project investments and the transparency and accountability to know where investments are flowing in an organization.

- *Increased awareness of technology's role in meeting a company's business objectives.* It is clear that projects must be aligned with business strategy. This problem is fundamental since recent industry studies have shown that 40 percent of capital investments are wasted mainly due to lack of alignment with business strategy.

- *Changing budgets, which require thoughtful reallocation.* "The essence of reality is scarcity" as companies have been reminded in the recent economic downturn. Less budget, fewer resources, yet business must go on.

Yet most organizations will adopt simplistic solutions based on input data and "nice charts" or will view portfolio management as a roll-up of projects into an umbrella group. It's not that easy. Why do some implementations drive portfolio value by as much as 30 percent while other attempts become just another failed project?

We look at seven proven best practices that were consistently used in successful PPM rollouts across over one hundred implementations at UMT:

1. Start at the top with senior management buy-in.
2. Don't overwhelm the organization with a big bang approach.
3. Develop a governance process.
4. Use proven PPM tools.
5. Develop a common currency to evaluate projects based on contribution to business objectives.
6. Optimize the portfolio against constraints to get the biggest bang for the buck!
7. Don't assume things will be okay. Monitor portfolio execution and benefits realization.

Any organization thinking of PPM should strongly consider using these while developing a PPM governance framework.

Start at the Top with Senior Management Buy-In

Because of continuing pressures to do more with less, senior management buy-in to a structured PPM process is essential to create awareness, provide support, build consensus as to organizational goals, and motivate stakeholders at all levels to participate effectively. Specifically this enables:

- *Focus on business objectives from the beginning.* Engaging business executives at the onset of the PPM process, from portfolio selection, ensures that business objectives are clarified early

in the planning cycle. As a result, consensus can be built between the management team over projects that support these
goals, and "squeaking wheel" (those that shout the loudest)
priorities are minimized.

- *Early application of the PPM framework to critical business needs.*
  The importance of buy-in at the senior level is especially critical in PPM governance. Early in the process, senior management can be educated in ways to engage and apply PPM
  during critical junctures as external or internal events necessi-
  tate investment level and direction modifications.

- *Establishment of communication forums.* Senior executive buy-in
  at this early stage also creates a defined forum for escalation of
  issues pertaining to portfolio delivery and provides executives
  with a tangible stake in ensuring the successful implementation of the portfolio.

Don't Overwhelm the Organization with a "Big Bang" Approach

Each organization is different in terms of its level of maturity and
ability to handle change. A phased approach should be used based
on the company's internal PPM maturity. Specifically, organizations
should:

- *Identify PPM focus areas through a gap analysis.* Maximize the
  chances of success with a gap analysis before applying any
  framework. The gap analysis provides an understanding of your
  current capability maturity versus industry best practices. Areas
  of greatest need are identified, and the customized target PPM
  environment is established for the organization. There are typically many valuable existing PPM processes that should be
  built on, not discarded.

- *Communicate within the organization using a proof of concept,*
  either in parallel to existing budgeting and planning activities
  or well before yearly planning. In many cases, participants in

the budgeting and planning process require tangible views of the value that PPM provides. A proof of concept is an excellent way to facilitate the communication of that value using data that participants relate to and with terminology specific to their needs.

- *Roll out PPM with less-than-perfect information.* There is never a good time to initiate a change process. Information is never perfect. You will always find opinions from those not interested in increased transparency that PPM may not be the right approach because of less-than-perfect data or an insufficient methodology. In fact, PPM is a process that engenders systemic and organization thinking and has self-correcting mechanisms that enhance results over time.

Whatever approach and tools are selected, never:

- Go too long without showing results. A perception that this approach is time-consuming is fatal.
- Run PPM in a "lab" environment without active business management support and participation. A perception that PPM is theoretical will cause a disconnect with the business client.

Develop a Governance Process

Project approval governance structures ensure that consistent processes are adopted throughout the organization. Governance structures should be tailored to the organizational environment.

Howard Rubin from the Meta Group says that "portfolio management without governance is an empty concept."[2] The need for a structured framework that supports decision making is absolutely essential.

Portfolio management implementations without a strong governance structure will struggle to be accepted and are unlikely to yield expected results. There are six critical factors to consider when establishing a governance structure. These are six pillars of governance (see Figure 10.3-1):

- *Timing:* When are decisions made: annually, quarterly, just-in-time, or over multiple years?

- *Decision style:* How is consensus achieved: in groups, by voting, or through a dictatorship?

- *Organizational level:* Who is involved in the decisions: the board, a multifunctional steering committee, a project management office?

- *Thresholds:* What are thresholds defined by: budgets, full-time equivalents (FTE), cross–business unit projects?

- *Decision criteria:* What other criteria affect decision making: financial impact, strategic impact, risk levels, architectural fit?

- *Decisions:* How do projects originate and get prioritized? How do they get funded? Who tracks their implementation?

Each of these areas must be understood to develop a governance structure tailored to the organizational environment.

FIGURE 10.3-1. Six Pillars of Governance

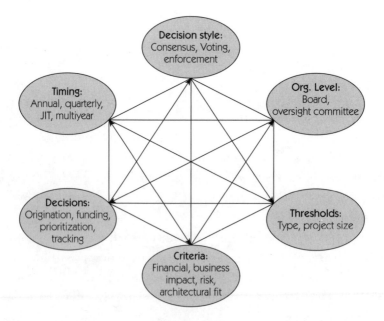

Use Proven PPM Tools

Project portfolio management tools are catching up to support the developing needs of the marketplace and are an essential part of any PPM implementation. They can determine failure or success in the PPM rollout.

As new vendors enter the growing market of portfolio management, software can be found in many forms, the bulk of which offer nothing more than project repositories with manual prioritization and nice graphical interfaces. To make multimillion-dollar project investment decisions, you really need a robust decision support tool that can help in these ways:

- Prioritize projects by their mathematically derived business value.
- Optimize against budget and resource constraints to select the best portfolio.
- Conduct what-if analysis using advanced portfolio intelligence.
- Drill down into reasons why the portfolio is not on the Efficient Frontier.
- Enable communication and sharing.
- Provide graphics and representations that are easy to understand and modify to reflect the ongoing changes in the portfolio.

The complex trade-offs of value, cost, resources, and risk require software that can mathematically weight, balance, and optimize a portfolio in a seamless manner. In selecting PPM tools, organizations should look not only at the breadth of functionality the tools offer, but also at the vendor's experience in PPM. With the evolving market for PPM tools and solutions, vendors with the most implementation experience are the ones who are likely to have the most sophisticated and scalable solutions.

Develop a Common Currency to Evaluate Projects Based on Contribution to Business Objectives

Once you have an inventory of proposed projects to consider, you must have a system to assign relative value to them. How do you compare a proposed customer relations management (CRM) project to a proposed storage area network? It's difficult, if not impossible, without a way to quantify previously qualitative beliefs, opinions, assumptions, and incomparable metrics. Without a rational system of quantitative comparison, decisions are made emotionally and by the most politically powerful or persuasive.

Yet quantitative financial gauges used alone are not enough, as they are lagging indicators that often fail to properly capture short-term benefits of certain business initiatives. Rather, translate company strategy into seven to ten business drivers and prioritize the drivers using conjoint analysis to determine their weighted importance. Next, determine the impact of proposed projects on business objectives, and mathematically derive a strategic currency from which one project can be compared to another.

Aligning projects to business strategy creates a visible link between the aim of the project and its intended benefits. It also allows all projects to be compared to each other based on a new system, a common currency.

Prioritization of the portfolio should be based on the degree to which each project supports organizational goals (strategic value). However, it is unlikely that the optimum project mix will consist simply of those projects that rank highest in this list. In order to optimize a portfolio, organizations should look to maximize the total strategic value their project portfolio can yield in relation to its constraints on resources.

Optimize the Portfolio Against Constraints to Get the Biggest Bang for the Buck

Scarcity is the essence of reality; you simply do not have the budget, skilled resources, technology, or organizational ability to undertake all project requests. So how do you select the best portfolio of proj-ects given these constraints? You could rank-order them based on their strategic value (that is, the common currency defined above) and select them in order until you run out of funds. Yet in most cases, there are multiple constraints, including limited competen-cies, project dependencies, mandatory projects, and more. In order to optimize a portfolio, organizations should look to maximize the total strategic value their project portfolio can yield in relation to all constraints, and this requires mathematical optimization.

Optimization is best seen through the use of an Efficient Fron-tier with which you can benchmark any proposed portfolio against the best you could possibly do given your constraints. (The Efficient Frontier concept is explained in Chapter 4.4.) The Efficient Fron-tier tool seamlessly looks across all of the possible portfolios and gives you the confidence to know where you are in comparison to the optimal solution, and what is holding you back from reaching it. (See Figure 10.3-2.)

FIGURE 10.3-2 The Efficient Frontier

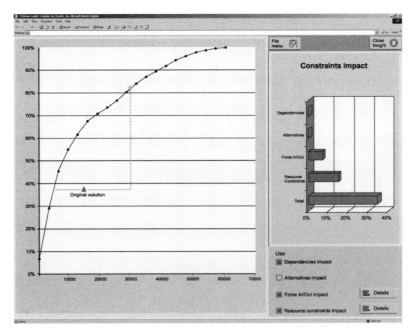

Moving to a fact-based decision model that enables identification of trade-offs between more and less valuable portfolio components leads to responsible decision making and maximum support of the company's business direction.

Don't Assume Things Will Be Okay; Monitor Portfolio Execution and Benefits Realization

Monitoring investments after they have been launched is one of the most critical parts of ensuring a successful PPM process. Portfolio agility, or the ability to stay current with your investment status and respond to changes, is a key driving force. With stricter audit and compliance rules, portfolio transparency is not only a luxury but an essential part of awareness that leads to corrective actions. Management has the ability to ensure that funding turns into the desired business results with an early warning system, using it to develop corrective measures and responses to potential issues.

Depending on the size of the portfolio, the monitoring and tracking of progress may be most effectively done through a dedicated PMO and PPM dashboard software. The responsibility of this function is to track the delivery of projects by assessing key indicators such as delivery to agreed milestones, mitigation of risks, resolution of issues, dependencies, adherence to change control procedures, and escalation of issues to senior management.

Dashboard or scorecard reporting is a practical way for PMO functions to provide senior management with key information. These reports highlight to executives whether their projects are progressing to plan or whether they need help, and give executives the opportunity to address any issues before they threaten to derail the project.

Summary

Using the best practices in the seven habits of effective PPM implementations will help you navigate the maze of IT portfolio management pitfalls no matter which methodology or tool set you choose.

By using these, you will fundamentally increase your chance of success in rolling out IT portfolio management.

Gil Makleff is managing director of UMT's U.S. business and a cofounder of the company. He has been a pioneer in driving Fortune 1000 companies to invest in and achieve their strategic goals by using portfolio management software and processes to support the alignment of IT and business. His background in computer science and consulting experience has been a key source of developing new ideas for the UMT Portfolio Manager™ software suite. In addition, he has been a major contributor to the development of the UMT tool set by distilling the needs of UMT's customers and translating them to software components. He graduated from Columbia University with a degree in computer science and holds an M.B.A. from the Stern School of Management at New York University.*

*Contributing authors: Mike Gruia, Angelie Gudka, Yorai Linenberg, and Brian Scully.

10.4

Project Portfolio Management Basics

PMI Knowledge and Wisdom Center

Though not a new concept, *project portfolio management* is a buzzword in recent project management literature. Similar to models of financial portfolio management in which investments are selected based on their potential for earnings or growth, project portfolio management helps to ensure that projects further the goals of an organization. A frequent distinction is that project management ensures that projects are done right, while project portfolio management ensures that the right projects are done. How this is accomplished varies across organizations and involves a variety of methods from simple summary sheets and prioritization to complex software solutions.

Project portfolio management can be defined as "the art and science of applying a set of knowledge, skills, tools, and techniques to a collection of projects in order to meet or exceed the needs and expectations of an organization's investment strategy. It seeks to answer the questions What should we take on? and What should we drop? It requires achieving a delicate balancing of strategic and tactical requirements."[1] At a high level, portfolio management processes include cataloguing candidate projects, developing selection or scoring criteria that will allow ranking of projects, and validating or balancing the portfolio using visual displays or analyses that allow modeling of various options and adjustment of the portfolio.

Organizations typically initiate portfolio management in order to maximize the value of projects in terms of a company objective such as profitability, achieve a balance of projects (for example, high risk versus low risk, long term versus short term), or to ensure that projects align with the firm's business strategy. In addition to facilitating these goals, portfolio management offers the benefits of enabling decision making based on strategic data and priorities versus ad hoc decisions driven by the needs of the moment; the practice can also reduce wasteful spending caused by inefficient allocation of resources or duplicate projects as well as provide a reasoned and fair process for justifying project decisions. Portfolio management can also yield a repository of project information to audit projects' progression and facilitate organizational learning from previous strategy decisions. While portfolio management can offer numerous benefits, drawbacks include the tendency to rely on tools or automation to make decisions and the possibility of adding another layer of bureaucracy to an organization.

Interest in portfolio management is growing, but a recent survey indicates that maturity levels are not high at present; 23 percent of respondents to a Center for Business Practices survey rated their maturity at level 1, or ad hoc processes only. Thirty-one percent noted the existence of a database of projects whose value is assessed in terms of individual projects (level 2); 23 percent rated themselves at level 3 (project selection/prioritization occurs at department/business unit level).[2]

Developing an Inventory

Portfolio management is predicated on a focused strategic plan for the organization. Key organizational goals, organizational mission and vision, culture, and priorities form the foundation for selecting appropriate projects to further these goals. Given a strategic plan, first steps in the process of portfolio management include generating standardized understanding or minimal acceptance criteria for what constitutes a project for this initiative (for example, a mature portfolio might include projects lasting more than six months) and developing an inventory of existing and proposed projects; the inventory should capture business case or justification information on each project.

Recommendations for information to capture vary but typically include some of the following: estimated financial impacts, risk factors, resource requirements, key players, dependencies, type of project (growth/strategic, compliance/mandatory), time-tables, major milestones, customer benefits, and utilization and pipeline data, as well as basic project identification information. This exercise alone, and the resulting repository, can prove highly valuable in focusing a company's efforts and uncovering redundancies. Because collecting standard data to allow comparisons is vital for portfolio management, a standardized template and process for recording project brief information should arise from this exercise.

Creating an inventory often also includes developing a catalogue of organizational data including resources (both labor and material resources such as equipment), skills availability, and standard financial rate information. Capturing such information assists in determining resource allocations once projects are selected.

Developing Selection Criteria

An organization must also establish weighted evaluation criteria for ranking projects; criteria arise from the organization's strategic plan and goals. An often-cited example of selection criteria, for example, is that used by Hoechst Chemical Corporation, which employs a scoring model that includes a number of strategy-related questions to ensure that strategic fit is examined; some metrics include likelihood of commercial success and synergy with company operations. Projects can also be diagrammed in an objectives matrix in which they are scored based on contribution toward an organizational objective (for example, "no contribution, supports, or fulfills"); the matrix table yields scores for how well a project supports objectives as well as the weight of an objective in a portfolio. Still other models use less complex, procedural metrics such as, "Are deliverables past due?" and "Is the project on schedule?" Whatever model is developed, it is critical that scoring is consistently applied and that the model is easy to understand and follow and is clearly communicated. Most project portfolio management literature also advocates that a high-level executive committee make scoring decisions to ensure a big picture focus and mitigate bias that might occur if project team members evaluate candidate projects.

Balancing the Portfolio

Another major facet of portfolio management is balancing or optimizing the portfolio; scoring elucidates high-priority projects, but balancing focuses on the optimal mix. Bear in mind that balancing portfolios involves just that: optimizing an entire portfolio, not just individual projects. Visual displays such as bubble diagrams allow flexibility in modeling options and can reveal levels of strategic alignments, overall risk, and resources committed. Quadrant diagrams also can be used to plot projects based on various factors, including potential for return and level of risk. A frequently discussed model places projects in the quadrants of "Bread and Butter," "Pearls," "Oysters," and "White Elephants" (see Chapter 7.2). Keeping resource allocation in mind is important to effective balancing.

Portfolio management is an iterative process. Once a portfolio is optimized, it must be continually monitored so that fit with objectives is maintained as businesses change. Organizations typically hold periodic portfolio review meetings to model options and make decisions about new and continuing projects. Ideally, these meetings work in coordination with project reviews and an organization's gating process.

10.5

Integrating Project Portfolio Management with Project Management Practices to Deliver Competitive Advantage

James S. Pennypacker, Patrick Sepate

Today's businesses find it increasingly important to execute projects efficiently—to do things right—bringing to the customer the expected quality and benefits desired from each project. They find it equally important to optimize their portfolio of projects—to direct the right resources to do the right things—in order to meet the organization's strategic goals. To accomplish this, best practice organizations integrate project management and project portfolio management (PPM) practices to tie the executive decision process to resource allocation and day-to-day project execution (see Figure 10.5-1).

Project Management and Project Portfolio Management

Project management is the application of knowledge, skills, tools, and techniques to project activities to meet project requirements. Project portfolio management is similarly the art and science of applying a set of knowledge, skills, tools, and techniques but to a collection (or portfolio) of projects in order to meet or exceed the needs

FIGURE 10.5-1 An Organization's Strategy Is Executed
Through Projects. Project Portfolio Management Is the
Key to Aligning Projects with the Strategy

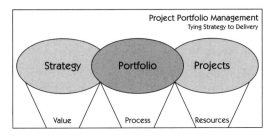

and expectations of an organization's investment strategy. Both PM
and PPM are focused on helping to meet or exceed stakeholder
needs, but they differ in the stakeholders and focus.

The stakeholders for individual projects (project management)
include business owners, business sponsors, and often the end user
of a project's output. These stakeholders are specifically concerned
with satisfying their own business requirements and needs and controlling cost and schedule. When their projects slip or exceed budget, they want to know what activities drove the variances.

The stakeholders for the PPM process include financial management, senior business executives, and ultimately the stockholders of
the organization. They are concerned with optimal investment of
scarce company resources and typically are interested in return on investment, strategic alignment, and risk profile of the portfolio. To satisfy both sets of stakeholders, organizations must define an integrated
process that links project management and portfolio management
practices.

Why Project Portfolio Management Important

Applying effective PPM practices is becoming increasingly critical
to business organizations. All organizations, large and small, must select and manage their investments and execute their projects wisely

to reap the maximum benefits from their investment decisions. PPM enables businesses to:

- Provide a structure for selecting the right projects and eliminating wrong ones
- Allocate resources to the right projects, thus reducing wasteful spending
- Align portfolio decisions to strategic business goals
- Base portfolio decisions on logic, reasoning, and objectivity
- Create ownership among staff by involvement at the right levels
- Establish avenues for individuals to identify opportunities and obtain support
- Help project teams understand the value of their contributions

Although there is compelling evidence to justify the use of PPM, few organizations today have established a mature project portfolio management process. Recent research from the Center for Business Practices (CBP) found that only a small percentage of organizations actively manage their projects as a portfolio (see Figure 10.5-2).

Integrating Project Portfolio Management and Project Management Practices

Integrating project management and PPM allows organizations to select the best portfolio of projects that are aligned with business strategy, monitor their performance, and iteratively reprioritize the portfolio as business conditions and budgets change. The project management process begins with initiation of a project, followed by planning, execution and control, and closing processes (see Figure 10.5-3). These processes comprise activities that are performed for effective project management and also provide a phased approach throughout the life of a project.

FIGURE 10.5-2 Only a Small Percentage of Organizations
Actively Manage Their Projects as a Portfolio

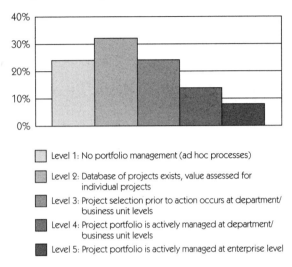

Level 1: No portfolio management (ad hoc processes)

Level 2: Database of projects exists, value assessed for
individual projects

Level 3: Project selection prior to action occurs at department/
business unit levels

Level 4: Project portfolio is actively managed at department/
business unit levels

Level 5: Project portfolio is actively managed at enterprise level

FIGURE 10.5-3 The Project Management Processes
as Defined in a Guide to the Project Management Body
of Knowledge (PMBOK® Guide)

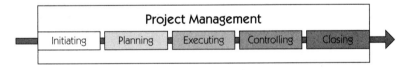

Source: Project Management Institute, *A Guide to the Project Management Body of Knowledge* (Newtown Square, Pa.: Project Management Institute, 2000).

Prior to project initiation, it is essential to create a process for identifying and structuring potential projects, screening these entities, and managing the valuation from a benefit and cost focus. This preproject stage, often designated as opportunity assessment, may be conducted by business sponsors, business liaisons, program managers, or other representatives who have the skills and knowledge to define business benefits and estimate associated costs. In this stage, projects are screened to ensure they pass minimal criteria—that they fit the organization's strategy and that they are feasible. Mandatory projects are also identified in this stage (for example, projects that must be implemented for the organization to function adequately).

Optimizing the Project Portfolio

Project portfolio management has five phases: portfolio inventory, analysis, planning, tracking, and review and replanning. These phases are dynamic, iterative, and ongoing (see Figure 10.5-4) and must be managed artfully depending on project life cycles as well as organizational issues, like budget cycles.

Initial project requests enter the portfolio inventory, where project data is captured and organized for portfolio analysis. The inventory includes active projects, proposed projects, and projects that are on hold or delayed. The inventory will have information about all projects in the portfolio, including schedule and cost estimates, budgets, dependencies, strategic initiatives, expected bene-

FIGURE 10.5-4 The Portfolio Management Process Is Ongoing and Iterative

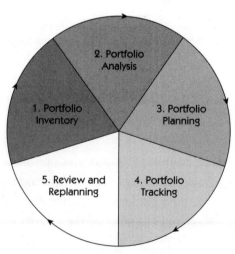

fits, risk, relative priority, value, and ranking. The inventory will also have information about available resources, roles, costs, skills, and other needed organizational information.

The portfolio is analyzed, periodically reviewing projects for their fit, utility, and balance: Do the projects fit the organization's strategy? Do they have value? How do the projects relate to each other, and how can the project mix be optimized? Portfolio analysis is crucial to prioritizing the portfolio and maximizing the value to the organization given its resource constraints. Organizations may prioritize projects based on a variety of criteria: financial, technical, strategic, and risk. Interactions among the projects in the portfolio are considered, including interdependencies, competition for resources, and timing. A variety of decision-making techniques and tools are used to help formulate the problem and facilitate the analysis of alternative solutions. Through multiple iterations, trade-offs are considered and final adjustments made to arrive at the optimal project portfolio.

Once projects are selected and initiated, they begin the project planning phase. Here resources are allocated and projects are scheduled. This project management process is integrated with the portfolio planning process, where resource allocation and schedule decisions are made, taking into account the whole portfolio of projects.

In tracking the portfolio of projects, metrics are captured to assess the performance of each project. And depending on the type, these projects must pass decision gate evaluations to determine whether to continue with the project, put it on hold, or kill it altogether.

Reviews of the project portfolio involve a reverification of the projects' critical success factors—including resource availability and the continued validity of the business case—with the business sponsors. In addition, shifting business, technology, and market conditions can rearrange priorities. Those decisions also require a realignment of the project portfolio, which may or may not affect other projects in the portfolio. Replanning may be required, including changes in resource allocation and scheduling.

This iterative nature of portfolio optimization requires that project reviews, program reviews, and portfolio reviews be held on a regular basis. These reviews provide a forum for studying the alternatives and help to build organizational buy-in for the portfolio. Integrating project management and PPM is necessary for developing an optimal project portfolio. Figure 10.5-5 illustrates a conceptual model for integrating PM and PPM.

Project Portfolio Management and Program Management

Linking business strategy directly to project prioritization and selection is often difficult to accomplish and manage over the long term. To facilitate the linkage, many organizations have established a program management function that provides a level of organiza-

FIGURE 10.5-5 Project Portfolio Management Is an Iterative Process That Occurs Throughout the Project Management Life Cycle Through Project and Portfolio Reviews

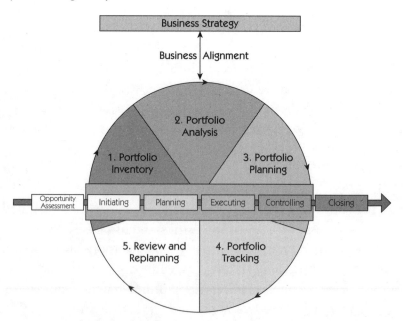

tion between business strategy, portfolio management, and project management. Program managers are responsible for establishing and managing programs, which comprise projects that support some common goal or objective. Prioritization of projects may then occur within a program, across programs, or at the program level across the enterprise.

Project Portfolio Management Software

There are a number of software tools that can be used to support the PPM process. Each year software developers improve the functionality of the tools to help the portfolio manager organize projects and programs, formulate the portfolio options, and analyze alternative scenarios. Pivot tables, bubble charts, resource allocation algorithms, and risk-reward diagrams provide the portfolio manager with a plethora of options and analytical capabilities. Recently software tools such as Microsoft Project 2002 Professional and Pacific Edge's Portfolio Edge have given portfolio managers robust tools for building, analyzing, and tracking the portfolio.

Analytic software—for example, software that uses the Analytic Hierarchy Process (AHP)—is still used successfully for prioritizing projects against appropriate strategic factors. In addition, a number of software vendors provide tools that help in financial analysis and return-on-investment calculations. Today's tools are becoming extremely valuable in tracking and analyzing a portfolio, especially as the disciplined project management provides a basis for collecting the information and data needed to plan and track the portfolio.

Project Portfolio Management and the Strategic Project Office

A number of organizations have established strategic project offices (SPOs, sometimes called enterprise project management offices) to improve project management practices across their organizations. The SPO, a relatively small, strategic group, connects executive vision with the work of the organization. Its strategic functions include assessing and promoting project management maturity, creating a project culture, integrating processes and systems enterprisewide, ensuring enterprisewide project quality, managing resources across projects and portfolios, and project portfolio management.

In many organizations, the SPO owns the PPM process. The SPO ensures that an organization's projects are linked to strategic plans. It may be involved in facilitating the prioritization and project selection processes, and typically it is intimately involved in resource allocation decisions. The SPO also coordinates tracking of the current portfolio, analyzes portfolio performance, and is instrumental in administering the decision gate process for all projects. The SPO ensures that the organization's project portfolio continues to meet the needs of the business, even as these needs continue to change over time. It serves as the critical link between business strategy and execution of tactical plans.

We recommend that organizations consider creating an SPO at the enterprise level, if one is not already in place, to help establish and manage the enterprise portfolio of projects and programs.

Summary

Project portfolio management is an important process that helps organizations prioritize, select, and manage their portfolio of projects. It links business strategy with tactical decisions in determining which projects should be included in that portfolio. Effective PPM provides a structured approach for selecting an optimal portfolio of projects—one that maximizes the organization's goals (revenue, profits, strategic goals, or something else), while providing the capability to manage the project portfolio as part of an ongoing, iterative process that takes into account changes in resource availability as well as shifting business, technology, and market conditions.

While efficient project execution is an essential factor in a business's success, in today's competitive environment successful project execution by itself is not enough. Sustainable competitive advantage won't come only from working efficiently on projects; organizations must also work on the right projects. Project portfolio management provides a consistent way to select the right projects—those that together offer the greatest value and contribution to the strategic interests of the organization.

James S. Pennypacker is the director of PM Solutions' Center for Business Practices and coeditor of *Project Portfolio Management* (1999) and *Managing Multiple Projects* (2002).

Patrick Sepate is the director of customer solutions for PM Solutions and is responsible for its project portfolio management practice.

Notes

Foreword

1. R. M. Wideman, *A Management Framework for Project, Program and Portfolio Integration* (New Bern, N.C.: Trafford Publishing, 2004), p. 181.

Chapter 1.1

1. R. M. Wideman, *A Management Framework for Project, Program and Portfolio Integration* (New Bern, N.C.: Trafford Publishing, 2004), chap. 13.

Chapter 1.2

1. Stage-Gate® is a registered term.

Chapter 2.1

1. Stage-Gate® is a registered term.

Chapter 2.2

1. Stage-Gate® is a registered term.

2. H. A. Levine, *Practical Project Management: Tips, Tactics, and Tools* (New York: Wiley, 2002).

Chapter 2.5

1. "Case Study: The Efficient Frontier: AXA Financial Inc.," *CIO Insight,* June 1, 2004.

Chapter 3.3

1. Stage-Gate® is a registered term.

Chapter 3.4

1. G. A. Moore, *Crossing the Chasm* (New York: HarperCollins, 1991), and *Inside the Tornado* (New York: HarperCollins, 1995).

2. Moore, *Inside the Tornado.*

Chapter 3.6

1. Q. W. Fleming, *Cost/Schedule Control Systems Criteria: The Management Guide to C/SCSC* (Burr Ridge, Ill.: Irwin, 1992).

2. Q. W. Fleming and J. M. Koppelman, *Earned Value Project Management* (Newtown Square, Pa.: : Project Management Institute, 1996).

3. For additional pragmatic approaches to earned value analysis, see H. A. Levine, *Practical Project Management: Tips, Tactics, and Tools* (New York: Wiley, 2002).

Chapter 4.1

1. B. Tregoe and J. Zimmerman, *Top Management Strategy* (New York: Simon & Schuster, 1980); G. Steiner, *Strategic Planning* (New York: Free Press, 1979); M. Porter, *Competitive Strategy* (Boston: Harvard Business School Press, 1986).

Chapter 4.3

1. T. L. Saaty, *The Analytic Hierarchy Process: Planning, Priority Setting, Resource Allocation* (Pittsburgh: RWS Publications, 1996).

2. E. H. Forman and S. I. Gass, "The Analytic Hierarchy Process—An Exposition," *Operations Research*, 2001, 49(4), 469–486. E. H. Forman and M. A. Selly, *Decision by Objectives: How to Convince Others That You Are Right* (River Edge, N.J.: World Scientific, 2001).

3. Paraphrased from T. L. Saaty, *Fundamentals of Decision Making and Priority Theory with the Analytic Hierarchy Process* (Pittsburgh: RWS Publications, 1994).

4. Saaty, *Fundamentals of Decision Making*, p. 339.

5. L. D. Dye and J. S. Pennypacker, *Project Portfolio Management: Selecting and Prioritizing Projects for Competitive Advantage* (Westchester, Pa.: Center for Business Practices, 1999), p. xi.

6. For example, R. J. Graham and R. L. Englund, *Creating an Environment for Successful Projects: The Quest to Manage Project Management* (San Francisco: Jossey-Bass, 1997); J. P. Lewis, *Mastering Project Management: Applying Advanced Concepts of Systems Thinking, Control and Evaluation, Resource Allocation* (New York: McGraw-Hill, 1998).

7. Note in particular the efforts of Glenn Mazur and Richard Zultner of the Quality Function Deployment Institute (www.qfdi.org). Mazur and Zultner have successfully applied AHP to quality function deployment implementations, new product development PPM, and Design for Six Sigma new product design efforts. Also note R. J. Calantone, C. A. Di Benedetto, and J. B. Schmidt, "Using the Analytic Hierarchy Process in New Product Screening," *Journal of Product Innovation Management*, 1999, 16(1), 65–76, and M. L. Liberatore, "An Extension of the Analytical Hierarchy Process for Industrial R&D Project Selection and Resource Allocation," *IEEE Transactions on Engineering Management*, 1987, EM-34(1), 12–19.

8. M. Jeffery and I. Leliveld, "Best Practices in IT Portfolio Management," *MIT Sloan Management Review*, 2004, 45(3), 41.

9. Paraphrased from P. Weill and J. W. Ross, *IT Governance: How Top Performers Manage IT Decision Rights for Superior Results* (Boston: Harvard Business School Press, 2004).

10. M. Light, "Project Portfolio Management in Reach" (paper presented at the Gartner Project Portfolio Management Summit, July 12, 2004), p. 12.

11. For a complete treatment of the balanced scorecard, see R. S. Kaplan and others, *Balancing the Corporate Scorecard* (Boston: Harvard Business School Press, 1998).

12. For specific details on the scales of measurement, refer to Saaty, *The Analytic Hierarchy Process*.

13. Matthew L. Liberatore of Villanova University was one of the first writers to make the connection between AHP and optimization. For details, see Liberatore, "An Extension of the Analytical Hierarchy Process for Industrial R&D Project Selection and Resource Allocation."

14. Note in particular David Hillson's work in this area. D. Hillson, "Use a Risk Breakdown Structure (RBS) to Understand Your Risks," in *Proceedings of the Project Management Institute Annual Seminars and Symposium* (Oct. 3–10, 2002). [http://www.risk-doctor.com/pdf-files/rbs1002.pdf]. Hierarchic risk structures like the risk breakdown structure are easily measured and leveraged with the AHP.

Chapter 4.4

1. TechRepublic and T. Smith, *IT Project Management Research Findings* (Louisville, Ky.: TechRepublic, 2000).

Chapter 5.1

1. R. J. Graham and R. L. Englund, *Creating an Environment for Successful Projects* (San Francisco: Jossey-Bass, 2004).

Section 7

1. Stage-Gate® is a registered term.

Chapter 7.1

1. "Fast, Focused, Fertile: The Innovation Evolution, Cheskin and Fitch: Worldwide, 2003." [www.fitchworldwide.com].

2. See new product performance results in R. G. Cooper, *Winning at New Products: Accelerating the Process from Idea to Launch*, 3rd ed. (Reading, Mass.: Perseus Books, 2001); American Productivity and Quality Center, *New Product Development Best Practices Study: What Distinguishes the Top Performers* (Houston: American Productivity and Quality Center, 2002).

3. The term *Stage-Gate*® was coined by the author in the 1980s and is a trademark of the Product Development Institute, www.prod-dev.com.

4. The APQC benchmarking study is a major study into new product performance and practices by the premier benchmarking institute in the United States. For more details on the benchmarking study, see American Productivity and Quality Center, *New Product Development Best Practices Study*, and R. G. Cooper, S. J. Edgett, and E. J. Kleinschmidt, *Best Practices in Product Innovation: What Distinguishes Top Performers* (Newtown Square, Pa.: Product Development Institute, 2003). The APQC benchmarking results cited in this chapter have also appeared in recent journal articles; see, for example, R. G. Cooper, S. J. Edgett, and E. J. Kleinschmidt, "Benchmarking Best NPD Practices—Part I: Culture, Climate, Teams and Senior Management Roles," *Research Technology Management*, 2003, 47(1), 31–43; R. G. Cooper, S. J. Edgett, and E. J. Kleinschmidt, "Benchmarking Best NPD Practices—Part II: Strategy, Resource Allocation and Portfolio Management," *Research Technology Management*, 2004, 47(3), 50–59; and R. G. Cooper, S. J. Edgett, and E. J. Kleinschmidt, "Benchmarking Best NPD Practices—Part III: The NPD Process and Decisive Idea-to-Launch Practices," *Research Technology Management*, 2004, 47(6).

5. See A. Griffin, *Drivers of NPD Success: The 1997 PDMA Report* (Chicago: Product Development and Management Association, 1997).

6. Griffin, *Drivers of NPD Success*.

7. The term *Stage-Gate*® first appeared in print in R. G. Cooper, "The New Product Process: A Decision Guide for Managers," *Journal of Marketing Management*, 1988, 3(3), 238–255. An earlier version was outlined in previous works; see, for example, R. G. Cooper, *Winning at New Products* (Reading, Mass: Addison Wesley, 1986). *Stage-Gate*® is now a legally registered trade name in a number of countries.

8. Problems and challenges in project selection and portfolio management were uncovered in several studies. See Cooper, Edgett, and Kleinschmidt, "Portfolio Management in New Product Development: Lessons from the Leaders—Part I"; Cooper, Edgett, and Kleinschmidt, "Portfolio Management in New Product Development: Lessons from the Leaders—Part II"; and R. G. Cooper, S. J. Edgett, and E. J. Kleinschmidt, "Best Practices for Managing R&D Portfolios," *Research-Technology Management*, 1998, *41*(4), pp. 20–33. A second major benchmarking study, undertaken with the Industrial Research Institute, into portfolio management practices probed portfolio management practices and performance. Results are in R. G. Cooper, S. J. Edgett, and E. J. Kleinschmidt, "New Product Portfolio Management: Practices and Performance," *Journal of Product Innovation Management*, 1999, *16*(4), 333–351; and R. G. Cooper, S. J. Edgett, and E. J. Kleinschmidt, "Portfolio Management for New Product Development: Results of an Industry Practices Study," *R&D Management*, 2001, *31*, 361–380.

9. American Productivity and Quality Center, *New Product Development Best Practices Study*; Cooper, Edgett, and Kleinschmidt, *Best Practices in Product Innovation: What Distinguishes Top Performers*; Cooper, Edgett, and Kleinschmidt, "Benchmarking Best NPD Practices—Part I: Culture, Climate, Teams and Senior Management Roles"; Cooper, Edgett, and Kleinschmidt, "Benchmarking Best NPD Practices—Part II: Strategy, Resource Allocation and Portfolio Management"; Cooper, Edgett, and Kleinschmidt, "Benchmarking Best NPD Practices—Part III: The NPD Process and Decisive Idea-to-Launch Practices."

10. Parts of this section are taken from R. G. Cooper, "Overhauling the New Product Process," *Industrial Marketing Management*, 1996, *25*, 465–482.

11. The assessments are from American Productivity and Quality Center, *New Product Development Best Practices Study: What Distinguishes the Top Performers*. Similar results have been reported in other studies. See, for example, S. Mishra, D. Kim, and D. H. Lee, "Factors Affecting New Product Success: Cross Country Comparisons," *Journal of Product Innovation Management*, 1996, *13*, 530–550; X. M. Song and M. E. Parry, "What Separates Japanese New Product

Winners from Losers," *Journal of Product Innovation Management*, 1996, *13*, 422–439; X. M. Song and M. M. Montoya-Weiss, "Critical Development Activities for Really New Versus Incremental Products," *Journal of Product Innovation Management*, 1998, *15*, 124–135; C. A. Di Benedetto, "Identifying the Key Success Factors in New Product Launch," *Journal of Product Innovation Management*, 1999, *16*, 530–544. For a comprehensive review of factors that lead to success in new product development, see R. G. Cooper, *The PDMA Handbook of New Product Development*, 2nd ed. (New York: Wiley, 2004).

12. American Productivity and Quality Center, *New Product Development Best Practices Study*; Cooper, Edgett, and Kleinschmidt, *Best Practices in Product Innovation: What Distinguishes Top Performers*; Cooper, Edgett, and Kleinschmidt, "Benchmarking Best NPD Practices—Part I: Culture, Climate, Teams and Senior Management Roles"; Cooper, Edgett, and Kleinschmidt, "Benchmarking Best NPD Practices—Part II: Strategy, Resource Allocation and Portfolio Management"; Cooper, Edgett, and Kleinschmidt, "Benchmarking Best NPD Practices—Part III: The NPD Process and Decisive Idea-to-Launch Practices."

13. The rugby analogy was first introduced in B. Uttal, "Speeding New Ideas to Market," *Fortune*, Mar. 1987, pp. 62–66.

14. Some of these practices are explained in Cooper, *Winning at New Products*; Cooper, *The PDMA Handbook of New Product Development*; R. G. Cooper "Third-Generation New Product Processes," *Journal of Product Innovation Management*, 1994, *11*(1), 3–14.

15. American Productivity and Quality Center, *New Product Development Best Practices Study*; Cooper, Edgett, and Kleinschmidt, *Best Practices in Product Innovation: What Distinguishes Top Performers*; Cooper, Edgett, and Kleinschmidt, "Benchmarking Best NPD Practices—Part I: Culture, Climate, Teams and Senior Management Roles"; Cooper, Edgett, and Kleinschmidt, "Benchmarking Best NPD Practices—Part II: Strategy, Resource Allocation and Portfolio Management"; Cooper, Edgett, and Kleinschmidt, "Benchmarking Best NPD Practices—Part III: The NPD Process and Decisive Idea-to-Launch Practices."

16. American Productivity and Quality Center, *New Product Development Best Practices Study*; Cooper, Edgett, and Kleinschmidt, *Best Practices in Product Innovation: What Distinguishes Top Performers*; Cooper, Edgett, and Kleinschmidt, "Benchmarking Best NPD Practices—Part I: Culture, Climate, Teams and Senior Management Roles"; Cooper, Edgett, and Kleinschmidt, "Benchmarking Best NPD Practices—Part II: Strategy, Resource Allocation and Portfolio Management"; Cooper, Edgett, and Kleinschmidt, "Benchmarking Best NPD Practices—Part III: The NPD Process and Decisive Idea-to-Launch Practices."

17. For more information on the use of lead users in idea generation, see E. A. Von Hippel, S. Thomke, and M. Sonnack, "Creating Breakthroughs at 3M," *Harvard Business Review*, Sept.-Oct. 1999, pp. 47–57.

18. R. Sears and M. Barry, "Product Value Analysis—Product Interaction Predicts Profits," *Innovation*, Winter 1993, pp. 13–18.

19. For voice of-customer methods and idea generation, see P. Lindstedt and J. Burenius, *The Value Model: How to Master Product Development and Create Unrivalled Customer Value* (Sweden: NIMBA AB, 2003).

20. For more information on fast-track versions of Stage-Gate®, see Cooper, *Product Leadership*, and Cooper, *Winning at New Products*.

21. For more information on Stage-Gate® for technology and platform developments, see Cooper, *Product Leadership*, and Cooper, *Winning at New Products*.

22. L. Yapps-Cohen, P. W. Kamienski, and R. L. Espino, "Gate System Focuses Industrial Basic Research," *Research-Technology Management*, July-Aug. 1998, pp. 34–37.

23. The concept of disruptive technologies (or radical innovations) was first developed by MIT researchers in the 1960s and later popularized by Christensen. See C. M. Christensen, *The Innovator's Dilemma* (New York: HarperCollins, 2000).

24. Milton D. Rosenau Jr. (ed.), *PDMA Handbook for New Product Development* (New York: Wiley, 1996).

25. For a sample scorecard for technology development projects, see R. G. Cooper, S. J. Edgett, and E. J. Kleinschmidt, *Portfolio Management for New Products*, 2nd ed. (Reading, Mass: Perseus Book, 2002).

26. Cooper, *Winning at New Products*, has become the authority for task forces in designing a Stage-Gate® framework.

27. SG-Navigator™ is available from Stage Gate Inc. at www.stage-gate.com.

28. Accolade™ is a comprehensive decision support system for Stage-Gate®. It was developed and is sold by Sopheon Inc. See www.sopheon.com. SG-Navigator™ is a somewhat simpler electronic version of Stage-Gate®, available from Stage Gate Inc. at www.stage-gate.com.

Chapter 7.2

1. This chapter also draws on R. G. Cooper, S. J. Edgett, and E. J. Kleinschmidt, "Portfolio Management in New Product Development: Lessons from the Leaders—Part I," *Research-Technology Management*, Sept.-Oct. 1997, pp. 16–28; R. G. Cooper, S. J. Edgett, and E. J. Kleinschmidt, "Portfolio Management in New Product Development: Lessons from the Leaders—Part II," *Research-Technology Management*, Nov.-Dec. 1997, pp. 43–57; R. G. Cooper, S. J. Edgett, and E. J. Kleinschmidt, "New Problems, New Solutions: Making Portfolio Management More Effective," *Research-Technology Management*, 2000, 43(2), 18–33; and R. G. Cooper, S. J. Edgett, and E. J. Kleinschmidt, "Portfolio Management: Fundamental to New Product Success," in P. Beliveau, A. Griffin, and S. Somermeyer (eds.), *The PDMA Toolbox for New Product Development* (New York: Wiley, 2002).

2. Portfolio management is defined in Cooper, Edgett, and Kleinschmidt, "Portfolio Management in New Product Development: Lessons from the Leaders—Part I."

3. P. Roussel, K. N. Saad, and T. J. Erickson, *Third Generation R&D: Managing the Link to Corporate Strategy* (Boston: Harvard Business School Press and Arthur D. Little, 1991).

4. Some statistics cited in this chapter are from a major study on portfolio management practices and performance study. See R. G. Cooper, S. J. Edgett, and E. J. Kleinschmidt, "New Product Portfolio Management: Practices and Performance," *Journal of Product Innovation*

Management, 1999, *16,* 333–351; and R. G. Cooper, S. J. Edgett, and E. J. Kleinschmidt, "Portfolio Management for New Product Development: Results of an Industry Practices Study," *R&D Management,* 2001, *31,* 361–380.

5. Parts of this section are taken from R. G. Cooper, "Maximizing the Value of Your New Product Portfolio: Methods, Metrics and Scorecards," *Current Issues in Technology Management,* 2003, *7*(1).

6. R. G. Cooper, S. J. Edgett, and E. J. Kleinschmidt, *Portfolio Management for New Products,* 2nd ed. (Reading, Mass.: Perseus Book, 2002).

7. Much of this section on road mapping is taken from Lucent Technologies. See R. E. Albright, "Roadmaps and Roadmapping: Linking Business Strategy and Technology Planning," in *Proceedings, Portfolio Management for New Product Development, Institute for International Research and Product Development and Management Association* (Fort Lauderdale, Fla., Jan. 2001). See also M. H. Meyer and A. P. Lehnerd, *The Power of Platforms* (New York: Free Press, 1997).

8. For more information on platforms, see Myer and Lehnerd, *The Power of Product Platforms.*

9. Cooper, Edgett, and Kleinschmidt, *Portfolio Management for New Products.*

10. The example is taken from a case study in the American Productivity and Quality Center (APQC) benchmarking study on new product best practices. R. G. Cooper, S. J. Edgett, and E. J. Kleinschmidt, *Best Practices in Product Innovation: What Distinguishes Top Performers* (Product Development Institute, 2003) [www.prod-dev.com]; R. G. Cooper, S. J. Edgett, and E. J. Kleinschmidt, *New Product Development Best Practices Study: What Distinguishes the Top Performers* (Houston: American Productivity and Quality Center, 2002) [www.apqc.org].

11. E. Roberts and C. Berry, "Entering New Businesses: Selecting Strategies for Success," *Sloan Management Review,* Spring 1983, pp. 3–17.

12. More detail on the methods outlined in this section can be found in Cooper, *Product Leadership*; and Cooper, Edgett, and Kleinschmidt, *Portfolio Management for New Products.*

13. T. Faulkner, "Applying 'Options Thinking' to R&D Valuation," *Research-Technology Management*, May-June 1995, pp. 50–57.

14. R. G. Cooper, S. J. Edgett, and E. J. Kleinschmidt, *R&D Portfolio Management Best Practices Study, Industrial Research Institute* (Washington, D.C.: Industrial Research Institute, 1997); R. G. Cooper, S. J. Edgett, and E. J. Kleinschmidt, "Best Practices for Managing R&D Portfolios," *Research-Technology Management*, 1998, *41*(4), 20–33.

15. Cooper, Edgett, and Kleinschmidt, "New Product Portfolio Management: Practices and Performance." Cooper, Edgett, and Kleinschmidt, "Portfolio Management for New Product Development: Results of an Industry Practices Study." Faulkner, "Applying 'Options Thinking' to R&D Valuation."

16. Bubble diagrams with "value" measured qualitatively are recommended in Roussel, Saad, and Erickson, *Third Generation R&D*.

17. P. Evans, "Streamlining Formal Portfolio Management," *Scrip Magazine*, Feb. 1996; and D. Matheson, J. E. Matheson, and M. M. Menke, "Making Excellent R&D Decisions," *Research Technology Management*, Nov.-Dec. 1994, pp. 21–24.

18. Based on Roberts and Berry, "Entering New Businesses: Selecting Strategies for Success."

19. Cooper, Edgett, and Kleinschmidt, "New Product Portfolio Management: Practices and Performance." Cooper, Edgett, and Kleinschmidt, "Portfolio Management for New Product Development: Results of an Industry Practices Study." Faulkner, "Applying 'Options Thinking' to R&D Valuation."

20. Cooper, Edgett, and Kleinschmidt, "Best Practices in Product Development: What Distinguishes Top Performers" and "Improving New Product Development Performance and Practices."

Chapter 8.1

1. E. Goldratt, *Critical Chain* (Great Barrington, Mass.: North River Press, 1997).

2. L. Leach, *Critical Chain Project Management* (Boston: Artech House, 2000).

3. E. Goldratt, *What Is This Thing Called the Theory of Constraints?* (Great Barrington, Mass.: North River Press, 1990).

4. W. Deming, *The New Economics for Industry, Government, Education* (Cambridge, Mass.: MIT Center for Advanced Engineering Study, 1993).

5. See the laws of the Fifth Discipline in P. Senge, *The Fifth Discipline* (New York: Doubleday, 1990).

6. W. Dettmer, *Strategic Navigation* (Milwaukee, Wis.: ASQ Quality Press, 2003).

7. See Dettmer, *Strategic Navigation*, for more information on these tools.

8. Leach, *Critical Chain Project Management*.

9. Goldratt, *Critical Chain*.

10. M. A. Cusumano and K. Nobeoka, *Thinking Beyond Lean* (New York: Free Press, 1998).

11. I am indebted to Eli Shragenheim for much of the thinking in this section. He led a productive discussion of an Internet discussion group to clarify many of the points addressed here.

12. Leach, *Critical Chain Project Management*.

Chapter 9.1

1. P. O'Connor, " Implementing a Stage-Gate Process: A Multi-Company Perspective," *Journal of Product Innovation Management*, 1994, *11*, 183–200. See also R. G. Cooper. "Speeding Up the Process: A Third Generation Approach." Note that Stage-Gate® is a registered term. R. Cooper, *Winning at New Products* (New York: Basic Books, 2001).

2. J. Katzenbach and D. Smith, *The Wisdom of Teams* (New York: McKinsey & Company, 1993); S. Wheelwright, "Organizing and Leading Project Teams," in S. Wheelwright and K. B. Clark, *Revolutionizing Product Development* (New York: Free Press, 1992).

3. *The PDMA Toolbook for New Product Development* (New York: Wiley, 2002), p. 331.

4. A. Wood, "Crompton: Trying to Rebuild Confidence," *Chemical Week,* July 14, 2004, pp. 19–21.

5. R. G. Cooper, S. J. Edgett, and E. J. Kleinschmidt, *Portfolio Management for New Products* (Ontario, Canada: Portfolio Study McMaster University, 1997) and *Portfolio Management for New Products* (Reading, Mass.: Perseus Books, 1998).

6. P. A. Koen and others, "Fuzzy Front End: Effective Methods, Tools, and Techniques," in *The PDMA Toolbook for New Product Development.*

7. B. Ausura, "The Debate Corner," *PDMA Visions Magazine,* 2003, 27(4), 15.

8. Cooper, Edgett, and Kleinschmidt, *Portfolio Management for New Products.*

9. B. Hayes, G. Pisano, D. Upton, and S. Wheelwright, *Operations, Strategy, and Technology: Pursuing the Competitive Edge* (New York: Wiley, 2004).

10. Hayes, Pisano, Upton, and Wheelwright, *Operations, Strategy, and Technology: Pursuing the Competitive Edge.*

11. S. Wheelwright and K. Clark, *Revolutionizing Product Development* (New York: Free Press, 1992).

12. Katzenbach and Smith, *The Wisdom of Teams.*

13. Wheelwright and Clark, *Revolutionizing Product Development.*

14. The original snapshot form was obtained at a Connecticut Time to Market meeting in 1995 where a presentation by Xerox contained what was called a snapshot form. This form was customized for use in-house.

15. As of August 2004, as this chapter is being written, Six Sigma and Design for Six Sigma are major initiatives being implemented throughout the corporation, including mapping into the stage-and-gate and portfolio management systems in the various businesses.

16. The Industrial Research Institute (IRI) is the foremost business association of leaders in research and development working together to enhance the effectiveness of technological innovation in industry.

Founded in 1938 through the National Research Council, it comprises senior executives from a diverse range of industries whose member companies are investing over $70 billion annually in R&D worldwide. The IRI is the only cross-industry organization providing the R&D community with insights, solutions, and best practices in innovation management developed through collaborative knowledge creation. For more information, visit iriinc.org.

17. T. Say, A. Fusfeld, and T. Parish, "Is Your Firm's Tech Portfolio Aligned with Its Business Strategy?" *Research Technology Management*, 2003, 46(1), 32–38.

18. Cooper, Edgett, and Kleinschmidt, *Portfolio Management for New Products*.

19. F. P. Boer, *The Valuation of Technology: Business and Financial Issues in R&D* (New York: Wiley, 1999) and F. P. Boer, "Risk Adjusted Valuation of R&D Projects," *Research Technology Management*, 2003, 46(5), 50–58.

20. Wheelwright and Clark, *Revolutionizing Product Development*.

Chapter 9.2

1. "Q&A with Bob Napier, CIO at Hewlett-Packard," *CIO Magazine*, Sept. 15, 2002. http://www.cio.com/archive/091502/napier/html.

Section 10

1. C. H. Kepner and B. B. Tregoe, *The Rational Manager* (New York: McGraw-Hill, 1965).

Chapter 10.1

1. D. J. Cohen and R. J. Graham, *The Project Manager's MBA: Translating Project Decisions into Business Success* (San Francisco: Jossey-Bass, 2000).

2. More details on the use of the calculator are contained in Cohen and Graham, *The Project Manager's MBA*.

Chapter 10.2

1. "Too Many Projects in the Development Pipeline Hurt Successful Launch Rate for Medical Device/Equipment Companies," *Business Wire*, Feb. 19, 1998.

2. K. M. Carillo, "Is It All a Project?" *Information Week*, Feb. 23, 1998, pp. 100–104.

3. H. A. Levine, "Reaching Out: It's That Enterprise Thing Again!" *PM Network*, Apr. 1998, p. 23.

Chapter 10.3

1. META Group 2003.

2. H. Rubin, "Portfolio Management: How to Do It Right," *CIO Magazine*, May 1, 2003.

Chapter 10.4

1. L. D. Dye and J. S. Pennypacker, *Project Portfolio Management: Selecting and Prioritizing Projects for Competitive Advantage* (Westchester, Pa.: Center for Business Practices, 1999).

2. PM Solutions, Center for Business Practices. [http://www.pmsolutions.com/articles/pdfs/general/industry_news.pdf].

Index

A

Accolade, 317

Accountability, 457, 458, 482

Accounting systems, traditional *versus* theory of constraints, 359–363

Action planning, in Stage-Gate framework, 287

Actual Cost (AC) or Actual Cost of Work Performed (ACWP), 46, 125, 126, 127, 128–129

Advanced Projects, 389

Agility, 490

Alternative scenarios, 166–168

Alternative solutions, 377

America Online, Inc. (AOL), 50, 392, 447–455; background on, 447; implementation at, 448–454; lessons learned at, 454–455; objectives of, 447–448; principles of, 448; project portfolio management at, 447–455; project prioritization at, 449–450; results at, 454–455; tools of, 451–452

American Productivity and Quality Center (APQC), 282, 283, 294, 297, 332

Analytic hierarchy process (AHP), 5, 155–175; background on, 155–156; execution management in, 172–173; forecasting in, 172, 173–174; methodology of, 156–158; performance measurement in, 173–174; project portfolio management applications of, 158–175; for project selection and prioritization, 65, 72, 135–136, 158–175, 251; risk assessment in, 171–172; steps in,

159–173; strategic alignment in, 161–165, 174; tools for, 163, 164, 172–173, 251, 503; validity of, 156; value of, 174–175

Anchored scales, 410–412, 414

Annual discount rate, 148–149

Applications Pathway gate, 314

Asset allocation models, 269–271

Audit, of current process, 315

Authorization document, 40

Automotive manufacturing plant, 477

AXA/Equitable Financial, 79, 247, 251, 255, 256, 260

B

Balance: in new product development portfolio, 322, 331–333, 345–350; portfolio, 38–39, 109–110, 171, 174, 205, 226, 495; in ranking, 64–65; resource, 38–39; risk and, 101–102

Balanced scorecard approach, 36–37, 64–65, 162; for new product development, 335, 343–345

BCG strategy model, 345

Benefits: in analytic hierarchy process, 167; in discounted cash flow model, 147, 152–153; evaluating and ranking, 35, 36–37, 38, 63–65, 147, 435–436; prequalification for, 95–99; of transformation projects, 114

Best practices: in IT project portfolio management, 242–265, 482–491; in Stage-Gate framework, 284–285, 289–298

Q

R